HAUGHEY

Also by Bruce Arnold

NON-FICTION

A Concise History of Irish Art
Orpen: Mirror to an Age
What Kind of Country
Margaret Thatcher: A Study in Power
An Art Atlas of Britain and Ireland
William Orpen
The Scandal of Ulysses
Mainie Jellett and the Modern Movement in Ireland

FICTION

A Singer at the Wedding
The Song of the Nightingale
The Muted Swan
Running to Paradise

HAUGHEY

His Life and Unlucky Deeds

BRUCE ARNOLD

HarperCollins*Publishers*

HarperCollins*Publishers*
77–85 Fulham Palace Road,
Hammersmith, London W6 8JB

Published by HarperCollins*Publishers* 1993

2 4 6 8 9 7 5 3 1

A catalogue record for this book is
available from the British Library

ISBN 0 00 255212 4

Set in Linotron Janson by
Rowland Phototypesetting Ltd
Bury St Edmunds, Suffolk

Printed and bound in Great Britain by
HarperCollinsManufacturing Glasgow

I have done the state some service, and they know't;
No more of that. I pray you in your letters
When you shall these unlucky deeds relate
Speak of me as I am; nothing extenuate,
Nor set down aught in malice.

Othello, William Shakespeare

Contents

LIST OF ILLUSTRATIONS   ix

ACKNOWLEDGEMENTS   xi

PROLOGUE: Unlucky Deeds   1

I   A Child of the 1920s   7

II   A Seat in the Dáil   16

III   Man of Justice   29

IV   A Mohawk   45

V   The First Leadership Contest   55

VI   The Covert Republican   71

VII   'Arms and the Man'   80

VIII   The Arms Trials   93

IX   'A Part of My Life'   102

X   From the Back Benches   110

XI   In the Political Wilderness   121

XII   The Hard Road Back   133

XIII   Lynch Under Threat   144

XIV   Party Leader and Taoiseach   155

XV   'A Better Way of Doing Things'   164

XVI   The Stardust Fire   175

XVII   Into Opposition   185

XVIII   The Year of GUBU   197

XIX   Out of Power   213

XX   The Fall of Garret FitzGerald   228

XXI   Converted to Rectitude   236

XXII   The Beef Scandal   250

XXIII   Resignation   274

EPILOGUE: The Next Generation   287

INDEX   300

List of Illustrations

Photographs courtesy of the *Irish Independent* unless stated

between pages 36–37

Haughey in 1966.
Outside the Four Courts during the Arms trial in November 1970 with Neil Blaney.
Haughey gives his press conference after the Arms Trial acquittal.
Haughey at the time of his trial in 1970.
Being congratulated by Dublin postman Ned Brennan.
Lynch's 1977 Government.

between pages 132–133

Aerial view of Abbeville.
Innishvichillane Island.
Haughey and Brian Lenihan leaving Dublin, 20 May 1980.
With George Colley in 1980.
Margaret Thatcher with Haughey and Lenihan, December 1980.
Triumphant having survived the leadership challenge of February 1983.
Cartoon from *The Irish Times*, 22 January 1992.
The Boss, at the Fianna Fáil Ard Fheis, March 1991.
Haughey with Bernard Cahill, chairman of Aer Lingus (The Irish Times/*Matt Kavanagh*).
Cartoon in *The Irish Times*, 7 November 1991.

between pages 228–229

Sean Doherty and his wife, Maura, at his press conference, 21 January 1992 (The Irish Times/*Frank Miller*).
Cartoon in *The Irish Times*, January 1992.
Haughey at his January 1992 press conference (The Irish Times/*Matt Kavanagh and John Carlos*).
Haughey's hands at the press conference (The Irish Times/*Peter Thursfield and John Carlos*).
Campaigning on behalf of his son, Sean, at St Brendan's Church, Coolock, in Dublin North-Central, 1992 (The Irish Times/*Paddy Whelan*).

Acknowledgements

I was not in Ireland for the 1957 general election, when Charles Haughey first entered the Dáil, but witnessed the presidential election two years later, which was combined with a referendum on proportional representation. Eamon de Valera became president, and Sean Lemass succeeded him as leader of Fianna Fáil and Taoiseach. In 1961, within one month of the general election which led to Charles Haughey's first appointment as a member of an Irish government, when he became Minister for Justice, I joined *The Irish Times*, and the following year I replaced Jack White as *Guardian* correspondent in Dublin, writing about Irish politics for a number of years for that newspaper. For thirty years I wrote about Irish politics for various publications, but principally, from 1972, for the *Irish Independent*. I owe a great debt of gratitude to the various editors for whom I worked, among them Basil Clancy, editor of *Hibernia*, Nicholas Leonard, editor of *Business and Finance*, Hector Legge of *The Sunday Independent*, Bartle Pitcher, managing director of Independent Newspapers, who invited me to join the group and write about politics, Aidan Pender, who edited the *Irish Independent* in the 1970s, and his successor, the present editor, Vincent Doyle. It is never easy to explain what their support means, or how it operates in a day-to-day way. Trust would be the one-word answer, often silent, unquestioning, but essential. And of all the many colleagues to whom I owe a debt, it is probably greatest to them, and in particular the two *Irish Independent* editors.

During that whole period I kept good documentation of meetings, correspondence, press conferences, and complete files of everything I wrote. I have drawn extensively on this primary material, much of it recorded in Leinster House, in the Dáil and Senate chambers, and in what are euphemistically called 'the corridors of power'. And I was in the habit of writing a private journal of events which has been widely drawn on for this book.

The literature for the period is not extensive and individual works which have been useful, or have been directly quoted, are cited in the text. The best historical accounts are J. J. Lee's *Ireland 1912–1985* and Roy Foster's *Modern Ireland 1600–1972*. Several political journalists have written more directly about Haughey and his era, and the outstanding titles, much quoted where relevant, are *The Boss: Charles Haughey in Government* by Joe Joyce and Peter Murtagh, *The Party: Inside Fianna Fáil* by Dick Walsh, and *The Haughey File* by Stephen Collins. They and many other political journalists have shown admirable courage in covering the period which I have dealt with in this book, and in addition to those who have written books about aspects of Irish politics during the period I would acknowledge the very considerable contribution of two with whom I worked closely: Vincent Browne and Geraldine Kennedy.

Many who gave more specific assistance, directly related to aspects of this book, and including politicians and men and women in public life, do not wish to be acknowledged, and attempting to separate and thank the rest would be an invidious pursuit. I am grateful to the many who offered help and advice, who checked details, who enriched or changed my judgements and perceptions. The man and his life are presented essentially in a political context and the final judgements about him and his actions are my own. But the work of political comment and biography would be impossible without the constant checking which is the unseen activity of political writing and the willing assistance which was given to me over many years is here gratefully acknowledged.

PROLOGUE

UNLUCKY DEEDS

Speak of me as I am[1]

C HARLES HAUGHEY handed over the leadership of his party and of the Government of the country on Tuesday, 11 February 1992. In an emotional speech in the Dáil he chose Shakespeare, and *Othello*, from which to draw an epitaph for a career and for a life:

> I have done the state some service; they know't
> No more of that –

and went on to speak with feeling of a lifetime's work in politics, of 35 years as a member of the House, of his predecessors and even of his own achievements, which he summarized as service to all the people, 'to the best of his ability'.

The quotation from Shakespeare was briefer than it might have been. Haughey curtailed it, for obvious reasons. No matter, the commentators picked up on it and published the following day Othello's even better-known lines appealing for a fair press after his departure:

> I pray you in your letters
> When you shall these unlucky deeds relate
> Speak of me as I am; nothing extenuate,
> Nor set down aught in malice.

Unlucky deeds they had certainly been. In any assessment of Haughey's career in politics, the question of luck arises. One single example looms large above the rest and was pure misfortune. This was the Stardust Fire, in 1981, which caused the Fianna Fáil Ard Fheis to be abandoned

[1] The quotations at the head of the chapters throughout this book are taken from William Shakespeare's play *Othello*.

at the beginning of its deliberations on the Saturday morning. Although this event, tragic in its impact on so many lives, was of passing significance in Haughey's career, it did more than terminate the annual conference of the party; it also denied him the platform to a general election he would have won, thus transforming his own career and future. But that election was deferred, the Maze hunger strike followed and when he did go to the country, in the summer, he lost. It was the first of many defeats, the hardest to bear and the one that most clearly resulted from bad luck.

But a general assessment of Haughey's career can only partly be based on unlucky deeds. He periodically demonstrated appallingly bad judgement. He judged wrongly the Arms Crisis of 1969 and landed himself in court, charged with conspiracy. He misjudged the fall of the FitzGerald administration, in January 1982, and reacted badly to it and the events that followed. He misjudged the general election in November 1982. And by far the greatest misjudgement of his whole career was his decision to go to the country in May 1989, choosing to have an 'unnecessary' and unwanted election in which he dropped four seats and was forced into coalition. This set in train his downfall.

Charles Haughey was Fianna Fáil leader from December 1979 to February 1992 and formed his first administration on assuming that leadership. He fought five general elections as leader of the party, and lost two of them outright. Of the others he was able to form two Fianna Fáil administrations with minority support. The last election fought by Haughey resulted in the party going into coalition for the first time in its history. Moreover, this coalition was with his strongest critic Desmond O'Malley, leader of the Progressive Democrats. In none of the elections did he achieve an overall majority for his party, something which his immediate predecessor, Jack Lynch, had achieved so convincingly in 1977. This meant that at no time did he have the stability of single-party rule for a full Dáil term. For a man who had spent thirty-five years as a deputy, twenty years as a minister and twelve years as leader of his party with four terms as prime minister, this was a cruel exercise in political punishment.

Many people in the country had felt relief at Charles Haughey's consistent inability to win any kind of convincing electoral mandate; many had voted in the various elections to achieve such an outcome. The very existence of the Progressive Democrats derived from a split within Fianna Fáil directly related to Haughey's own autocratic and personalized style of government; and throughout his active political life this had induced in people who knew him or worked with him reservations about, and at times fear of, his willingness to observe democratic requirements within his own party and in the country.

Ten years before becoming leader of Fianna Fáil, Charles Haughey had been dismissed by his predecessor, Jack Lynch, and had been brought before the courts on charges of conspiring to import arms illegally into the State. Though acquitted, he was exposed by the trial as having apparently been motivated by strong republican sympathies. And soon after becoming leader of Fianna Fáil, in 1979, he demonstrated a desire to make fundamental changes in the country's policy on Northern Ireland, with a view to achieving a united Ireland. Combined with his early approach to the economic problems of the country, this represented an odd set of political choices and his management of them alienated a significant proportion of the electoral support which had held steady behind Fianna Fáil during the previous two decades.

Charles Haughey can be seen, therefore, as a compromised candidate for leadership from the outset, bearing within himself mistakes and flaws. He brought to the leadership of his party, when he won it in 1979, a whiff of sulphur, a hint of danger, a sense of threat. And these handicaps remained with him throughout the succeeding twelve years. Quite simply, many were afraid of him, those closest to him, including his colleagues within the governments he formed, often more fearful than the rest. And this seemed to protect him through the various challenges which inevitably followed his electoral and other failures.

He became renowned for his ability to survive. Survival at the head of his own party, the largest in the State since 1932, gave him a rather crumpled passport to power, even if it did not result in any overall majorities. And he devoted much attention to the problems of dominating the Fianna Fáil organization, recognizing that this was the key to the formation of successive administrations. In the end it was his own party which dismissed him.

He is a man of immense charm with a compelling physical presence, despite his smallness of stature. This has caused many to liken him to Napoleon. He moves with economy of gesture and energy. His well-tailored suits conceal a plumpness not unlike that of the French emperor. His handshake is without warmth or commitment; a soft, limp paddle of flesh is offered disdainfully and received humbly. Into his eyes are concentrated all his feelings and they are essentially cold and suspicious; the stare is reptilian. On public occasions the eyes flicker ceaselessly over the assembled company, giving always the impression that nothing whatever is missed. He becomes animated at political events and his look can take on fire and excitement. But it is in response to adulation that this happens, transforming an otherwise suspicious, guarded and threatening demeanour. Under pressure the lids of his eyes lower and he views the hostile world through narrow slits. During much of his political career it seems that he has seen the world as unremittingly hostile. It never has been such; indeed, quite the opposite, with his party, former leaders, the electorate, his political opponents, the public generally and women in particular, giving him repeatedly the benefit of the doubt over his behaviour and his actions. Yet the abiding image is of a human being under siege.

The public mask he always wears is of sober dignity and prudent judgement. Yet behind this there is anger and abuse, foul language to those closest to him and an abiding sense that, when criticized or attacked, the motivation is personal and vengeful. On many occasions, under pressure, he has claimed vilification; it is a favoured defence, obviating clear and convincing answers to the legitimate questions which have faced him throughout his career.

One query persistently made concerns his wealth. By any standards he is a wealthy man. Independent assessments by accountants indicate the need for a current, pre-tax income of £500,000 annually to main-tain the large mansion in north county Dublin, extensive land, an island off the west coast with a house built at great expense, bloodstock, an ocean-going yacht, regular riding to hounds, a connoisseur's taste in wines which is lavishly indulged, love of fine clothes and a reputation for affairs with many women. Yet he has been a full-time public rep-resentative for thirty-five years and has been the holder of office, and therefore fully a public servant on modest remuneration for twenty of those years.

He worked successfully as an accountant before accepting his first ministerial appointment. What is known of his ownership of wealth-yielding, taxable income bears little relationship to the perceived levels of private expenditure. And it never has done. At a point in his career when he held the powerful position of Minister for Finance, he sold his house Grangemore at a substantial financial gain, the land which he sold becoming one of the large new housing estates on the north side of the city. With part of the proceeds he bought Abbeville. This is often pointed to as the source of his wealth and was at the time the subject of fierce political criticism. It has remained a benchmark for some kind of supposed relationship between power and wealth involving Haughey, Fianna Fáil and the development of a new style in politics with new standards. It has no such relevance and hardly relates at all to the sustained scale of Haughey's wealth. Though this has been raised regularly, during elections, with explanations sought by journalists, Haughey's extensive wealth and how it was accrued has remained an enigma.

He has reputedly had many love affairs, is clearly attracted by pretty women and is enormously attractive to women. It is more difficult to assess his relationships with men, or his capacity for friendship unconnected with politics and power. Many of those who worked closely with him were drawn into involvement, whether in a Fianna Fáil Party context or within the Civil Service, and found themselves in positions of trust or collaboration simply because they were there at the time, or performed some immediate task sufficiently well to impress a man who came to be known as 'The Boss', with very real implications of instant obedience and constant availability. Despite the sometimes accidental nature of the initial encounter or association, those who worked with him stayed with him, notably his principal speech-writer and political researcher Martin Mansergh, his cultural adviser Anthony Cronin, and his press secretary P. J. Mara.

This book deals with the political life. It does not attempt to invade the intense privacy with which Haughey surrounded his personal life, his financial affairs and wealth, his love affairs, his family, his friends. To a marked degree, many, though not all, of those with whom I spoke about him were reluctant to be identified or publicly thanked. This reticence is as understandable now as it was throughout the period from 1962 until the last days of his leadership, during which I informed myself about him and wrote about him and his unlucky deeds. My gratitude for all help received is as comprehensive now as it was during the whole of that fascinating period in Irish history.

CHAPTER I

A CHILD OF THE 1920s

Come, come:
You'll never meet a more sufficient man.

MUCH OF THE THINKING of Charles Haughey's generation
was shaped more by the events that *followed* Ireland's independence than by those that brought it about. His views
on Northern Ireland and on Anglo-Irish relations, his attitudes towards
Fine Gael, all of these were strongly conditioned by a tragic sequence
of events in Irish history, beginning with the the signing of the Treaty
in December 1921. This single event, which achieved independence
for the twenty-six southern counties of Ireland, while at the same time
ratifying the future existence of the remaining six counties of Northern
Ireland within the United Kingdom, shaped Irish political life for the
rest of the twentieth century. The Treaty should have healed the long
years of struggle to bring about an independent state. Instead, the
Treaty divided the country from top to bottom, created the foundations for two bitterly opposed political parties, led to an immediate
and savage civil war, and continued for many years to be not just the
basis for the confrontations that developed within democratic politics,
but also the excuse for the continued existence of a guerrilla organization – the IRA – which exists to this day. The most bitter period of
all stretched from four years before Charles Haughey's birth up to the
late 1920s, when he was still no more than a child. And he must have
viewed these years through the fortunes and career of his father, a
man whose life, from well before independence until he resigned from
the army in 1928, was professionally engaged in the military underpinning of power. It was a modest involvement. Nevertheless, his
father's life, in the space of those early years of the State's history,
gave a geography to the son's understanding of his country: Castlebar
in the west of Ireland, Swatragh in Northern Ireland, and Dublin, the
cradle for all his future energies and identity.

The tragic events of those early years were the product of a compromise in the Treaty of 1921, signed by Michael Collins and the other signatories (but not by de Valera), only under threat from Britain of renewed war 'within three days', as Lloyd George dramatically put it. The Treaty confirmed acceptance of a separate Protestant state on the island of Ireland, loyal to Britain and in certain important areas subject to the parliament at Westminster. It also assured, for the 26 counties, continued membership of the British Empire and entailed an oath of allegiance to the King, who would maintain a representative in Ireland, the Governor General, and there would be other ties in areas of security. A modest loophole, the Boundaries Commission, gave some prospect of a future reconsideration of the divided nature of the island of Ireland, but not much. The Irish Free State came into existence with certain fatal flaws and these fired an indignation fierce enough to provoke an immediate civil war and to shape political life for many years afterwards. For a dedicated minority, the compromise of 1921 represented a justification for challenging, on a permanent basis, the peaceful development of a constitutional democracy in either part of Ireland.

This grouping, from which may be traced modern Sinn Fein and the Provisional IRA, was there from before the start of the Irish Free State. The famous statement by Liam Mellowes[1], a militarist republican opposed to the Treaty, that 'we who stand by the Republic still will I presume rebel against the new government that would be set up if this Treaty is passed', set in 1921 a standard of divisiveness that has been present ever since.[2]

The shaping of Charles Haughey's beliefs about his country and its history, which were always arguably more republican than they appeared on the surface, relates very much to this violent, still-confused period of Irish history and to the career of his father.

Charles Haughey was born in Castlebar, County Mayo, on 16 September 1925. He was the third son of Sean, or 'Johnnie', Haughey, a commandant in the Irish Army, and his wife, Sarah, whose maiden name was McWilliams. She used the Irish form of his name, Cathal, and he also frequently signed himself in this way. There were seven

---

[1] Liam Mellowes (sometimes spelt 'Mellows') (1892–1922) was born in Liverpool and brought up in Wexford. His politics were radical, his idealism rigidly republican and extreme, rejecting the Treaty as a betrayal. He fought in the Four Courts, was arrested in September and executed in December 1922.
[2] See J. J. Lee, *Ireland 1912–1985: Politics and Society*, London, 1989, pp. 50, 56–7.

children in all: of the sons Padraig, the eldest, associated later with his brother, particularly in the late 1960s; Sean worked for Dublin Corporation and became assistant city manager; and Eoghan became a priest in the Oblate Order and a teacher at Belcamp College. There were three daughters, Bride, Maureen and Eithne. At the time of Charles's birth his father was attached to the 4th Battalion, Western Command, 2nd Brigade. Two years earlier he had been based in Ballina, in command of the 63rd Battalion. The Haugheys did not come from Mayo, however, but from County Derry, where Sean had been active in the War of Independence. In January 1919 he was second-in-command of a South Derry battalion of Irish Volunteers. In 1922 he was in command of a brigade. Sean Haughey is reputed to have smuggled a consignment of rifles from Donegal to Derry early in the Civil War, on the orders of Michael Collins and expressly for the defence of the nationalist areas in the city, and in other areas of the newly created Six Counties. This was the response from Dublin to rumours of pogroms against Roman Catholics, especially in Belfast.[1] When the Treaty was signed it conferred legitimacy on the Irish Republican Army (IRA), and opened the way for those who wanted to be transferred to the State's new army. Sean Haughey did this and moved to the Curragh, for training. He was there when the Civil War broke out and there he remained.

Having come from one of the most republican areas of Northern Ireland[2], and having fought for independence there, Sean Haughey, along with many others, found himself transformed, almost overnight, from being an officer in a rebel army into being an officer in the army of a new state in which the threat of civil war was already ominously present. This created understandable tensions within what had become the regular army of the Free State. It also precipitated the infiltration of that army by anti-Treaty forces at a time when its commander-in-chief, Michael Collins[3], well aware of the coming conflict, was urgently expanding the force. His military position at the time – the early

---

[1] See unsigned article, entitled 'At Home with the Haugheys', in 'The Haughey Years', supplement to *The Irish Times*, 31 January 1992.

[2] Swatragh is in the eastern part of County Derry, midway between Cookstown and Coleraine. It is divided from the county town by the Sperrin Mountains, the countryside being very deserted.

[3] Michael Collins, the dynamic and convincing leader of the Pro-Treaty side, Cabinet-member and military genius, was forced by the growing threat of civil war to relinquish political duties in the summer of 1922 in order to concentrate on winning over the support and loyalty of the existing army, weeding out the anti-Treaty factions and recruiting.

summer of 1922 – was precarious. He had an army of approximately 8,000 men, not all of them armed, and their strategic positions needing careful consideration and in some cases swift reorganization. The recruitment that took place helped to save the State from a long-drawn-out war, but also created problems for the future. From a standing army of 8,000 men the regular Free State Army expanded to 55,000 men by the time the Civil War ended, the vast majority of whom then had to be demobilized. From August 1922, following Michael Collins' death at Béal na Bláth, Richard Mulcahy became commander-in-chief and hence responsible for this major problem of winding down the armed forces.[1]

Sean Haughey's position in all this appears to have been stable enough, in terms of his career. We know nothing of his attitudes. He was 'ordered to remain'[2] in training on the Curragh when the Civil War broke out, in 1922. Subsequently he followed a conventional army career. There seems to have been no great objection to the fact that he was working within the security forces of an increasingly 'law-and-order' administration in the mid-1920s, often deployed against those whose objectives remained precisely the ones with which he had grown up. Though this may have had a bearing on his relatively early resignation – he was only in his twenty-ninth year when he resigned his commission – it is more likely that the inducements used to scale down the huge army of the State once peace was restored were responsible, as was a period of ill-health. The inducements for people to leave the army included the provision of farms from properties which had been taken over by the Land Commission.

There were inextricable links between politics and the army in the early years of the State, resolved to some extent by the firmness of the administration formed after the deaths of Arthur Griffith and Michael Collins, an administration that was determined to establish clear dividing lines between the different institutions of the State, making the army answerable to the executive. Collins had been the epitome of the

---

[1] Richard Mulcahy (1886–1971) joined the Volunteers shortly after their formation in 1913 and fought in 1916, being subsequently interned. He was elected to the Westminster Parliament in 1918, supported the 1921 Treaty and, after commanding the Army during the Civil War, became Minister for Defence. His political career led him to the leadership of Fine Gael after W. T. Cosgrave's resignation in 1944, but he proved unacceptable to the coalition partners in 1948 as head of government and served in both inter-party administrations as Minister for Education.
[2] The phrase is used by Martin Mansergh, *The Spirit of the Nation: The Speeches of Charles J. Haughey*, Ed. by Martin Mansergh, Mercier Press, Cork, 1986, p. xxxi.

military and political leader combined, a suitable role in any struggle for independence, but increasingly redundant and dangerous once that independence has been achieved.

Normal politics, however, took much longer to restore. The Liam Mellowes line vitiated democracy through the 1922 and 1923 elections, remaining a shadow over the two elections of 1927 and even after the watershed of 1932, when Fianna Fáil took over from the Cumann na Gael government.

In the 1923 general election, republicans contested seats throughout the country, using Sinn Fein as their political organization. It was an extremely bitter time. Something in the region of 13,000 republicans, who had been on the losing side, were either in internment camps or in gaol; many more were 'on the run'. There was sustained harassment of republican supporters, including election workers, by the Free State Army, de Valera himself being arrested and gaoled. Nevertheless, Sinn Fein did well, winning 44 seats.

There is no indication that this was an additional reason why Sean Haughey resigned his army commission in 1928, but the scorn with which his son subsequently viewed that 1920s ruling tradition would indicate a deep aversion, shared by other members of the family, the Northern republican roots playing a significant part in family friendships and associations and shaping basic political beliefs. On one occasion in the Dáil a leading Opposition deputy attempted to suggest that Haughey had belonged at university to a political organization associated with Fine Gael; the vehemence with which he rejected this was absolute.

For whatever reasons, Sean Haughey did not become involved in Free State politics as they were developing in the period immediately after his departure from the army, in 1928. This departure came at a crucial time. It may have been his father's early career that coloured Haughey's own attitude to the Defence Forces. Years later, in a Dáil debate in 1958, he pleaded eloquently for increased expenditure on the Defence Forces in general and on the FCA[1] in particular. 'It has always seemed to me that it would be a very good thing that our young men from the ages of seventeen to twenty should go into the FCA and have an opportunity of being inculcated with patriotism, proper

[1] Fórsa Cosante Aitiúil, or the auxiliary defence force, a successor to the Local Defence Force (LDF) which was the Irish equivalent to the Territorial Army in Britain. The FCA was set up in 1946 and attracted a wide membership.

national ideals, a sense of discipline and all the other advantages that
go with military training at that early age . . . a lot of young men who
find themselves caught up in movements [a reference to the IRA]
without realizing fully what is involved in the ultimate, would never
get into these difficulties if the career of a member of the FCA were
made more attractive and interesting.'[1]

Sean and Sarah Haughey both came from Swatragh, in County Derry,
where their families had lived for generations. Martin Mansergh, in his
edition of Charles Haughey's political speeches,[2] says that descent in the
Haughey family can be traced back to the Uí Neill, kings of Ulster.
There is a wider association with the O hEochaidh clan, which inhabited
a considerable area of mid-Ulster. Members of the clan were kings of
Ulidia up to the end of the twelfth century and one of the O hEochaidh
kings fell at Clontarf, fighting with Brian Boru.

After resigning from the army, Sean Haughey settled for a short
time in Sutton, a suburb on the north side of Dublin, before moving
to a farm in Dunshaughlin, County Meath, where Charles Haughey
had his first schooling. There were still members of the family in
Swatragh and Charles also spent periods there living with his grandmother, at times going to the local school at Corlecky. In 1933 the
family settled in Donnycarney and it was from there that he went to
the Christian Brothers' primary school, Scoil Iosef, in Marino, and on
to the St Joseph's Christian Brothers' Secondary School at Fairview.
The family house in Donnycarney remained as such until well after
the death of Sarah Haughey on 13 September 1989, at the age of 87.
Two daughters, Eithne and Maureen, who worked in business, lived
there with their mother. The house was corporation-built in the 1930s
on the corner of Belton Park Road and Belton Park.[3] This was then
an area of new corporation building, on the very fringes of the city.
Beyond it lay what was left of several of the great estates of the eigh-
teenth century, one of which, Abbeville, was one day to become
Haughey's home. The standards of construction in the newly created
suburb were impressive and the area has since become a settled and
attractive example of housing on the north side of the city, dominated
by the huge Roman Catholic church.

[1] *Dáil Report*, 25 March 1958, col. 894–5.
[2] Ed. Martin Mansergh, op. cit.
[3] The house was number 12. In the 1992–3 telephone directory it was still listed as the
home of Mrs S. Haughey and is still, presumably, a family home.

He was a distinguished pupil and good at sport. He played GAA[1] games with some success and was an able scholar, taking first place in the Dublin Corporation Scholarship examination while at St Joseph's, and winning a scholarship to the National University. While still at school, in his fifteenth year, he joined the Local Defence Force, transferring to the FCA when it was founded, in which he became a lieutenant. He remained a member until his election to the Dáil, in 1957, and for a time considered the army as a career, but was dissuaded from this by his family.[2]

He was a student at University College, Dublin, from 1943 to 1946, with a bursary in commerce, graduating with an honours degree in that subject and opting, on impulse, for accountancy as a profession. He had no Fianna Fáil roots, but at university met Maureen Lemass, whom he was to marry on 18 September 1951. Maureen Lemass was the eldest of Sean Lemass's four children. At the time of her meeting with her future husband, her father had been Minister for Industry and Commerce in five successive administrations throughout the whole period of Fianna Fáil rule, since 1932. By the early 1940s, when his daughter was at University College, Dublin, with Charles Haughey, Sean Lemass was an obvious, but not the only, candidate to succeed de Valera as party leader. There were three other children: Peggy, Noel[3] and Sheila. Maureen Lemass read commerce at university. Once married to Charles Haughey she kept a deliberately low profile, devoting herself to home and family. Friends describe her as a gentle and patient woman. She rarely participated in political events, disliking public occasions and taking no part in politics at all. She shares with her husband an interest in horses and in later years has given much support to riding for the disabled.

---

[1] The GAA, or Gaelic Athletic Association, ran a complete sporting system in the Republic of Ireland from its foundation, in 1884. The main sports were hurling and Gaelic football. Haughey played both for the school, for Leinster Colleges teams, and then went on to play for two Dublin clubs, the St Vincent's Hurling and Football Club, and Parnell's Gaelic Football Club, for which, in 1945, he won a Dublin Senior Football Championship Medal. The GAA exercised a ban on non-Irish games, so that members were forbidden to play 'English' games, such as rugby. Effectively it introduced a political and to some extent sectarian divide in sport throughout Ireland, North and South.
[2] Vincent Browne, *The Magill Book of Irish Politics*, Dublin, 1981, p. 157.
[3] Noel entered politics in 1956 and was deputy for twenty years and a junior minister from 1969 to 1973. His death in 1976 precipitated a by-election which was won by his widow, Eileen, who then served in the Dáil and later as an MEP. Peggy married Jack O'Brien, who was an officer in the Irish Army and successively aide-de-camp to his father-in-law and then to Jack Lynch. In the turmoil of the Arms Crisis, and specifically because of Sean Sherwin's departure from Fianna Fáil, Jack O'Brien had differences with Jack Lynch.

Haughey's instincts, deriving from his Christian Brothers education, from sporting experience, from family background and from his friends at university, were decidedly republican, and an incident which took place in May 1945, on Victory in Europe Day, gives some indication of this. In celebration of the ending of the war in Europe, students at Trinity College flew the Union Jack from the flagpole facing College Green. Charles Haughey, with a friend, Seamus Sorohan, who was then a law student and later became a barrister, burned another Union Jack on a lamp-post outside the college, an action which led to a minor riot.

After graduating in 1946, he was articled to Michael J. Bourke, of Boland, Bourke and Company, obtaining his associate membership of the Institute of Chartered Accountants in 1949, when he was also called to the Bar, becoming a fellow in 1955. In 1950, with Harry Boland, he established an accountancy practice, remaining an active partner until his first political appointment, in 1960.

Charles Haughey was recruited into Fianna Fáil in 1947 by Boland and another schoolfriend, George Colley. Both were the sons of Dáil deputies of the time. Harry Boland's father, Gerald Boland, was Minister for Justice; Harry Colley, George Colley's father, represented Dublin North-East and the branch of the party which Haughey joined was in that constituency.[1] Ten years after joining, Charles Haughey was to unseat his friend's father and take the Dublin North-East seat in the general election of 1957.

Haughey was active in cumann affairs from the start. He became involved in the writing of a policy pamphlet called *Férinne Fáil* for young members of the party. When Richard Moylan retired as cumann secretary, Charles Haughey took his place. His first attempt to get elected to the Dáil was in the general election of 1951, when he stood in the Dublin North-East constituency with the two outgoing deputies, Oscar Traynor and Harry Colley. Eugene Timmons, who was later to be his running-mate in a number of elections, was also on the party ticket. Haughey obtained 1,629 first-preference votes but failed to get elected. He had two further unsuccessful attempts at election, in the general election of 1954, where he marginally improved his first-preference support to 1,812 votes, and in the 1956 by-election, occasioned by the death of the former Dublin Lord Mayor, Alfie Byrne. The seat went to Byrne's son.

[1] Fianna Fáil's organization is based on the *cumann*, meaning 'club' or 'association'.

Charles Haughey's father died in 1947. Although it seems that his political sympathies would have been with the Fianna Fáil Party, there had been no association during his lifetime and there is even an indication that political focus in the family was on Northern Ireland and on Northern politics during Charles Haughey's childhood. During the time they lived in Donnycarney, in the mid-1930s, his parents, according to him, 'kept open house for friends and visitors from the North'.[1] This would have been against the general political trend of the period, hinting at an association with republican objectives designed to complete the business of independence for the Six Counties by reversing the establishment of the Stormont Government of 1920 and bringing all 32 counties under Dublin rule. But it is no more than a hint.

In Charles Haughey's career this end became a declared objective, shaping his policies in power, conditioning his responses in opposition and inspiring many of the most significant speeches he made. From the time of his father's death, a career was steadily built within the framework of the politics of the day and in association with the largest political organization in the country; but during the previous 22 years a different set of associations had prevailed against a background of national change and adaptation to the reality of an Ireland permanently divided into two parts.

---

[1] Ed. Martin Mansergh, op. cit., p. xxxi. Though the editor of this selection of speeches throughout Charles Haughey's career specifically says that the Fianna Fáil leader 'did not see any part of it prior to publication', he makes a specific exception in respect of the details of those early, childhood years.

CHAPTER II

A SEAT IN THE DÁIL

in such cases
Men's natures wrangle with inferior things,
Though great ones are their object.

T
HE TEN-YEAR PERIOD, from the time Charles Haughey joined
Fianna Fáil to his successful winning of a Dáil seat in 1957,
was probably the least stable period politically for Ireland since the State's foundation. Indeed, in the eyes of many people,
there was a loss of confidence amounting almost to complete
despair.

From the end of the Second World War, in 1945, there had been
a succession of administrations, all of them short-lived, with neither
side able to stay in power for a second term. After his long and
unbroken sixteen-year rule, from 1932 to 1948, which included six
successive elections in which he first gained then retained power,
Eamon de Valera lost in the 1948 general election and a coalition
Government was formed under the leadership of John A. Costello.[1]
The principal partnership, which was to become central to all future
non-Fianna Fáil coalitions, was between Fine Gael and Labour. But
in fact Fine Gael, with only 31 out of the 147 seats in the Dáil, was close
to being at a record low in its political fortunes. Labour had 19 seats
and, in order for these two parties to form a government, they needed
the additional participation of a new grouping, Clann na Poblachta.
This party, formed only two years earlier and led by Seán MacBride,[2]

[1] John A. Costello (1891–1976), a lawyer and former Attorney General in four administrations up to 1932, was not especially active in politics, though he had held a Dáil seat
since 1933. He was a compromise choice, seen as the only significant figure able to unite
the disparate elements in the new Government.
[2] Seán MacBride (1904–88) was the son of John MacBride and Maud Gonne. He was
secretary to Eamon de Valera, was called to the bar and founded, in 1946, Clann na
Poblachta, which formed part of the first Inter-Party Government, in which MacBride
was Minister for External Affairs. He had a distinguished international career subsequently and received, among many honours, the Nobel Peace Prize.

had ten seats. Even this was not enough in an 147-seat Dáil in which Fianna Fáil had 68 seats and the additional support of independents, of whom there were no less than 22, added to the potential instability of the new administration.

It was not unsuccessful. Early on, Costello made the significant constitutional change of declaring Ireland a republic. This was announced in somewhat odd circumstances, at a press conference in Ottawa during an official visit by Costello to Canada, and there was some question as to whether a Government decision had been made prior to the Ottawa statement. Domestically it revitalized the 'National Question', putting an entirely new focus on the political parties and their will in respect of partition, Anglo-Irish relations and the future shape of a country passing through a crisis of confidence. It was a challenge, by a new, untried, compromise political leader, to the towering figure of Eamon de Valera. As Lee[1] puts it, 'It stole Fianna Fáil's Sunday suit of constitutional clothes. Who were the real republicans now?' Costello was head of the administration, though not leader of Fine Gael. Seán MacBride had objected to the then Fine Gael leader, Richard Mulcahy,[2] as Taoiseach on the grounds that Mulcahy had led the Free State side in the Civil War after Michael Collins' death. MacBride, who saw himself as the guardian of a purer form of anti-partition republicanism than even de Valera espoused, could not stomach the idea of working under the former leader of troops who had given so harsh a time to republicans in the 1920s. The very existence of MacBride's party, Clann na Poblachta, was in part based on dissatisfaction by republicans in the country with the absence of any progress on partition. Since Fianna Fáil had been in power for sixteen years, this meant dissatisfaction with de Valera. De Valera was concerned at the possibility that the unlikely partnership of Costello and MacBride would deprive his own party of its verbal republicanism by specific actions, not just in declaring a republic, but by leaving the Commonwealth, which took Ireland a step further away from Britain than India, which also became a republic in 1949, and by refusing to join NATO on the grounds that partition precluded it.

There were other noteworthy achievements under John A. Costello's first administration, but the coalition fell apart over the so-called

[1] J. J. Lee, op. cit., p. 300.
[2] Richard Mulcahy had succeeded William T. Cosgrave in 1944 as party leader and remained in that position until 1959, when James Dillon took over.

'Mother-and-Child'[1] scheme as a result of the Government and the Roman Catholic Church coming into conflict. This was a *cause célèbre* in Irish political history, demonstrating the power and effectiveness of Roman Catholic Church intrusion into law and the administration of the country's health services. Seán MacBride had nominated Noel Browne as Health Minister on the formation of the first Inter-Party Government. Browne attempted to introduce a state maternity health scheme which was to operate without a means test. The Church, which was heavily involved through Catholic religious orders in the running of hospitals, opposed government intervention in this area and the bishops denounced state health care for all mothers and children as 'a ready-made instrument for future totalitarian aggression'. Browne's radicalism added fuel to the controversy, but his colleagues in government failed to back him and the scheme was abandoned. He later published his correspondence with the bishops, to the delight of Unionists in Northern Ireland, who republished the exchanges as clear evidence of 'Rome Rule' in the Republic of Ireland. John Costello, the head of that administration, commented wryly, 'The public never ought to have become aware of the matter.'[2] Fianna Fáil did not win an overall majority in the general election called in 1951 and so led a shaky minority government that lasted just three years in office, and were again defeated and replaced by an administration led by Costello.

The second so-called Inter-Party Government, which lasted from 1954 to 1957, was potentially more stable than the 1948–51 administration. From a low point of 31 seats in 1948, Fine Gael had grown to 50 seats and, in coalition with Labour, which had 19 seats, comfortably exceeded the rather miserable 65 seats won by Fianna Fáil.[3] The two parties, which had worked well together in the earlier 'rainbow' coalition, seemed set to run a full term and indeed to introduce sensible reforms and to combat effectively the economic stagnation that had dogged successive administrations since the ending of the Second World War. But the 'old trouble', of defining and dealing with 'the

---

[1] The 'Mother-and-Child' scheme was introduced by Dr Noel Browne, only 33 when he became Minister for Health on his first day as a Dáil deputy. A brilliant, resourceful and inventive politician, though one whom many found difficult to work with, Browne stood up to the Church over State involvement in the care of children. The Government, cowed by the Church, failed to back him; his party leader, Seán MacBride, forced his resignation and the crisis brought down the Government.

[2] See R. F. Foster, *Modern Ireland 1600–1972*, pp. 571–2.

[3] In the whole period from 1932, when they won their first general election, to the present, this was the lowest number of seats won by Fianna Fáil in any election.

National Question', returned. A militant republican campaign in Northern Ireland and in Britain, involving bombings on the Border and bombs on the British mainland, was initiated in 1956. Costello's hostility to the IRA campaign and his use of the Offences Against the State Act to arrest and imprison them created insupportable internal strains between Fine Gael and Seán MacBride's Clann na Poblachta. MacBride withdrew the support of his party and then tabled a motion of no confidence in the government, forcing a general election in March. It took place in unfavourable economic circumstances and de Valera won an outright majority for the first time in ten years.

Charles Haughey had fought the high-profile by-election, occasioned by the death of Dublin's Lord Mayor, Alfie Byrne, a year before and was well placed when the general election of 1957 was called in February. He won a Dáil seat for the first time. He was to retain it for the rest of his political career. The election was a turning-point in his fortunes. The election itself was a political watershed for Ireland. It was the last of the old-style elections, fought out at public meetings and rallies, despite the fact that it took place in February. There was no television. There were abrasive, attacking speeches, posters and placards, and much pounding of the pavements and roadways of Ireland.

Not only had the television service not been started, but radio broadcasting itself was a branch of the Department of Posts and Telegraphs, came under the direct control of the minister and was staffed by civil servants. Far from inducing party political pressures or making it a key element at election time, it had the reverse effect; it was insulated from politics. 'Radio Eireann staff members were expected as civil servants to take no overt part in politics and the station took a strictly neutral position simply by broadcasting no political material at all.'[1] It is hard to imagine Irish elections under such a handicap. In 1960, when the Broadcasting Authority Act transferred the control from a government department to 'semi-State' status, and opened the way for television, which was in place for the 1961 election, all changed irreversibly. But in 1957 the newspapers bore the burden of political comment and argument, and pushed the candidates themselves on to the streets. Political rallies in the dusk in College Green, with the penetrating voice of the 75-year-old Eamon de Valera, the stentorian

[1] See Basil Chubb, *The Government and Politics of Ireland*, Stanford (California) and London, 1970, p. 134.

tones of Sean Lemass, or the powerfully persuasive, magic harmonies of James Dillon, set the tenor of campaigning. These speeches were reported in the long, sober, unbroken columns of the national daily newspapers. Paper was scarce, advertising limited, the lavish coverage of later elections was not even a glint in the eyes of party organizers. Only the main events, leaders' speeches, major rallies and meetings, were brought to public attention by the press. Not that people were unaware; newspapers were an arm of information, not head and legs as well, and personal campaigning was dominant. Fianna Fáil won exactly half the seats. Sinn Fein, with five per cent of the votes and four seats, stayed out of the Dáil, giving de Valera his overall majority. Fianna Fáil increased its vote from 578,000 to 593,000, though in percentage terms this represented an increase from 43.4 per cent to 48.3. Fine Gael dropped 10 seats. Labour, its image seriously damaged by association with the economic constraints of Costello's Finance Minister, Gerard Sweetman,[1] dropped from 19 to 12 seats. Seán Mac-Bride's party, which had been so prominent in the first Inter-Party Government and had then been responsible, in no small measure, for precipitating the 1957 general election, was virtually wiped out, with MacBride himself losing his Dáil seat.

One of the casualties in that general election was George Colley's father, Harry Colley, who lost his seat to Charles Haughey, then making his *fourth* attempt to get into the Dáil. Though George Colley had been responsible for bringing Haughey into Fianna Fáil, he was not then a Dáil deputy, nor did he at the time intend to become one. At that stage he had decided to practise as a solicitor, a possible indication of the poor view he had of the future of a politician.

The 1957 general election was Eamon de Valera's greatest electoral triumph. He had passed through a ten-year period of uncertainty and instability, unable to deliver the kind of victory that his party demanded, unable to offer practical leadership on the 'National Question' and lamentably short of ideas on how Ireland's economy was to be revitalized. Indeed, it is questionable whether Eamon de Valera perceived revitalization as necessary at all; he had a home-spun respect for the economic status quo, thinking that it underpinned social

[1] Gerard Sweetman (1908–70) had a short but impressive political career and showed considerable courage in addressing Ireland's economic crisis during the period of the second Inter-Party Government. He spotted the talent of T. K. Whitaker and appointed him secretary of the Department of Finance and head of the Civil Service in 1956.

stability. The practical side of party affairs, including the orchestration of policy, was in the hands of Sean Lemass[1] and others. To some extent de Valera was increasingly seen as blocking the progress of the next generation within Fianna Fáil and notably inhibiting Sean Lemass from introducing a more progressive programme of industrial and economic development. But though de Valera achieved a resounding victory, it was in fact more a vote of no confidence in the other parties, since the victory was achieved without any massive swing.

Ireland stood at a crossroads in 1957. Though the election had been precipitated by historical issues, the campaign itself had concentrated on the economy and the future, and within Fianna Fáil the focus of attention was on this and on the Budget which was immediately brought in by James Ryan.[2]

Charles Haughey made his maiden speech on 14 May, identifying himself with principles of economic growth and the motivation of profit. He offered the examples of Britain and the United States, whose industrial and commercial expansion was essentially funded out of profit and contrasted this with the Irish situation, where too few industrialists were making any real profit at all. If industrialists were offered profit as a motive for their commitment to the country's growth and prosperity, members of the Civil Service were exhorted to abandon their traditional approach of remaining the aloof and remote dispensers of regulations, the wider purpose of which they had never considered to be their business. 'If we are to achieve national recovery, it will involve a tremendous national crusade. It must be made clear to our civil servants that they also must take part in that crusade.' He proposed that there should be a new scheme, the State building factories for the purpose of renting them to new enterprises. It would solve 'one of the biggest' of all problems for new businesses – the finding of premises. It would also give a boost to the building industry.

Charles Haughey's maiden speech gave a good summary of his father-in-law Sean Lemass's economic thinking, which was to direct the fortunes of the country for the next decade: greater incentives for commercial enterprise, the direct involvement of the State in

---

[1] Sean Lemass (1899–1971) had been deputy leader of party and of government, in and out of power, since 1945. He was the obvious successor, though others – James Ryan, Sean MacEntee, Frank Aiken – were not inconsiderable figures.

[2] James Ryan (1891–1970) had been in the Department of Health in de Valera's previous administration, when Sean MacEntee was in Finance. Ryan was less conservative, more attuned to future needs, and possibly more under Lemass's influence.

motivating the private sector, the encouragement of the building industry and the generation of a broad national crusade aimed at recovery, and involving everyone in a harmonious spirit of enterprise.

Though Sean Lemass is always given credit as the architect of this policy, which was to shape Irish economic development throughout the 1960s, much of it was already in place when he came to power. The crusade to which Charles Haughey referred had already started. At the head of the Civil Service there was already a man with outstanding leadership qualities, dedicated entirely to the country's welfare and the detailed planning over what should be done was well advanced.

Kenneth Whitaker,[1] as Secretary of the Department of Finance, was the enlightened choice of Gerard Sweetman, Finance Minister in the outgoing Inter-Party Government, who had broken with precedent in persuading his ministerial colleagues to pass over more senior figures in the department on the grounds that Whitaker was the most qualified man for the position. His career had already been outstanding and he was ready to make the same kind of unconventional choices of staff as had been made in appointing him. 'I knew I could put together a team of willing collaborators who would be very able. I knew there were people I could touch who would be glad of a release from the rather narrow confines of their own responsibilities. We had economists. In the Department of Finance itself I brought in as many good officers as I could, no matter what their rank. One must try to transcend the hierarchical system.'[2]

Sean Lemass's first and most important contribution was to deliver the full backing of the Fianna Fáil Party, eliminating any political obstructions that might hinder Whitaker's own detailed planning. Lemass himself had a plan. It derived from the post-war Italian Vanoni Plan, a ten-year project of economic recovery in that country which Lemass had read about in the newspapers. He had then obtained a copy of it from the Italian Embassy in Dublin. Charles Haughey himself has told an attractive homespun story of his father-in-law's extensive reading during the period in opposition, 1954–7, which resulted in

---

[1] Kenneth Whitaker (b. 1916) joined the Irish Civil Service in 1934 and moved to the Department of Finance in 1938. He became Secretary of the Department on 30 May 1956.
[2] Author's interview with Dr T.K. Whitaker, August 1986. The interview was undertaken on behalf of John F. McCarthy, whose book, *Planning Ireland's Future: The Legacy of T. K. Whitaker* (Dublin, 1990), quotes extensively from it and also gives the best account of the lead given to politicians in the late 1950s and through the 1960s by this enlightened man and his collaborators.

his being sent out on Monday mornings to buy the various books on development and economics which Lemass had read about over the weekend.[1] The Italian example led to what became known as 'The 100,000 Jobs Speech', given to Fianna Fáil party members and supporters at a dinner in Clery's Ballroom on 11 October 1955. It was, in Lemass's own words, 'a rather amateurish attempt'. It failed to convince the party as a whole. It offered hostages to fortune, in that Lemass broke the basic rule of survival as a forecaster: he combined the figure, 100,000 jobs, with a deadline – five years. The party view was that such an approach was both unwise and unnecessary, and that it was better to keep all options open until they were back in power.

Lemass deserves credit more for his belief in a national debate on the country's economic future at the time than for being the originator of any really fundamental ideas about the structure and detail of what should be done. He believed that it 'would be politically wise for Fianna Fáil to try to restore the country's morale regardless of the party in power', a view that was not shared so generously by his party and in later years was reversed with damaging effect by his son-in-law when he became leader of Fianna Fáil and was in opposition, during the period 1982–7. Lemass envisaged public spending to create jobs, not to energize Irish industry. What he did achieve – and it took time – was a shift away from negative preoccupations and from rigid or narrow perceptions about how objectives were to be achieved. Policy on the Irish language was changed: the programme aimed at its protection rather than its restoration, and by means of persuasion rather than coercion. Lemass also faced more realistically than his predecessors the fact that the aim of reunification of the two parts of Ireland was more an excuse for pointless rhetoric than for any concrete proposals, and he set out to remedy this. Though these were still the primary objectives of the Fianna Fáil Party and constituted its claims to being 'the Republican Party', they needed and got a measure of change in their presentation to the public.

Fine Gael carried no such ideological luggage, giving Sweetman a freer hand, reinforced by the fact that Costello himself was not burdened by traditional worries over power in the future. He was there to do a job, the best possible, and concentration on the economy was logical to him. He was also prepared to be more experimental, not bound by conservative and doctrinaire thinking. The main proposals

[1] Ed. John F. McCarthy, op. cit., pp 25–8 and 67.

for industrial growth included the use of tax incentives to encourage exports and government investment in plant by way of grants which would help new industries to start up. It must have been particularly galling to lose power when a serious economic programme had actually been set in train and then to watch it be taken over by the great pragmatist, Sean Lemass.

Whitaker was the great bridgehead between Costello and Lemass and their administrations. He recognized the need for a national consensus on future development, which in turn would allow for rapid progress after an era of stagnation. The country, whichever side was in power, needed to be won over to the main investment objective, which was to attract the enterprise for Ireland's economic development from Britain and the United States, and to fund it properly. Lemass himself needed to come to terms with the idea that serious planning and motivation could be left in the hands of civil servants. Their role was to give public endorsement and the executive the backing necessary to the smooth operation of a large and complex public-service bureaucracy still largely based, in 1957, on the Whitehall system.

Whitaker was not alone in preparing the groundwork for planning. John A. Costello had as his adviser in his own department Charles Murray,[1] who was responsible for a guideline memorandum of some importance in January 1957, since it linked Irish economic planning with events in Europe and was prepared essentially to better the country's chances in future trading arrangements, either with a European Free Trade Area, or with the more restrictive 'Community' which came into existence just two months later with the signing of the Treaty of Rome. Whitaker and Murray had, for three months, already been working well together on this planning process when the change of government occurred, in March 1957, and by December Whitaker was able to explain the project in sufficient detail to his Minister for Finance, James Ryan, to obtain Government confirmation of broad inter-departmental backing for its finalization.

Whatever their shortcomings, *Economic Development*[2] and the sub-

---

[1] Charles Murray (born 1917) was just a month younger than Whitaker; they joined the Civil Service in the same year, 1934. Murray served with the Revenue Commissioners and in the Department of Agriculture before moving to the Taoiseach's Department, where he remained until Lemass took over from de Valera, in 1959, when he went to Finance. He was assistant secretary there until 1969, when he took over as secretary.

[2] *Economic Development* was a study of the Irish economy; *The Programme for Economic Expansion* was the White Paper produced from it and was published on 11 November 1958.

sequent White Paper revolutionized thinking in Ireland and set the country on a course of recovery which coincided with steady growth in world trade. The key elements represented a fundamental change in the way in which the economy had been managed since the 1930s. Protectionism and rigorous control of public spending, extending even to capital projects, were replaced with a new programme for the economy which brought down tariffs and placed major emphasis on investment, from both domestic and foreign sources. Tax incentives, increased emphasis on grants for capital investment, which had been in place since 1956, improvement of grasslands, the encouragement of foreign businesses to set up in Ireland and the encouragement also of foreign and domestic business collaborations, were all written into the programme. There was to be more use, where necessary and if carefully monitored, of supplementary capital resources drawn from international institutions such as the World Bank. As Whitaker said, many years later, 'The chief significance, I think, of what was done was, first, to free the Government of the day from the shackles of outmoded self-sufficiency policies and orient them fully towards free trade and, second, by showing, as we said, that "a dynamic of progress awaited release in agriculture, fisheries, industry and tourism", to regenerate confidence in our ability to manage our affairs successfully. That mismanagement recurred at times can scarcely be laid at our door.'[1]

Charles Haughey was then little more than a spectator. Yet his subsequent career as a politician, his reputation on economic matters, his frequent invocation of Sean Lemass's approach to the economic problems of Ireland as an ideal and his own later involvement in several subsequent national economic plans and programmes, all were formed in his first years in active politics. He became convinced of the *appeal* of planning and programming. He saw at first hand the creation of the dynamic approach which Whitaker had identified and watched it spread through the country, performing very much as had been projected. And to the end of his career, plans and programmes were an essential ingredient. Yet their character changed and his own capacity for genuine planning, embracing a vision that stretched ahead over a number of years, is open to serious question. Nothing characterizes Charles Haughey's early days in the Dáil so much as his own personal dynamism; he was driven by ambition to get on; his words and actions

---

[1] Whitaker speaking at a reception to mark the publication of *Planning Ireland's Future*, ed. by John F McCarthy, op. cit.

were fuelled by very remarkable intellectual ability. This made him impatient and in a sense intolerant of those less able around him. Such attitudes are not conducive to the patient realization of objectives over the lifetime of an administration and beyond. Unlike Lemass, whose personal ambitions were modest and who thought in collective, national terms about economic and social progress, his son-in-law was far more focused on himself and on the short, rather than the long, term.

In 1957 Haughey entered the Dáil. In 1959 Eamon de Valera resigned as Fianna Fáil leader and as Taoiseach to stand for election as president of Ireland, and was replaced by Lemass. Notwithstanding the fact that the economic programme predated the 1957 general election, the changeover from de Valera to Lemass represented an equally significant watershed, between the paternalistic style of the party's founder-figure and the pragmatic materialism of his successor. As a politician who was publicly to set his sights on the leadership of Fianna Fáil within the space of less than ten years, Charles Haughey drew equally from the examples of the two men. The paternalism of de Valera appealed to him; so too did the emphasis which de Valera placed on the so-called 'National Question' of reunification. If de Valera was authoritarian – though authoritarian in a subtle and persuasive way – then Charles Haughey was to be much more so, embracing an extreme independence of decision-making and of action which ultimately contributed to his downfall. If Lemass was a materialist and a pragmatist, then Haughey was that too, later turning his father-in-law's serious interest in planning into a much more token use of the idea of a national plan, and in fact pursuing only a loose and variable economic programme in the periods of power from the late 1970s into the 1990s. But in those early days as a deputy he was keenly interested in the details of economic planning and Haughey's close interest in planning is reflected in his contributions to debates. His maiden speech[1] demonstrated an impressive grasp of the programme which was then still in the process of being completed for publication. He stressed the practical needs of Irish industrialists by referring to the idea of advance factories, built by the state before an occupant had been identified. This approach, already adopted in Northern Ireland, would give valuable employment and an impetus to industrial development, Haughey said, and he went on saying it in subsequent speeches

[1] *Dáil Report*, 14 May 1957, col. 1197.

in a way that provoked cynicism. Indeed, the advance factories were the butt of many jokes and deputies all had their pet stories to tell. 'There are three such factories already in my county,' one deputy told Haughey in a Dáil exchange. And went on to say that the crows were building in one, the pigeons flying through it; the machinery was kept oiled, a caretaker was in residence – but there were no jobs.[1]

Speaking on an Undeveloped Areas (Amendment) Bill, in July 1959, Haughey referred to the competition for investment which was taking place throughout Europe and the impact on this of the Common Market, within whose tariff barriers much new industrial investment would be concentrated. Ireland was in competition with Common Market countries and with the United Kingdom (which included Northern Ireland): 'We are not just one country endeavouring to attract industrialists to our shores; we are now more and more in a keenly competitive situation where other communities are alive to the desirability of attracting foreign participation and are actively going out to secure it.'[2] He was keen on other investment and development schemes, and on the committee stage of the previous year's Finance Bill had moved an amendment to reduce tax liabilities on market gardening and to exempt it from Schedule D taxation in Gaeltacht areas altogether, as an incentive for western development and the creation of employment.[3] The amendment was opposed by James Ryan, who expressed himself generally opposed to income tax reliefs. In particular, he was alarmed at the prospect of rival claims from Gaeltacht and 'Congested Districts' industries, from enterprises other than market gardening, and from other parts of the country. Later in the same debate Ryan, who was an avuncular figure within Fianna Fáil and well liked, commented on the two busy 'tigers' who had been harrying him throughout the extended exchanges: 'I have to admit that the two Deputies who did most of the speaking – Deputy Sweetman and Deputy Haughey – know more about income-tax than I do.'

Haughey showed considerable ability in his early speeches, which were wide-ranging, well-informed and enthusiastic. Even after becoming Parliamentary Secretary to the Minister for Justice and taking on the considerable burden of putting through the large backlog of legislation from that department, he continued to contribute on

[1] Fintan Coogan, of Fine Gael, *Dáil Report*, 29 April 1959, col. 1209.
[2] *Dáil Report*, 8 July 1959, col. 815.
[3] *Dáil Report*, 18 June 1958, col. 225–8.

economic issues. In a speech on the Budget, in April 1961, he said:
'Since I have interested myself in economic matters I have always been
aware of the fact that the greatest single stimulus one can give to an
economy is to reduce direct taxation. That is the ideal aimed at by all
economists and all Ministers for Finance.'[1] It was a worthy objective
and direct taxation came down that year, as it had done two years
before that. But Haughey, when he came to power, lost sight of that
ideal and was much criticized for crippling levels of direct taxation.

He frequently spoke out, as a backbencher, in criticism of proposals
being put forward by ministers and developed a style of argument
with Opposition deputies which was often impressive, and at times
humorous. Occasionally, he gave hostages to fortune. In a speech on
12 March 1958, on a budgetary provision, he expressed a clear grasp
of the necessity for prudence in economic strategy. 'There is no doubt
about it . . . that in 1956 the country ran into a serious financial crisis
which very seriously threatened the whole basis of our finances as a
nation. Until such time as the Government, by careful, determined
hard work can restore soundness in the nation's finances, we cannot
go ahead and achieve the expansion of employment which we require.'

In June 1957, in an exchange with Jack McQuillan about fisheries
policy, later a pet subject with Haughey, he said: 'I may be naïve. I
will probably become cynical and opportunist, like the deputy, but
that may be some time yet.'

Charles Haughey was, of course, drawn closer to both the routine
and the drama of economic events in the years 1957–65 by virtue of
the fact that he had married into the Lemass family. After his marriage
to Maureen Lemass on 18 September 1951, they lived first in Raheny,
a suburb on the north side of Dublin city, in a house called Cill Eanna.
The eldest child, Eimear, was born in 1955, Conor in 1957, Ciarán
in 1960, and Seán in 1961.

[1] *Dáil Report*, 26 April 1961, col. 1075.

CHAPTER III

MAN OF JUSTICE

Mere prattle without practice
Is all his soldiership. But he, sir, had th'election.

S EAN LEMASS invited his son-in-law to become Parliamentary
Secretary to the Minister for Justice in May 1960. According to
Haughey, Lemass told him: 'As Taoiseach it is my duty to offer
you the post of Parliamentary Secretary and as your father-in-law
I am advising you not to take it.' This apparently light-hearted
approach on the part of both men to Haughey's first important political post conceals a number of conflicts and complications over the
appointment. Sean Lemass, according to both Kevin Boland and Neil
Blaney as well as Haughey himself, was opposed to the appointment.
But in the Boland and Blaney versions, the offer was unqualified. Their
view was that Oscar Traynor,[1] who had been Minister for Justice since
1957, persuaded Lemass to appoint Charles Haughey as his parliamentary secretary. But the Secretary of the Department of Justice, Peter
Berry,[2] in his diaries[3] contradicts this, maintaining that Traynor was
strongly opposed to the appointment and that between himself and
Haughey there was considerable tension, possibly aggravated by the

[1] Oscar Traynor (1886–1963) took part in the 1916 Rising, fought in Dublin in the Civil
War, was first elected to the Dáil as a Sinn Fein candidate in 1925 and remained within
Sinn Fein, standing in that interest against Fianna Fáil before joining the party to be first
elected as a Fianna Fáil deputy in 1932. He was a member of all Fianna Fáil governments
from 1936 until he retired from politics in 1961.
[2] Peter Berry (1910–78) was a civil servant with the Department of Justice for 44 years,
serving under every Minister for Justice from Kevin O'Higgins on, and as private secretary
to two ministers as well as to the Secretary of the Department in the 1930s and 1940s. He
was thus privy to State security matters from a very early stage in his career. He did not
become Secretary of the Department until February 1961, but, because of the prolonged
bouts of ill-health his predecessor suffered, he was effectively Department Secretary from
a much earlier stage.
[3] 'The Peter Berry Papers' (published in *Magill*, May–July 1980) were his memoirs based
on his diaries which covered these years. He also gave detailed background information on
the Arms Crisis in the May and July issues of the monthly magazine (q.v.).

fact that both men represented the same constituency at the time.

Oscar Traynor was seventy-five years old and, after de Valera, the oldest member of the Government. He was becoming increasingly deaf and was both secretive and sensitive about this. He found the ministerial workload heavy and two measures were particularly onerous during the early part of 1960: the Intoxicating Liquor Bill, which was a substantial piece of legislation, comprehensive and in part a consolidation; and the Criminal Justice Amendment Bill, which was concerned with certain aspects of penal reform, including changes to the parole system and the introduction of 'sleep-in-work-out' arrangements for certain categories of prisoner. Traynor told the Secretary of the Department of Justice that Lemass had offered him a parliamentary secretary to ease the burden and asked him to select deputies who might be suitable. Berry chose four names, among them Seán Flanagan.[1] Flanagan declined the offer; Lemass thought the other three unsuitable and put forward the name of his son-in-law.

Lemass may well have advised Haughey privately not to accept but, according to Berry, Lemass told Traynor that Haughey would almost certainly refuse anyway, since his accountancy practice was busy and expanding and to accept junior ministerial rank would cause considerable loss of earnings. Traynor had real misgivings, 'and said that if he had had the remotest idea that he would be saddled with Deputy Haughey he would have turned down the offer in the first instance.'[2] Traynor told Berry that his own misgivings, which amounted to 'a decided aversion', were shared by Gerald Boland, who had been Traynor's Fianna Fáil predecessor in the Department of Justice,[3] and also by several senior ministers. Gerald Boland, whose son, Harry, was in partnership with Charles Haughey and had been responsible for bringing him into the Fianna Fáil Party and into the same constituency as

[1] Seán Flanagan (1922–93) was a solicitor and a noted sportsman who captained the Mayo team in Gaelic football in 1950 and 1951, when Mayo won the All-Ireland title. As with many other similar achievers, Flanagan then went into politics and represented Mayo from the 1951 general election up to 1977, when he lost his seat. He became an MEP in 1979.
[2] *Magill*, June 1980, p. 48.
[3] Gerald Boland (1885–1973) was born in Manchester, the son of a Parnellite who was fatally injured in a fight with Healyites for possession of the offices of the *United Irishman*. Gerald was a Volunteer who fought in Jacobs' biscuit factory in the 1916 Rising and was one of the founders of the Fianna Fáil Party, standing as a deputy for the Roscommon constituency. He was a minister in every government from 1933 to 1948, serving as Minister for Justice from the outbreak of war in 1939 and returning again to that Department in 1954. His record against the IRA was stern to the point of being draconian.

Oscar Traynor, was particularly outspoken in his criticisms of the proposed new appointee, not only to Traynor, but to Berry himself, giving it as his opinion that 'Mr Haughey would yet drag down the party into the mire'.[1] Berry's own view, based on the opinions of others, was that Charles Haughey was of 'first-class intelligence with initiative, application and tenacity'. Despite the reservations, Haughey was appointed.

Clearly, Haughey was already arousing strong feelings. Traynor, with other senior members of the Fianna Fáil organization, took exception to Haughey's way of life. It was as simple, and as complicated, as that. Even as early as 1960, Haughey kept horses and rode to hounds. He was photographed at times wearing a top hat, but in any case always correctly turned out. He developed expensive tastes. He had a cellar of fine wines, dined frequently and lavishly in Dublin's best hotels, and seemed at pains to demonstrate his success in an ostentatious way, and to display quite clearly an association between wealth and power. It marked him, in the public mind, for the rest of his political career. His taste in food and drink was the subject of endless comment. Gossip columnists reported on the restaurants he visited, the dishes he liked, the wines he drank. He developed a taste, unsurprisingly, for Dom Perignon champagne and in one of her Saturday columns, Angela Phelan wrote: 'It seems only yesterday that he used to turn up at the most intimate parties in the better mews houses in Ballsbridge carrying his own Dom Perignon, wrapped in brown paper. Those were the days before he discovered Cristale [sic].'[2] At this stage in his career there was not much power, but there was the expression of nepotism in his nomination by Lemass and it confirmed precisely what Haughey himself seemed to want: the image of a man travelling fast along a predetermined and rather special inside track.

This would have been absolute anathema to a man of Oscar Traynor's background, as it would also have been to many others in the Fianna Fáil organization. Haughey represented the fleshly side of economic progress, the opportunism and flashiness of planning and programming, the fruits of being in control, the short-term and essentially personal advantages of creating 'a dynamic'. He was distinctly ahead

[1] *Magill*, June 1980, p. 48
[2] Angela Phelan, *Irish Independent*, 4 January 1992. She presumably means Roederer 'Cristal'.

of the pack. No other politician at the time came near him in terms
of fulfilling the image of 'the men in mohair suits'. That reference,
which, as the 1960s progressed, was also to attach itself to others,
notable among them Donogh O'Malley, was not to be achieved with
quite the dash that Haughey brought to his dress and his behaviour.
He seemed to want 'style' in a comprehensive way that embraced 'old'
wealth as well as 'new'. Side by side with the image of the mohair suit
was the quite different image presented by hunting and horses generally. And it was all much admired, just as success and wealth were
admired at the time as a mark of Ireland's recovery. Haughey definitely
stood for a new Fianna Fáil and his appointment, very much it seemed
with Lemass's blessing, gave credibility in the party to the idea of a
partnership between wealth and business success, power and the
direction of the nation's affairs.

Oscar Traynor planned to give up his Dáil seat at the next general
election and during 1960 handed over some of his legislative duties to
his parliamentary secretary. But it was done reluctantly. Haughey's
approach to the problem that existed between himself and his Minister
was to identify blocks of work which he could take over and complete
without having to refer to Traynor. According to Berry, Traynor was
reluctant to let go, but did so over the presentation of legislation in
the Dáil. It seems also that he allowed Haughey to take over the
political administration of the programme of law reform. But Lemass
emphasized, when announcing the appointment, that 'there is a very
considerable congestion of work there, including a great deal of legislation which it is desired to have enacted. This is a temporary arrangement to facilitate Government business.'[1] Haughey was not, therefore,
an initiator, as so often claimed, but a facilitator in putting through
the backlog of legislation.

In November 1960, Haughey introduced and steered through the
Dáil two pieces of legislation, the Charities Bill and the Rent Restrictions Bill; in January 1961 he took the second stage of the Civil Liability Bill and the Defamation Bill; and in May and June 1961 he acted
for the Minister on the committee stage of the Courts Bill and on a
supplementary piece of Courts legislation which was introduced at the
same time. A good deal of parliamentary time during 1960 was devoted
to the Intoxicating Liquor Bill. Among other things this piece of legislation abolished the *bona fides*, public houses on the arterial roads out

---

[1] *Dáil Report*, 10 May 1960, col. 899.

of Dublin which enjoyed special licence facilities for *bona fide* travellers, hence the name. They were used instead by students and thirsty citizens generally, who travelled out from town after city establishments had closed their doors. By the late 1950s the number of car-owning young people had created a mass exodus to these hostelries and an extensive abuse of the loophole in the law.

The Civil Liability Bill was a significant piece of legislation. It is thought not to have originated in the Department of Justice, but to have been the work of the noted academic, Glanville Williams. It affected the law of tort and altered the burden of responsibility: prior to its enactment, if a plaintiff was to any degree responsible for the events which led to a particular accident, he or she could not recover costs at all. This was changed to a shared responsibility, with proportionate recovery of damages. The legislation also introduced the concept of damage for bereavement. This piece of legislation did not find its precedent in the United Kingdom, which was often the case, but was one in which Ireland moved independently, drawing example from America and Europe, which was also to be the case with the Succession Bill, an equally important measure which came at the end of Haughey's period in Justice.

Quite clearly, these pieces of legislation had been in train for some time and in fact much else that was to follow had been written and prepared before Haughey came into the Department of Justice. But he brought to the presentation of legislation a dynamic confidence and his speeches were well-researched, forceful and often eloquent as well. He demonstrated an easy grasp of detail, he handled interruptions well, was never flustered and his many exchanges, some of them quite sharp, are a pleasure to read.

His impact was such that the original appointment as parliamentary secretary, which Lemass had stated, on 10 May 1960, would be temporary, became the subject of parliamentary questioning in March 1961, when Richie Ryan asked the Taoiseach when the temporary appointment would be terminated, or whether his Minister for Justice would resign, so saving the taxpayer £5,000 a year. Lemass indicated that the need for a parliamentary secretary had been proved and that he did not envisage terminating his son-in-law's appointment 'for quite a long time to come.'[1] Up to that point, he said, in the Department of Justice, a great deal of work had been 'neglected over many years

---

[1] *Dáil Report*, Wednesday, 22 March 1961, col. 1003.

by reason of the inability of successive Ministers for Justice to over-
take it'.

Right at the start, Charles Haughey had defined for himself an area
of responsibility which fundamentally changed perceptions about the
country's law and introduced an unfamiliar, reformist image to the
Fianna Fáil Party and to these two Lemass administrations. It was a
good start.

There were lighter moments. On one occasion, a lengthy exchange
took place on the introduction of new titles for judges, in Irish, to
replace the English style of address which one deputy described as the
'unctuous ballyhoo and other trappings that the British left behind
them'. It was proposed, in the Courts Bill, to address a judge as 'A
Bhreithimh', a group of judges as 'A Bhreithiána' and the Chief Justice
as 'A Phríomh Bhreithimh'. One Opposition deputy, the lawyer
Patrick J. Lindsay, the greater part of whose life, even then, was spent
in the Courts, described the arrangement as 'codology', while Deputy
T. F. O'Higgins, later to become Chief Justice, wondered what would
happen should the judge be addressed by someone with a lisp.[1]

The legislative work ran side by side with the much more dramatic
responsibilities in the Department of Justice for matters of State security. These had been particularly acute from 1957, when the IRA had
initiated a violent Border campaign requiring strict security responses,
and were still a major problem for the Government during Charles
Haughey's period as parliamentary secretary, although it was almost
certainly an area which Oscar Traynor would have kept under his own
direct control.

In the closing stages of his first period as parliamentary secretary,
the conflict with Traynor worsened, not only in the Department, but
also in the constituency and within the Fianna Fáil Parliamentary
Party. Traynor knew there would be a general election before the end
of 1961. In fact he was no longer a Dáil deputy when he performed
his last act as Minister for Justice, which was to attend the unveiling
of the memorial to Kevin Barry and other patriots in Mountjoy Gaol
on 8 October 1961, after the general election. Three days later the
new Dáil met and Charles Haughey was nominated Minister for Justice
by his father-in-law.

Peter Berry, who had formally been Department Secretary since
the beginning of the year, was a stickler for constitutional and legal

[1] *Dáil Report*, 22 March 1961, cols. 1112–3.

proprieties and had consistently run foul of previous Justice Ministers.
He now confronted the new political head of his department in circumstances that are instructive about the way power operates within the
Irish system. The details are also illuminating about the political
approach to problems which Haughey adopted. Believing himself to
be the ultimate authority within his Department, Haughey sought to
have a person to whom he owed a political favour appointed to a
position that carried a small emolument in the form of a capitation
grant. Unfortunately, he had given this undertaking while still Parliamentary Secretary, only to discover that Oscar Traynor, as Minister,
had already given the job to another man. When he became Minister
he sought to put this situation right by trying to make a parallel
appointment, thus honouring his obligations. Berry opposed the new
appointment on the grounds that the second capitation grant was not
in the public interest and that he, Berry, would not be able to make
the payment. Haughey insisted that his decision be implemented, to
which Berry replied by giving an undertaking that he would make the
appointment. But he then told the Minister that, under the 'Treasury
Rules' which had been inherited from the Whitehall system and which
prevailed throughout the Irish Civil Service, he would require the
direction from the Minister to be in writing and went on to say that
he would have to report it, both to the Minister for Finance and to
the Committee of Public Accounts. Haughey withdrew his insistence
and the direction was not given. Berry was about to take his summer
holiday and thought it prudent to give the facts to the Assistant Secretary of the Department. It was a wise move. 'On my return the Assistant
Secretary told me that he had received a ministerial directive to appoint
the second man to the post, that he had informed the Minister that
he was aware of the Accounting Officer's refusal earlier and that the
Minister would be liable to a personal surcharge. He said that the
Minister was furious with me, not alone for my refusal, but for fore-
warning the Assistant Secretary, thus causing the Minister to lose
face.'[1]

Berry gives an account of a second occasion when he was in conflict
with his new Minister, again over an appointment, but ending this
time in a kind of Pyrrhic victory for Charles Haughey, who had insisted
on another appointment that ran counter to a selection board recom-
mendation, which came to the Department of Justice from the

---

[1] *Magill*, June 1980, pp 45–6.

Commissioner of the Police. The result was a compromise, with the new Minister's reputation damaged within the police force and Berry himself perplexed that Haughey did not seem to have grasped the essentials of the relationship between the permanent officer in charge of each department and the political appointee: 'The Minister had not come to an understanding yet, apparently, that the Secretary [of a Government department] was an office holder in his own right, appointed by the Government under the Ministers and Secretaries Act, 1924, and that he should not be obliged to act as a rubber stamp for the Minister in official matters'.[1]

Despite these strictures, Berry had a high regard for Haughey as Minister. In Berry's view, he combined great ability with a dynamic approach to the job and in his first month drew up a ten-point programme for the Department. 'He was a joy to work with and the longer he stayed the better he got.'[2]

According to a more junior civil servant in the department at the time, Haughey had stimulating capacities for bringing forward new ideas about changes in the law, having them investigated and for standing firmly behind commitments over legislative reforms, despite the often fierce public reaction which could emerge and could intimidate weak politicians. This was particularly the case with the Succession Bill, which created great fears about the inheritance of land, particularly among farmers.

Haughey applied himself to three essential problems. The first was the underfunding of the Department of Justice. Where successive previous Ministers for Justice had shown neither courage nor determination, Haughey pushed successfully for greater Department of Finance funding for the development of resources in his first Government job. He gave a high priority to defeating the IRA's campaign of violence on the Border. And he expanded the programme of reform.

The Government, perhaps mindful of the events that had led up to the 1957 general election, where Costello's firmness against the IRA had cost him votes and lost him the support of noted republicans like Seán MacBride, had held back from full confrontation. But on 23 November 1961, though he commanded only a minority position in the Dáil, Sean Lemass considered his position safe enough to set up a special criminal court staffed by army officers. This court took a

---

[1] ibid., p 46.
[2] Peter Berry, ibid., p. 48

Haughey in 1966

Outside the Four Courts during the Arms Trial in November 1970 with Neil Blaney

Haughey gives his press conference after the Arms Trial acquittal

Haughey at the time of his trial in 1970

Below: Being congratulated by Dublin postman Ned Brennan after the Arms Trial verdict. Brennan won a Dáil seat in the first, February election of 1982 and lost it again in November in the second election of the same year

Part of Lynch's 1977 Government: (*clockwise, from bottom left, excluding obscured*) Sylvester Barrett, Brian Lenihan, George Colley, Bobby Molloy, Desmond O'Malley, Gene Fitzgerald, Jim Gibbons, Gerard Collins, Padraig Faulkner, Charles Haughey, Anthony Hederman (Attorney General) and Padraic Lalor. The Taoiseach was sitting to the right, out of picture tough line and a number of IRA suspects were sentenced before the end of the year. It brought to a rapid end the Border campaign. The IRA had had enough. The order was given to 'dump arms' and, in a statement, 'the attitude of the general public' was given as the foremost factor behind the decision.

In his own ministerial statement, which followed the announcement of the ending of the IRA's campaign of violence, Charles Haughey referred to the 'deep resentment' felt by the people of the Republic at partition, but condemned as foolish the attempts to resolve this through violence. He hinted at an amnesty and in fact one followed swiftly, with all IRA prisoners then in detention being released, including six who were part of 'Northern [i.e. Northern Ireland] Command'.

On law reform generally, Haughey's record, during four and a half years in the Department of Justice, is one of energetic implementation of a wide range of measures and is arguably his best performance in terms of changing life for the ordinary citizen and attempting to enhance the prospects of the disadvantaged. He saw social justice as part of the country's general advance during years of recovery after demoralization and loss of confidence. He placed his own work on legal reform firmly within the context of economic progress and development. In his first major speech on the subject, given to a Fianna Fáil party meeting in September 1962, he presented an image of the party in the public mind as the political grouping that met the two objectives equally. 'People think of us first as the party which built the factories, put our ships on the sea and our aeroplanes in the sky, fostered our agriculture and planted our forests. They sometimes overlook, not unnaturally I suppose in the circumstances, the fact that ours is an organization with great and aspiring social objectives.'

The programme of reform, largely instigated by Haughey, was formalized in a White Paper, published in January 1962. Later that year he said: 'I wanted to see a programme of law reform on a wide scale, a re-examination of our penal system with emphasis on the causes and possible cures of juvenile delinquency, an examination of our probation system . . . the provision of legal aid for poor persons in criminal cases and whether the costs of litigation could be substantially reduced . . . In particular, it is intended that all our statute law will be contained in Acts of the Oireachtas. The implementation of this programme is being pursued steadily and systematically.'[1]

---

[1] *Dáil Report*, 27 November 1962, col. 81.

Charles Haughey's attitude on penal reform was expressed in the context of debate rather than legislative action, however, and, though it was based on humanitarian concern for the individual and a wish for his or her rehabilitation, he achieved little in this area. The views he gave early on after his appointment as Minister had an urgency about them which remained unfulfilled. The objectives which he outlined were essentially aspirational, aimed at turning Irish prisons into 'places where everything possible is done to ensure that as many as possible of those who have been committed to them will be returned to society fitted to adapt themselves to the life of normal useful citizens'.

In fact little was done by that administration, or indeed subsequent ones, to bring this about. He had set up a committee earlier in 1962, apparently as a result of a party resolution at the previous year's conference of the Fianna Fáil organization and had urged it to come forward with recommendations as and when they were worked out, and not to wait on any final, comprehensive report. And there were serious problems, he said, including apprenticeship needs, the custody and treatment of juvenile offenders, of both sexes, and the psychiatric care of habitual offenders, mentally retarded prisoners and sexual offenders.

Eighteen months later, in a speech to law students,[1] his approach had changed, virtually out of recognition. Haughey was replying to a paper presented to the debating society by the student auditor, who had contrasted the situations in Britain and Ireland, praising British penal reforms and condemning 'the enthusiastic, devoted corps of people who are labouring in this field in this country', and on whose behalf Haughey felt he had to speak out. The main reliance expressed in the speech, for progress on reform that would place Ireland in the mainstream rather than on the margins – and this was the criticism which the student auditor voiced in his paper – was on a watching brief on international developments.

The urgency was gone; the emphasis was on penal reform being 'to a very large extent uncharted territory' and full of 'difficulties, complexities and uncertainties. Even now very little has in fact been scientifically established. Attractive ideas, theories and experiments have a way of ending in failure, and disillusionment comes often even

---

[1] Inaugural Meeting of the Law Students' Debating Society of Ireland, 28 February 1964.

to the most enthusiastic.' There was, he said, the need to have 'plenty of informed public discussion'. There was brief mention, at the end, of the committee that had featured in his speech eighteen months earlier, with its charge to deliver recommendations on a piecemeal basis. But there was no sense of this having created the dynamic of action which his words at the time, given to an audience of party faithful, seemed to invite. Instead, for law students who would become more directly involved in the kind of legislation initiated in the Department of Justice, the tone was defensive, and the hard facts of achievement or specific intent were thinly spread within the bland text. One of these recommendations, for a Prison Welfare Service, was to be implemented 'within the next few weeks', and there had been minor adjustments in prison training facilities.

There was also to be a system of 'warnings' for juveniles, rather than their prosecution, mainly, one suspects, because there were no custodial provisions whatever for young offenders. There was, however, an after-care institution for young people which had been set up by the Roman Catholic Archbishop of Dublin, John Charles McQuaid, whose role in all aspects of social life was dominant at the time to the point of being authoritarian. This institution represented, in Haughey's view, 'a really important and significant development'. Into the bargain, it was free: 'The fact that it is being provided on a voluntary basis without any cost to the State is something at which in these modern times we can only marvel.'

One of the guiding principles Haughey presented was 'the belief that the application of punishment should be a process whereby a person proceeds from a state of guilt brought on by the crime, through repentance and expiation back to a state of freedom and liberation from guilt. It follows from this that our procedures must be reformative and redemptive and that the primary purpose of punishment must be the rehabilitation of the offender.' Nothing that was included in the law reforms at this time seriously addressed the problems implicit in these words.

The period was one of rising prosperity and a low crime rate, arguably a good time for reform, when funds would be forthcoming and demands and pressures relatively light. In fact this climate of progress was used as an excuse to do little or nothing. No important legislation affecting the country's prison system was introduced during Haughey's time in the Department of Justice. His reforms lay elsewhere. The target was massive and of course remains largely unfulfilled to this

day. It was typical of the man to identify a comprehensive programme
and in a sense to revel in what might be done. The character of his
mind was such that he could embrace large schemes swiftly and clothe
them in the kind of compelling colour and detail which brought them
vividly to life. The nature of his political vision depended on the public
outline of that vision's complete territory and also of the targets which
might in the end be achieved. And he was to use the same approach
throughout his political career, both in ministerial issues and responsibilities, and in presenting his larger vision as party leader. In his particular approach to the presentation of large schemes he lacked caution
and subtlety, declaring at the outset of any project or design what it
would ultimately achieve and often clothing this in imaginative and
glowing terms. Then came the laborious stages of construction and
the necessary processing of the design. This always proved less attractive and the character of his subsequent statements would often shift
in mood and tone, away from the defiant, wholly positive initial set
of claims and towards a more conditional, vague and aspirational
interpretation. His prologue to events was always confident, broadly
stated and filled with a sense of easy and early achievement, as though
the natural and well-regulated programme for the state was being
prudently and efficiently implemented by the solid resources of civil
servants under the wise guidance and direction of dedicated politicians.
The reality, in the Department of Justice, as was the case in other
departments as well, was that he was dealing with a massive backlog
and a Civil Service starved of funds. It has been said, with some justification, that up to that point the department had lacked the driving
force of an ambitious and able politician. Certainly Charles Haughey,
despite initial misgivings about his appointment, provided this drive.
But it was only part of what was needed, and still left many problems
that drive and ambition alone could not solve.

It could also be argued that, with the ending of the IRA campaign
of violence, which had resulted in murders on the Border, the abolition
of the death sentence might have been made an absolute reform, rather
than a qualified one. But Charles Haughey, introducing the Criminal
Justice Bill in the Dáil in 1963, announced the retention of the death
penalty – though it was never to be implemented again – for several
categories of offence, especially the murder of diplomats and members
of the Garda. It was argued that it would be a deterrent.

If the full range of legislative measures introduced at this time is
analysed, then the overall achievement constitutes a valuable process

of tidying up and of bringing the law up to date rather than anything that could be characterized as fundamental social reform. Much of the legislation Haughey introduced was already in an advanced stage of preparation by the time he arrived in the Department. Even the Succession Bill, often singled out as a major contribution to reform, is thought to have been the work of an assistant secretary in the Department. Introduced in 1964, it was completed after Haughey's departure. It went a considerable way towards safeguarding the inheritance rights of widows and their children and began a process of improving the position of women in Irish society, which was to be further advanced by pressure from women's groups in the 1970s and by Ireland's membership of the European Community.

Haughey concerned himself with the value of women in the political life of the country. In a speech to Fianna Fáil women in February 1964 he referred to the need for increased female representation in the Dáil and made the radical proposal that women deputies should play an active role in vetting legislation in which they had a special interest. At the time there was no prospect of this happening. In a Dáil of 147 deputies there were four women; they increased by one in the 1965 election and were reduced again after the 1969 election to three.

Haughey's social concern was sometimes stretched to embrace extreme situations, one of which involved a tinker woman, the mother of twelve children and expecting her thirteenth, who had been committed to prison for begging in the streets of Galway. None of the promised reforms of the prison system had taken place and, under pressure from the leader of the Labour Party, Haughey took the easy way out and ordered her release.[1]

The quality and extent of Charles Haughey's reformist zeal during his period as Minister for Justice matched the central idea that Sean Lemass brought to leadership of the party and the country. He strove to get Ireland moving again and to encourage a desire for change and a general spirit of consensus. Both George Colley[2] and Donogh

[1] *Dáil Report*, 13 February, 1964, col. 1076.
[2] George Colley (1925–83), who was born in the same year as Haughey, was a lifetime colleague within Fianna Fáil until his untimely death, under surgery, in 1983. His father, Harry Colley, was unseated by Haughey in the 1957 general election, at which time George Colley had not decided on politics as a career. He subsequently became a minister under Lemass and Minister for Industry and Commerce, then Finance, under Jack Lynch. He competed for the party leadership against Haughey in 1979.

O'Malley[1] in the Department of Education, and Brian Lenihan,[2] who succeeded Haughey in Justice, had reformist ideas and to some extent took actions that invited criticism, notably from the Roman Catholic hierarchy. They tested the new climate, which was markedly different from the atmosphere in Irish social, medical and educational fields which had prevailed during the two previous decades, and their achievements were of some significance. Lenihan achieved reforms in censorship. O'Malley initiated far-sighted changes in education, though these were subsequently modified. Colley effectively stood his ground in a confrontation with the Church over the problem of school closures.

In Justice the reformist requirements were for absolute improvements in the lot of certain categories of people, partly through straightforward changes in the law, but also through fundamental updating of institutions such as prisons and the provision of a far wider range of facilities designed to bring about social change. This was where the scope for real reform lay. In the end the emphasis remained on legalistic rather than on institutional reforms. Almost thirty years later the capacities of the Irish penal system to punish firmly and fairly, to rehabilitate and reform, to deal with young male and female offenders, to cope with begging, child abuse, petty crime and other ills which greater social awareness has laid bare, are wholly and woefully inadequate. Haughey summarized it in a lengthy address in Luxembourg in March 1964: 'a complete overhaul of civil law, criminal law, court practice and procedure and of other legislation.'[3] At the time the advisory committee, which Haughey had set up in 1962, was its principal mechanism for reform. Eventually, some thirteen years later, the process was more sensibly placed in the hands of the Law Reform Commission, which was also an advisory body, but presided over by a senior

---

[1] Donogh O'Malley (1921–68) represented Limerick in the Dáil from 1954, serving as Minister for Health and then Education. He was responsible for introducing free post-primary education.
[2] Brian Lenihan (b. 1930) served as Minister for Justice under Lemass, taking over that department from Haughey. He was subsequently Minister for Education, for Transport and Power, Foreign Affairs, Agriculture, Forestry and Fisheries, and again Foreign Affairs at the time of the two Haughey–Thatcher summit meetings. He stood unsuccessfully for the presidency in 1991 and was defeated by Mary Robinson.
[3] Inaugural address to the spring session of the International Faculty of Comparative Law of the International University of Comparative Sciences at Luxembourg. Quoted by Martin Mansergh, op. cit., pp. 40–7. Mansergh, quite properly, says that the speech was the most comprehensive ever made on law reform by an Irish Justice Minister.

judge, dealing with reform on a planned, subject-by-subject basis.[1] Charles Haughey's work between 1960 and the end of 1964 laid the ground for this process, but he was vastly over-ambitious in how he saw the objectives being achieved. He identified measures where he did make fundamental advances in specific legislative terms, including the Extradition Bill, then before the Dáil, which abolished the requirement of a *prima facie* case before the extradition of an accused person, and the Succession Bill.

Charles Haughey's political character, during the first half of the 1960s, involved certain easily defined strands. The first of these was a loose identification of himself with the ideas of economic progress and development which were being pursued by his father-in-law. These reflected the positive climate of expansion and optimism of the period. He was not closely identified, apart from the role he played within the Government, as one of the team of ministers directly involved in the country's economic planning and management. He played no strongly outspoken or public role on economic issues, though he spoke about them in speeches at party functions. These speeches were couched in very general terms and were not particularly distinguished or precise, but he broadly favoured Fianna Fáil's revitalization programme.

Secondly, he established a reputation as a reformist minister within his own Department and certainly gave to his work great energy, dynamism and intellectual grasp of what was required. The actual programme of legislation emanating from the Department was impressive and continued after his departure.

Thirdly, he became interested in the arts and was supportive of a broad range of cultural developments, from traditional music, architecture, poetry and writing, to galleries and painters. He led the 'New Men' in the Government. They were himself, Donogh O'Malley and Brian Lenihan, and they were associated with commercial and business interests that were regarded as responsible for getting Ireland moving again. Within Fianna Fáil there was admiration for this, even from traditionalists such as Neil Blaney and Kevin Boland, and from the more passive politicians, among whom one would number Jack Lynch and Patrick Hillery.

Charles Haughey had firmly established himself as a politician of

[1] The Commission was established by the Law Reform Commission Act of 1975 and came into existence in 1977, with Judge Brian Walsh as its first president.

strength and purpose by the end of 1964. And it was perhaps for this reason, when the Minister for Agriculture resigned, that Lemass moved him, without any delay, into that Department.

CHAPTER IV

A MOHAWK

So shall I clothe me in a forced content,
And shut myself up in some other course
To Fortune's alms.

THE APPOINTMENT OF Charles Haughey as Minister for Agriculture was not a well-judged move on Lemass's part. Haughey knew little about agriculture and, unusually, was on record as acknowledging the fact.[1] Neither his background nor his temperament suited the job and he subsequently turned out to be ill equipped to deal with the crisis that faced the Government in respect of the farmers. Paddy Smith[2] resigned from the Lemass Government on 8 October 1964 in protest at what he saw as concessions to the trade union movement, over a strike of maintenance men and more broadly over what he considered to be an over-emphasis on industrial development at the expense of the country's largest and most profitable industry – agriculture. In spite of the fact that Whitaker's first Programme for Economic Development had run its full term and had been succeeded by a second programme, introduced in July 1964 by Lemass, the beef industry alone within the agricultural sector earned more than all industrial exports put together, including tobacco and beverages (mainly whiskey and Guinness). Industrial exports exceeded agricultural exports for the first time only in 1969.

The resignation was accompanied by a strong attack on the trade

---

[1] *Dáil Reports*, 28 May 1958, col. 785, speech on the Finance Bill. His otherwise clear and effective analysis of the economic situation at the time ignored agriculture, reflecting the general attitude. Then and subsequently agriculture was the poor relation in terms of economic planning, leading to the unrest which faced the Government in the early 1960s.

[2] Patrick Smith (1901–92) was a farmer from Cavan, the youngest of eight children and a Dáil deputy from 1923. He fought in the War of Independence and was condemned to death in 1921. He was one of Lemass's staunchest supporters and the quintessential Fianna Fáil man. When once asked what clubs he belonged to or interests he had he replied, 'One of the founder members of the Fianna Fáil organization and I find this supplies all my interest in this field.'

union movement. But it was more than a mere protest. Smith represented the older, rural-based traditions in the party which were dependent on small farmers for political power. He was mistrustful of the growing liaison between Fianna Fáil and the new business class, mistrustful also of the apparent shift in power to younger, urban-based deputies, who seemed to be losing contact with the older traditions of the party.

The Dáil was in recess at the time of Smith's resignation, which by Irish standards was a momentous event. At first Lemass simply could not believe that a member of his Government was standing down on a fundamental matter of principle and Smith had to force acceptance on him by making the matter public. 'If we are to judge from the newspapers and radio,' James Dillon,[1] the leader of Fine Gael, told the Dáil, 'Deputy Smith seems to have been constrained to place it in the hands of everyone else in the country before he could persuade the Taoiseach to admit it had been placed in his.'[2] But Lemass then acted swiftly, appointing Haughey within hours, then moving Brian Lenihan to replace Charles Haughey in the Department of Justice, and promoting George Colley to replace Lenihan in the Department of Lands, as Parliamentary Secretary with responsibility for fisheries.

The Dáil exchanges gave Dillon the opportunity to underline what he saw as the inappropriate appointment of city deputies to farming and fishing responsibilities, but the Fine Gael leader then veered off into a row about a recent by-election in Roscommon and the main attack on Government disunity was left aside. Brendan Corish, the leader of the Labour Party, unsuccessfully sought a repudiation of Smith's diatribe against trade unionists and there the matter rested.

In the 1960s the population of the State became mainly urban, but Charles Haughey's public comments were essentially anodyne on the urban-rural split. Those who sought to emphasize it 'could do very real damage to national morale and to our solidarity as a modern community',[3] he said in a speech at the time. Because the shift from

---

[1] James Dillon (1902–86) was himself a merchant, with a chequered political history which included involvement in several organizations before the setting up of Fine Gael, in the mid-1930s, which he then left for a time on the issue of Irish neutrality. He was pro-British, colourful in manner and copied Churchill in much of his parliamentary style. He was the son of John Dillon, who led the Irish Parliamentary Party after the death of John Redmond.
[2] *Dáil Reports*, 3 November 1964, col. 93.
[3] Speech to the inaugural meeting of the Dublin Institute of Catholic Sociology Debating Society, 21 November 1964, Ed. Martin Mansergh, op. cit., pp 49–51.

the land into the towns had been relatively recent in Ireland, there were strong bonds between urban and rural communities. 'Ideally our people in the town should look back to the land with affection and sympathy while our farming community should look with pride and hope on what is being achieved in our towns and cities.'[1] Though the Second Programme had already been published at this stage, Haughey suggested in the same speech that any 'reassessment of national objectives' would need to include 'a great new stride forward in agriculture'. But neither he nor anyone else in government had any very clear ideas about how this great new stride was to be defined. In anticipation of possible membership of the EEC there was academic acknowledgement of the inevitability that Irish farms would need to be enlarged by amalgamation and that agriculture as an industry, however large a segment of trade it occupied and however successful, would not be capable of supporting the large numbers that had depended on it since the State's foundation. The kinds of reforms implicit in this were not tackled by Haughey, however. Though his emphasis was on increasing farmers' incomes 'by every means available to us', the means he listed – better prices, better productivity, better technical methods, and the eradication of disease – did not include the fundamental reforms that farming then needed.

The farmers' grievances ran deep, however, and were not focused on such apparently trivial issues. Irish farmers were tolerably well organized, under the leadership of Rickard Deasy, and were in a militant frame of mind. For at least a year there had been agitation over the absence of any Government plan for agriculture. In addition, Deasy was highly vocal on the issue of land purchases by foreigners. He put a figure of 10,000 to 12,000 acres a year on land being bought by non-nationals. Marches in various parts of the country, with a major march on Government offices in Merrion Street, Dublin, in protest at prices for agricultural goods, fomented a confrontation which Charles Haughey handled in a somewhat high-handed fashion.

He was Minister for just eighteen months. The farmers camped in Merrion Street, defying the police. The Government sat out the confrontation, well aware that there was nothing that could be done, in the short term, to improve the basic position of Irish farmers. Indeed, that position had been substantially worsened by Harold Wilson's victory in the British general election on 16 October, which

[1] Ibid.

he had won by the narrow margin of four seats. Because of Britain's own problems, Wilson imposed a 15 per cent levy on imports, which applied to the Republic.

With attention focused on Ireland's trade isolation and the country's excessive dependence on trade with the United Kingdom, Lemass and the relevant ministers in his Government – including Haughey – responded by pursuing better trading relations with Britain and establishing the Anglo-Irish Free Trade Area Agreement,[1] which was a substantial advance in relations between the two countries. The negotiations had already been given considerable impetus by the historic meeting between Sean Lemass and Captain Terence O'Neill, the Northern Ireland Prime Minister,[2] at Stormont on 14 January 1965: the first of its kind since the establishment of the two parliaments on the island of Ireland in 1921. The invitation came from O'Neill. The acceptance letter was addressed to 'Stormont Castle, Dublin'. A postal worker crossed out Dublin and pencilled in: 'Try Belfast'. O'Neill made a return visit to Dublin a month later.

Lemass was ambivalent about the North. In O'Neill's own words, 'Mr Lemass continues to brood about the partition issue'.[3] The ambivalence was real enough; Lemass recognized the pragmatic need to live in peace and harmony with the Northern Ireland state. At the same time, as a good republican leader of the most republican party in the south he needed to make the appropriate noises about re-unification, purely for domestic political reasons. He brooded in Tralee in a positive fashion in July 1963, when he recognized that the will of the majority in Northern Ireland favoured the Government and Parliament as they existed in the Six Counties; but then his brooding in Washington, in October, concerned the traditional Republic of Ireland demand, that Britain should change its attitude and abandon support for a partitioned island of Ireland.

Charles Haughey was closely identified with the whole Lemass ethos at this time. He shared Lemass's view on Northern Ireland, that eco-

---

[1] This Agreement was signed in London on 14 December 1965.
[2] Terence O'Neill (1914–89) was Prime Minister of Northern Ireland from 1963 to 1969, having served in previous administrations and as an MP in Northern Ireland since 1956. He was raised to the peerage as Lord O'Neill of the Maine in 1970.
[3] O'Neill was speaking in Newcastle, County Down, on Friday, 19 October 1963. He wanted to discourage Southern statements about 'the ultimate reunification of Ireland', 'the evil of Partition', and references to 'the Six County Area'; this he saw as an inappropriate description of a sovereign state.

nomic co-operation offered the best way of achieving rapprochement between North and South. He was also at one with Lemass on the Republic's aspirations for closer ties with Europe – including eventual membership of the EEC – and on an active Government role in economic development. Just one year before his second Government appointment, to the Department of Agriculture, he was interviewed, not just as an example of the type of politician 'concerned primarily with the development of social and economic systems which will be fair, effective and healthy', but 'because he is the one among the Young Men of the present administration who has advanced the furthest.'[1]

The administration itself had achieved much and Lemass himself was seen in the country as a whole with something that came close to affection. He was a gruff, pragmatic figure, clipped in his speech and generally decisive in his actions. He presided over change with the essential virtue of being a reconciler, so that he sought to amalgamate the different factions in his own party, the different classes and groupings in the country, behind a broad, progressive nationalism which operated at the level of a better economic and social life deriving from economic programming and the growth of Ireland's trade. He made the appropriate gestures on what were regarded as the broader national issues. There was a renewed commitment to the Irish language, in terms of spreading its practical use, which few believed would work; there was far too much emphasis on Ireland's international objectives for that. His policy of North–South appeasement had startled the country, though it had been initiated by O'Neill. The meeting had presented Lemass with a fortuitous pre-election opportunity. He was careful to reassure everyone, in the statement issued after the Stormont meeting in January – particularly addressed to the people of the Six Counties – that the discussions had not included constitutional or political issues. Lemass was anxious to emphasize the economic and social advances of the country after two terms of Fianna Fáil rule.

Haughey added his own voice to this process, in a much-publicized speech to the Irish Club in London on St Patrick's Day, shortly before the general election was called. The British Prime Minister, Harold Wilson, was in the audience, as was Cardinal Heenan. Haughey laid some emphasis on the passionate desire of Irish people to see reunification and even threw into his argument the ancient apophthegm, to the effect that 'England's difficulty was Ireland's opportunity', but then

---

[1] *Hibernia*, December 1963, p. 15, interview with John Dillon.

set it aside in favour of 'an entirely different concept', that of treating
the whole region – in other words, the British Isles – as indivisible.
'We wish to go forward into the future with Britain in a spirit of
mutual co-operation, not on either side seeking what advantage can
be gained over the other but how we can collaborate to our mutual
advantage.'

This was the tone in which the April 1965 election was fought. It
is indicative of the high regard in which Lemass was held that a leading
political opponent, David Thornley,[1] wrote of Lemass as having
'worked wonders'. Over both party and country 'hangs the supremely
successful image of the leader – not a charismatic figure in the Dev
mould, but a superbly gifted political tactician lurking behind the pro-
jection of an avuncular, pipe-smoking Mr Plain.'[2] The historian J. J.
Lee, in an equally brief but pithy assessment of Lemass's character
and his capacity to hold on to power after de Valera's departure and
deliver a rejuvenated Fianna Fáil to his successor Lynch, suggests that
'the reputation of Lemass does not finally rest on either his electoral
record or on his record as party leader. It was neither his manner of
gaining power, nor his manner of holding it, that distinguished him
uniquely among Irish prime ministers. It was his manner of using it.'
His style was in the doing of it: he was by nature quiet, gruff, un-
dramatic, brief in his public statements. He was comparatively small of
stature, but heavily built; his lined face with moustache, closely cut
hair and lack of expressive reaction epitomized the prudent businessman and cautious judge of when to act. The family owned a drapery
business in Capel Street, but lived at the time of his birth in what was
then countryside, at Ballybrack. And Lemass worked in the business
between his dramatic activities in the GPO and later the Four Courts.

The recipe offered by Lemass worked extremely well. He led his
party into the election on a platform of solid achievement really for
the first time in its history. Time and again, under de Valera, elections
had been called to exploit division or disorganization within the Opposition; they had been snap affairs, shrewd coups which had short-
term tactical advantages, often to cover up the lack of progressive or

---

[1] David Thornley (1935–78) was born and educated in England, then at Dublin University,
and was an associate and supporter of Noel Browne in elections in the 1950s. He then
became a leading intellectual force within the Labour Party, radical in his views to the point
of losing the party whip by his support for Sinn Fein, and too radical to get office in the
1973–77 coalition, after which he lost his seat, dying a year later.
[2] *The Irish Times*, 1 April 1965

reformist policies. This approach would have been anathema to Lemass, who had a remarkable capacity for presenting the advantages he and his party offered in a way that suited the demands of the country at the time. Lemass's great disadvantage was that he had served for too long under de Valera's leadership and had come too late into his own. Modern though he was in many of his attitudes, and above all in the dynamism he brought to Ireland's economic resurgence in the first half of the sixties, he belonged among the Founding Fathers of the State and was surrounded by a new generation already dominated by the talented sons of his colleagues, many of whom were withdrawing, or had withdrawn from active politics, many more of whom had passed on.

Nevertheless, public regard for Sean Lemass was reflected in the outcome of that April 1965 general election, where an increased turnout delivered an improved vote for the Government and gave Lemass an overall majority.

It was perhaps typical of the man that almost immediately he began to look to the future of the Fianna Fáil Party and to prepare for a handover of its leadership. 'It is time I passed on. I don't want to become a national monument around the place!' he is reported to have said in 1966.[1] Apart from having taken up with considerable determination and resourcefulness the central issue of the country's economic rescue and then development, Sean Lemass did not have a vision of the future, or of how to extend economic recovery into other social and cultural fields. He had no fundamental answers on agriculture, beyond finding markets; on Northern Ireland, although his meeting with O'Neill was a sensational event, his thinking did not extend beyond friendly co-operation; on world or Western defences he was broadly in favour of a potential Irish commitment to freedom and democracy, but all carefully unspecified; his social policies were limited – he was not reformist, nor particularly enlightened; and even his economic planning, which was in any event a product of the Civil Service machine, which he valued and supported, was becoming increasingly a running commentary on world trading opportunities and how Ireland was responding to them, rather than a definitive process that would yield results. He believed in the adage that 'a rising tide lifts all boats' and it was followed by Fianna Fáil in a way that induced a certain *laisser-faire* conservatism. Lemass was less

[1] Michael Mills, 'Sean Lemass: A Profile', *Irish Press*, 18 January 1969.

conservative than his party and was faintly surprised by the climate of opportunity that developed and expanded from the late 1950s on, although always prepared to exploit it. But the fundamental climate of the Lemass era, 1959–66, was that of a benign paternalism that favoured organised labour – Lemass instituted regular, negotiated wage rounds for workers – and benefited urban, particularly Dublin, society, leading to the physical and population expansion of the city. There were less attractive side-effects, however; they included the unplanned demolition of many of its architectural treasures and the growth of financial self-interest which came to be a hallmark of Fianna Fáil supporters and members, including ministers.

Charles Haughey was inevitably associated with this side of Fianna Fáil. He became personally wealthy during the 1960s, at the end of the decade buying Abbeville, a fine, large eighteenth-century house, in part designed by James Gandon,[1] and standing on a large estate of some 400 acres. He was later to buy an island off the Kerry coast. Yet throughout this period he was a full-time public office-holder, on the relatively modest income then, and now, paid to members of the Government, and his capacity for acquiring substantial wealth has never been explained satisfactorily.[2] Haughey's mother, though she was very proud of his success, had some difficulty with her son's growing power and somewhat ostentatious wealth. She thought it wrong to visit him at Abbeville and declined to become involved in any way with the life pursued in this large mansion only a couple of miles from the house where she had raised her family. Other members of the family felt a similar diffidence.

Within Fianna Fáil the association of power with wealth and success was symbolized and clearly flaunted by Taca, a fund-raising organization of 500 businessmen who 'enjoyed ostentatious dinners in the Gresham Hotel',[3] and paid, at the outset of the organization, £100 per evening. Tim Pat Coogan, editor of the *Irish Press*, coined the epithet for them 'the Men in the Mohair Suits'. It stuck. Kevin Boland,

[1] James Gandon (1743–1823) was a pupil of William Chambers who was brought to Ireland to design the Custom House by John Beresford, Commissioner of Revenue, who then commissioned Gandon to work on Abbeville.
[2] His opposite number in Northern Ireland, Harry West, Minister for Agriculture, was dismissed, 26 April 1967, on the grounds that private land deals in which he was involved conflicted with his position.
[3] See Dick Walsh, *The Party: Inside Fianna Fáil*, Dublin, 1986, p. 82. Walsh gives a good account of the various factions in the party during the 1960s and the leading political figures.

who was one of Taca's officers, went one better: he called the mohair-suited ones 'Mohawks'.[1] Apart from Charles Haughey, who was to become the greatest mohawk of them all, its prominent figures included young progressives such as Donogh O'Malley and Brian Lenihan, but also Neil Blaney[2] and Kevin Boland, who had a more traditional, republican image. This did not make Blaney any less committed to the support group, and he also became spokesman for Taca, defending it in a brilliant speech at one of the Fianna Fáil Ard Fheis-anna when there was a fairly strong move to have it disbanded on the grounds that it gave the wrong image for grass-root supporters. Blaney had the reputation within the party of being something of an organizational wizard, both locally and nationally. He was also a man who saw himself as a future leader.

Taca was a slick and sophisticated response to the economic boom of the 1960s. Its leading members enjoyed the new prosperity which they had engineered and they flaunted their power and success by dining lavishly in the best Dublin hotels – the Russell Hotel was the most opulent and the most favoured – in the company of self-made men, particularly builders, speculators and successful architects, who were tearing down much of Georgian Dublin and replacing it with neutral glass-faced office blocks which were often rented back to government departments at the highest possible rates. A favoured, late-night place for meeting was Groome's Hotel, in Parnell Square, also patronized by actors and writers, the odd district justice, and by other backbench and rural politicians. Drink and promises were exchanged there with equal enthusiasm and in roughly equal quantities. The company could be entertained by many stories, among them Donogh O'Malley's latest exploits, ' "See the arrows, guard?" sez I, on this one-way street. 'To tell the truth, guard, I didn't even see the bloody indians." '[3]

The hotel was owned by Patti Groome and her husband, Joe, who was a founder member and a vice-president of the Fianna Fáil Party. It seemed that these men and their ostentatious style represented the new soul of Fianna Fáil, destined to take over from Sean Lemass when

[1] Dick Walsh, op. cit., p. 84.
[2] Neil Blaney (b. 1922) succeeded his father, who had fought in the War of Independence and the Civil War, in the Donegal North-East seat in 1948. He became Minister for Posts and Telegraphs in March 1957, moving to Local Government in December of that year. He succeeded Haughey as Minister for Agriculture in 1966.
[3] Dick Walsh, 'The Haughey Years', The Irish Times, 31 January 1992.

his leadership came to an end. And they certainly presented themselves as being firmly in control of the party's future. Yet they also created suspicion and resentment. There were the occasional sinister stories, rumours of guards being offered the choice between a drink and a transfer. The picture which emerged indicated not only control over party affairs, but the close association between politics and success, wealth and power, to the point where this small elect among politicians in power were identified as running Ireland for their own ends.

CHAPTER V

THE FIRST
LEADERSHIP CONTEST

Why, there's no remedy. 'Tis the curse of service:
Preferment goes by letter and affection,
And not by old gradation.

I N 1966 IT BECAME CLEAR that it was Lemass's intention to hand
over the leadership of party and country in good time for his
successor to build a proper power base and prepare in good time
for the next general election. Lemass was sixty-six and, it seemed, in
reasonable health. He was a family man, liked playing poker and had
no obsessions about power. He had been active in public affairs, as a
revolutionary in the early days (not many other politicians still active
in the mid-1960s had been involved both in the Easter Rising and the
Civil War by the age of twenty-two) and later as an elected politician
from 1925. He had brought on a new generation and it was obvious
that the next leader would be drawn from among those who were
prominent in that new group of men – there were no women – who
had been first elected since the Second World War. It was a good
time for such a transition, stable, positive and productive. The faltering
fifties had given way to two successive Fianna Fáil governments under
which much had been achieved. It looked as though future control of
power would rest with the party. It also looked as though the party's
leading younger figures offered capable future Taoiseachs. The choice
ranged across a broad spectrum, from those like Jack Lynch and
Charles Haughey, who were first-generation members of the party, to
those like Neil Blaney and George Colley, whose fathers had been in
it from the start. Together with Donogh O'Malley, Brian Lenihan,
Erskine Childers and Kevin Boland, they constituted a team of energetic men whose ideological range covered a considerable and impressive national programme. Fianna Fáil was too conservative,
perhaps, to embrace the radicalism of the mid-1960s Labour Party or

the burgeoning 'Just Society' instincts within Fine Gael; but it did reflect a broad, mid-60s Irish consensus out of which Lemass could comfortably foresee a sustained leadership of Ireland by the party he had helped to found.

Lemass had been advised to give up the leadership of the party, on medical grounds. He was not ill, but the potential strains were regarded as too much for him during any further sustained period in power. The story of his impending departure, on these grounds of medical advice, was leaked and appeared first in the *Irish Press*. It was then denied by 'Government sources', provoking fierce internal party debate. Lemass fostered this approach himself, it seems, in order to test the atmosphere within Fianna Fáil and bring to a head the pressures which were building up as a result of growing discussion and rumour. Jack Lynch,[1] Lemass's preferred successor, was the first to be told that Lemass was in fact stepping down and indicated, in return, that he would not be a contender. That weekend George Colley, who was Lemass's second choice, was in the United States when he was informed of the impending decision by Lemass, an obvious invitation to enter whatever contest might emerge and an indication that Lynch would not stand. Lemass viewed with some alarm the faction-fighting that developed once he announced his intention to hand over the leadership, turning rumour into fact. Despite Lemass's intentions for a clean, uncontroversial changeover, it looked as though the party was heading for an unprecedented battle, quite unlike the pre-ordained way in which the transition from de Valera to himself had taken place. More than anything else, this was the harvest reaped from bringing on so much talent and energy.

There were two candidates initially – George Colley and Charles Haughey – and both represented fairly well-defined factions in the Fianna Fáil Party. Colley was representative of the traditional wing in the party, its inspiration drawn from core values on the Irish language, on reunification and on broad republican ideals which were inherited from the historical fight for freedom. He believed in a party morality and dedication which derived its standards from an austerity close to

[1] Jack Lynch (b. 1917) was first a civil servant working in the Department of Justice, then a barrister. He entered the Dáil in 1948 and was Fianna Fáil Government Whip in the 1951–54 administration. He was successively Minister for Gaeltacht and then Education under de Valera, Industry and Commerce and then Finance under Lemass. He was an outstanding Gaelic games sportsman, winning all-Ireland medals in hurling or Gaelic football in six successive years, the only player ever to do so.

that of de Valera. Haughey was under a party obligation to take much of this on trust, but he represented a freer, more modern interpretation of Fianna Fáil as the organization best suited to get the country moving, build houses and factories, energize people, create and use wealth effectively. He represented the brash, progressive element which wanted to associate Fianna Fáil with businessmen and commercial objectives.

Haughey's campaign manager was O'Malley. Donogh O'Malley was more than just a brash promoter of a closer association of Ireland's new businessmen with the party. He was a man bubbling with thoughts and proposals. Lemass said of him once that he would come up with six ideas: four would be suitable only for immediate discarding; one might be for further discussion; but one would be quite brilliant. Haughey's well-rehearsed rhetoric about the future and positive prospects for the Irish economy under Fianna Fáil leadership gained the committed backing of deputies such as Brian Lenihan, Seán Flanagan and other younger members and was, of course, attractive to many Dublin TDs.

George Colley, perhaps the most traditionalist of the younger politicians in the party, had as his campaign manager Jim Gibbons, later to become his parliamentary secretary in the Department of Finance. He also had the significant backing of founder-figures such as Frank Aiken, Paddy Smith and Sean MacEntee. Finally, there was Neil Blaney, party organizer, grass-roots expert and very much a rural deputy, who was persuaded to stand by Kevin Boland.

Haughey's nominator was O'Malley; Colley's was James Gibbons. Neil Blaney, who represented another, rural-based party faction, then threw his hat into the ring. He knew that Colley and Haughey represented the party's extremes of conservatism and opportunism and that, without Lynch's candidacy, he might steer the middle course and defeat both contenders. It colours one's judgements, not just of the situation that had developed during the Lemass period, but also of the likely future developments and their impact both on Blaney and Haughey. It was a perception which had a profound effect on Haughey; he very much feared Blaney's claim on middle-ground support. Blaney represented, in Haughey's eyes, the biggest future threat to his political advance. Deep down, Haughey, the urbane, city-based architect of progress and dynamic action, saw too much of his own real character in Neil Blaney, the rabble-rouser and organization man, who knew who held the Fianna Fáil party power-strings in every county in Ireland. And he feared this knowledge and the rivalry it implied.

Lemass decided to ask Lynch a second time if he would stand. He was prompted by the divisions which were being created by the other contestants and by his own shrewd judgement that Jack Lynch was by far the best candidate for the job of leading Fianna Fáil. He also seemed to be backing this compromise leader in order to get over the dangers of faction-fighting in the party. And this view was reinforced, inadvertently, by Lynch himself, in an ill-judged remark to that effect.[1]

This false start in his candidacy for leader was later used by his rivals in the party, particularly Haughey himself, to imply an inadequate command over party loyalty. There arose the image of him having been called in to mend differences and to hold the position until some stronger figure emerged.

But Lynch was never a compromise candidate. True, he resisted the initial call; but when it was made again he discussed it with his wife, Maureen, close companion in his long political career and a formidable woman in her own right, and then decided to take on what was clearly going to be a vast challenge. His determination was reinforced within days of the party ballot when three deputations, mainly from Munster, went to Lynch and added their entreaties for him to let his name go forward. His consultation with his wife – a perfectly normal sharing of the decision with the person closest to him – was subsequently used as an indication of Lynch's prevarication and uncertainty, even of weakness, through dependence on a woman; it was anything but. He was a man who often delayed decisions; but when made they were firm and unequivocal.

Lynch was an obvious choice within the party. From his first political responsibilities as a deputy, which were as de Valera's assistant in Opposition, from 1948 to 1951, and then as Parliamentary Secretary to the Government, Lynch had been impressive. In 1957 de Valera made him Minister for Education. When Lemass took over from de Valera, in 1959, he moved Lynch to his own former Department of Industry and Commerce, where Lemass had made his own reputation, keeping him there during the subsequent administration, a clear indi-

---

[1] He spoke of being a compromise candidate after his election to the leadership (see Dick Walsh, op. cit., p. 91). Walsh claims that Lynch 'bitterly regretted' the use of the word and in no sense intended it to mean that he would relinquish control at an early stage. He in fact led the party for twice as long as Lemass and was more successful, electorally, than de Valera and much more successful in every way than Haughey.

cation of trust in his abilities. In 1965 he had given Lynch the most important job of all, as Minister for Finance. Lynch was told by Lemass of his intention to go before announcing the decision to other party members, an indication that he was the chosen successor. 'Lemass put his raddle-mark on me early on.'[1]

Lynch led no faction. He did not need to. He had the broad respect of a comfortable majority of deputies and he commanded almost unswerving devotion from Munster and particularly Cork city and county, as much for sporting prowess and personal charm as for political drive. But he had doubts himself and kept his counsel over the implicit invitation which Lemass's confidence suggested. Far from being uncertain or self-deprecating, other than in the sense that he was being chosen to follow two men of mythic standing in the country's fight for independence, Lynch could afford to sit, wait and conserve his energies, allowing others to rally their support, and to canvass and campaign, while he attended to his ministerial duties and waited for the actual contest. It was a sportsman's approach, almost laconic in its indifference to the swirl of activity, even prior to Lemass's announcement that he was stepping down.

As soon as Lynch announced his intention to stand, Haughey withdrew, as did Blaney. George Colley, on reflection, decided to remain in the contest and it went to a vote. Since this was the first leadership election within Fianna Fáil, no procedures existed. It was decided that, since the parliamentary party alone would vote on the leader's nomination of successor as head of the Government, the vote should be confined to Dáil deputies, with members of the Senate excluded. Lynch won handsomely, by 54 votes to 19.[2] 'The manner of his victory in the succession stakes epitomized his style. He came quietly through on the rails, giving the impression that he was merely out for a canter, while his frothing rivals churned up the ground in the centre.'[3]

Jack Lynch reconstructed the Government, making some sensible and important changes. He moved Haughey out of Agriculture and put him into Finance. He replaced him with Neil Blaney. He kept George Colley in Industry and Commerce, to which Lemass had

---

[1] See Dick Walsh, op. cit., p. 89.
[2] The nineteen who supported Colley included James Gibbons, who was later involved in the Arms Crisis, Bobby Molloy, later a founder-member of the Progressive Democrats, and at least three members of Lemass's Government.
[3] J. J. Lee, op. cit., p. 409.

moved him only four months before.[1] And he extended the role in Government of Erskine Childers.[2]

It has often been said of Lynch that he presided without controlling during the period between becoming leader of the party, and hence prime minister, in November 1966, and his first general election, three years later in 1969. It is an over-simplification. Jack Lynch adopted an entirely different style as party leader from his predecessor. He was much closer to de Valera than to Lemass in his approach – essentially passive, leaving the work of government to his ministers and relying on them to deliver. His decision to retain Colley in a key post resolved any potential split with his declared opponent in the leadership vote and he came increasingly to rely on Colley as one of his closer aides within the Government.

He was a constitutional politician who took seriously the principle of collective Government responsibility which de Valera had enshrined in the 1937 Constitution and he interfered as little as possible. Arguably, he was a lazy man. Certainly, in his ministerial days, his civil servants had found it difficult to get decisions out of him. But his first period of inherited power was entirely smooth and uneventful. It was not 'a period of anarchy', as has been suggested.[3] Lynch's relatively short periods of indecision during national crises were followed by forceful and comprehensive action.

Placing Haughey in Finance was an overdue move. From the very beginning of his parliamentary career, Haughey, an accountant by training, had displayed a better grasp of economic issues than he had of other national problems and he welcomed all the challenges and opportunities offered by the central and most powerful department in the Irish Civil Service. He was lucky in the timing of his appointment.

---

[1] In July 1966 a new Department of Labour was set up, with Patrick Hillery as Minister. Hillery was replaced at Industry and Commerce by Colley, who was replaced in Education by Donogh O'Malley. Seán Flanagan was brought into the Government as Minister for Health.

[2] Erskine Childers (1905–74) came from two distinguished Protestant Republican families. His father, Robert Erskine, was a British politician and author who settled in Dublin, was elected to the Dáil, fought on the Republican side in the Civil War and was executed. His grandmother was a Barton, her brother, like his father, a signatory of the 1921 Treaty. He was a Dáil deputy from 1938, served in several ministries, under de Valera, Lemass and Lynch, and became President of Ireland in 1973. He died in office the following year.

[3] See Vincent Browne, op. cit., p. 160. This popular view of the control of events being in the hands of Haughey, Blaney, Boland and Donogh O'Malley (until his death) is one which these men may have helped to create, in an effort to shorten Lynch's time as leader, but is not consistent with the facts.

Ireland was enjoying considerable prosperity and it was possible to have successive budgets, from 1967 to 1970, in which he was able to provide grants, incentives and tax reliefs across the board. He helped old-age pensioners with free electricity, free transport, free radio and television licences; he gave more money to the arts, to youth projects and to sport; he made special tax provisions for the disabled, improved medical tax exemptions and created a fund for West of Ireland development; he improved the working conditions for civil servants.

During the previous eight years he had developed a highly cultured image. Through his association with artists, patronage of painters and sculptors, and opening of exhibitions, he appeared to be a national patron of all artistic endeavour. This culminated in his introduction, in the Budget of 1969, of tax exemption for artists. The scheme provided for categories of excellence of work: paintings, works of sculpture, books, musical compositions and plays, if judged to be of sufficient 'cultural merit', had their earnings exempted from income tax. The criteria for qualification included the nature of the work, which had to be original and creative, and the quality: it had to have 'cultural or artistic merit'. The onus of judgement was handed to the Revenue Commissioners, who were permitted to consult with others 'competent to advise them'. The measure was given broad welcome, not just among artists, but within the population as a whole, and in its early implementation was interpreted very freely by the Revenue Commissioners. It encouraged many foreign artists to settle in Ireland, some of them specifically on short-term visits to ensure exemption on large earnings, others for longer periods. Frederick Forsyth, P. D. James, Peter Sellars, Gordon Thomas, Wolf Mankievicz, Robert Elegant, Malcolm Arnold and Anne McCaffrey all lived for periods in Ireland and benefited from the measure. It was done, Haughey said in his Budget speech,[1] both to encourage artists and to create a sympathetic environment in which the arts could flourish. He emphasized later that 'the taxation and financial aspects of this particular provision are of relatively minor importance. Ireland has had a long history of exporting her most creative people and I brought in this measure with a view to halting this intellectual drain and to underline the importance of the artist to the community in which he lives and the value of the contribution he makes... That artistic endeavour is singularly unrewarding in a

---

[1] The budget was introduced on May 7; the second-stage debate began on July 15. In both speeches he dealt with the measure. See *Dáil Reports*.

commercial sense is well known and to that extent the measure was much more important as a gesture than as an act of patronage.'[1] In its first three years 300 people qualified for tax relief. Seventy per cent were writers, 25 per cent painters.

The measure was claimed by Haughey as unique. 'We are entering a field in which there is no precedent or experience to guide us.' The impact was substantial and, though it took time to achieve the broader aim of creating a more positive and sympathetic environment for the artist, this budgetary decision created an undoubted forward surge in confidence and activity in the arts. Perhaps more deeply, Haughey's clear and unswerving personal commitment to artists and their work – he was then, and remained, an eclectic connoisseur and collector – gave confidence and dignity to those engaged in the appallingly difficult process of creative work.

He also showed at the time an interest in the development of science, launching the National Science Council at the beginning of 1968 and describing the event as an important landmark. It was the era in Ireland for the creation of such bodies. And Haughey's view of their function and accountability was very much in keeping with the Lemass philosophy, which was to give them as much autonomy as possible. It suited the 1960s, when the rising tide, which was lifting all boats anyway, made it possible to by-pass the question of accountability which would arise in more difficult economic conditions. When Haughey became Minister for Finance there were about forty-five State, or 'Semi-State', bodies, as they were known at the time, one-third of them 'non-trading', as he put it in a speech about their role and performance.[2] 'We have to allow these bodies to take calculated risks', he said, and he made a modest genuflection to the concept of the Dáil's public representatives deserving 'the greatest respect and consideration from any of these bodies'. But he was not prepared to envisage parliamentary answerability through an all-party committee. To counter the importance of the publicly elected deputy there was 'the great corps of dedicated and devoted people who give their services to these organizations'. This view was consistent with the Lemass philosophy and it was to become a standard interpretation of how democracy should work in Haughey's

[1] Address to the Harvard Summer School Institute, Harvard University, 12 July 1972.
[2] *Dáil Reports*, 22 February 1967. He was opposing an Opposition attempt to get an all-party committee established with powers to investigate these bodies and make them more answerable to the Oireachtas. Haughey favoured answers to the relevant minister only.

eyes as well. It actually by-passed democratic control and it involved vast sums of public money. So long as the servants of the semi-State companies remained servants, and also remained 'dedicated and devoted', all would be well. Either way, the Dáil was denied detailed access, interrogation and control.

There was more than a whiff of corporatism in this approach, which reflected Irish political traditions stretching back into the 1930s. There had always been a tendency for highly influential lobbies and group-ings, of which easily the most powerful was the Roman Catholic Church, to acquire special status by virtue of their services to society, which often gave them a special say in the running of the country. Little serious attempt at change in the fields of education or health, for example, where there was a substantial input from the religious orders, would have been possible in Ireland without the agreement of the Roman Catholic hierarchy. And this gave credibility to other special relationships, such as that between government and the Semi-State Sector.

The arguments in favour of political answerability were not based on any serious fault-finding. The strange character of the whole decade, seen with the benefit of hindsight, is its urbane optimism. Growth provided the revenues necessary for the kind of economic expansion which fed this. The Roman Catholic Church permitted these benefits, which in any case made its own work easier, drawing the line only on crucial family issues. And in the realm of politics there seemed to be no fierce challenges directed against ideologies, such as they were. Relative prosperity vanquished the more strident voices of the Left. It divided the two main Opposition parties. With the excep-tion of the farmers, who went on demonstrating and in some cases were gaoled, growth ameliorated hardship, increased a wide variety of social benefits, extended employment, turned the tide of emigration, produced the major watershed of Irish population decline – which had been continuing for almost a century – and spread an atmosphere in town and country of pride, self-confidence and optimism about the future.

Just before Lemass's departure as leader in September 1966 (and, it is thought, with his prior knowledge), Donogh O'Malley, in a speech which had not been cleared by the Government and which took the then Minister for Finance, Jack Lynch, and the whole country by surprise, announced the introduction of free post-primary education. It was a stunning objective to set, even today not fully realized. And it had major implications for the public, for the Roman Catholic and other Churches, for teacher organizations, and of course for the Minister for Finance.

Haughey spoke on the financial implications, which were immense, in June 1967.[1] The response to O'Malley's initial announcement had been highly gratifying. An anticipated 75 per cent response had been exceeded, with a 93 per cent participation in the scheme. Even without the State footing the bill, there had been an increase of 45,000 children attending secondary school in the three-year period, 1964–7. And so long as the country went on earning more money through foreign trade, this bill would be met.

However, problems began to arise in the third phase in economic development and the expansion of Ireland's trade, represented by accession to the European Economic Community. Ireland had been vetoed in 1963, along with Britain, with whom it shared a common currency and in other ways was too closely associated. In parallel with the United Kingdom, Ireland applied again in 1967. Again de Gaulle blocked Britain's entry and the Irish application was also shelved.

Success in two by-elections, won by Fianna Fáil in Cork and Limerick in 1967, reinforced party confidence. In March 1968 Donogh O'Malley, one of the most colourful and dynamic of the 'mohair-suited' ministers, died from a heart attack. He was only 47. Donogh O'Malley was in many respects the most attractive of the 'mohair-suited' brigade. He was approachable, open to ideas, willing to meet with people and discuss issues on which the government should act, not necessarily confining himself to educational matters. He was, like Haughey and because of his ministerial role, interested in culture and the arts. He was probably closer to Haughey than any other Fianna Fáil minister at that time, though Haughey's personal reaction to the death does not particularly reflect this. In the ensuing by-election his nephew, Desmond O'Malley,[2] who was to become the most formidable challenge to Charles Haughey's own political career, was elected to the Dáil.

But in anticipation of his first general election as leader of the party,

---

[1] Athlone, 24 June 1967; see Ed. Martin Mansergh, op. cit., p. 74.
[2] Desmond O'Malley (b. 1939) trained and practised as a solicitor, but was then prevailed on to stand for his uncle's Dáil seat, though in conflict at the time with Donogh O'Malley's widow, Hilda, who also wanted to be nominated by the party. Lynch made him Chief Whip after the 1969 general election and he became Minister for Justice at the time of the Arms Crisis.

Jack Lynch began to prepare early on, repeating Lemass's 'hands across the Border' initiative, with meetings in Stormont and Dublin with the Northern Ireland premier, Captain Terence O'Neill.[1] The first Civil Rights march followed in the summer and ended in a confrontation with Protestants, but then the two sides dispersed without incident. The second march, on Saturday, 5 October 1968, in Derry, was an entirely different affair. Blocked by a Home Office ban, by Protestant Unionists and by the police, it led to weekend riots with many injured, though with no deaths.

There was widespread concern in the Republic, but it did not become an election issue. If anything, it raised more questions within Fianna Fáil than between Fianna Fáil and the other parties. More than them, Fianna Fáil was tested by the events in the North in respect of its traditional answer to Northern problems. The debate did not really extend to a detailed understanding of the Six Counties, how they were governed and by whom, but was dominated by the simplistic view that the North itself was the problem and that the answer was to end partition and reunite the island of Ireland into a 32-county republic, governed from Dublin. This, of course, side-stepped the need for understanding that the protests in the North in 1968 were about the quite different problems of domestic civil rights and social reforms. In such contacts as took place between nationalist politicians from the North and politicians from all parties in the South, this point was repeatedly made. It was counter-productive for the Republic of Ireland to offer the reunification of the whole island as an instant solution to all ills. Lynch grasped this and was supported by a majority within the Government. A smaller but significant grouping, which included Neil Blaney, Charles Haughey, Kevin Boland and later on Micheál O Móráin and James Gibbons, 'tried to get an approach based on the fundamental reason for the existence of the political party to which we all belonged.'[2] Put simply, to end partition.

The repeated statement of this objective, counter-productive though it was in its impact on Northern Ireland, and indeed on British opinion, had considerable popular appeal in the South, and there were politicians in all parties who were quite vociferous in putting forward the

[1] On 11 December 1967 Lynch saw O'Neill at Stormont, followed on 8 January 1968 by O'Neill's visit to Dublin.

[2] Kevin Boland, 'Up Dev!', Dublin, 1977, p. 11. This book, written after the general election in June 1977 which saw Lynch sweep back to power with the largest majority in Fianna Fáil's history, is an important source for Government frictions and divisions in 1968–9.

nationalist answer. No one was more outspoken in this than Neil
Blaney, who persisted in making speeches that were at odds with what
Lynch himself was saying. Haughey's silence on the issue was a most
extraordinary phenomenon. Given that his supposed concern for
the nationalist minority in Northern Ireland was to lead him into
actions that would result in his dismissal from the Government, the
absence of any public expression of concern has always been a totally
bewildering aspect of his character at the time.

In the autumn of 1968 the differences between the two groupings
within Fianna Fáil became public, with Neil Blaney making strongly
republican speeches, attacking 'the bigoted junta' in Northern Ireland
led by Captain Terence O'Neill, but in effect attacking Lynch. These
views were then contradicted by Jack Lynch, who paid muted lip-
service to the party's views on partition, but then laid serious stress
on the need for reform in Northern Ireland. For a time the situation
seemed to stabilize in the North. O'Neill made his 'Ulster at the
Crossroads' speech on 9 December 1968, in which he appealed, with
considerable success, to moderate opinion in Northern Ireland to support the extensive reform programme which he had already announced.
In reality O'Neill had brought into the open the power struggle within
the Unionist Party, confronting his main critic, William Craig.
Strengthened by the public response, O'Neill dismissed Craig and
subsequently won a clear vote of confidence from his parliamentary
party. What he needed was time to set the reforms in train and the
Civil Rights movement was prepared to give him time. People's
Democracy, a much more militant group among whose leading activists were Bernadette Devlin and Michael Farrell, 'more a sect than a
party',[1] were determined not to give O'Neill the time to prove his
good intentions over reform. They decided on a protest march from
Belfast to Derry, their route passing through traditionally Protestant
territory. One of the most heavily Protestant parts of the march's
route was Burntollet. There, with police complicity and the apparent
involvement of individual police and 'B Special' officers, the marchers
were assaulted quite savagely in what became known as 'The Burntollet
Massacre'. O'Neill fell swiftly. Faced with disintegrating support
within his own party he decided on a general election which was
called on 4 February 1969. The results were inconclusive. The election
resolved nothing. His control over his own party was marginal. On 28

[1] See J. J. Lee, op. cit., pp 421-3.

April O'Neill resigned. 'You either succeed or you fail. I failed,' he said.

In March 1969 the Government published 'The Third Programme for Economic and Social Development', addressing the years 1969–72. Haughey was the principal political architect of this, though the main work on it was again undertaken by Whitaker, Charles Murray and Maurice Doyle.[1] Just before the programme appeared, Whitaker moved to the Central Bank, as its Governor, being succeeded by Murray as Secretary in the Department of Finance.

The Programme represented an election platform. During the second half of the decade there had been growing criticism of the whole approach adopted by Fianna Fáil under Lemass and Lynch. It was felt that the party, in its policies, had stressed economic progress to the neglect of social progress. Increased employment generated by economic development had been seen as the most powerful social benefit the government could bring to the country as a whole. It was now being argued by the Left that a simple reliance on the redistribution of the benefits of growth, was not a satisfactory role for government. To some extent this did happen. The initial benefits of Fianna Fáil's policy through the 1960s were to the strongest elements in society, serving the interests of business and of wealth. And it was this struggle between economic and social progress which gave character and direction to the general election of 1969; on balance, given the choice between Fianna Fáil achievement and the social recipes offered by the non-aligned Opposition parties, the electorate decided in favour of Fianna Fáil.

The 1960s had been progressive and enlightened – in comparison with previous decades. There had been no serious confrontation between Church and State. The heavy weight of excessive literary and film censorship had been lifted. The idea of the State playing a more decisive role in educational reform had been accepted. In December 1961 a national television service was inaugurated which brought into a growing number of Irish homes an intrusive, questioning and at times challenging view of the life of the people. The Church itself, under the impact of Pope John XXIII, also seemed progressive and more enlightened.

---

[1] Maurice Doyle, who also worked closely with Whitaker on the First Programme, was to succeed Murray as Secretary of the Department of Finance. He is currently Governor of the Central Bank.

One of Sean Lemass's last acts, as Taoiseach, had been to set up an all-party committee of elected politicians to consider possible reforms to the Constitution. In its report, published in December 1967, it recommended changes to Articles 2 and 3, which deal with the Republic's claim to Northern Ireland and the definition of the State's territorial extent and legal remit. It also recommended the introduction of a limited form of divorce and the ending of the special position of the Roman Catholic Church.

A referendum was held nine months later, but it did not reflect these proposals, and instead, in a piece of political opportunism that would have repercussions for a long time to come, proposed the simple abolition of proportional representation and its replacement by the 'first past the post' system. This again was rejected by the electorate.[1] In the climate of the time, the changes recommended by Lemass's constitutional committee represented an enlightened approach which was to evaporate in the face of Northern violence and the division of the communities in the Six Counties. And even when the troubles in Northern Ireland began, with the Civil Rights marches during 1968, the general election in the Republic effectively ignored the reunification issue.

Jack Lynch was remarkably well prepared and well placed for that 1969 election. With the exception of a somewhat sharp supplementary budget, which had been introduced at the beginning of November the previous year, all the ingredients for a steady continuation of broad economic and social policy were in place, and no hostages had been given to fortune in other areas. Indeed, following the failure of the referendum to replace proportional representation, the government had carried out a re-drawing of electoral boundaries – known as 'Kevin Boland's Gerrymander' – which was favourable to Fianna Fáil and on which the forthcoming electoral contest was to be based. Wisely, from the point of view of the party, Lynch aimed at achieving his first electoral mandate essentially on the policies that had served the party well during the whole decade. And the man he put in charge, as director of elections, was Charles Haughey.

The Opposition, on the other hand, was quite deeply divided on

---

[1] An attempt had previously been made in 1959, when de Valera's election to the presidency coincided with a referendum on proportional representation. Fianna Fáil campaigned for both; the electorate approved the de Valera choice for presidency, but rejected the proposed electoral reform.

ideological lines. The divisions were within Fine Gael and Labour as much as between the two parties that had now been defeated in three successive elections. Fine Gael, following the 1965 defeat, which led to the abrupt resignation of James Dillon, had chosen as leader Liam Cosgrave. Though initially involved in quite radical thinking within the party, which had produced as a new manifesto a document called *Towards a Just Society*, Cosgrave, in the period leading up to the 1969 election, had come increasingly under the influence of Gerard Sweetman, an able but conservative lawyer, and had moved away from the reformist figures in the party, among whom were Declan Costello and Garret FitzGerald. Though an effective constituency deputy and an experienced politician who had served in both Inter-Party administrations, he was a somewhat limited leader, facing difficulties in uniting his own party and unprepared for the still greater problems of leading the Opposition as a whole.

The situation in the Labour Party was not conducive to any joint programme with Fine Gael to put before the people. Brendan Corish himself was against coalition. He had become leader of the Labour Party in 1960 and in both the 1961 and the 1965 elections, without any pre-election pact with Fine Gael, had increased party strength in the Dáil. But in the 1965–9 period the party attracted even greater radicalism and the shift to the Left, implemented by new deputies, senators and party activists, threw up the spectre of Marxism, which was then exploited by Fianna Fáil to its own advantage. Part of the Labour Party's strategy was to attack the supposed use of power by politicians for self-advancement and this inevitably led to attacks, principally by Conor Cruise O'Brien,[1] on Charles Haughey, who was seen at this stage not only as the leading representative of this grouping in Fianna Fáil, but also as having gained his own personal wealth through being in power. During the campaign, O'Brien concentrated on a land deal concluded shortly before by Haughey, who sold his home, Grangemore, and bought Abbeville, with its large estate of some 400 acres. To this single land deal, admittedly a substantial one, has been repeatedly credited Haughey's wealth. It could in reality be no more than marginal. It allowed him to buy a larger estate and a much grander

---

[1] Conor Cruise O'Brien (b. 1917) started his career as a civil servant, first in Finance, then in the Department of External Affairs, which he left to join the United Nations in 1956. He became UN representative in Katanga in 1961. He wrote and lectured extensively during the 1960s, joining the Labour Party shortly before the 1969 election, and ran in the same constituency as Haughey.

house. But as a foundation for wealth on the scale enjoyed by Haughey during the next two decades, it could have been only of limited significance.

Haughey, though an appropriate target for O'Brien within the Dublin North-East constituency, was the wrong person to attack in national terms. It should have been the more difficult figure of Lynch. Haughey fought back against the criticisms, suggesting personal vilification, but not answering any of the specific points. He seized on every opportunity during that election to hammer home Fianna Fáil economic achievements and to present the not untruthful picture of the party in power having consulted effectively with the trade unions, which he repeatedly described as 'the real representatives of the workers'.[1]

Lynch won a comfortable majority of five. The election had focused mainly on the Labour Party and its increased emphasis on socialist policies. The party had put up ninety-nine candidates, their largest number, and were the main target for Fianna Fáil campaigning, with much made of the 'alien ideology' and of Communism within the party. In Dublin Labour increased its vote. But it lost in rural areas, where the 'Red' smear was more effective, dropping three seats. Fine Gael actually gained three seats, and Fianna Fáil gained two, despite a slight fall in the party's share of the vote. It was a clear victory, nonetheless, as much for the leader as it was for the party, because the campaign had revolved around his own countrywide tour, focusing on his personal appeal. Lynch had discovered during the campaign his own overwhelming personal popularity. Some of the credit, naturally, reflected on the director of elections, who was now widely seen as Lynch's main rival within Fianna Fáil. But the principal laurels went unquestionably to the leader, now clearly confirmed at the head of a party which would be securely in power for a full term.

---

[1] His election addresses during May and June 1969 contain trenchant criticism of the Left and of militant and disruptive minorities, and contrast these with the 'vocational and other groups' which are part of the progressive consultative machinery being employed by the Government.

CHAPTER VI

THE COVERT REPUBLICAN

We cannot all be masters, nor all masters
Cannot be truly followed.

A SOLID ELECTION VICTORY, a comfortable overall majority, no
fundamental changes in economic and social policy, and no
significant changes in the Government itself – this was the
reassuring picture for Jack Lynch in the aftermath of the 1969 contest. For Charles Haughey it represented privately a rather dismal
situation. Lynch could no longer be dismissed as either a compromise or an interim leader: he had unquestionably confirmed his
authority within both party and country and at fifty-one could
expect to go on being leader for ten years at least. Haughey was
eight years his junior. For anyone with a natural and relaxed view
of the likely political succession, the prospects for the second most
powerful politician in the country were promising. But 'promising'
was in no sense enough. Haughey's attitude to power was anything but relaxed, and by nature he was impatient. In the period
1966–9 he had often evinced a disdainful and dismissive view
of Lynch. He liked at that time to be regarded as the central figure
of power within Fianna Fáil, the decision-maker, the chancellor of
Ireland, controlling its finances and therefore with essential discretion over decision-making. Apart from combining this well-
constructed image of himself with that of a generous patron of the arts,
a man of culture and good taste, Haughey concealed all other
ambitions and in the aftermath of the election had to come to terms
with the realities of running a difficult and only moderately successful
economy.

Lynch made the fewest possible changes in his Government. Frank
Aiken, the only remaining veteran of the struggle for Independence
and the Civil War, stood down in the 1969 election and was replaced
at the Department of External Affairs – its name was shortly to be

changed to Foreign Affairs – by Patrick Hillery.[1] This necessitated other shifts. But the main ministries remained as before.

The nomination of the new Government was followed by the completion of outstanding business and the adjournment of the Dáil, for the summer recess, in mid-July. Decimalization was one of the matters dealt with in that short interim period and Dr Garret FitzGerald, a newly elected Fine Gael deputy for Dublin South-East, spoke on that issue on 9 July, fiercely attacking the methods proposed by Haughey for the implementation of this major change, which was to take place in 1971. Characteristically, the newly elected deputy – future leader of Fine Gael as well as future Taoiseach – dispensed with the formality of a maiden speech on his first day in the Dáil, in the debate on the nomination of Lynch as head of the Government, and instead embarked on a dazzling array of parliamentary questions, to Lynch and nine of his ministers. He spoke on three different Bills which were to be cleared up before the recess and also on the Finance Bill, during the final week of business before the summer holidays. On the decimalization measure the two men clashed repeatedly, FitzGerald picking at detail, Haughey presenting the broad strategy behind the change and defending the somewhat autocratic manner in which the designs for the new coins had been chosen.

It was a confrontation typical of many that were to follow between the two men. Haughey was by now one of the most experienced men in Lynch's Government – successful, assured and enjoying power again. FitzGerald was a self-confessed neophyte but, though new to the Dáil, had considerable Senate experience and was a powerful voice within Fine Gael. And his judgement and effectiveness, along with those of many other Opposition politicians, were soon to be tested on issues far more serious than the nature of coinage or the degree to which imitation of the way Britain was introducing a similar system mattered or not.

The anniversary of the Battle of the Boyne, 12 July, fell on a Saturday in 1969 and, in spite of the rioting the previous year, the Orange Order was permitted to organize and hold marches which led to riots in Derry, Dungiven and Lurgan. Shots were fired on both sides and

[1] Patrick J. Hillery (b. 1923) was a medical doctor who was in politics throughout his life, serving successively as Minister for Education, Industry and Commerce, Labour and Foreign Affairs, before becoming Ireland's first European Commissioner in 1973. He returned as President of Ireland in 1977 and served two terms.

two people were wounded. Then, on 14 July, there occurred in Northern Ireland the first death as a result of violence, caused by clashes between the Civil Rights movement and the RUC. There were further clashes that month and in early August there was serious rioting in Belfast. Even greater fears focused on the Apprentice Boys' march, which takes place in Derry every 12 August. James Chichester-Clark, the Northern Ireland Prime Minister who had replaced Terence O'Neill, was afraid to ban it in case his orders were defied, which might lead to a general breakdown of law and order. British Government responsibility, in the absence of Harold Wilson, who had gone on holiday to the Scilly Isles, rested with the Home Secretary, James Callaghan, and with Denis Healey, Secretary of State for Defence. They were relying, not on the small British Army presence, but, unwisely, on the RUC. There had been growing distrust of their fairness in the administration of the law since the so-called 'Burntollet Massacre' of January 1969 and this was aggravated by threats of revenge and punishment against Roman Catholics in Derry. Defence of the Bogside, a nationalist area in Derry which had been the scene of fierce conflict in October 1968 and in January and July 1969, became a priority and a Derry Citizens' Defence Committee was established, which ordered the erection of barricades.

The riots that followed, which lasted for a week and spread to Armagh and Belfast, were the worst up to that point and indicated clearly to the British Government that the British Army would have to be widely deployed in place of the RUC. As far as the Government in the Republic was concerned, this was a major crisis, requiring urgent decisions and practical action, with the need also for a reassessment of policy. At least, that was how it was seen by the more nationalist members. The Dáil had adjourned on 24 July, but the Government continued to meet, at times on a daily basis.

Lynch's judgement of the situation was simple, straightforward and entirely practical. He realized that the Government in the South could do very little in any event. He believed that it should not get involved in rhetoric, but should investigate the possibilities and options, and perhaps rectify the lamentable shortage of first-hand knowledge and awareness of what had been happening in the past, in Northern Ireland, and what the causes of the current situation were. Based on this, his instincts were that no overt action should be taken. But there were strong alternative pressures within the Government, arguing in favour of a more strident line, mainly in the form of rhetoric, but also including a demand for a modest deployment of troops. Lynch made a television address on Wednesday, 13 August, warning that 'the Irish Government can no longer stand by and see innocent people injured and perhaps worse.' Field hospitals, under Irish Army control, were sent to Border areas. This was done after consultation with the Chief of Staff and had a two-fold purpose. On the medical side treatment was provided for those Northern nationalists, many of them non-participants, who had been injured in incidents involving the Northern Ireland security forces and were reluctant to seek treatment in hospitals north of the border. They were free to seek help from the field hospitals. But the personnel manning these stations were also alert to the fact that certain groups in the South might be assembling arms for use in Northern Ireland against the security forces there; there was to be surveillance to monitor this and, if possible, to prevent the movement of arms.

The Minister for External Affairs went to the United Nations to urge on the Security Council the despatch of a peace-keeping force to Northern Ireland. A call was made for discussions between Britain and the Republic of Ireland on the future constitutional position of the North. The actual words used by Lynch were: 'It is our intention to request the British Government to enter into early negotiations'. The statement was first discussed at a Government meeting on 12 August, was substantially redrafted and considered again the next day before it was delivered. Lynch, however, deliberately departed from the agreed wording in his television announcement. In its agreed form it read: 'The Irish Government can no longer stand *idly* [my italics] by and see innocent people injured and perhaps worse.' Lynch, on his own judgement that this form of words was unnecessarily provocative, edited out the word 'idly'. But the original phrasing was leaked to the press and has since passed into the folklore of the period. In the eyes of many people it is 'remembered' as the actual version used, creating a long-standing wrangle over what had in fact been said. So successful was this sowing of the seed of idleness that it was regularly, and unfairly, thrown at Lynch in questions and debate.[1]

The hardliners within the Government 'scored the temporary and

[1] In a long and contentious exchange in the Dáil over a possible meeting between Lynch and Wilson on 24 Feburary 1970, Corish, after repeated questioning of Lynch, said: 'Just a minute. We take it therefore, that the Taoiseach and the Government are standing idly by?' *Dáil Report*, col. 1381.

illusory successes',[1] in Jack Lynch's television statement, of the UN demand, the deployment of a modest but military presence along the Border and the promise that the constitutional future of Northern Ireland would be discussed with Britain. In addition to the contents of that statement, the 13 August Government meeting made several far-reaching decisions.[2] The first of these was to establish a four-man sub-committee to deal with certain aspects of Northern Ireland affairs; three Border ministers, Neil Blaney and Joseph Brennan (both Donegal) and Padraig Faulkner (Louth) were on it, as was Haughey, apparently because of his alleged knowledge of, and interest in, the North. Haughey combined this with control of a special Northern Ireland relief fund of £100,000 voted by the Dáil, from which money was later made available for the purchase of arms. The Government also initiated an international propaganda campaign for which various publicity officers were recruited from the Semi-State organizations. This public relations project lasted into the late autumn and was wound up on 15 November, when the men and women concerned went back to their original duties.[3]

The role of the Government committee was to gather information and to report back. It had no mandate to take initiatives outside the general terms of that day's discussions. It did not meet as a committee, ever. No information was passed back to the Government as a whole. Virtually no information passed *between* its members, at least not formally, or to them as committee members. The only 'committee', as such, was made up of Haughey and Blaney. But the setting up of such a subsidiary grouping gave a nominal authority to its members which was then used, principally by these two, to initiate actions that were of a quite different order. Haughey, as Minister for Finance, held most power and he deployed it covertly, dealing most of the time on a one-to-one basis, both with fellow ministers and with those outside the Government who became involved in the attempt to import arms.

[1] Kevin Boland, op. cit., p. 11.

[2] Martin Mansergh, op. cit., p. 139, claims that the Government decision was made on August 16. 'Mr Haughey's role was to arrange for the speedy disbursement of the monies with a minimum of bureaucracy to persons or groups that could be vouched for as responsible and trustworthy.'

[3] Lynch announced these decisions in the Dáil on Wednesday, 19 November. Conor Cruise O'Brien made the point that their efforts around the world were superfluous to the real intent, which was 'to convince . . . our fellow Irishmen in the North' about the case for Ireland's unity. *Dáil Reports*, 19 November 1969, col. 1224.

Neil Blaney's position on that committee had, perhaps, the greatest legitimacy. Though he is often criticized for the controversial speeches he made on Northern Ireland, which created tensions within his party and apparent confrontations with Lynch, notably the Letterkenny speech of 8 December 1969, his record was consistent and the policies he pursued were close enough to the overall Fianna Fáil Party line to earn Lynch's *defence* of them against opposition criticism. Earlier in 1969 Blaney, in a speech in Cahir, had outlined three main strands of policy: that the constitutional claim to jurisdiction was real and not 'a legal fiction', the words used by Captain O'Neill; secondly, that the party was against partition; thirdly, that unity 'will always be an issue for the people of this country so long as the Border divides it'. Lynch, summarizing these points, said that they accorded fully with Government policy.[1] Indeed, part of Lynch's difficulty was this authentic strand of republican policy within his party running side-by-side with the covert actions which were to develop in the ensuing months.

Support of the nationalist community in Northern Ireland did not come only from the direction of the more militant republican wing of Fianna Fáil, however. Less than a month before the violence that produced the Government responses outlined above, Brendan Corish, the Labour Party leader, was exerting pressure on Lynch to meet Harold Wilson. Such a meeting had taken place in April, at the time of O'Neill's resignation, and Corish thought the violence precipitated by the celebration of the date of the Battle of the Boyne required another such meeting. But Lynch saw a subtle yet important difference: he wanted to act in support of the representatives of the minority community in Northern Ireland in their pressures on the Westminster Government, rather than being seen to go above their heads. 'I should like to make sure that the initiative that I take would benefit the people whose interests we have at heart.'[2] He went on: 'I suggest that the situation has changed ... A different series of incidents have taken place with perhaps a slightly different motivation.' This was undoubtedly the case, emphasized only the previous day, by the first death from Northern Ireland violence.

In the immediate aftermath of the weekend of serious rioting in Northern Ireland, Government meetings were a daily occurrence. The troubles in the North continued. The Bogside was, in Boland's words,

---

[1] See *Dáil Report*, 27 February 1969, col. 1933.
[2] Reply to Corish in the Dáil, 15 July 1969, *Dáil Report*, col. 467.

'still holding out'. He was becoming increasingly disillusioned at what he saw as the rejection of fundamental republican ideals. He believed that the objective of reunification should have been the basis of government policy at the time in responding to the Northern crisis.[1] On 15 August he announced his resignation to Government colleagues, during one such meeting, and went home. Haughey was among those who tried to make him reverse his decision, which would inevitably expose divisions within the Government. Their attempts were unsuccessful. But President de Valera was persuaded to intervene and summoned Boland to the presidential residence in the Phoenix Park. The effect of the meeting, in which de Valera applied pressures on Boland that seem, on the face of it, highly improper,[2] was that Boland 'suspended' his resignation in order to help avoid a public crisis that might, or so de Valera argued, have led to an election. Boland continued to attend Government meetings. He spoke only on issues connected with his own department and from time to time 'helped Blaney out with scribbled notes'.

At this time, in the increasingly violent circumstances that were developing in Northern Ireland, Haughey's concerns were essentially directed at their potential impact in the South. He was faced with the distinct possibility of the violence against the Roman Catholic minority creating a massive reaction in the Republic, which might make Lynch's position untenable. The person most likely to gain strength in the party from any discrediting of Lynch was Blaney. He was the outspoken militant in the Government. His speeches repeatedly provoked controversy. Into the bargain, he was the supreme grass-roots organization man and it was from this source that much of the unthinking tide of emotional concern about Unionist oppression and British suppression derived.

Haughey, who in other times, with his comprehensive grasp of economic policies and general leadership potential, would have been seen without question as the successor to Lynch, had no such claim in the violent atmosphere prevailing during the summer of 1969. He was outclassed by Blaney, whose republican credentials were solid and well-based. This gave birth to Haughey's covert republicanism at this

---

[1] Kevin Boland, op. cit., p. 12.

[2] There are no constitutional grounds for a president to intervene in this way. It was essentially to protect the Fianna Fáil Party from the threat of an election. It only came about because the president was a former leader of the party, knew Boland well and had known his father even better, thus making the persuasion almost a 'family' matter.

time and was the overriding motivation for his direct involvement in
Northern Ireland affairs; there was not, as so often has been stated,
any deep commitment to the Northern Ireland minority. Haughey
was more frightened of Blaney, as a future contender for the party
leadership, than he was of anyone else in the party. This had been the
case since the 1966 leadership contest, when Blaney had expressed
justified confidence that he would have beaten both Haughey and
Colley, but not Lynch. It became increasingly so as the Northern
Ireland situation deteriorated and as Blaney increasingly demonstrated
an approach at variance with Lynch's, and seemed able to make diver-
gent speeches without being disciplined for them. The Blaney threat
to Haughey's future prospects lessened by the end of 1969, but was
still a factor long afterwards.[1]

The idea that Haughey was a committed, if covert, republican, hid-
ing his convictions under a bushel until such time as they should be
revealed to the greater glory of some unpre-scripted dream about
Ireland's future, simply does not stand up. There is no evidence for
it. In fact, the contrary view is not only confirmed by his strong emphasis on Lemass-style economic solutions for Ireland, throughout his
early and middle period in politics up to that point, but also by his
tough anti-IRA stance when he was Minister for Justice. He had no
patience then with the militancy against the Unionist forces in Northern Ireland; he sought, as we have seen, to deflect young people in
the Republic away from the IRA and towards organizations such as
the FDA. And he was on record, more than once, as seeking to promote
peace and harmony, with both Northern Ireland and Britain.

He made no speech, before 1970, that indicated even a fraction of
the feeling and understanding for events in Northern Ireland which
were so central and so passionate a part of Neil Blaney's political
make-up. Haughey's covert republicanism, which really developed in
a slow and minimalist way between the Burntollet march, at the beginning of 1969, and the summer riots, was then accelerated for shrewd
and politically opportunistic reasons. He needed to maintain a watching brief on Blaney. He needed to control him, if he could, or at least
legitimately to watch over his movements, and certainly the best way

---

[1] The strange Haughey–Blaney relationship in some respects accounted for both the closeness of the two men, during the 'wilderness period' which followed Haughey's dismissal,
and their later antagonism, which in the end prevented Blaney's ever being drawn back into
Fianna Fáil.

of doing this was to work closely with Blaney on every initiative that the older and much cleverer politician undertook. As a result, when Haughey's involvement in the sequence of events that took place between August 1969 and May 1970 finally became public, it took everyone by surprise.

CHAPTER VII

'ARMS AND THE MAN'

When remedies are past the griefs are ended.

C HARLES HAUGHEY became involved with people who were endeavouring to import arms into Ireland to be given to the minority communities in the North. He acted throughout this period as a member of the Government, using his authority as a senior minister and the facilities of the Department of Finance to fulfil his supposed obligations as a member of the Northern Ireland sub-committee. But, as the person principally responsible for the special fund for the relief of distress in Northern Ireland, over which he had control, he did not keep the Government informed of his actions. This alone undermined the central responsibility he had to his colleagues and made a nonsense of the constitutional concept of collective Government responsibility. It did so at a time of major national crisis, with security in the North under constant threat, with lives being lost, people being injured, property being wilfully destroyed and an effective state of siege frequently existing in various parts of the Six Counties. It is not going too far to say that the Government in the South was undermined from within and that the person most directly and forcefully involved was Charles Haughey. Whatever else he did subsequently, and there was much for which he eventually became answerable, nothing was as damaging to the country as the actions in which he engaged during these months.

In Northern Ireland itself a serious attempt was made to grapple with the problems of security and reform. The British Government assumed control of Northern Ireland, the process beginning with the deployment of British troops, first in Derry, on 14 August, and then effectively taking control of security in the whole of the Six Counties within a week. Two key reports appeared in September and October. The first, the Cameron Report, blamed the Stormont Government for the grievances of Roman Catholics, notably on housing, and was critical of the RUC and the reserve force, the B Specials, for the breakdowns in security. Secondly, the Hunt Committee, which had been set up to propose changes in the security arrangements for Northern Ireland, recommended the reorganization of the RUC, with the disbanding of the B Specials and the setting up of a new reserve under British Army control, the Ulster Defence Regiment, which was inaugurated on 1 January 1970.

As an initial response it was respectable enough and certainly met the requirements of the Government in the South, as it did the demands of the elected nationalist politicians in Northern Ireland. There was of course a great deal still to be done; much of the injustice was endemic and prejudice was widespread. But as a surface response to militant yet straightforward Civil Rights protests and demands, the British Government had set in train the necessary changes.

It was adequate, as far as Lynch was concerned. And a majority of Government members thought the same. Kevin Boland makes quite clear[1] that there was no groundswell in the Fianna Fáil organization, at any level, for militancy and offers an anecdote[2] about a mustering of men in Donegal which involved supporters from Cork armed with two .22 rifles in the back of a Dáil deputy's car. On being sent home, they indulged in a bit of duck-shooting on the River Shannon at Rooskey on their way back. But widespread public concern had been aroused and, in the absence of any clear conceptions about what lay in the future, the republican debate raged within Fianna Fáil. Jack Lynch, on the one hand, sought to win the support of a sufficient number in Northern Ireland to make reunification possible by agreement. Neil Blaney, on the other hand, continued publicly to state that force could not be ruled out.

Lynch directed his message very clearly at both sides in Northern Ireland, despite contentious attacks on him within the Dáil that 'his only interest in the North is in the effects, or possible effects, of developments there on the political balance inside the twenty-six counties'.[3] Lynch concluded that particular exchange by saying: 'I think it would be wrong to have discussions or consultations only with the Nationalist Party. That would be rather divisive in my opinion.'

Blaney's inflammatory rhetoric offered encouragement to the IRA

---

[1] See Kevin Boland, op. cit.
[2] Ibid., p. 12.
[3] Conor Cruise O'Brien, *Dáil Report*, 2 December 1969, col. 2.

to resume the military action which had been discontinued as a result of Charles Haughey's measures in 1962, when, as Minister for Justice, he had set up the special military courts. Since then the organization had pursued a left-wing programme, aimed at political reform, and the men of violence had drifted away. Now they came back, and many more with them. Recruiting took place in the autumn of 1969, in Belfast and elsewhere, and in greater numbers than at any time since the 1920s. Cathal Goulding, who was chief of staff of the IRA, was mentioned in a security report as having met Charles Haughey well before the split in the IRA that led to the setting up of two factions: the Official and Provisional IRA and the equivalent two political wings, Official and Provisional Sinn Fein. This split can be dated to 11 January 1970, when the last party conference before the split divided on the issue of elected representatives entering any of the three parliaments – at Stormont, Westminster or Leinster House.

In fact the attempt to import arms for the defence of the nationalist community in Northern Ireland was well advanced by this stage and already involved leading members of the IRA. As early as October 1969, to the certain knowledge of Charles Haughey, James Gibbons, the Department of Justice, the Special Branch and Army Intelligence, there were meetings with leading members of the IRA, when they were promised money and arms.

The critical encounter took place in Bailieborough, County Cavan, on Saturday, 4 October 1969. It had been arranged by Captain James Kelly, an army intelligence officer, and Cathal Goulding. Kelly, at that stage, was already the subject of several security reports to the Secretary of the Department of Justice, Peter Berry, from the Special Branch, implicating Kelly with subversives and with promises of money and of arms. Berry had an intelligence report of the Bailieborough meeting on the morning it was to take place and endeavoured to contact his own minister, Micheál O Móráin, and the Taoiseach, Jack Lynch. Failing with both of these he telephoned Charles Haughey, almost certainly informing him of his failed attempts to make contact with the Taoiseach or his own minister. Haughey visited Berry in the nursing home where he was undergoing tests. Berry knew of Haughey's membership of the Government's Northern Ireland sub-committee – which incidentally did not include his own minister – and more generally identified Haughey as having a broad concern for what was happening in the North. Additionally, since the two men had worked together satisfactorily, it seemed a sensible choice for Berry to contact Haughey.

According to Berry,[1] Haughey showed interest in the sources of this information, the police contacts and the general reliability of these. This was perhaps not surprising. What the Minister for Finance did not tell the Secretary of the Department of Justice was that two days earlier the head of Army Intelligence, Colonel Michael Hefferon, with Captain James Kelly, had been at Haughey's own home, Abbeville, for a meeting prior to the Bailieborough encounter. At this earlier meeting Kelly had been promised £500 as expenses for the meeting and contingent activities. Haughey later denied that he had made arrangements for the payment.[2] Captain Kelly later described the Bailieborough meeting as 'the genesis of the plan to import arms'.[3]

Peter Berry received a full report on the Bailieborough meeting. This included the information that Captain Kelly, 'in front of known members of the IRA', had promised £50,000 for the purchase of arms. At this stage, in the autumn of 1969, there had already been small illegal importations of arms, including one through Dublin Airport, which had been allowed to go ahead to the point where the consignment was moved by the IRA to a hiding-place in the Dublin Mountains.

Berry again tried, this time successfully, to arrange a meeting with Lynch, which took place in the Mount Carmel nursing home, where Berry was still undergoing tests, on 17 October 1969. Berry claimed that he gave a full report on the information he had at that time. Lynch, while acknowledging that the meeting took place, recalled it only in general terms, including the reports of other activities, and expressed some concern that, if anything illegal was going on, Berry should deal with it. It was a highly unsatisfactory encounter. There were frequent interruptions by Berry's medical attendant, who had to remove and replace certain vessels being used for bodily drainage. The attachments to his nose and throat made basic communication very difficult, since Berry was to some degree incoherent, and in the end

---

[1] *Magill*, June 1980, p. 34.
[2] See ibid. See also 'Report of Public Accounts Inquiry Number 19 – 1971/72'. Para 4102 Hefferon gives evidence about payment; Para 9148 Haughey denies knowledge of £500 payment. See, in addition 'Pink Book' Committee of Public Accounts, published by Stationery Office, December 1970; Book of Evidence from the two Arms Trials; and *Dáil Reports*.
[3] *Magill*, June 1980, p. 34.

Lynch entirely lost patience and walked out, inviting Berry to deal with the matter himself.

Berry is thought to have been worried at the possibility of his own death while undergoing these tests for a serious medical complaint. Given the circumstances surrounding his minister, and the nature of what he knew, he understandably considered that this meeting with Lynch was essential. Lynch later raised the matter of the involvement of the army with the Minister for Defence, James Gibbons, who in turn discussed it with Colonel Hefferon.

In November 1969 Seamus O Tuathail, editor of the *United Irishman*, a republican organ which reflected IRA activity and thinking, published a well-informed article claiming that there was a conspiracy involving senior members of the Fianna Fáil Government and their supposed attempt to gain control of the Civil Rights Movement in Northern Ireland. Haughey, Boland and Blaney were named as the 'spearhead of the conspiracy . . . to subvert the Civil Rights Movement': 'The finance for the take-over job involves large injections of Fianna Fáil money channelled from Messrs Blaney, Haughey and Boland . . . These Fianna Fáil politicians are doing their best to disrupt Civil Rights and anti-Unionist forces in the North whose successes have been politically highly embarrassing to them. Other questions arise. Is this plan an official Fianna Fáil plan? How much of this work has been financed directly by Government money?' Photographs of the three ministers appeared in the paper with captions under each suggesting 'He knows'. There was also a photograph of Lynch with the caption: 'Can he not know?' Political journalists all saw and discussed the article, and simply dismissed it.[1]

O Tuathail queried the extent to which what was going on was official and how much of it was financed with taxpayers' money. He knew that Seamus Brady, a journalist who was close to Neil Blaney and who undertook work for him in his department, was also carrying out propaganda work under the cloak of the programme of such action decided by the Government in August of that year, as part of the response to the rioting. Brady had been responsible for a newspaper called the *Voice of the North* and had also written a pamphlet called *Terror in Northern Ireland*.[2]

Lynch denied the allegations made in the *United Irishman*, as he also

[1] *United Irishman*, November 1969.
[2] For a fuller account of the events at this time see Dick Walsh, op. cit., pp. 95–110.

later denied any detailed knowledge of the Bailieborough meeting. On Berry's own evidence the encounter was unsatisfactory.[1] Moreover, Berry, who kept a diary, was in the habit of adding to it and refining it, in the light of subsequent events, making it a less than reliable document, notwithstanding its great interest.

Berry was a stickler for correct procedures, as we have seen in the context of Haughey's early days in the Department of Justice. His Lynch encounter, in Mount Carmel, was exceptional. Throughout this period he tried repeatedly to act through his minister, Micheál O Móráin, who in a sense becomes a crucial, though negative, force and was decidedly unhelpful.[2] O Móráin was a colourful, West of Ireland politician who could be quite brutal to his political opponents, one of whom, in his own constituency, he named 'the Maggot Durkan'; another prominent group – the new intellectuals who revitalized the Labour Party in the second half of the 1960s – he characterized as 'Left-wing political queers from Trinity College and Telefís Eireann'. He drank heavily at this time, was often unwell and continued – against convention – to run his legal practice in Castlebar. Out of a sense of loyalty to an old de Valera veteran, Lynch kept him on. It was a mistake. O Móráin was later to assert that he passed on to Lynch the security reports coming to him from Berry. Kevin Boland is equally emphatic that O Móráin informed the head of the Government of developments during the period from the Bailieborough meeting, in October 1969, to the time of his resignation in May 1970. But Lynch denies this, and Berry's eventual action, in going to de Valera in April 1970, seems to confirm this, as do his assertions that O Móráin was at times incoherent, listless and unaware of what was being said to him.

Kevin Boland, however, maintains that Lynch repeatedly ignored O Móráin in order to rid the Government of Haughey and Blaney. 'The Taoiseach was playing a devious game, which a conscientious man like Moran could not be expected to suspect.'[3]

---

[1] Berry was undergoing complicated tests. When Lynch arrived, two doctors and two nurses were present. When they left, a nurse repeatedly came in to siphon off liquid with a tube through his nose to his stomach and Lynch quickly became impatient, and told him: 'This is impossible. I will get in touch with you again.' And the encounter was terminated. There was no further meeting between the two men until the Arms Crisis in April 1970.

[2] Micheál O Móráin (1912–84) was a solicitor. He was first elected in 1938 and was given his first ministerial appointment, to the Gaeltacht, by de Valera, to which Lemass added the responsibility for Lands in 1959. Lynch made him Minister for Justice in 1968, in the reshuffle which followed Donogh O'Malley's death.

[3] Moran was the anglicized version of the name. Kevin Boland, op. cit., pp 46–7.

Charles Haughey became increasingly involved in a situation where people close to himself were engaged in the complicated and difficult business of international arms dealing, cross-Border intelligence, IRA activities, politics in Northern Ireland, the Civil Rights Movement and Fianna Fáil Party intrigues. At the same time he was running the most powerful, and possibly the most complicated, Department of State in the country. The closest secrecy cloaked activities relating to Northern Ireland and, unlike Neil Blaney, Haughey made no public utterances in support of a different, more militant policy in the Fianna Fáil Party than the one being pursued by Lynch. Unlike Blaney, he had no profile at all on the matter.

Haughey's knowledge of Northern Ireland was really quite limited. He had placed himself at the centre of Government control over Northern policy, such as it was, on the strength of childhood visits to Derry and the fact that his parents were born there. He had not, however, maintained personal or political ties with the North, unlike Blaney, and had no contacts with experienced nationalist or opposition politicians, either in Derry or Belfast.[1] Because of his covert attitude, amounting almost to paranoia, about being seen to have strong or informed views on how policy should be shaped, his access to further background information was limited to narrow and somewhat suspect sources. He relied, when he could get it, on casual Irish Army and other intelligence, which itself was pretty limited, about the deteriorating security situation. The situation was also changing rapidly and insufficient attention was paid to IRA infiltration of legitimate relief and aid organizations. His great strength, what made him of value to all groupings involved in what was deteriorating into a conspiracy, was his stature within the Fianna Fáil Party and in the country, and his crucial role in controlling funds, propaganda, reorganization of the Defence Forces and Government sub-committee deliberations. His Government colleagues, Neil Blaney and Kevin Boland, who despised Lynch's policy-line and saw the developing situation as one in which Fianna Fáil would fulfil its republican destiny, reunite the country and enjoy its finest hour, made him an attractive addition to their caucus.

[1] At this stage, opposition in Northern Ireland was fragmented, only later amalgamating into the Social, Democratic and Labour Party, and even then retaining within its umbrella organization the distinctive and uneasily linked voices of men such as John Hume, Gerry Fitt and Paddy Devlin.

The initial intention – to find, buy and bring in arms, and then ship them to Northern Ireland, for the minority population – even if it never had Government sanction, seemed more appropriate to the circumstances of August 1969 than it did to the winter that followed. What began as a response to the appeals of many different groups from the North, ranging from Citizens' Action Groups and the IRA to politicians and Church leaders, at a time of great crisis and amidst genuine fear and terror of assault and death, then took well over six months to come to any conclusion. By that stage the IRA, which had shown itself to be ineffective against the earlier attacks on nationalist areas, had been repossessed by its former militant veterans – those who had left it when Marxist theorizing and agitation had replaced the campaign of violence in the early 1960s, and who in turn had divided into Official and Provisional wings of the movement. In effect the old guard – the Officials – with their links between Dublin and Belfast, involving Cathal Goulding, were ousted as irrelevant. The new movement, focusing all its attention on Northern Ireland, was that much less accessible from Dublin and certainly from politicians like Haughey. They used him; he failed to see that this was the case. It is questionable whether his focus, when he looked across the Border, was anything but blurred.

The British Army, since April 1969, had been taking over security duties. The Cameron and Hunt findings had begun to be implemented. And still no arms had been secured, though the money had been promised and a chain of individuals, all working more or less in the dark, was fumbling its way towards disaster.

Funds for the relief of distress were dispersed. Whether it was proper or not, sums were paid out to people manning barricades, and therefore unable to go to work or draw unemployment benefit. This happened in various trouble-spots in Northern Ireland, mainly in Belfast, and accounted for roughly one-third of the £100,000 relief fund. A similar amount was spent on attempted and actual arms purchases. These were unbelievably inept. Among others, 'Jock' Haughey, Charles Haughey's brother, was involved in fruitless negotiations in London. IRA contacts in the United States were reactivated and arrangements made there for arms shipments to Ireland. These were then abandoned as being too slow and an alternative deal, organized by Neil Blaney through a Belgian business friend, Albert Luykx, went ahead.

Some of the episodes were not unlike a bad Graham Greene thriller. Blaney was a central figure and worked closely with John Kelly, a

Belfast republican[1] who, when travelling by train between Belgium and Germany, with £3,000 in a paper bag, thought he was being challenged for it by a Customs officer, who simply wanted to see his passport, and was on the point of giving it up. Through Albert Luykx, Kelly met Baron William Regniorers, whom he renamed 'Bill the Baron', and in turn was introduced to Otto Schleuter, a Hamburg arms dealer, who arranged delivery of Czech automatic weapons, rifles, pistols and ammunition.

Obtaining the arms was an easy matter compared with getting them into Ireland. First efforts involved an attempted rendezvous at sea, off the Kish lighthouse, fifteen miles due east of Dublin Bay. Three times small vessels went out, but waited in vain. Then it was decided to bring the arms in 'officially', with Haughey asked to organize the Customs clearance.

The consignment was due into Dublin Port from Antwerp on 25 March 1970. Clearance was arranged. Captain James Kelly and John Kelly were at Alexander Quay at 7.30 in the morning and watched the unloading. Some flak jackets were brought ashore, but no arms. Though listed on the manifest, the packages had been stopped by Belgian Customs because they did not have any export licence. Captain James Kelly intended to retain a measure of control over the consignment, shipping it to Donegal. John Kelly, however, fully intended taking over the arms on behalf of the IRA and bringing them first to a convent outside Dublin and then, in small consignments, into Northern Ireland.

Following this failure to bring in the arms by sea, the shipment was switched to air transport. Initially, it was intended that a chartered aircraft would bring them in on 7 April. This arrangement, made between Captain James Kelly, Albert Luykx and Otto Schleuter, in Hamburg, fell through. Then, on 12 April, Schleuter attempted to get clearance for the importation of arms *and* ammunition on a *passenger* flight from Frankfurt to Dublin. It was against IATA regulations to ship ammunition on passenger flights and the splitting of the consignment was ordered. Then, when the transport superintendent at Dublin Airport heard of security arrangements being made at Vienna, where the consignment was originating, the shipment was cancelled. At that

---

[1] John Kelly came south from Belfast during the riots there and became a central figure in North–South liaison work with Captain James Kelly. He was responsible for receiving money, transmitting it to the North and ensuring its distribution in nationalist communities.

stage, through clearances issued from Haughey's Department of Finance office, through his personal assistant, Anthony Fagan, the arrangement was for no Customs or other interference once the consignment was landed. It would be handed over to 'J. Kelly', whose lorry would take the arms directly from the plane. A repeat of the City of Dublin disposal arrangements would have meant that the arms would have become the property of the IRA soon after the landing.

In the face of yet another collapsed endeavour, Captain James Kelly and Albert Luykx became frantic for a new solution and told John Squires of Aer Turas[1] that they had been commissioned to bring in guns and ammunition for the use of the police and army. Squires asked them about their 'end-user certificate'. Not only did they not have one; they did not know what such a document was. And when he heard that Luger pistols were involved, a weapon not used by either force in the Republic, he reported his suspicions. Word reached Berry, on Friday, 17 April, and he immediately imposed 'a ring of steel' on Dublin Airport, reporting what he had done to his minister. 'You'd think we were in fucking Casablanca or somewhere', was O Móráin's comparatively coherent remark to the Secretary of his Department.

Despite the reaction of John Squires to the inept handling of the importation, there were others involved who still regarded the proposed arms consignment, which Kelly and Luykx had already departed to Vienna to bring back, as legitimate. One of these was the airport Customs superintendent, Thomas Tobin, who reported to Anthony Fagan, asking for guidance on the surveillance and whether or not the arms were still to be let through, and under what conditions.

This led immediately to Haughey's direct involvement yet again. He telephoned Berry, on the morning of Saturday, 18 April, to arrange for the importation to be let through. Haughey later indicated that he was unaware of the contents of the consignment. Berry maintained that Haughey gave him an undertaking that, if the security 'ring of steel' was relaxed, he would guarantee that the consignment would go directly to Northern Ireland. Haughey also tried to make telephone contact with Chief Superintendent Fleming of the Garda Special Branch, who reported this to Berry and was ordered to accept no such calls. In addition, John Kelly, James Kelly's wife – in his absence in Vienna – and Colonel Hefferon, of Army Intelligence, were all

[1] A small independent airline, specializing in freight and bloodstock, and having, as one of its main clients, Aer Lingus.

informed of the security developments. Berry blocked any further communication. He considered his own position, which was complicated.
Firstly, there was the fact that two ministers, Blaney and Haughey,
seemed to be directly involved in an attempt to import arms and
ammunition illegally; secondly, James Gibbons, Minister for Defence,
was at least partly involved; thirdly, his own minister, Micheál O
Móráin, when able to focus on events, seemed to be treating the whole
matter as an entertaining drama; and, finally, Lynch himself, to the
extent that he knew what was going on, seemed disinclined to act.
Berry went, once again, to de Valera, who said his only course of
action was to go to the Taoiseach, telling Lynch that de Valera was
aware of what was going on. Lynch was enraged by this and de Valera
himself was distressed at being involved in the crisis.

Haughey realized that the operation was collapsing and told
Anthony Fagan that it should be called off. Kelly, in Vienna, already
knew, from his wife, that things had gone seriously wrong. On Sunday,
19 April, he sought guidance, through Fagan, from Haughey as to what
he should do and was told of the cancellation of all plans. Haughey was
now faced with a quite different set of problems, severely aggravated
by the fact that on the Monday night, 20 April, as the result of an
accident, he went into hospital. He was said to have fallen off his horse.
He may in fact have fallen off a piece of drainage guttering.[1] There
are several versions of how he came to suffer multiple injuries[2] but,
however they were inflicted, they were serious enough to keep him in
hospital for more than a week and this meant that the Budget statement, due to be delivered to the Dáil on Wednesday, 22 April, had to
be delivered for him by Lynch. At the beginning of business in the
Dáil the actual announcement made by Lynch was: 'Before leaving his
home this morning the Minister for Finance met with an accident
which has resulted in concussion. He is now in hospital and has been
ordered to remain under medical observation for some days.'

The events which then brought the arms crisis to public attention do
not shed much credit on any of the participants. Because of Haughey's
injuries Lynch was unable to see him and he decided also to postpone
any confrontation with Blaney. On the Thursday of that week Blaney

---

[1] He showed the present writer a gap in the guttering above a stable door and claimed that
he had tried to dismount on his way into the stable by lifting himself off the saddle by
gripping the gutter, which then broke.
[2] Haughey suffered a fractured skull, broken clavicle and chest injuries.

held a meeting in his office with James Kelly, Colonel Hefferon, who was no longer head of Army Intelligence, having retired a few weeks earlier, and the Minister for Defence, James Gibbons. Micheál O Móráin was also to have been present, but had collapsed at a public function the previous evening and was indisposed. He went into Mount Carmel Hospital the following morning, Friday, 24 April, and a Government statement was issued saying that his condition would necessitate a stay 'of some weeks' and that 'under medical direction he is not to receive any visitors or to enter into any communication with anybody'.[1] It was Blaney's view that, because no guns had been imported, there could be no prosecutions. It was not until the following week, on Wednesday, 29 April, that Lynch was notified that he could see Haughey. Before going to the hospital he summoned Blaney, told him what he knew of the attempted importation of arms, including Blaney's role in the affair, and asked for his resignation. Blaney refused. Lynch then went to the Mater Hospital and told Haughey the same facts, asking him also for his resignation. Haughey wanted time to consider his position.

Lynch faced enormous difficulties still. Though dismissal was clearly the only alternative open to him if the two men refused to resign, such a course of action would lead to a massive public crisis and would have other implications, including the possibility of criminal proceedings of the gravest kind. He clearly needed again to go over the facts governing the long, complicated and inept sequence of events dating back to the previous October, and involving himself in various meetings at which different parcels of information had been delivered to him. He held meetings with Berry, with the Attorney General, Colm Condon,[2] accompanied by the heads of the Special Branch and Army Intelligence, and with Captain James Kelly. It was Lynch's intention to confront Kelly and Blaney at this meeting, but Kelly refused to let himself become involved in a situation where he would be accusing Blaney and did not attend.

In this series of meetings, Lynch seems to have been ensuring that he had the necessary grounds, not just for the dismissal of two senior Government ministers, but also for the ensuing controversy and the possible legal action which would follow. It has been represented that this was in fact prevarication and that Lynch did not intend to proceed

[1] Micheál O Móráin resigned on 4 May.
[2] Colm Condon (b. 1921) was appointed Attorney General in 1965.

against the two men. Peter Berry reportedly was of this view.[1]

Blaney attended the Government meeting on Friday, 1 May when Lynch reported to the Government on the illegal attempt to import arms, that allegations had been made against two ministers to the effect that they were involved, and that the two ministers had denied this. The matter was, for the present, closed. Blaney knew it was not over; Boland believed that it was and favoured going to the Mater Hospital to tell Haughey.

By the time that Government meeting took place, the leader of the Opposition, Liam Cosgrave, was in possession of details concerning the attempted importation of arms. It is thought that details were leaked to him in reaction to the perceived view that Lynch did not intend to move against the ministers involved and that this leak came from the Special Branch. Instead of confronting Lynch, Cosgrave tried to persuade a journalist, Ned Murphy, who worked for the *Irish Independent* and wrote a column for the *Sunday Independent*, to publish details. When this failed, and only then, Cosgrave went to Lynch, on the evening of Tuesday, 5 May. Lynch summoned Blaney and asked for his resignation again. When Blaney refused, Lynch told him that he would be requesting the President to terminate his appointment. Haughey was dismissed in the same manner. Kevin Boland resigned. A government statement was issued at 2.50 in the morning. It merely stated that the two senior ministers who had been dismissed 'do not subscribe fully to Government policy in relation to the present situation in the Six Counties'.

[1] See *Magill*, May 1980, p. 54, where Berry is reported to have been told by Lynch, at a meeting on Thursday, 30 April, that the matter was ended and that there would be no 'repetition'.

CHAPTER VIII

THE ARMS TRIALS

Where is this rash and most unfortunate man?

CHARLES HAUGHEY'S POLITICAL CAREER was in ruins. He had hopelessly misjudged an international crisis and had behaved in a manner that seriously aggravated the difficulties faced by the three governments. His actions had certainly helped the IRA, lending weight and support to the militant faction, and then increasingly to those who were to become the Provisional IRA. The organization's central role in future events in the Six Counties was established during this period and was hugely strengthened by the support given from within the Government.

For a period of more than six months Haughey had ignored an essential constitutional obligation on any Irish minister, that of the 'collective authority' of the Government, enshrined in Article 28.4 and requiring that the actions of individual ministers have the formal endorsement or backing of a Government decision. Given the seriousness of the situation in Northern Ireland throughout the period from August 1969 to the spring of 1970, this was particularly grave. And judged objectively, the autonomy that Haughey arrogated to himself at this time is by far the most astonishing and reprehensible aspect of what had now become known as the Arms Crisis. Others were at fault. But it was Haughey who controlled the funds, who exercised most authority, who was therefore the one most directly responsible to his Government colleagues and the Taoiseach about detailed and day-to-day events – and who told them all nothing.

No collective Government decision was made that could conceivably have sanctioned the use of funds 'for the relief of distress' for the purchase of arms and ammunition to be handed over to private citizens. Many of the other decisions, involving discussions with other ministers and senior civil servants, and the issuing of instructions to police and army personnel, also fell outside the framework of what the Government had decided in the middle of August 1969.

This poor judgement of the situation was matched by an equally poor judgement of people. There never was an adequate analysis of the logic and value of the scheme to bring in arms and to make them available to ordinary citizens for the defence of nationalist communities. Yet Haughey seems to have dealt exclusively with those firmly committed to one solution and was oblivious to the fundamental changes that took place during this six-month period. Once locked in the course of action that was initiated at the Bailieborough meeting, in October 1969, Haughey became as much the victim of tunnel vision as those around him and seemed quite unable, right to the end, when he was brought before the courts charged with conspiracy, to disentangle himself from an increasingly ill-conceived, ill-managed, amateurish operation.

Perhaps the poorest judgements of all were those he made about himself. He seemed, at this time, to reverse his whole evolution as a politician. His father-in-law had broken fresh ground, in the early 1960s, with the exchanges between himself and O'Neill, which represented the abandonment of the sterile political pursuit of an ending to partition. In its place an entirely different policy of mutual and, if possible, profitable co-operation was established, which made possible a decade of economic development. It also favoured Fianna Fáil's three successive general election victories. From his first days in the Dáil, right through to his introduction of the Third Programme in March 1969, Haughey had been identified more directly with this than any other politician and had built his whole political reputation on this perception of the country's best interests. For no more than a mess of pottage he had thrown it all away.

Once the events became public, Lynch acted with clear determination, blocking any attempts to reverse what he had done and forcing the party into unanimous endorsement of his interpretation of policy. This was his first priority. Indeed, following his statement in the early hours of 6 May, the whole issue of the attempted importation of arms remained the subject of widely discussed rumour in the corridors of Leinster House, unconfirmed by any Government source. Apart from explaining to the Dáil, when deputies met that morning, his right to nominate and to seek the dismissal of ministers, Lynch concentrated on the issue of party loyalty, in particular how it related to Northern policy as expressed by himself. He sought an immediate adjournment in order to inform the President and complete the formalities of proposed Government changes, setting a late hour for reassembly of deputies, at ten that evening. This was to allow for a more important, and possibly more contentious, formality – the special meeting of the Fianna Fáil Party, set for six o'clock. Again, the objective was confined to the single issue of his right as leader to hire and fire as he saw fit, and the demand that he was entitled to make on all party members for their loyalty. Kevin Boland worked hard during the same period trying to persuade Neil Blaney and Charles Haughey to come together and agree a joint course of action that would block Lynch. But he failed, in part because Haughey was unable to respond.

Lynch achieved the unanimous support of Fianna Fáil and a carefully worded statement was issued claiming that 'each of the three former ministers, deputies Neil Blaney, Kevin Boland and Charles J. Haughey, and the former Parliamentary Secretary, deputy Paudge Brennan, expressed unreservedly his loyalty to the Fianna Fáil Party and the Taoiseach.'[1] Haughey's own expression of loyalty must have been obtained from his hospital bed in the Mater and conveyed to the party meeting. One writer described the event as 'probably the most remarkable example of an Irish party's instinct for self-preservation overcoming its internal divisions, an example of pragmatism without parallel in the history of constitutional nationalism in Ireland.'[2]

Lynch was strengthened enormously by the statement of loyalty. It meant he could go into the debate that evening without any immediate fear of defeat on a vote of no confidence. The Labour Party and Fine Gael were uncertain about how they should proceed and had not worked out an agreed strategy. Lynch was disposed to let them have whatever debate, or debates, they wanted, to be continued for as long as they saw fit, but insisted that the subject would be the formal motion nominating his new Government ministers. This was consistent with the party statement and avoided a *vote* on the wider matter which was shortly to be introduced, though of course the debate itself would inevitably range much more widely, covering party agreement over policy and the extent of party disaffection.

Lynch had this in mind when naming names. On the issue of subscribing to policy, Lynch put the two men who had resigned, Kevin Boland and Paudge Brennan, firmly with Blaney and Haughey,

---

[1] Paudge Brennan (b. 1922) was the son of a Fianna Fáil politician and had represented Wicklow since 1954. He was Parliamentary Secretary to the Minister for Lands. He had resigned his position earlier that day, in sympathy with Neil Blaney.

[2] Dick Walsh, op. cit., p. 115.

suggesting a smaller grouping than in fact was perceived from outside the party, where speculation suggested at least ten who were dissatisfied with Northern Ireland policy as expressed by the leader. He then briefly stated to the Dáil that he 'had information which purported to connect them [Haughey and Blaney] with an alleged attempt to unlawfully import arms, on the basis of which information I felt it was my duty to request their resignations as members of the Government.' He went on to say that 'not even the slightest suspicion should attach to any member of the Government in a matter of this nature.' Lynch then gave a short account of the period of delay between first asking for their resignations and finally exercising his right to dismiss them.

Haughey made a statement from his hospital bed, rejecting any idea that he had been guilty of a breach of trust and denying absolutely any involvement with arms. 'The Taoiseach informed the Dáil that he requested my resignation on the grounds that he was convinced that not even the slightest suspicion should attach to any member of the Government. I fully subscribe to that view. So far as I have been able to gather, the Taoiseach received information of a nature which in his opinion cast some suspicion on me. I have not had the opportunity to examine or test such information or the quality of its source or sources. In the meantime, however, I now categorically state that at no time have I taken part in any illegal importation or attempted importation of arms into this country. At present I do not propose to say anything further except that I have fully accepted the Taoiseach's decision as I believe that the unity of the Fianna Fáil Party is of greater importance to the welfare of the nation than my political career.'

The denial was a mistake. Distant from the debate and discussion in the Dáil, unaware of the extent of public knowledge and disquiet, and at odds with the testimony contained in speeches by other members of the Government sympathetic to him, Haughey locked himself into the narrow confines of a claim that he knew nothing and had done nothing. He effectively became silent, leaving the extensive and unending speculation to others. Where it mattered – in respect of divisions within the Government during the previous ten months – the only views made public were those of Boland and Blaney. Boland, while dismissing the newspaper reports about the attempted and illegal arms importations, went on to say that such 'importation into the part of this country in which the writ of this Government does not run is not illegal as far as I am concerned. It is our duty to advise against it but it is not our business to interfere, and any co-operation with the security forces of the country that continues to occupy six of our counties is, in my opinion, intolerable.' He also said that 'it would be unpardonable for us to take any action to frustrate the efforts of our people in the Six Counties to protect their lives and property.' Neither Boland nor Blaney favoured force in order to achieve reunification; both favoured force as a defence against British Army or Northern security forces' action against the minority nationalist community.

The two-day debate, which began on the morning of Friday, 8 May, and concluded with a division at eleven o'clock the following evening, involved 69 speakers, almost half the deputies, although only sixteen were from Fianna Fáil. Once Lynch had heard Boland and Blaney he knew he would win comfortably. The margin was 73–66. Though Opposition demands for a general election continued, the prospect of any breakdown in Fianna Fáil support for the Lynch Government receded. A 'no confidence' motion, put down by the Opposition the following week, was comfortably defeated by Lynch and by the end of that week the papers dealing with the attempted importation of arms were handed to the Attorney General, Colm Condon. On Wednesday, 27 May, James Kelly, John Kelly and Albert Luykx were arrested and charged with conspiracy to import arms. On Thursday, Charles Haughey and Neil Blaney were arrested and charged with the same offence. On 2 July the charges against Neil Blaney were dismissed. The other four men were returned for trial.

Kevin Boland, outraged at this public humiliation of the party and of all it stood for in his eyes, reacted strongly to the charging of the two former ministers and accused Lynch of 'felon-setting'. He sought a special conference of the Fianna Fáil Party with the express purpose of getting rid of Lynch. The party expelled Boland, though eleven voted for him, among them Haughey, Blaney and Paudge Brennan. Four others are known to have supported Boland: Des Foley, Sean Sherwin, Flor Crowley and Lorcan Allen – the first was also later expelled, the second joined Kevin Boland in forming a new party which subsequently failed, while the two others remained as backbench deputies.[1] Boland had earlier resigned from the national executive of the party, and his father, Gerry Boland, who was a vice-president and trustee of Fianna Fáil, also severed all connections. When the son's resignation was

[1] Flor Crowley lost his Cork seat in the 1977 general election and became a senator. It was from there that he worked, during 1979, to ensure Haughey's victory in the leadership struggle.

announced, Blaney was asked to comment. 'It isn't over yet,' he said.

Haughey recovered slowly from his extensive injuries. He made no public statement during the period between his dismissal and the first Arms Trial. How could he? He knew nothing and he fully supported the Fianna Fáil Party and its leader. The first trial commenced on Tuesday, 22 September 1970, before Mr Justice Andreas O'Keeffe. Charles Haughey, Albert Luykx, James Kelly and John Kelly were charged with conspiring, between 1 March and 24 April 1970, to import illegally 500 pistols and approximately 180,000 rounds of ammunition. On the sixth day the judge was accused of bias by counsel for Albert Luykx, to which O'Keeffe took grave exception. The jury was discharged and a new trial ordered. It opened on Tuesday, 6 October, before Mr Justice Henchy. It lasted fourteen days.

Charles Haughey was obliged to remain consistent with his statement of 8 May, denying all knowledge and all involvement. This meant that there was a fundamental disagreement between Haughey and the other defendants, all of whom admitted that they had attempted to import the arms and ammunition, but maintained that what they had done had been legal, since it was sanctioned by the Minister for Defence, James Gibbons.

This placed Gibbons and his evidence at the centre of the trial and led to a major conflict between himself and Haughey, in particular over a specific conversation between the two men, either on 17 or 20 April 1970. At this meeting Gibbons made clear to Haughey that arms and ammunition were to be imported through Dublin Airport and that the Departments of Defence, Justice and Transport and Power were aware of this. Gibbons laid responsibility at Haughey's door and asked him to stop the importation. He recalled, in evidence, Haughey using the phrase 'the dogs in the street are barking it', meaning that knowledge of the attempted importation of arms was spreading rapidly. Haughey, according to Gibbons, promised to stop the process 'for a month'. Gibbons replied: 'For God's sake, stop it altogether.'

Haughey accepted that the meeting in his office had taken place, but denied the conversation. He accepted that the importation of 'a certain consignment' had been called off, an admission corroborated by Anthony Fagan, his personal assistant in the Department of Finance, but not that he knew what the consignment contained. Although several Government departments and their senior ministers, as well as officials of Customs and Excise and Aer Lingus, were all involved, it was Haughey's personal defence that he did not know what it was they were all so concerned about.

Unsurprisingly, Judge Henchy saw in this a fundamental conflict of evidence and, in his summing-up, indicated that either Gibbons or Haughey was guilty of perjury.

Apart from anything else, Haughey's claim that he had no role in the conspiracy meant that he could not plead, as the other defendants had, that it was all done as part of Government policy. Their claim of Government backing, even in general terms, fell to pieces completely. The idea that the Government sub-committee on Northern Ireland (which had never operated as such and had in fact never met at all) had given justification for arms importation collapsed. The idea of the relief fund for Northern Ireland distress and the joint action by Haughey and Gibbons in respect of the Defence Forces, and their involvement in Border relief, all became detached from the isolated issue of buying and bringing into the Republic of Ireland arms and ammunition to be passed to the minority community in Northern Ireland. This isolation turned the attempted importation into a criminal act. Captain James Kelly was legitimately shattered by this and felt betrayed and tainted, notwithstanding the fact that he and his co-defendants were all acquitted of conspiracy to import arms illegally on Friday, 23 October.[1]

Charles Haughey misjudged this moment of acquittal also. Jack Lynch was in New York, addressing the United Nations on the occasion of its twenty-fifth anniversary. In his speech he included something of Northern Ireland policy. Within an hour of the jubilant scenes in the Four Courts, when the verdict of not guilty was announced, Haughey called a press conference and challenged Lynch as party leader, suggesting that his statement of policy on Northern Ireland, which had formed part of his speech to the UN, did not represent party policy. He was intent on a head-on collision and on Lynch's resignation. 'Those responsible for the débâcle have no option but to take the honourable course open to them,' he said. 'I think there is some dissatisfaction about the leadership at the moment. The Taoiseach's position is something that will be decided by the

---

[1] The charge of conspiracy failed on the grounds that three of the four men before court believed they were acting under formal direction from a member of the Government, with Government approval, while the fourth did not reveal to them the fact that he was acting independently, without Government knowledge or approval.

parliamentary party.' Haughey, flushed with victory, swayed by the
crowds of jubilant supporters swirling around him in the main hall of
the Four Courts building and then carrying him shoulder-high out
into the thronged streets, misread completely the real climate in the
Fianna Fáil Party and in the country. He spoke of the warmth and
extent of the support he had received, throughout the ordeal of the
Arms Crisis, from its very beginning up to the acquittal. 'I don't believe
in counting heads,' he assured his huge audience. He would have been
wiser had he carried out such a count before issuing his challenge.

Lynch issued a statement in New York saying that he was confident
about any leadership challenge. He gave a press conference himself
the following day, saying that the attempted importation had not been
disproved and that the effort to bring in the arms had been made; also,
that Blaney was involved. He returned to Dublin after the weekend
and was met by a massive show of strength in his support. More than
fifty deputies, twenty-seven senators, two former and highly respected
colleagues of de Valera's – Frank Aiken and Sean MacEntee – as well as
every Government minister with the exception of two who were out of
the country, turned up at Dublin Airport and ranged themselves behind
Lynch. During the course of a crisp and confident press conference
Lynch made much of the careful and prolonged investigations that had
been carried out and warned that there would be an intensification of
the inquiries since the sources of the funding for the purchase of the
arms needed to be tracked down. There was a justified fear that public
money had been used and this needed clarification.

When the Fianna Fáil Party met the following day, Haughey's
unexplored head-count, so easily dismissed the previous week, turned
out to consist of five men, including himself and Neil Blaney. Even
then, his own confrontation collapsed, as did that of his former
Government colleague, when both he and Blaney pledged that they
would vote for Fianna Fáil in the 'no confidence' motion that was to
be debated later that week.

Kevin Boland was, and remains, distressed by all this. He had
attempted to get co-ordinated action from Blaney and Haughey when
the Arms Crisis first burst upon an unsuspecting public. He tried again
at the time of the trial. Anticipating an acquittal, he had letters prepared
which were to go to every branch of Fianna Fáil throughout the
country, designed to initiate pressure for a special party conference
that would confront Lynch as leader. Again, Haughey and Blaney
could not be brought together to agree on a joint course of action and

the letters were never sent.[1] Boland is fierce in his book, *Up Dev!*, in condemning the apparent ineptitude of Lynch in allegedly receiving so much information about the proposals to import arms and yet doing nothing. Yet he is silent on the greater ineptitude among minis-ters of the Government of which he formed a part in not reporting formally on the amazing things they were doing independently of each other, and not reporting back on their supposed activities undertaken in the name of Government decisions made in August 1969. In an honourable commitment to the terms under which he had stood repeatedly for his Dáil seat in the Fianna Fáil interest, Kevin Boland had already decided, having been expelled from the party, that he would resign his seat on the same day as the debate and he so informed the Ceann Comhairle.[2]

Lynch maintained his tough stance in the warnings he gave, at the conclusion of the parliamentary party meeting, of the possibility of a general election, should the 'no confidence' motion be carried against him. And in a rare show of menace, directed primarily at deputies on his own side, he concluded his speech in the debate: 'I do not want any deputy to go into the lobby with me to buy time, because I am not in the market for buying or selling time.'

At that stage in his political fortunes, however, it was all that Haughey could buy. He was totally discredited. He had betrayed country, Government, party and himself. By the skin of his teeth he was still within the organization, still a member of Fianna Fáil and still a Dáil backbencher. He had in fact bought time by knuckling under, pledging confidence in a man whose policies he rejected and whose leadership he sought to overthrow. All he had was the tenuous and fragile residue of a political career that stretched back twenty-three years, encompassed several high offices of State and a huge breadth of performance and experience, but which had come now to nothing.

[1] See *Magill*, July 1980, p. 22.
[2] The Ceann Comhairle, or speaker, announced the resignation before the division. There were Opposition calls for an immediate by-election. Lynch complied, moving the writ straight away.

CHAPTER IX

'A PART OF MY LIFE'

In following him, I follow but myself.
Heaven is my judge, not I for love and duty,
But seeming so for my peculiar end.

'IT ISN'T OVER YET.' Blaney's words were to echo for a long time to come, his scepticism overshadowing the year to November 1971 and then subsequently haunting Haughey much more, and for much longer, than they did the man who had uttered them. Lynch saw out the year of the Arms Crisis and of the Arms Trials comfortably in command of the first essential – his own political majority. He could afford to shed some support. The majority of seven, which he had attained in the Opposition's 'no confidence' motion on 4 November 1970, had been comfortable enough to allow him not to compromise with members of his own party. When they did depart – either through resignation or dismissal – the direction they took was into political outer darkness, for Lynch, on any perceptible political spectrum involving the North and republicanism, stood firmly between them and the Opposition. There were, in any case, no political parties on the republican or nationalist Right for them to join, unless they formed such parties themselves.[1] They would not in any way strengthen the Opposition parties. They would not vote *against* Fianna Fáil. The worst they could do was to deplete Lynch's majority and edge him towards a general election.

During the year that followed, everyone concentrated on the money. The Opposition, having failed to dislodge Lynch, began a process of harassment through debate. The performance of Fine Gael and Labour had not been particularly accomplished during the crisis itself. Liam

---

[1] This in fact is what happened. Kevin Boland, after resigning from Fianna Fáil, formed a party called Aontacht Eireann. Sean Sherwin was one of its members. Neil Blaney was approached, but declined to join. The party did poorly at the 1973 general election and subsequently failed completely.

Cosgrave's own uncertainty, clearly indicated by his handling of the Garda letter, was matched by the retreat into verbiage that characterized many deputies both from his party and Labour. Long and well-crafted speeches, some of them brilliantly delivered, many others deeply boring, ranged over the whole nature and character of Fianna Fáil – its people, its policies, its lack of direction, its disunity. Curiously, however, the hunt was really directed against Fianna Fáil, rather than against Lynch. In successive debates, and in the numerous exchanges provoked by parliamentary question, there emerged an indefinable sympathy with Lynch, an unspoken expression of support for him *against* elements in his own party. And Lynch responded with speeches that at times outclassed those of the best of his critics. There was, for example, a homespun directness about his summer recess definition of civil rights: 'Civil rights are the other man's rights; his right to do something that may not sit well with me but which I am bound to respect for my sake as well as for his sake. To me, any Irishman is an Irishman. I am convinced that our society is capable of moving away from unnecessary restrictions both in the interests of doing so for its own value and in the interests of doing so for our country's progress in unity and peace. Society is constantly in a state of perfecting itself. Its instruments are Parliament and Government. Therefore our duty is clear.'[1]

In reality, the two Opposition parties had been given time and opportunity, by Lynch's survival, to come to terms with the electoral failure of the 1969 Labour Party strategy, which had rejected the idea of coalition. A certain solidarity developed as a result of the crisis within Fianna Fáil and it was helped by the shared intellectual sympathies of politicians such as Garret FitzGerald and Conor Cruise O'Brien. They had common cause in hunting Haughey and in attempting to discover whether he had funded the purchase of arms, and where the money had originated.

This information about money might reasonably have been expected to emerge as a result of continuing investigations during 1970. During the debates that took place when the crisis broke, in the spring of 1970, Lynch had been taxed over the source of funds, being asked if they had come from votes for the Secret Services, from the Department of Defence, or from the Department of Finance. He told the Dáil that he had received assurances that no exchequer funds had been paid out.

[1] *Dáil Report*, 28 July 1970, col. 2173.

The Dáil Committee of Public Accounts[1] found that the money had come from the Department of Finance, had been transferred through the Irish Red Cross Society to bank accounts in fictitious names, and had then been dispersed, part of it into Northern Ireland, part of it for the purchase of arms. Garret FitzGerald, who sat on the committee, has summarized the essential political points: 'The committee produced a final report that clarified to a degree that process by which state funds authorized by the Minister for Finance, Charles Haughey, had been used to finance an attempt to import arms illegally. On the basis of the evidence we had been able to unearth despite the unco-operativeness of some witnesses, we brought our Fianna Fáil colleagues on the committee to accept that if three Ministers, Neil Blaney, Charles Haughey and Jim Gibbons, had "passed on to the Taoiseach their suspicion or knowledge of the proposed arms importation" the misappropriation of part of the money spent on arms might have been avoided, with a rider to the effect that the committee was not satisfied that the decision of Charles Haughey as Minister for Finance to make available a specific sum of money from the Fund for the Relief of Distress in Northern Ireland was justified.'[2]

Haughey continued to deny knowledge of the purchase of arms by Captain James Kelly and readily agreed, in his own evidence to the committee, that the Fund for the Relief of Distress in Northern Ireland, for which he was responsible, would have been totally inappropriate for such a purpose.

Lynch delayed the setting up of the committee, using the excuse of the further investigations. Demands by Brendan Corish, in May, and by Liam Cosgrave in October, were blocked and it was not until December that the committee began its deliberations. This timing suited Lynch. He faced his first post-Arms Trial Ard Fheis early in 1971 and knew that this particular annual conference of the Fianna Fáil organization would be a difficult affair, with confrontations from the grass-roots over the events of the previous year and the possibility – remote though it was – that he would face serious challenges to his leadership. In the weeks preceding the event, the deliberations of the committee brought to public notice the issue of public funds having been misused. On the Wednesday of the week in which the Ard Fheis opened, Padraig ('Jock') Haughey, Charles Haughey's brother – who

[1] The Committee was set up in December 1970. It reported in July 1972.
[2] Garret FitzGerald, *All in a Life: An Autobiography*, Dublin, 1991, pp 96–7.

had acted as an intermediary, together with John Kelly, in negotiations in London over arms, which came to nothing – refused to answer questions put to him by the committee and was cited for contempt. He was later given a six-month sentence, suspended pending appeal.[1] On appeal to the Supreme Court the sentence was quashed on the grounds that the statutory provision under which it was imposed was unconstitutional.

There was some blood-letting at the Ard Fheis, with a powerful, pro-Lynch speech by Patrick Hillery, many bitter speeches both for and against the current interpretations of Fianna Fáil republicanism, and a predictable triumph for the leader at the end. Yet still it was not over. A key figure in the whole story, and one whose knowledge of events at the time, together with his actions based on that knowledge, raises questions to this day, was James Gibbons, who had been Minister for Defence and was now in charge of the Department of Agriculture. He told the committee on 21 April 1971 that he had known on 30 April 1970, from Captain James Kelly, that the funds used by him and carried to Europe in a paper bag, had come from the Fund for the Relief of Distress in Northern Ireland. This was two weeks before Jack Lynch told the Dáil that no funds from this source had been used to purchase arms.

Gibbons' evidence had no immediate relevance, apart perhaps from contributing to Kevin Boland's final departure from the Fianna Fáil organization, when he resigned his ordinary party membership and founded Aontacht Eireann, only one other Dáil deputy, Sean Sherwin, joining him. It also further enraged the pro-Haughey faction within Fianna Fáil and led to speeches critical of Government policy on Northern Ireland from Paudge Brennan and Neil Blaney. Blaney claimed that he knew the names of twenty-five deputies and senators who had supplied guns to Northern Ireland in August 1969. Des Foley, another outspoken critic of Lynch's leadership, attacked Northern Ireland policy in an autumn speech and then resigned. Lynch let pass the defiance of his policy, and of his view that no one else should enunciate an alternative.

The policy differences and the militancy of a tiny minority in Fianna Fáil had become largely irrelevant. Events in Northern Ireland had increasingly exposed the emptiness of the militant republicanism within Fianna Fáil. Its main exponents had been expelled or had

---

[1] The case became a leading authority on the question of Court of Tribunals.

departed. And the consistent attack from Opposition deputies, with particularly forceful and sustained criticisms being mounted by Conor Cruise O'Brien and Garret FitzGerald, had continued to bring reality face to face with an often indifferent and ill-informed public in the South. Haughey himself had become a very low-profile politician indeed. He took part in none of these post-Arms Trial debates in the Dáil. O'Brien captured well his image at the time in an adjournment debate on the Northern Ireland situation. 'I do not know whether Deputy Haughey is still to be associated with this group [he had referred earlier to supporters of Neil Blaney in Fianna Fáil] or not. Deputy Haughey has an abstracted look about him these days as if he were solving some difficult mathematical problem, perhaps a problem connected with re-entry.'[1]

In November, when a motion of no confidence in the Minister for Agriculture, James Gibbons, was tabled by the Opposition, deliberately designed to flush out those within Fianna Fáil who were opponents of Lynch and who would find it impossible to support Haughey's arch-enemy within the Government, Lynch acted. When Neil Blaney and Paudge Brennan, unable to stomach that course of action and to pledge confidence in Gibbons in the Dáil vote on 4 November, abstained, they were expelled.

Charles Haughey pre-empted the Dáil debate in a statement issued three days earlier, which effectively preserved his future membership of Fianna Fáil and placed firmly in the past all differences, all recollections, all overt challenges: 'I intend to honour my party pledge and vote in favour of the Government motion of confidence on Wednesday next. I will do so because the only alternative to a Fianna Fáil Government at present is political chaos. In the best interest of the country, therefore, I believe I must put aside all other considerations at this time. I have been represented as having challenged for the leadership of Fianna Fáil. I have not done so. What I did was to invite those responsible for the present divisions to take what seemed to me the only course open to them. In Fianna Fáil we have serious differences over policies and personalities. I believe these can only be solved through the ordinary democratic party process and that this must be done. A general election would solve nothing. Fianna Fáil is the organization on which the nation's future depends. My aim, therefore, will be to do everything I can to restore its unity and reaffirm its purpose

[1] *Dáil Reports*, 21 October 1971, col. 236.

so that it may successfully carry on its work for the nation. Fianna Fáil is too much a part of my life for me to take any other course.' Without having referred to him, or the issue of truth between them both, Haughey pledged confidence in James Gibbons. It was a humiliating conclusion to the most devastating period in his life, yet it was carefully constructed. And it is a quite remarkable mark of his tenacity that from that low point he should have managed to fight back and take over the leadership of the party eight years later.

He had been demolished by a superior tactician. Much has been written about Lynch's handling of Haughey, his uncertainty, his pre-varications, the extent of what he knew, when he knew it and why he did not act earlier. The truth will elude us always, since neither Lynch nor Haughey has ever given even partial versions of the events. These have been filled in around them on countless occasions, raising innumerable questions, but eliciting no answers. The crucial questions mainly concern timing and judgement, since on the vast majority of facts – about meetings, the disposal of funds, the giving of undertakings and the passing of information – there is plenty of corroboration.

In Lynch's case the overriding consideration was the survival of stable government in the Republic, at a time of acute crisis throughout Ireland, North and South. In his judgement such survival required his continued leadership of the administration and his firm control over the Fianna Fáil Party. It had been demonstrated clearly enough in party debates, in the year before the riots of August 1969, that he faced opposition. And after the crisis, Government meetings had set in train the not very satisfactory Southern responses to Northern terror and panic: given the difficulties of sustaining a peaceful policy, putting pressure on Britain to bring in reforms and making sure that world opinion was enlightened represented all that could be done. All, that is, short of active involvement in Northern affairs through the pro-vision of aid in the form of arms, or in any other way that favoured the growth of terrorist organizations. Lynch drew the line on this with increasing clarity as these organizations grew in determination, during the autumn and winter of 1969–70. But this did not resolve the prob-lems within his own party, which were less concerned with alleviating distress north of the Border than with bringing him down, since he stood in the way of other men who considered themselves much stronger and more determined republicans.

The evidence is clear enough about Lynch's meeting with Berry, in Mount Carmel in October 1969, and from then on he had at least some idea of a plot. Confronting it then would have been futile and counter-productive. It would undoubtedly have precipitated the challenge to his leadership that was publicly explicit, in the speeches being made by Neil Blaney, and was implicit in the actions and meetings of which Lynch had at least some inkling. And had that confrontation taken place, on the miserable evidence of a few meetings and promises, there is a fair chance that Lynch's authority would have suffered and that his opponents would have been immeasurably strengthened. The course of their own actions, and their determination, would have been stiffened and the Fianna Fáil Party divided more evenly than in fact it was. The unseating of Lynch might have been a more difficult proposition, but the disdain with which he was treated by members of his Government, whose disregard for constitutional propriety created a bizarre scenario of cloak-and-dagger activity, is worthy, not of Graham Greene, but of Victorian melodrama. With party blood-letting, all came right in the end. But the process of letting time induce an increasingly inept performance was a very significant factor in Lynch's judgement. It was cruel, but it was politically sound. Neither then nor later could Lynch show his hand. The arguments were, and are, too strong in favour of straightforward challenge and confrontation, even if judgements about the impact of this are woefully misguided or short-sighted. Lynch needed to carry the country and the party through a period of crisis. Majority opinion in the country was behind him. As it turned out, the same was true within Fianna Fáil. But no one had tested this and the nature of power does not necessarily reflect the obvious when leaders are challenged and leadership changes. Lynch felt the overriding need to control potentially violent reactions in the South, to alter perceptions about what should be done in the North and to carry the country with him. It is astonishing that when the general election of 1973 arrived his defeat was so narrow. A couple of hundred votes, in a few key constituencies, and he would have been returned for another period in office. And less than five years later, in the election of 1977, his victory was the greatest of any politician in the State's history.

The more Lynch broadened his appeal and extended his control of the Fianna Fáil Party through expulsions and the resignations his firmness encouraged during the lengthening period from August 1969 into 1971 and 1972, the more Haughey was driven into silence and isolation. From his Mater Hospital endorsement of Lynch as party leader, 'the unreserved loyalty' that followed immediately after his and

Blaney's dismissal, up to the humiliating vote of confidence in James Gibbons, Haughey held on to the one thing that offered him political survival in the future: his membership of the Fianna Fáil organization. At the very beginning of that same period, in his statement, again issued from the Mater Hospital, he closed all avenues for debate and discussion by an absolute denial of involvement in any conspiracy. In time those avenues became totally congested, isolating the whole Arms Crisis issue like a deserted and crumbling mansion in a forgotten parkland. It invited endless speculation and became the subject of extensive further investigation which, as we have seen, was revived in particular by *Magill* magazine in 1980, the year that followed Charles Haughey's victory against George Colley for the leadership of Fianna Fáil. And new information came to light at that time, though much of it of a confused and unverifiable kind, since Peter Berry, whose diaries were the basis of the new investigations, was by then dead.

These investigations failed to arrive at any basic conclusions on what had happened. No other investigation has achieved this. There will never be a definitive account. The mansion will continue to crumble, the avenues will remain clogged and, as time passes, the ghosts will increase in number.

CHAPTER X

FROM THE BACK BENCHES

Reputation is an idle and most false imposition; oft got
without merit and lost without deserving. You have lost no
reputation at all, unless you repute yourself such a loser.

DESMOND O'MALLEY'S[1] name came to the fore in 1970 when
he was appointed Minister for Justice to replace Micheál O
Móráin. He was to remain firmly at the centre of the Arms
Crisis for the following two years, through the Arms Trials, the succession of dismissals and the period of tense security worries which
immediately preceded the 1973 general election. He was correctly
perceived, from the moment of his appointment to Justice, as being
implacably opposed to what Blaney and Haughey stood for, in respect
of the North.

At the time of his first appointment by Jack Lynch, Desmond
O'Malley was a relatively new deputy, having been elected in the
by-election that followed the death of his uncle, Donogh O'Malley,
in 1968. Ironically, Neil Blaney and Charles Haughey worked
extremely hard to get O'Malley elected in this by-election.[2] To some
extent he was seen as their protégé, but not for long. His admiration
for Lynch, reinforced by his reasonably sound knowledge of Northern
Ireland politics, grew steadily.

After the general election the following year, Jack Lynch appointed
O'Malley Parliamentary Secretary in his own Department. This meant

---

[1] O'Malley was a solicitor until he gave up his legal practice on winning the 1968 by-election.
He was Chief Whip for a year before being appointed Minister for Justice. He held ministries,
mainly in the field of industry, trade and commerce, between 1977 and his resignation from
Haughey's Government in October 1982.
[2] Limerick was a difficult constituency, with a strong Labour vote. The by-election was
fiercely fought: Blaney, with a reputation as a powerful electoral organizer for the party,
was put to the pin of his collar to think up stratagems to embarrass the other sides and
reduce their vote. Even with the presence of himself and Haughey, O'Malley was only
narrowly elected.

that he was Chief Whip throughout the period during which the Arms Crisis was gestating and attended all meetings of the Government, though not participating in its deliberations. He was there because it was his job to implement decisions that affected party organization, the planning of parliamentary business with the Whips of the other parties, and the ordering of business in the Dáil. This meant that, on a daily basis during Dáil sittings, it was his responsibility to know where deputies were, how to contact them and generally what was going on in the party. Though Lynch had a press secretary, O'Malley, to at least some journalists and others outside the party, would have been a prime source of information about what was happening. Most importantly of all, he became closely associated with Jack Lynch, almost his *alter ego*. There was no question about his views on Northern Ireland; married to Patricia McAleer, from Tyrone, he had a good understanding of Northern affairs and was committed to the Lynch view.

Despite being present for Government meetings and taking good note of the divergence of views over Northern Ireland policy which emerged in Government discussions, notably from August 1969 on, he was 'simply amazed'[1] at the revelations that immediately preceded Haughey's dismissal, and of which O'Malley was aware only 'a couple of days' before he was made Minister for Justice. Other members of that Government were more vocal in their opposition to Lynch's line and O'Malley assumed that Haughey's involvement in the Government sub-committee was reasonable simply on the grounds that as Minister for Finance his responsibilities for the provision of finance to back up decisions made him a necessary participant.

O'Malley's time as Minister for Justice was extremely difficult, embracing security threats that required new and controversial legislation. But before these arose he was confronted with specific problems connected with the Arms Trial and with the investigation by the Committee of Public Accounts, many of the witnesses coming under his Department, including Chief Superintendent John Fleming. Peter Berry asserts[2] that O'Malley instructed Fleming to be totally frank at the Committee hearings, but told Berry that the Official Secrets Act would preclude him from giving any information of serious value and that he would not be releasing him from the constraints of this Act.

---

[1] Dick Walsh, *Des O'Malley: A Political Profile*, Dingle, Kerry, 1986, p. 30.
[2] 'The Peter Berry Papers', published in *Magill*, May–July 1980.

He further recommended that Berry should not appear at all, but the former Secretary of the Justice Department did give evidence in the form of a 'consultation' with the committee and revealed to them, against the wishes of both Lynch and O'Malley, details of the meeting he had had with Jack Lynch concerning the Bailieborough encounter between Captain James Kelly and representatives from Belfast republican groups. This attempt to constrain Berry was not revealed until 1980.

More controversial were the meetings between O'Malley, as Minister for Justice, and Charles Haughey, *after* he had been charged with conspiracy and *before* the trial took place. Haughey approached O'Malley at the races and sought a meeting, which was held shortly afterwards. This was an indiscretion on O'Malley's part. What occurred has not been disclosed. Peter Berry believed that it concerned Berry's evidence in the forthcoming trial. O'Malley later regretted that he had allowed the meeting to take place: 'I suppose, in retrospect, I should not have met him, but it's easy to say that many years after the event. I am sure more serious errors of judgement have been made, by me and by others, than that particular one.'[1]

O'Malley expressed in his actions, more than any other minister between 1970 and 1973, more even than Jack Lynch himself, the spirit of the party and the country in the post-Arms Crisis period. The opposition to the IRA was resolute and backed up by tough legislation. Nationalist feelings, which were given every reason by events to spill over into renewed support for the men of violence, were channelled instead into political and diplomatic pressures on the British, and the slow and at times painful education of the Irish public in the realities of Northern Ireland life.

Haughey had no role at all in this. The period, for him, was one of almost complete political isolation. Yet he was a party member and a deputy, a former minister of considerable experience in a number of different Departments of State, and he was determined on rehabilitation. He spread his interests over a broad front. He spoke on the economy, on Ireland's social objectives, on the development of the food-processing industry, on tax reform within the European Community and on wildlife. In one of his infrequent incursions into Northern Ireland policy – on which the making of 'political' statements was jealously guarded by Jack Lynch – Haughey wrote an article calling

[1] Dick Walsh, op. cit., p. 30.

for the intervention of the United Nations in Northern Ireland. Perhaps most substantially of all, he developed further during this period his interest in, and support for, the arts.

It was a self-imposed regime of rehabilitation, difficult to undertake at first, but made easier through practice. It was also helped by continued support for him within the Fianna Fáil organization, which provided him with platforms. But Haughey was undertaking more than just a broad recovery of political image based often on bland territories that offered scope for a mixture of rhetoric and vision. He was also working out future policies, or the broad ingredients for them, in anticipation of a return to the top. He spoke and acted as though this were an inevitability. He cultivated relationships with journalists and broadcasters. He painstakingly built a network of support wherever it seemed possible.

The speeches are not very good. They are bland and full of platitudes. Political speeches as a general rule are hollow, but from a man who had set his heart, yet again, on rising back through the party to the top, they offer no serious analysis of Fianna Fáil's shortcomings and chart no new departures from the essentially *laisser-faire* philosophy which Haughey himself had pursued in power. They do not inspire. They do not offer a vision for the future.

A plausible approximation to social objectives is expressed in his belief that all the projects and every course of action, in the development and expansion of a modern economy, 'must be subjected to both an economic and a social test, before being implemented'. But the kind of test is not spelled out and the machinery capable of carrying out such a monitoring is not envisaged.[1] And there is more generally a wide gap between broad objectives and how they are to be achieved.

On Northern Ireland, Haughey restructured his republicanism to exclude direct support for the nationalist minority, which had led to his involvement in the Arms Crisis and had caused his downfall, and aimed it instead at the British presence in Northern Ireland. This entailed the espousal of an idea first put forward at the crisis Government meetings in August 1969, included in the statement drafted by the Government, and then expressed by Lynch, in his speech on 13 August; namely, that there should be a United Nations force in the

[1] See 'The New Tension of Change' speech given to a Fianna Fáil meeting in Wynn's Hotel, Abbey Street, Dublin, 10 December 1970, and quoted in Ed. Mansergh, op. cit., pp 142–5.

North. The British response – a flat rejection – was demonstrated in practical terms, the following day, when the British Government sent 300 men of the Prince of Wales's Own Regiment in to Derry, the first British troops to be deployed in the North. For the first few months the British Army enjoyed a kind of honeymoon period. They were seen as protectors from sectarian violence and worked well to establish good community relations, particularly in the Catholic ghetto areas. But inevitably this phase ended. Riots became a matter for army control and occurred mainly, though not exclusively, in the Catholic areas. Brian Faulkner replaced James Chichester-Clark as Prime Minister of Northern Ireland in March 1971, and in August, following riots in which fifteen people died, he introduced internment.

Haughey saw this as an opportunity to involve himself once again in Northern Ireland affairs and to reactivate the more militant republican arguments in the South. He issued a statement[1] which revived Fianna Fáil partitionist thinking. It was also the basis of what was to become his own future policy on the North. Central to this was the failure of Northern Ireland as 'a political entity'. He did not use this expression until 1980, but it was implicit in his strong condemnation of the situation that had led to internment: 'the cynical experiment of partitioning Ireland has ended in total, tragic, failure.' He wanted the Dáil recalled. He wanted once again the United Nations Security Council to be asked to put a peace-keeping force into Northern Ireland. He went so far as to reject the policy that was being followed by Lynch and Fianna Fáil, one which was broadly supported by the other parties in the Dáil: 'On Monday we reached a point where it became crystal clear that a policy of looking to the British Government to ensure reform and an end to injustice while the British Army kept the peace has failed.'

It was a fruitless gesture – the phrases emotive, but the logic defective. The British had already vetoed the idea of any United Nations involvement, which would have been tantamount to a declaration of incapacity, and therefore of an intent to withdraw. The British had also implemented reforms and in part had addressed the problems of injustice. The British Army peace-keeping activities in the North, though they were shortly to lurch into the disaster of Bloody Sunday, were nevertheless the best peace-keeping programme the

[1] Haughey's statement, issued later in the week beginning Monday, 9 August 1971, is given in full in Ed. Mansergh, op. cit., pp 155–6.

South could expect, infinitely preferable to making it an international concern.

Haughey's statement had the added drawback that it was a seasonal argument. Every August, the likelihood of grounds being offered for heightened emotions and exploitative rhetoric had, tragically, become increasingly strong. Faulkner's decision to introduce internment demonstrated this, adding to the concern and reinforcing the need for restraint in the South. Given Haughey's complete silence on Northern affairs during the previous two years, the statement was provocative and damaging. It was provocative on the domestic front, where Lynch had effectively assumed all responsibility for Northern policy and needed his statements to be clearly seen in that light; and damaging in how Britain perceived that policy being implemented. Successive British Governments – for by now the problem of Ireland had passed through the uncertainties of Harold Wilson's Labour government's direction into the control of Edward Heath's Conservative administration – had witnessed unprecedented instability in the Republic of Ireland. Their worst fears – of the defeat of Jack Lynch by a cabal of strongly militant republicans within the governing party who seemed, on the face of it, to have been prepared to act outside the law, as far as Northern Ireland was concerned – had been averted. But fears of some kind of rebirth, or reactivation, of the thinking that lay behind the successive confrontations within the Fianna Fáil Party over the previous two years were still very real in Whitehall and they focused primarily on Charles Haughey as the only serious politician left within Fianna Fáil whose views still, it was assumed, diverged from party policy. He had, after all, said quite specifically, in his statement before the vote of confidence in James Gibbons, that 'serious differences over policies and personalities' existed and would have to be worked out democratically. The eventuality of this was treated seriously by the British.

Yet Haughey had to express his Northern Ireland policy views, such as they were. His sights were now set on the leadership of Fianna Fáil. His sense of destiny was unimpaired. He had demonstrated this clearly enough, if unwisely, in the immediate aftermath of the Arms Trial. He had reaffirmed it just over a week afterwards, in the Gibbons statement. And it was central to his thinking during the period remaining before the next general election. What it now needed was the clothing of public views and policies on a wide agenda of matters facing the Irish people. And difficult though it was to intrude into territory specifically reserved by the party leader, Haughey seized on the opportunity offered by the internment decision to speak out.

His wider arguments, encompassed in his article for *This Week*, were presented skilfully. He characterized the British Army as 'engaged in a campaign of repression', involving brutality and indiscriminate shooting, and never again able to be impartial. Therefore a substitute – the United Nations – was needed. He presented the spectre of cost, as seen by the people of Britain, together with the decline in army morale, and pointed to an inherent contradiction between the views of the G.O.C. Northern Ireland, General Tuzo,[1] who believed that there could be no military solution without a political one, and those of Edward Heath, who at that time 'apparently refuses to entertain any serious political initative until there is a military victory'. Haughey's belief was that the introduction of the United Nations would 'provide that temporary calm which would be the best background for serious and constructive political discussion'. Unfortunately, the article was seriously flawed in that it offered nothing in the form of an agenda for such discussion – no ideas, no proposals. His words contained a more malignant flaw, in the form of a doomsday proposition: 'For both Ireland and Britain, the present situation, tragic though it is, is fraught with even more terrifying possibilities, like shooting incidents across the border resulting in fatalities. Once this has happened, reconciliation and political initiatives would be irrelevant.'

Lynch let breaches of party discipline occasioned by statements on Northern Ireland pass. He was as conscious of the forthcoming general election as Haughey and needed to present as much unity as possible. Moreover, there were serious problems developing which needed extremely cool judgement. There was a widespread expectation that Fianna Fáil, after all that it had gone through, would be defeated. And the fact that Lynch had needed, and had bought in the toughest circumstances possible, time to prepare for a general election had also given the Opposition scope for preparing some sort of joint agenda for government. Although it turned out in the end to be quite haphazard in its formulation, the prospect of a joint Fine Gael–Labour coalition was ominous. If Lynch lost badly, his leadership would be challenged. If he lost at all, he would face difficulties. And in the circumstances,

---

[1] General Sir Harry Tuzo (b. 1917) was GOC Northern Ireland from 1971–73, the worst period, as far as violence was concerned, in the Six Counties.

no doubt motivated still by the need to end divisions and questions and fully reunite the party, he looked for an electoral victory once again.

His other reason for ignoring Haughey's Northern Ireland intervention was its essential irrelevance. On 12 August 1971, he had countered Haughey's internment statement with a much more fruitful proposal – that the Stormont form of government should be replaced by an administration embracing the concept of power-sharing between the two Northern Ireland communities. The Social, Democratic and Labour Party of Northern Ireland, under what was then effectively a collective leadership of men from the smaller parties which had come together to represent the Catholic nationalist minority, had already boycotted Stormont in July, and Stormont's future – certainly in the eyes of the British – was already in the balance. Lynch, who at this stage was better informed about the situation in the North than any other Southern politician, demonstrated most effectively his confidence in his own position in the Republic by adopting this line of argument at a time of growing violence and distress. The worst August rioting so far took place that year and, following the announcement of internment, when 300 were arrested, fifteen died in further riots. There were streams of refugees now crossing the Border. The first forty had been accommodated in a camp in County Cork. But now camps were opened in Border counties and the numbers escalated to 4,500. John Hume[1] and Ivan Cooper[2] were arrested while taking part in a peaceful demonstration in Derry. The bombing campaign caused growing carnage in Belfast. Throughout, Lynch maintained a cool and open stance in respect of the British Government. He held meetings with Heath, and then with Heath and Brian Faulkner, in London, in September 1971. Both domestically and in respect of the United Kingdom as a whole, Jack Lynch, through these meetings and the patient process of speeches and statements issued in Ireland and internationally, had laid the foundations for Sunningdale and for the

---

[1] John Hume (b. 1937) is the leader of the Social, Democratic and Labour Party and a leading Northern Ireland nationalist politician. He is a member of the Westminster and European parliaments.

[2] Ivan Cooper (b. 1944) was a founder member, with John Hume, of the SDLP and an independent member of the Stormont parliament from 1969 until the formation of the new party. He was a major figure in the Civil Rights movement in Northern Ireland. He was Minister of Community in the short-lived power-sharing administration of January–May 1974.

longer-term pressures which would always have at their heart the concept of Northern Ireland never returning to the simple Unionist majority rule which had so abused and divided Northern society since 1920.

At the end of 1972, in a by-election – admittedly in Lynch's own home territory of Cork – the Fianna Fáil Party won comfortably, with 53 per cent of the vote. It looked amazingly as though Lynch, despite the traumas of the whole period since the summer of 1969, might yet win the general election which, though not required until the summer of 1974, was expected some time early in 1973.

On the plus side the economy was sound. The population was rising, close to three million once again (the census of April 1971 showed a 3.3 per cent rise on the 1966 figure). Ireland had successfully negotiated EEC entry, Lynch himself signing the Treaty of Accession, in company with the Minister for Foreign Affairs, Patrick Hillery, on 22 January 1972, and this was followed, on 10 May, by a five-to-one referendum vote in favour of Ireland's entry. There had been modest reforms, including proposals for the restructuring of the Civil Service, the lowering of the voting age and the removal from the Constitution of the reference to the special position of the Roman Catholic Church, although that special position in the country precluded quite modest social change, such as the introduction of contraception, despite radical protests and the more cogent work being undertaken in the Senate by an independent member elected for one of the Dublin University seats, Senator Mary Robinson.[1]

The lowest point of all, as far as Northern Ireland was concerned, developed during 1972. Bloody Sunday, on 30 January, when thirteen people were shot dead by the British Army, was followed by a march to Merrion Square, where the British Embassy was then burnt down. Brian Faulkner refused to accept the transfer of security to Whitehall and his Government was dissolved, with direct rule being imposed from Westminster and William Whitelaw becoming the new Secretary of State for Northern Ireland. His immediate involvement eased the situation. He granted amnesties, lifted the ban on marches, released many from internment, closed down the prison ship, the

---

[1] Mary Robinson (b. 1944) was a barrister and lecturer in the Law Department of Trinity College. She became a trenchant and effective voice on the extension of social, family and human rights during the 1960s and early 1970s. She joined the Labour Party in 1976 and ran for a seat in the 1977 general election, unsuccessfully. She remained a senator and was elected President of Ireland in 1990, the first woman to hold the office.

Maidstone and made himself available for talks on a wide – some would say too wide – basis of accessibility.

Haughey's thinking had no real place in this tense and clotted chronology. Indeed, it is ironic that his first significant contribution to Dáil debates since May 1970 came in the immediate aftermath of the passage of the amendment to the Offences Against the State Act, in December 1972, and was on the subject of wildlife.

The violence that spilled over into the South, with bombs in Dublin and Monaghan, causing deaths and widespread injury, an extension of the endemic violence in the island as a whole, reflected badly on all who had been soft on the individuals and organizations operating outside the constitutional and democratic process. It was a time for strict law-and-order thinking. Desmond O'Malley had already put through an Emergency Powers Act, allowing for the transfer of republican prisoners from civil to military custody; and had invoked, in June, Section Five of the 1940 Offences Against the State Act, which authorized the setting up of the Special Criminal Court for the trying of terrorist offences. Then, in November, in order to facilitate the conviction of members of illegal organizations, an amendment to the same Act was proposed. This provided that if a garda [police] chief superintendent expressed the 'belief' that a person was a member of the IRA it would be sufficient evidence to convict. The proposal was controversial and the Opposition were deeply divided. They were opposed on grounds of the measure's infringement of civil liberties, with the additional argument that existing legislation had not been employed extensively enough. No doubt there were Opposition politicians who also saw in this approach the possibility of weakening Lynch's position in the country, and in particular with the republican factions within Fianna Fáil, by characterizing his as a 'law and order' administration, determined to crush nationalist expression. The divisions within Fine Gael were between those supporting Liam Cosgrave, who favoured the new and tougher legislation, and those – a majority – opposed to it on civil liberty grounds. The Labour Party's opposition was virtually unanimous. Jack Lynch sensed the electoral advantage of this and was contemplating a dissolution and a law-and-order election when two bombs exploded in Dublin, killing two men and injuring 127 people. The growing threat of a revolt within the Fine Gael Party, which would have toppled Cosgrave, was immediately pre-empted by this. Fine Gael opposition to the bill was withdrawn. Only Labour voted against and the situation passed, ironically with Liam Cosgrave's position strengthened.

Lynch's opportunity to call a snap general election, on the issue of law and order and against a divided opponent, passed. His general political strength, and his supremacy at the time, did not. And when he sought a dissolution of the Dáil and went to the country, in February 1973, the Fianna Fáil Party actually increased its vote by half of one per cent. He was defeated by a single factor: the joint programme of Labour and Fine Gael, and the resultant transfer of votes throughout the country under the proportional representation system.

The result demonstrates the remarkable degree of stability that had been restored following the protracted and in some respects inconclusive national crisis between 1969 and the February dissolution. Jack Lynch returned with 68 seats, a drop of six from the 1969 total of 74.[1] Fine Gael won 54 seats, four more than in 1969, while the Labour Party gained one to finish with a total of 19.[2] It may seem contradictory, but Lynch's defeat – which included two constituencies where seats were lost by the slenderest of margins – was something of a triumph. He had shed deputies; he had seen a new party formed by dissident Fianna Fáil members; his second candidate in Donegal had been squeezed out by Neil Blaney, yet he still maintained the basic strength of Fianna Fáil, uncompromised by any policy concessions to his enemies within the party, including Haughey, and came back in an assured position to continue as party leader. He was firmly in control. Haughey was as firmly in the wilderness and destined to remain there at Jack Lynch's discretion.

[1] The Ceann Comhairle, or Speaker, who was Fianna Fáil in the two previous Dáils, is automatically returned without contest and is not included in these totals.
[2] The election usefully illustrates the peculiarities of the Irish proportional representation system. The percentage share of Labour Party votes, for example, fell substantially – from 17 to 13.5 per cent – but because of effective transfers from Fine Gael, it increased its total number of seats. Fine Gael, whose share increased by only one percentage point, also benefited from the vote transfers.

CHAPTER XI

IN THE POLITICAL
WILDERNESS

Therefore put money in thy purse.

THE ARTS preoccupied Haughey increasingly during what
might be described as 'the Wilderness Years'. He was genuinely and personally interested in the artists themselves and,
by giving expression to this in the 1969 Finance Act, through the tax
relief on creative work, he had, in one dramatic and far-reaching piece
of legislation, established for himself a unique status among artists
throughout the country and, indeed, abroad as well.[1] He was widely
seen as their 'champion', the only politician with a commitment that
was practical, constructive and based on the idea of self-help. It did
not interfere with existing aids to the arts. Instead, it added an attractive
new dimension.

But the measure really solved only one small problem within the
arts: namely, to make personal income go further for those artists who
were able to earn enough to qualify. It did not really address the much
more central problem of poor funding prejudicing the development
of a wide range of disciplines within the arts, inhibiting the regional
spread of artistic endeavour and leaving many of the major institutions
desperately short of funds. All it really did was to complicate the
argument about aid to the arts: the choice between state resources
being applied to them generally, through the mechanism of the Arts
Council, or the much more direct device of giving to artists a real
benefit on their earnings. As regards the first option, state resources
were limited and there was the additional problem of administration.

[1] Many of those who benefited most from the tax exemption were artists – writers in particular – who came to Ireland simply because it was a reasonably civilized tax haven specially
designed for them. With one or two exceptions, they remained uninvolved in the country's
cultural life, interested essentially in preserving their wealth.

During the 1960s the Arts Council had been dominated by its director, Father Donal O'Sullivan, who ran it in an authoritarian way with a strong emphasis on patronage as a funding mechanism, directed too closely towards the visual arts, and aimed too closely at a limited group, mainly of painters, who were already seen as doing better than the rest. The Council had its own collection, made up of these purchases, and there was considerable controversy over the absence of a clear policy for the arts and the spread of very limited resources over a growing number of demands. That itself was a separate issue, shortly to be addressed by the incoming National Coalition Government. The second option, of influencing directly the artist's earnings, through tax relief, also had its drawbacks, in that the income levels of most struggling painters and writers remained to a large extent unaffected. Initially this was a strength; no one could argue effectively against the measure, which seemed to have beneficial potential for the arts in the country, despite the fact that it created a unique status, hard to define, hard for the Revenue Commissioners to administer.

Neither of the two options involved any significant expenditure. Funding for the arts through the Arts Council was an uncontroversial Dáil vote. The amounts involved in individual artists claiming tax relief were also expected to be small. Nevertheless, by making the provision, Haughey had transformed public perception of the role of the artist in society in a dramatic and irreversible manner. That nothing further was done about the arts, during the remaining three years of Lynch's administration, is unsurprising, given the circumstances. But the need had been recognized and the first piece of legislation to be introduced by the new Cosgrave Government was the Arts Bill, a measure designed to reconstitute the Arts Council.

It was debated during 1973 and passed in 1974. It was neither far-reaching nor controversial, save in one particular: Cosgrave, who moved the measure himself and took much of the debate on his own shoulders, had included a section that gave the Taoiseach – whose Department administered the Arts Council – the right to appoint all sixteen council members. This led to a division at the committee stage, which the Government carried.

Haughey should have been well prepared for this Bill, yet in the event his lengthy contribution was quite confused. His earlier Finance Act provision for artists had attracted considerable interest outside the country. In the summer of 1972, as a result of it,[1] he had been invited by the Harvard Summer School Institute to give an address on the relationship between the State and the Arts, and the lengthy paper he delivered was later claimed unequivocally as 'Charles Haughey's most important statement on the role the State should play in relation to the Arts'.[2] At the time, the sum of money dispensed by the Arts Council was put by him at around $200,000 and the total paid out by the State on all artistic and cultural activity was around $3 million – 'one quarter of one per cent of the national budget'. And he embraced in this some fairly important institutions, such as the National Library, National Museum and National Gallery.

Haughey recognized the need for a comprehensive policy for Ireland on the arts, declaring it 'an integral part of good government in a modern community'. Yet he devoted by far the greatest part of his Harvard address to the problem that he had already, in essence, solved, that of transferring at least some of the financial advantage in the State's commitment to the arts from institutional funding to help for the individual.

In that Harvard speech, Haughey was developing the notion which was to lead, in due course, to the establishment of Aosdána.[3] The Irish poet, Anthony Cronin,[4] has written lyrically of struggling along the cliffs beyond St George's Head, in Kilkee, County Clare, with Charles Haughey, in 1972, debating the issue. It revolved around one 'pretty salient fact', according to Cronin, that 'governments and government agencies tended to favour organizations over individuals and performances over creativity'.[5] The Harvard speech refers to the high costs of putting on performances of operas, ballets and symphonies, or of mounting retrospective exhibitions of the works of dead artists, which are described as mainly the subsidizing of *audiences*. This helped the

---

[1] Martin Mansergh states that 'the invitation was surely a product of [Haughey's] decision . . . to free creative artists from tax liability'. Op. cit., p. 164.
[2] Ibid.
[3] Aosdána is an organization of up to 150 artists (it reached this total in the late summer of 1992, when it was announced that an increase in the total admissible number was being considered). They are eligible, as a result of membership, for a state grant or pension, means-tested. All the arts are represented.
[4] Anthony Cronin (b. 1926), poet and author, later became Arts Adviser to Haughey in several administrations and for many years was responsible for his speeches on cultural and other matters.
[5] Anthony Cronin, *How Aosdána Began*, Dublin, 1990. This short pamphlet, its pages unnumbered, became controversial shortly after its publication (see below).

'producing and performing artists', as opposed to the creative artist in the narrow sense. Haughey had made special provision for the creative artist in his financial legislation three years earlier and Aosdána was an attempt to extend this help. At very considerable length the speech deals with this problem, expatiating on the difficulties of identifying individual talent, whether it is the younger practitioner, 'demonstrating that peculiar quality called promise', or 'lonely middle-aged geniuses ... who have somehow missed the bus'.

The speech, which ranged widely over the works and vicissitudes of Rembrandt, Blake, Goldsmith, Rimbaud, Alfred Austin, D. H. Lawrence, Diego Rivera, Soutine, Modigliani and Michelangelo – to name only a selection – is more a demonstration of Cronin's wide reading on the difficulties of the creative artist than it is a constructive outline of a national policy for the arts. The implicit proposal, for a kind of college of creativity with pensions for chosen artists of merit, did not materialize for some years. The speech ended with a plea for priorities in the disposal of taxpayers' money, which raised of course the spectre of Ireland's lamentably poor performance in the field of the arts and the very low level of help of any kind whatever. Without the restructuring of aid generally, the scheme for identifying the creative genius who had not productively demonstrated his talent on his own, whether young or middle-aged, and then giving him finance 'to create', was a poor starting-point in elucidating a national policy for the arts in Ireland.

It was one thing to be speaking to the Harvard Summer School Institute; quite another to be faced with actual legislation on the arts. When Liam Cosgrave brought in the 1973 Arts Bill, in late October, it offered Haughey a golden opportunity to fill a considerable void. Not only was he right, in pointing out the absence of any comprehensive policy on the arts and the obvious need for such a policy – as he had done at Harvard – but in addition he stood almost alone among politicians of all parties in having a genuine commitment to the arts and artists, and a record in power to prove it. It could be argued that the occasion was not the most opportune; it was of a kind to attract a backbencher only and was marginal for serious opposition politics. But when not in power politicians can rarely choose the ground they fight on and Haughey needed an issue in which altruism, good judgement and knowledge of the subject would clearly distinguish his contribution to the debate.

The background to the Bill was complicated. During the whole post-war period there had been virtually no legislative change to the artistic and cultural environment. The leader of the first Inter-Party Government, John A. Costello, had brought back from England the distinguished art historian Thomas Bodkin,[1] to advise on a broad range of issues, including the constitution and working of the National Gallery of Ireland, the National Museum, the National College of Art and art education generally, the role of design in industry, and the acquisition and preservation of historic sites and buildings in the country. Bodkin produced an outstanding report.[2] It was almost totally ignored. He did not propose a government department with responsibility for the arts, but he did recommend civil service responsibility, through a section of one of the departments – preferably that of the Taoiseach – and it was only as 'a less ambitious approach' that the idea of 'a small autonomous body' to advise the Government emerged. This body became the Arts Council of the 1951 Act. With the exception of the legislation which established the National College of Art and Design, there were no Bills at all covering any of the issues that had been considered by Bodkin in his report. All reliance was placed on the 'small autonomous body'. Worse was to follow. The intended advisory range of the new council was not properly structured in the legislation. By placing it outside the Civil Service, in Costello's words 'free from the trammels' of procedure, its powers were reduced. And it had no clear ministerial direction: it would be 'subject merely to the Government'. Indeed, Costello seems to have lost interest in it. He embraced in its remit guidance on postage stamps, State ceremonies, art exhibitions, even 'design of advertisements in furtherance of the tourist traffic'. And he benignly anticipated that 'every Department of State which requires its advice will be able to go to it and get from it advice and assistance and direction'.[3] This rarely, if ever, happened. The Arts Council became a mechanism for the distribution of very modest State funding for the arts.

[1] Thomas Bodkin (1887–1961) was a lawyer who was called to the bar in 1911 and practised for a time. He became director of the National Gallery of Ireland from 1927 to 1935, but then took up the Barber Professorship of Fine Arts, in Birmingham, and was the first director of the Barber Institute until his retirement in 1952. He was offered the directorship of the Arts Council, which was a product of his own recommendations to the Inter-Party Government, but he declined.

[2] 'Tuarascáil Ar Na hEealaíona In Eirinn', Report on the Arts in Ireland, Professor Thomas Bodkin, 30 September 1949.

[3] Dáil Report, 24 April 1951, col. 1293. The second stage was moved in April, the committee stage in May, and the Bill was passed in July.

Liam Cosgrave's purpose was to transfer to his own Department the power to appoint *all* the members of the new council, which would have a full-time director (he had previously been part-time) and a part-time chairman. Haughey made the longest speech in the debate. But though he was critical of the narrow terms of reference and called for a comprehensive policy on the arts, he found himself unable to offer his own proposals, and pleaded inadequate 'resources' for the Opposition for this. Even on the Bill's specific proposals he was unsure of himself. He could not make up his mind as to whether one arts council was sufficient, putting forward the idea that three might be better, one for music, one for the plastic arts, and one for literature. Nor was he sure where responsibility should be located. On balance he favoured the Department of Finance over the Taoiseach's Department, but had no clear idea about ministerial responsibility.[1] He had certainly read the previous debates and was fully aware of the broad, if unfulfilled, objectives contained in the 1951 Act. Yet he failed to address the policy implications of this lack of fulfilment and when the Bill went to committee stage he merely repeated that he would have preferred the complete replacement of the 1951 Act rather than its amendment by the new measure.

It was a lame performance. The principal Opposition speaker was John Wilson,[2] then spokesman for Education, who was uncritical of the measure, save in respect of the limited funding for the arts, which he wanted increased. Padraig Faulkner,[3] who had been Minister for Education and responsible for the legislation expanding the National College of Art into a college of art and design and providing it with new premises, took up the main Opposition criticism, which was directed at the Taoiseach's right to appoint all council members. This effectively left Haughey, as a backbencher, with the opportunity to demonstrate fundamental and far-reaching policy ideas embracing all the arts, thereby fulfilling his earlier interest and concern. That he did not do this was the result of an innate confusion exemplified in the Harvard

[1] When he became Taoiseach he favoured keeping the arts within the Taoiseach's Department.
[2] John Wilson (b. 1923) was a schoolteacher and university lecturer before entering politics. He represented Cavan from 1973 and served in all the subsequent Fianna Fáil administrations, becoming deputy leader of the government, following Brian Lenihan's dismissal in 1990, and withdrawing from the Dáil in the November 1992 general election.
[3] Padraig Faulkner (b. 1918) was a national schoolteacher first elected to the Dáil in 1957 and made Minister for Education in 1969.

speech. In his discussions with Anthony Cronin he had moved away from the broad objectives of constructing a comprehensive policy and instead had moved towards the narrow target of aid for artists themselves, albeit transcending the limited powers of the Arts Council.

The failure is all the more surprising, since Haughey had been associated with the idea and practice of planning and policy from his earliest political experiences. He had witnessed, almost at first hand, at the end of the 1950s, the operation of dedicated public servants constructing the kinds of policies in the economic field which were then the basis for dynamic developments of a complex kind. Then, in Justice, he had been given the opportunity to apply much-needed political drive to similarly positive and complex proposals by civil servants. In the Department of Finance he had become directly responsible for programming as an expression of policy. In no sense was he unaware of the need, in the political field, for responsibilities to be shouldered by public servants so that a measure of groundwork could be offered to the relevant ministers, or indeed the head of the Government, to implement. He was not alone in his wealth of experience in this; but he stood almost alone in his recognition of the need for precisely the same approach to be applied to the arts. No other politician, before or since, has been as well placed as Haughey, both then and during his twelve-year period in power, to deliver a broad policy on the arts and then implement it through legislative and administrative decisions. What has actually been achieved is meagre in the extreme. What Haughey did was to turn away from the extensive range of cultural and artistic problems at every level in Irish society and confine himself instead to the slow and laborious process of bringing Aosdána, Ireland's equivalent of the Académie Française, into being.

Haughey was in the fortunate position, as a backbencher, of being free to range over most issues. He spoke well and with confidence. There was no great precision in his utterances during the period between the election of 1973 and his return to the Fianna Fáil front bench as spokesman on Health, at the beginning of 1975. But this did not inhibit his views or his criticisms.

One of the highest profiles within the National Coalition Government was that of Dr Conor Cruise O'Brien. From the same constituency as Haughey, he was an implacable critic of Haughey. His appointment gave him unenviable responsibilities for the telephone services in Ireland at the time, which were lamentably bad. And he took these up with some determination, initiating a number of highly significant technological advances. But his other, and much more controversial, responsibility was for broadcasting. Combined with his outspoken views on Northern Ireland and his fiercely antagonistic attitude towards emotive republicanism, which was still a significant feature of comment and debate, it was inevitable that he became a focus for controversy, particularly over the issue of control of the national radio and television network, Radio Telefis Eireann.[1] This came under the RTE Authority and O'Brien was to make significant changes in the law, increasing its degree of autonomy but reinforcing the powers by which spokespersons from proscribed or subversive organizations could be blocked. In the early months of the National Coalition the issue which greatly interested O'Brien was whether RTE should operate a second channel, or simply rebroadcast the BBC or some other chosen British channel to the western parts of Ireland, which was deprived by distance of this free service. He put forward a 'freedom of the airwaves' argument on grounds both of the cost to RTE of running a second channel and of the plurality of ideas and views.

Haughey elected to enter this debate, as he did so many others, without any clear views himself about how the conflicting issues should be resolved. There were two quite different agendas. On the one hand the simple and understandable feeling, in the west, that the people were neglected. Starved of entertainment and variety of choice, they wanted something official and legal done. On a quite different level there were questions of propaganda, national culture and identity, and the actual survival of RTE in the face of 'freedom of the airwaves' competition.

Haughey expressed serious fears about the survival of RTE in the face of such competition and laid the blame at O'Brien's door. At the same time he did not wish to be seen as restrictive over the dissemination of alternative points of view. He was critical of RTE. Competition from British channels could turn RTE into 'a heavily subsidized white elephant' or render it a 'defunct symbol of an unachieved national ambition'. Haughey had his own prescription: 'Put more Irish life on to our screens, put a much greater proportion of available budgets into creativity and less into the bureaucratic machine which has been built up.'

---

[1] The station, first known as 2RN, then as Radio Eireann, had opened a television channel in 1962. For east-coast viewers British and Scottish broadcasting was readily available, making them multi-channel areas. For the west, the choice was much more confined.

O'Brien had, in his period at the Department of External Affairs, been involved in information services and under Liam Cosgrave he had been asked to assume certain responsibilities with respect to the Government Information Bureau, which up to then had been directly under the Taoiseach. Muiris Mac Conghail[1] had been appointed the new head of this bureau and was to become a close associate of O'Brien's during the National Coalition Government's period in power. Haughey foresaw difficulties in the change and may have been thinking of the August 1969 Government statement when he said: 'I have seen what damage can be done, what public confusion caused by something coming out from the Government not fully explained or correctly interpreted.' Haughey opposed at that time radio or television coverage of the Dáil and Senate. He wanted deputies to speak 'with all the sincerity they possess, and from conviction', and felt that television coverage would induce members to 'strike poses and adopt attitudes for public consumption'.

He was not finding it altogether easy to discover what pose he should himself be adopting. His fundamental objective was still rehabilitation. He had survived within the party. He had erected a wall of silence around the events of 1969 and 1970 by never speaking about any aspect of the Arms Crisis. Periodically it came up during the following five years, in part because there was the unresolved matter of a fundamental disagreement between himself and James Gibbons about evidence. But it was fading from public memory and was being replaced by a new Charles Haughey – the dedicated politician who spoke on a broad range of subjects with authority. Though he sat on the back benches, the term 'backbencher' did not ever fit him. He was a potential leader in exile, in waiting, and he filled the time effectively. He had a cultivated stance of cultural and artistic awareness, and of commitment, not just in his speeches but also in his regular presence at art exhibitions and other functions. His speeches made little serious contribution to the issues under debate, but they were extensive, confident and urbane. Judged rigorously, they were at times confused and they fell all too easily into the classic mode of demanding better from those in power without specifying in any detail as to how this should be structured or financed.

In this Haughey conformed to the general performance of his party during this early period in Opposition. Fianna Fáil had been in power

[1] Muiris Mac Conghail (b. 1941) had previously worked in RTE as a producer and director.

for sixteen years prior to the 1973 election and had survived the greatest crisis in its history. It was licking its still unhealed wounds and recovering. While other senior figures in the Fianna Fáil Party were largely restricted to their briefs as spokesmen, however, Haughey did have the freedom to speak on virtually any issue, with the exception of Northern Ireland, where Jack Lynch largely reserved to himself statements about policy, including the changes in favour of power-sharing that were being promoted by Liam Cosgrave's Government and which were being given their public character by Conor Cruise O'Brien and Garret FitzGerald in particular. The National Coalition Government had in fact achieved considerable progress in developing Anglo-Irish relations during its first year in office, leading to the signing of the Sunningdale Agreement on 9 December 1973. Though this was to founder, all too swiftly and tragically, early the following year, its fate was more a product of problems in Northern Ireland and of Edward Heath's own electoral difficulties in Britain, than it was of the restrained opposition which Jack Lynch expressed at the time.

The very strength of Lynch in power – his ability to impose, through a combination of firmness and persuasion, a new policy approach on the North – was a handicap in Opposition. Traditional Fianna Fáil republicanism, expressed in renewed pressures for reunification and reinforced by Neil Blaney, who was now an outspoken independent deputy on the back benches, added to the perception that the party was not delivering good, strong opposition. Lynch had his own timetable. He appointed, in October 1973, a new and very able General Secretary, Seamus Brennan.[1] And this marked the beginning of the long haul back to power. But Lynch was fairly clear in his own mind that the Cosgrave administration would run the full term, and set his agenda accordingly. His economic adviser, and the man who was to become his principal electoral strategist, was Martin O'Donoghue, who had worked closely with Lynch since 1970. Also on board were a highly effective press officer, Frank Dunlop, appointed by Lynch, and a lawyer, Esmonde Smyth, who were responsible for an unusual innovation for the party – policy documents.

Haughey shared Lynch's perception that the timetable for a return

---

[1] Seamus Brennan (b. 1948) was an accountant and management consultant with excellent organizing abilities and was only 25 when he took on the key role in preparing the party for the next general election.

to power should allow for a full term for the Cosgrave administration. If Fianna Fáil then failed to win once again, the question of a change of leadership would immediately arise. In that event his full rehabilitation to the front bench would be a better point of departure in the challenge for succession.

From the very start, the National Coalition had surprised everyone with its performance. The auguries had been inauspicious. Labour and Fine Gael had come together with a hastily concocted 14-Point Programme for Government. Only a few months before, the major party, Fine Gael, had emerged from a near-chaotic situation, over the amending legislation to the Offences Against the State Act, when Liam Cosgrave's leadership had been under threat. And the prospective tensions between the two parties, and within Fine Gael, gave little sense of stability. Yet almost within weeks Cosgrave had established his own authority, virtually beyond dispute, and had placed talented men in the key ministries, with a genuine programme of legislative work which was impressive. It included many changes in social reform, encouraged and in some cases dictated by Ireland's membership of the EEC. It covered the arts, as we have seen; it included promised changes in taxation, among these being the introduction of a wealth tax; and it embraced the politically sensitive area of constituency reforms, where the Coalition was thought to have blocked the possibility of Fianna Fáil returning to power. When the climate was further tested in a series of five by-elections, during that first flush of coalition power, Fianna Fáil did badly. There was a distinct feeling that the power of the party had been broken. Even later, when the Coalition had suffered setbacks as a result of the oil crisis, the expectation remained that if the two parties held together and offered themselves again on a joint programme, they would win.

In these circumstances, Haughey's cultivated stance was carefully promoted within the party and among journalists. He spent a great deal of time travelling the country for party functions, or just to visit. Dick Walsh described him as being engaged in a 'half pilgrimage and half recruitment drive, motoring alone or with some helpful friend to towns and villages he once would not have visited without the accompaniment of a band ... but never ... did he permit himself the luxury of a sentence, publicly uttered, which could be considered disloyal. Making common cause with those who, for one reason or another, did not hold party office, or with officers who were out of favour with headquarters, as well as with any local representatives who cared to meet him – and very many did – he crossed the familiar territory again and again and sat and smiled and waited.'[1]

With journalists he sat and talked, never about the Arms Crisis, always about the inherent instability of coalition and the need for Fianna Fáil's return to power, not with himself as leader, but with his central involvement in government. His persuasive personality, rather than any decisive ability in Opposition, won him friends and there was growing support for the idea of his return to the front bench, as early as the occasion of the first annual conference of the party in Opposition and essentially for the good of the party: 'Much of the focus of political interest [at the conference] will be upon those figures who can either frustrate or resolve the party's internal divisions. And at the top of this list is Mr Haughey's name. His words and his attitude will be weighed very carefully by those delegates – and they are the vast majority – who believe that no really effective opposition, and therefore no eventual return to power, can be achieved without the unity of the Fianna Fáil Party being firmly and publicly cemented together once again.'[2]

There was another problem, in some ways more difficult to resolve: this was the adamant refusal of James Gibbons to serve on the front bench with Haughey. Lynch wanted to be even-handed and bring both men back, so that there would be no residual division left to rankle. After all, Gibbons had been George Colley's close ally and supporter. A planned reshuffle was indicated by Lynch in August 1974. By Christmas it was still being debated, and publicly all the emphasis was on the obvious question – 'Will he, won't he, bring back Haughey?' – rather than the more subtle issue of resolving all the party's internal difficulties. Haughey, Lynch later claimed, had been a brilliant minister with a great future and it would have been unjust and un-Christian to have penalized him indefinitely. There had been no disloyalty. There was no grumbling antagonism over the key issue of Northern Ireland. If there had been a time when his future within Fianna Fáil had been at risk, then it was over. On 30 January 1975, in an even-handed gesture of reconciliation, both Charles Haughey and James Gibbons were brought back to the Fianna Fáil front bench, Gibbons as spokesman on Agriculture, Haughey as spokesman on Health.

---

[1] Dick Walsh, *The Party: Inside Fianna Fail*, Dublin 1986, p. 137.
[2] The present writer, *Irish Independent*, 16 February 1974.

Aerial view of Abbeville, Haughey's home in north County Dublin

Innishvichillane Island, Charles Haughey's island off the Kerry coast

Haughey and Brian Lenihan leave Dublin
for Haughey's first meeting with
Margaret Thatcher as Fianna Fáil leader,
20 May 1980

With George Colley in 1980

Margaret Thatcher with Haughey and Lenihan at
the Dublin Castle Summit, December 1980

Above: Triumphant having survived the leadership challenge of February 1983

Left: Meanwhile Haughey is at his press conference denying knowledge of the 1982 phone-tapping

Below: The Boss – Haughey's customary salute, at the Fianna Fáil Ard Fheis, March 1991

Haughey with Bernard Cahill,
chairman of Aer Lingus

A cartoon in *The Irish Times* two
days before the November 1991
no-confidence motion,
which he won

With Albert Reynolds,
October 1991

CHAPTER XII

THE HARD ROAD BACK

How poor are they that have not patience!
What wound did ever heal but by degrees?

RESPONSIBILITY FOR HEALTH in Opposition isolated Haughey
and gave him no central role in the party's planning for the general election, which could be expected within two years of
Haughey's reinstatement.[1] Such control, of strategy and organization,
was firmly in the hands of a comparatively small group comprising
Lynch himself, George Colley, Desmond O'Malley and Martin O'Donoghue. This was an intentional isolation. While Lynch had paid tribute
to Haughey's ability in justifying his return to the front bench, referring
to his ministerial abilities and the idea of forgiveness, the predominant
motive was party unity. Haughey was to be part of the Opposition team,
part of the electoral effort in a general way, and thus a contributor to
party unity and the presentation of a solid Opposition front in the Dáil;
but he was not to be central to the all-important economic strategy.

It could be argued that this was a mistake, although it is difficult to
see how any closer integration would have been workable. Haughey's
perceived stance on the economy, not unlike that of Sean Lemass,
remained a carefully judged mixture of doctrinaire economic thinking
combined with a positive, dynamic view about the implementation of
this. He was essentially conservative when engaged in the objective
analysis of national economic needs and felt simply that a positive
attitude on the part of the government, linked to a definite plan of
action, was sufficient to energize the economy. There was a major
economic crisis in the year of his return to the front bench, 1975, and
it was of an unprecedented severity. Very high inflation, running close
to 25 per cent, rising unemployment, which, for the first time since
1942, exceeded 100,000 in January of that year, a mounting current

---

[1] In fact it came in the midsummer of 1977.

Budget deficit and high levels of Government borrowing, had all followed the oil crisis, which grew out of the Yom Kippur War of 1973.
And despite his main duties, on health matters, Haughey had much
to say on the economy as well.

He despised economists. He despised journalists who fed on
economic forecasting and official pronouncements. Such analytical
documents, Haughey disdainfully remarked, were 'fine-combed by
commentators and leader-writers in search of an encouraging phrase,
sentence or paragraph on which some sort of hopeful message can be
based ... It is all pathetically passive; like the soothsayers of old por-
ing over the sacrificial entrails in an effort to predict the course of
events over which they have no control.'[1]

His own recommendations, though they did have a positive ring
about them, were not too precise, either. Moreover, they were consistent with much that was being said by the very economists whom
Haughey condemned for their passivity. He sought an interpretation
of the key elements affecting the economy, notably recognition of
the growth in population and reduced emigration creating growing
demands for employment. This was a much-debated issue at the time,
Ireland, in contrast with many other European countries, having produced a population 'bulge' in school-leavers, which was to remain a
major problem for those trying to create employment for many years
to come. And he reiterated warnings about the need for confidence
within industry and business. This second point was provoked by the
impact of a world oil crisis on a government which had embarked on
wealth taxation proposals that were unpopular and which Fianna Fáil
characterized as anti-investment. Haughey's proposal for a return to
planning, with 'a national plan of economic progress', also incorpor-
ated a view which he was to develop further in later years; this was
the direct involvement of the trade union movement in the process of
constructing the economic system needed by the country, later to
become his 'social partnership' of employers, workers and Government. At the time the trade union movement was perceived as a threat
to stability which would seek 'its own ends independently' if not
involved in the planning process.

Haughey's particular *bête noire* among economists was, understandably, Martin O'Donoghue and, though he ties his words to 'official

---

[1] 'The Economic Crisis and the Need for Planning', speech given to the Dublin Society of
Chartered Accountants, 5 November 1975, Ed. Mansergh, op. cit., p. 203.

sources', it is fairly certain that he was alluding in part to O'Donoghue in a reference in the speech to 'a very definite impression of the official economist, like Diogenes, clutching his lantern, peering into the statistical gloom and searching for some faint sign of the longed-for upturn . . .' O'Donoghue, with his bald head and severe, penetrating gaze, bore a marked resemblance to the traditional representation of the Athenian philosopher who, when consulted by Alexander the Great about his economic problems, replied: 'You could move away out of the sun, and not cast a shadow on me.'

O'Donoghue, who remained as Lynch's own economic adviser after the 1973 election, had initially been drawn into the Fianna Fáil back room at the time of Haughey's dismissal from the Government by Lynch. In remaining as adviser to the party leader in Opposition, O'Donoghue's position had changed, becoming more political, enabling him to play the role of key strategist and in due course assume the position of orchestrator of the coming electoral programme. Into the bargain he accepted a nomination for the Dáil in the Dun Laoghaire constituency.

He was very much the back-room boy, working equally well with party organizers, such as Seamus Brennan and Frank Dunlop, as with George Colley and Desmond O'Malley. He was closest of all to Lynch himself and was able to construct an economic strategy which was undoubtedly to be the principal factor in the defeat of the National Coalition. Two of its ministers, Richie Ryan[1] and Justin Keating,[2] were bogged down in legislation that was either unpopular or ill-judged or both. Cosgrave himself, having seen the collapse of his Northern Ireland initiatives, was increasingly concerned about security and unsure of how to approach the general election which initially seemed likely to turn out in their favour in the summer of 1976. This was a good deal earlier than required, but Fianna Fáil was doing very badly in Opposition, while the Coalition's performance, despite the economic crisis, was really quite strong. Then things changed and a mood of uncertainty developed, manifesting itself, in part, in Cosgrave's responses to the murder by the Provisional IRA of Christopher Ewart Biggs, British Ambassador in Dublin, on 23 July 1976.

[1] Richie Ryan (b. 1929) was Minister for Finance and close to Liam Cosgrave. He was involved in extensive taxation reform during this period.
[2] Justin Keating (b. 1930) was Minister for Industry and Commerce. At the time, 1976–7, a major piece of mining legislation, resulting from the State's involvement in Bula mines, dominated Dáil business.

At Cosgrave's insistence, the Dáil was recalled to implement a package of emergency legislation, some at least of which seemed, in the circumstances, draconian.[1] The President, Cearbhaill O Dalaigh, exercising his constitutional powers to refer legislation to the Supreme Court, sent two of the Bills there. Though they were found to be constitutional, there was clear endorsement of his right, if not his duty, to take this action. But the referral, unfortunately, was not seen in the same light by the Minister for Defence, Paddy Donegan,[2] who provoked a constitutional storm by referring to the president as 'a thundering disgrace'. O Dalaigh resigned; Donegan didn't; Cosgrave sat tight; and the credibility of the National Coalition was, from that point on, irreversibly damaged.

It was a period of subtle politics between Lynch and Cosgrave, including the question of the future of Northern Ireland. Cosgrave, following the collapse of the Sunningdale Agreement, and with Harold Wilson in power in London unwilling to pursue any new initiative and with a Secretary of State for the North who relied essentially on the military, adopted a narrow security approach, avoiding any new and positive political initiatives. Fianna Fáil went through a brief but unhappy flirtation with a more hardline brand of Opposition republicanism, emanating from the spokesman on Foreign Affairs, Michael O'Kennedy, who drafted a statement which the party endorsed. It sought from Britain a commitment to withdraw from Northern Ireland. Lynch himself was unhappy about it.

The immediate motive for the hardline shift was a by-election in West Mayo, where it was thought traditional republicanism, expressed in the form of a demand for a British 'declaration of intent to withdraw', would help the party. It had the opposite effect. Despite the release of Tiede Herrema, the kidnapped Dutch businessman working in Ireland, the day before polling,[3] Lynch knew that the mood in the country was unresponsive to the line which O'Kennedy had fostered

[1] There were three measures: a motion invoking a new 'national emergency' as a result of terrorist acts; a Criminal Law Bill, amending various roadblock provisions and increasing maximum sentences; and an Emergency Powers Bill, which extended the period during which suspects could be held.
[2] Patrick S. Donegan (b. 1923) was described in the political directory of the time as 'company director, miller, farmer, publican' and was appointed Minister for Defence by Cosgrave in 1973.
[3] Tiede Herrema, a Dutch businessman, had been kidnapped several weeks before. A secret deal with his kidnappers, Eddie Gallagher and Marian Coyle, secured his release, though the terms of the agreement were not made known until later.

and that it should not be pursued. At the same time, once decided on by the party, and issued, the policy statement was better left on the table, while the real emphasis was switched to the economy.

The Fianna Fáil Party was resoundingly defeated in the by-election by Enda Kenny, of Fine Gael, the death of whose father, Henry, had provoked the contest. Yet only a week after this defeat, Charles Haughey spoke out in carefully considered terms, supporting the idea of a British declaration of intent to withdraw and calling for the British 'to indicate that the Irish problem is to be a matter for the Irish'. Haughey was to some extent guided by political developments at the time in Britain and believed, wrongly as it happened, that British devolution of independent assemblies for Scotland and Wales would be conducive to the changes which he claimed that he wanted in Northern Ireland. But he was also wary of the profile which Michael O'Kennedy gave himself by being the prime mover in the creation of a new Northern Ireland policy for the party based on the idea of a 'British declaration of intent to withdraw'. Both Haughey and Colley were seen at the time as contentious successors to Lynch, neither of them capable of sustaining the unity of the party. Lynch himself felt this and favoured Desmond O'Malley as successor. O'Kennedy, who was then just forty and three years older than O'Malley, was laying down an alternative challenge and using Northern Ireland as his potential platform. Haughey took up the idea.

It was the wrong attitude, at the wrong time, and bore little relevance to British thinking, the actual circumstances in Northern Ireland, or the political instincts of the vast majority of people in the Republic, who had generally come to the conclusion that the Sunningdale strategy, of a form of agreed power-sharing between the Protestant and Roman Catholic communities in the Six Counties – even if not possible in the short term – was the right way forward. Nevertheless, Haughey sustained his position during the early part of 1976, participating fully in the debates on the Criminal Law Jurisdiction Bill, a measure which grew out of Sunningdale, and allowed for trial and prosecution in the Republic for offences committed in Northern Ireland, and vice versa, as an alternative to extradition. It was party policy to oppose this Bill, mainly on grounds of the measure's legislative flaws or unworkability – which proved in the event to be correct – but Haughey's own speeches, demonstrably based on his claim to a Northern background, went further, edging into the territory of expressing political judgements on the consistent failure of the Northern administration itself to work properly, or indeed at all, and well beyond the legalistic issue of whether the proposed legislation had any real chance of defeating terrorism.

It is difficult to analyse Haughey's motives in all this. Martin Mansergh suggests, in an introductory passage to the speeches on the Criminal Law Jurisdiction Bill, that his position on Northern Ireland issues 'openly reflected his Northern family background'.[1] Yet the rub of politics at the time was about something quite different: the very presence of Haughey within the Fianna Fáil Party Front Bench, while he still appeared to espouse views on the North that were inconsistent with those of Lynch and were in fact in sympathy with the objectives of the Provisional IRA, which also wanted a British declaration of intent to withdraw, was part of Haughey's internal strategy. The more militant republican line had developed a policy of its own within Fianna Fáil and this had become 'official'. One might query why Haughey was voicing it. Part of the answer lies in the poor state of Fianna Fáil's parliamentary performance. The party had made no real showing in Opposition. On the overall legislative programme, which included a number of socially important measures deriving from Ireland's membership of the European Community, there were few arguments open to it. For sixteen years it had enjoyed power, not without some complacency, and for the last three of those it had governed through a period of crisis. Ill-used to opposing at all and bewildered in the face of what was at heart a dynamic partnership, uncertain about what should be its new 'core values', Fianna Fáil was open to the kind of policy change which Michael O'Kennedy had fostered and virtually defenceless against the comeback which Haughey was making.

Conor Cruise O'Brien was one of the most consistent and outspoken of Haughey's critics at this time. He saw in the change on Northern Ireland an incipient drift back towards a policy not unlike that being followed by the militant republican organizations north and south of the Border, and he said as much, in articles and broadcasts at the time, claiming that there was 'a distinction without a difference' between Fianna Fáil and Provisional IRA policy on Northern Ireland. The bitterness between O'Brien and Haughey, constant throughout the 1970s, became a notable feature of the 1977 general election.

It was a well-planned campaign by Fianna Fáil, with a carefully wrought election manifesto – the first in their history – and a strong

[1] Ed. Mansergh, op. cit., p. 213.

emphasis on creating employment and reducing taxation. The document was starry-eyed in what it promised on employment, prodigal in what it offered in tax reliefs and has been condemned ever since for the adverse impact its subsequent implementation had on Ireland's economy. Yet its excessive generosity has to be judged in the context of the times, which were tense and unstable for everyone and particularly worrying for Lynch. He faced challenges to his position from three sides. Firstly, there was the National Coalition, which had held together and was campaigning, for the first time in Irish political history, for a second term with the same basic recipes. Secondly, unprecedented setbacks in the economy had to be addressed by Lynch with a set of alternatives to those being offered by Ryan, Keating and others in the Fine Gael–Labour Coalition. Thirdly, and of greatest significance to Charles Haughey, a Fianna Fáil victory was essential if Lynch's own leadership and the party's basic policies were to be preserved. In power, he knew he could restore the moderate Northern Ireland line, supportive of the minority and of its wish to achieve a form of power-sharing in any restored Northern assembly. In Opposition a second time, he would not be there to achieve, restore or preserve anything at all.

If you haven't shaken hands with Jack Lynch, you haven't lived, politically speaking, in Ireland. The muscular, knuckle-crunching grip of a great sportsman who has 'pressed the flesh' through every townland in Ireland became the decisive personal factor in the election of 1977. From the very start he totally outclassed Liam Cosgrave, who, halfway through the contest, seemed to give up the unequal struggle, not appearing at rallies and developing a 'sore throat'. Though Jack Lynch crossed and recrossed the country, it was in no sense a barnstorming performance. It was totally different in character from the kind of electioneering which the party had favoured in the past and to which, in changed circumstances, it would return in the not too distant future. Lynch, endlessly gracious and deprecating in manner, did not seem the dynamic leader of men and, whether taking tea with nuns in the crimped, starched formality of the convent parlour or discussing sport in the smoke-laden, distempered air of the bars in country-town hotels after meetings, his deep-rooted charm and affability became the greatest political asset of the party.

Haughey, who in the past had so often been 'on the road' in the party's electoral interest, was this time a minor figure, fighting a contentious corner on his own, defending his record against the cyanide of Opposition disdain. He still had the resource of his own personal vote in his constituency to fall back on and invoked it midway through the campaign, on 31 May, in response to attacks against him by Conor Cruise O'Brien, which appeared in the pages of *The Times* and were then repeated in a BBC interview. 'That Dr Cruise O'Brien should go to the London *Times* to launch a piece of character assassination against a fellow Irishman is not surprising in view of that newspaper's role in Irish history. What has astounded many, however, is that the Irish national radio station should, within a matter of minutes, rebroadcast verbatim the vicious personal attack made on me by Dr O'Brien on BBC radio.'[1]

Despite the indication of some opinion polls, then somewhat simplistic in their format, the gathering of press, radio and television journalists attending a final joint press conference, in the Shelbourne Hotel on Monday 13 June sporting virtually all the ministers in the Government, felt that the Coalition would win a second term. On the Sunday before polling, 12 June, political correspondents taking part in a radio discussion which virtually concluded the coverage of the campaign were unanimous in their view that the coalition would be returned to power. And at that final election press conference the vast majority of those present who had been following the campaign and commenting on it came to the same conclusion. There were good reasons for this. The 1974 Electoral Amendment Act, which had substantially revised the constituencies, was thought to have favoured the coalition parties with a possible six extra seats. Despite errors of judgement made by Cosgrave and Donegan, among others, the general performance on the economy had been solid enough. And Fianna Fáil's performance in opposition seemed insufficient to counteract this balance in favour of a coalition which had successfully held together. Even the impressive election campaign run by Lynch failed to change this view and Lynch's own prediction about the outcome was modest. The party might, he said, get 77 seats, 'a number chosen, some thought, rather for its historical associations than as the end-product of electoral arithmetic, though that is what it probably was.'[2]

The result was an outright victory for Fianna Fáil, with a total of 84 seats, giving the party an overall majority of twenty seats. Fine Gael

[1] Statement issued by Haughey, 31 May 1977, and quoted in Ed. Mansergh, op. cit., p. 241.
[2] Basil Chubb, 'Analysis of Results', in Ted Nealon and Frank Dunlop, *Guide to the 21st Dáil and Seanad*, Dublin, 1977.

dropped from 54 to 43; Labour dropped two seats, to 17; and four independents were returned, Neil Blaney and Joe Sheridan being re-elected, Mick Lipper winning a seat in Limerick, and Noel Browne coming back into the Dáil from the Senate, where he had held one of the three Dublin University seats. The Fianna Fáil success was based on a 4.4 percentage increase in their vote, to 50.6 per cent, a result achieved only once before, in 1938.

From Haughey's point of view the outcome of the election was dismal. Lynch recorded the greatest electoral success in the State's history. He was comfortably in control, free to form what government he liked, to stay for as long as he liked and to be answerable to no party pressures on policy, on the extent of his leadership, or on the use of any individual, even one as able as Haughey. In Lynch's judgement Haughey would contribute best, from everyone's point of view, in a job that was demanding and absorbing, but detached from other ministries, and neither involved in the country's economy nor in the sensitive territories of security, Northern Ireland or foreign affairs. He was given his front bench job of Health, to which was added Social Welfare.

Cosgrave resigned the Fine Gael leadership and was replaced by Garret FitzGerald. Brendan Corish resigned the leadership of the Labour Party and was replaced by Frank Cluskey.

It was a watershed election in a number of different ways, the most obvious of these being that it spelt the end of prediction commentary based on guesses and hunches and the advent of opinion-poll fore-casting, precisely because the media had ignored the evidence of the opinion polls with a massive degree of complacency. From early in 1976 regular opinion-poll findings, which were available and pub-lished, indicated that a Fianna Fáil victory would be virtually certain. Instead, on the basis of the by-elections and as a result of the constitu-ency revisions, politicians and commentators stuck with the view that the coalition had been copperfastened into power.

The causes of victory and defeat, as always, are complex. Fianna Fáil had much in their favour. Above all, there was Jack Lynch's personality: at this stage in his political career, he towered head and shoulders above colleagues and opponents. His personal tour of the country, mammoth in scope, persuasive in the abilities he brought to it to appeal directly to ordinary people and compelling because of what he had gone through, was a major factor. So too was the meticulous and thorough planning of the campaign by the party.

It is often said, however, that governments lose elections, oppositions rarely win them. Not only did the coalition fight an anaemic campaign, particularly in the case of the Taoiseach, failing to combat the ideas and promises put forward by Fianna Fáil, it also had lost the confidence of the electorate in the single most important area of all – the economy – many months, if not years, before. Apart from the high piont of the Mayo West by-election, which coincided with the ending of the Tiede Herrema kidnap, the National Coalition had trailed Fianna Fáil in the opinion polls substantially because of economic policy. The parties in power had suffered the early setback of the 1974 oil crisis which followed the Arab–Israeli war and had had a destabilizing effect worldwide. Their economic policies, which included proposals for new forms of taxation on wealth, were at odds with the conservative disposition of the electorate and failed over the difficult middle years 1974–6 in assuaging doubt and fear. And this situation, aggravated by high inflation, tough budgetary measures and difficulties over creating new employment, lay behind a loss of confidence which was never effectively made up. It spread to traditional supporters of the coalition parties, with rural Fine Gael voters doubting the wisdom of the party's taxation proposals and with urban Labour Party supporters increasingly unhappy at the levels of unemployment and the rising tide of inflation.

The election was a watershed from the point of view of deeply held traditional loyalties. The result showed clearly that voters would respond on bread-and-butter issues and that the electorate, more urban-based, more volatile, would switch support much more readily from now on. Secondly, it was a watershed in that it demonstrated the effectiveness of clear, clean professionalism in politics. Fianna Fáil ran a very professional campaign; neither of the coalition parties seemed aware of the term.[1] Finally, it was readily apparent from the result that the manipulative re-drawing of the constituencies had rebounded against the coalition and that the lesson for the future was for a more independent approach to this problem. What no one could have known then was that this would be the last time a Fianna Fáil leader would win an outright majority. Jack Lynch had set impossible targets for a successor and the man most interested in this problem, Charles

---

[1] Garret FitzGerald, who succeeded Liam Cosgrave after the election, took immediate note of this lesson and set up a new party headquarters and effective constituency organizations and appointed proper professional staff to run the Fine Gael Party.

Haughey, came back into a Dáil where he was almost as marginal as he had been after his downfall. When the Dáil met early in July the hill he had to climb, in order to displace the party leader and take over, was of mountainous proportions.

CHAPTER XIII

LYNCH UNDER THREAT

A finder out of occasions; that has an eye can stamp and
counterfeit advantages, though true advantage never present
itself.

I T WAS CLEAR, during the first half of 1978, that Jack Lynch would
resign as leader well before the next general election, and quite
possibly before the elections for the European Parliament, scheduled for June of the following year. It was also clear that the two main
candidates in the succession would be George Colley and Charles
Haughey. Colley was undoubtedly the favourite. 'Charles Haughey's
biggest handicap is the question mark over his ability to deliver back
to deputies the votes which will keep them in their seats . . . a consistent number of grass-roots supporters of Fianna Fáil are prepared to
declare openly that they would not continue to support the party if it
was led by Charles Haughey . . . The phenomenon of such antipathy
is unusual in Irish politics, even more unusual in Fianna Fáil politics,
the party having a capacity, second to no other, for closing ranks on
all the deepest issues. It must weigh heavily in the minds of deputies.'[1]

It did weigh heavily in the minds of deputies. There was an acceptance
of the idea of a team led by George Colley, with Desmond O'Malley
and Martin O'Donoghue as his close associates, succeeding Lynch. And
throughout this first phase in office, following the 1977 landslide victory,
Haughey was on the sidelines, his only contribution to public political
life his timid and lugubrious performance in the introduction of legislation to control and regulate the availability of contraceptives. 'This
delicate, sensitive and fundamentally important matter', as he described
it to John O'Connell, whose own view was then more down-to-earth,
was an example of Haughey's pusillanimous approach on critical issues.[2]

[1] Present writer, *Irish Independent*, 6 May 1978.
[2] *Dáil Report*, 1 February 1978, col. 368. John O'Connell, a doctor with experience of
practising in the poorer parts of Dublin, was radical on most health issues. See footnote
below, on page 154.

The takeover of the party began in earnest during 1979. It was, for the Government, a year of misfortune which began with three major industrial disputes – national bus and postal worker strikes, and farmer protests against a two per cent levy on their income – and went on to the June elections for the European Parliament in which Fianna Fáil did badly, winning only 5 of the 15 seats. There were more deep-seated problems to be tackled, however. White Paper targets for the economy were not being met. Workers responsible for industrial relations strife were simply not amenable to the appeals and exhortations coming from Government ministers and from Lynch himself. And while some members of the Government were grappling with the workers, their complaints about taxation and the construction of a 'national under-standing', Desmond O'Malley was grappling with a second oil crisis. In such circumstances the introduction, by Haughey, of his Health (Family Planning) Bill at the end of February 1979, though it had taken close on two years to produce, seemed almost a minor triumph. The Bill – which he described as 'an Irish solution to an Irish problem' – was flawed and further amending legislation was subsequently required. But it was an agreed measure, endorsed by the Fianna Fáil Party,[1] and Haughey was seen as having accommodated the needs of the majority in the country.

Enmity still rankled between Haughey and Gibbons. And in the climate of disaffection which was developing, Gibbons played a curious 'stroke', voicing qualms of conscience about the Family Planning Bill and challenging the party Whip while remaining Minister for Agricul-ture. Neil Blaney and others were swift to point out the special relation-ship which Gibbons and Lynch enjoyed, since no action was taken against the former when he abstained on the vote. No one supported him. But he seemed almost to thrive on the isolation, leading people to speculate whether there was 'unfinished business' connected with Haughey and the Arms Crisis, words that still had to be spoken. 'I have thought out every eventuality of the decision not to support the Bill', he said at the time.[2] The most striking eventuality was his survival, in marked contrast with the succession of expulsions, including Blaney's, that had attended such action in the past.

---

[1] This was no small achievement. A previous Bill, introduced by the Cosgrave administration, had been defeated, notably because Cosgrave himself and his Minister for Education, Richard Burke, had voted against their own piece of Government legislation! The Fianna Fáil Bill was introduced in the Dáil on Wednesday, 28 February 1979.
[2] Interview with the author, May 1979.

But if there was a faint whiff from the hidden embers still smoulder-
ing five years on, there was a distinctly more active approach within
that section of Fianna Fáil sympathetic to the replacement of Jack
Lynch with Charles Haughey. It derived from a steady and quite rapid
decline in party confidence about future electoral prospects. To some
extent George Colley was responsible for this. His introduction in the
Budget, early in 1979, of the two per cent levy on farmers, designed
to ensure an across-the-board tax contribution as a demonstration that
they were paying their fair share, came without warning and provoked
anger in the party, particularly among rural deputies. Modifications
were sought and agreed, and deputies went back to their constituencies
to explain the scheme, only for it to be completely withdrawn. The
deputies' rage at this incompetence was aggravated sharply by the
reaction of urban workers, who engaged in massive demonstrations
against the PAYE system. At one stroke, it seemed, both urban and
rural voters had been alienated in substantial numbers. At one point
it was estimated that close on a million people were on the streets
demonstrating against taxation inequities.[1]

The blunder was critical to Haughey's succession prospects. Up to
this point, Martin O'Donoghue had been the dominant voice in economic policy and had strongly opposed the levy in Government discussions. But Colley, supported by Gibbons, forced the issue and got
his way. Backbenchers felt that they had been treated with contempt.
O'Donoghue himself was so annoyed that he asked Lynch to excuse
him from being present at meetings with the farming organizations,
when the modified terms of the levy were discussed and then when
its suspension was decided. Considered together with Gibbons's
behaviour, it seemed that Lynch had lost his grip; it seemed also that
the party was no longer democratically run, but had fallen into the
hands of a small oligarchy, less and less in touch with backbenchers
and the grass-roots. The lamentable outcome of the European elections and the miserable local election results of the same day, were
all too public the expression of disillusionment. Fianna Fáil support,
which in 1977 was over 50 per cent, dropped to 34 per cent, an
unprecedented low point and an irreversible setback for Jack Lynch.

He had decided by this stage to resign, but not until after his six-
month European Community presidency, which began on 1 July. It

[1] See Vincent Browne, 'The Making of a Taoiseach', *Magill*, January 1980. This is one of
the best accounts of the events in 1979 which led to Haughey's leadership victory.

was a kind of prison, that first Euro-presidency, preventing Lynch from addressing internal problems and from giving the Government a much-needed reshuffle. At the party meeting that followed the election result, there was no satisfactory response to backbench dismay and the many proposals on party organization and policy that were made. That evening the so-called Gang of Five[1] held its first meeting and began to plan for the replacement of Jack Lynch with Charles Haughey.

Up to this time there had been growing backbench discussion about the future of the party, though in the main it was inconclusive and disorganized. The focus now, after George Colley's misjudgement had led to electoral disaster, was that Haughey had the best prospects of winning a majority as leader. There was a growing conviction within the party that, notwithstanding the Arms Crisis, Haughey's general abilities would confound all his critics, once he gained power, and that he would be a better leader than Lynch. Those who held this view were still in the minority; but there were growing numbers, either in support of it or increasingly dissatisfied with the inaction of the current leadership. However, though it was the intention of Jackie Fahey and Thomas McEllistrim, with the help of Mark Killilea, Albert Reynolds and Sean Doherty, to organize for the succession of Haughey, their first moves specifically avoided this question. They planned a caucus meeting for immediately after that weekend, in order to get things moving before the summer recess. It was handled with admirable discretion, even secrecy. And the strict, self-imposed rule that there should be no discussion about the leadership. The state of the party and its future prospects were to be aired, and those who emerged as sympathetic to change would then be recruited for further action.

The conspiracy – for such it was – worked admirably and is described in some detail by Vincent Browne. 'The caucus was organized with magnificent calculation. First, no time was set, so that if there was a leak from the gang of five, the caucus could be called off without any loss of face. Then it was agreed that nobody should be seen to be calling the meeting – the word should be surreptitiously spread around the corridors of Leinster House among deputies thought to be generally sympathetic to the aims of the convenors. On the following

---

[1] The members were Jackie Fahey (Waterford, first elected 1965, and a parliamentary secretary 1970–3, but not reappointed in 1977), Thomas McEllistrim (North Kerry, first elected 1969, succeeding his father), Sean Doherty (Roscommon, first elected 1977), Albert Reynolds (Longford-Westmeath, first elected 1977), and Mark Killilea (Galway West, first elected 1977).

Tuesday, when the Dáil resumed, it was decided to hold the caucus meeting at 4 p.m. in the parliamentary party room and then, to lend a touch of ambiguity to the affair, the meeting was postponed to 5 p.m. The four – Killilea was late – simply went around the corridors asking their colleagues if they had heard there was a meeting taking place and if they knew what it was about.'[1]

The strategy worked. Jackie Fahey took the chair and imposed some kind of order on the wide-ranging debate, blocking any discussion on the leadership of the party, concentrating instead on its general lack of direction and of electoral appeal. Lynch heard of the caucus meeting and confronted it at the party meeting the following day, promising greater openness, more debate. Though the caucus held no further meetings – it would have implied non-acceptance of Lynch's assurances – the conspiracy continued. Its purpose became two-fold. There was never any doubt of the Gang of Five's commitment to Haughey as the next leader of Fianna Fáil. That had been present from the start. What now became of primary importance was to speed up the departure of Jack Lynch. There is irony in this. Lynch himself had decided to go after the six-month European presidency term ended, on 1 January 1980. He could not reasonably go before that. Nor could he announce his intentions so far ahead. But public disaffection within Fianna Fáil surfaced, aimed at achieving what was going to happen anyway, and inflicted damage in the process.

The conspiracy became more general. Sile de Valera,[2] Eamon de Valera's granddaughter, was drawn in by Jackie Fahey when she spoke at a function in his Waterford constituency. 'He had an opportunity of sounding her out there. She revealed deep disenchantment with Jack Lynch, notably on Northern policy, and she became deeply involved at an early stage.'[3] Northern Ireland policy had not been a notable issue of discontent among the Gang of Five. Nor had it been the subject of much debate at the caucus meeting or the subsequent parliamentary party meeting. Now it became central.

Sile de Valera made a speech in Fermoy, early in September, ostensibly designed to raise the republican issue, but in fact 'part of the

---

[1] Vincent Browne, op. cit., p. 32. Browne listed 33 deputies attending the meeting. He claimed in the article that 28 of them subsequently voted for Haughey in the leadership contest.

[2] Sile de Valera (b. 1954) was a teacher, first elected to the Dáil in 1977, and its youngest member. Her uncle, Vivion de Valera, was also a deputy.

[3] Vincent Browne, op. cit., p. 34.

general conspiracy to escalate tension within the party.'[1] The script was circulated on Thursday, 6 September, in advance of delivery the following Sunday. Lynch asked de Valera to let him see it on the Friday morning, read the script, pointed out certain passages which he described as not opportune in the current political climate in Northern Ireland, but did not wish to exercise censorship. This is her version. He later told the Dáil that he had asked her to withdraw it.

Central to what she said in Fermoy was the Fianna Fáil Northern policy requirement that Britain should make a declaration of intent to withdraw. This was not contrary to the party line, merely changing the emphasis. First enunciated in 1975, at Michael O'Kennedy's instigation, and retained by Lynch as part of the Northern Ireland policy 'package' through the 1977 general election and beyond, the pressure for a British declaration of intent to withdraw had spawned various versions and interpretations of the meaning of republicanism. As far as Lynch was concerned, such a speech by a backbencher was a hostage to fortune, not unlike the inaccurately quoted 'We shall not stand idly by' statement of August 1969.

The thrust of de Valera's speech was a general plea for the restoration of a more dynamic republicanism within Fianna Fáil. The burden of its content was more suited to a party in opposition and its hidden purpose was really to voice the frustration of a 'party in opposition' – the one within Fianna Fáil, trying to hasten the departure of Jack Lynch and to replace him with Haughey. She delivered it well; more importantly, she defended it well when it became the subject of a special meeting of the Fianna Fáil Parliamentary Party, in Leinster House at the end of September. In the meantime its impact had been quite out of proportion to its substance and had provoked widespread debate and discussion, both inside Ireland and abroad. One of the exchanges at the time was between Conor Cruise O'Brien and the former British Ambassador to the United States, Peter Jay, who had called for British Government support for a united Ireland. This, said O'Brien, 'unwittingly and unintentionally encourages the IRA to keep up its killings ... the message, as received by the IRA, is "OK, keep it up, boys, we're winning." '[2] O'Brien, who always chooses his words with care, had in mind the latest atrocities: the murders, by the IRA,

[1] Ibid.
[2] Interview with Conor Cruise O'Brien, BBC 'News at One' programme, Thursday, 20 September 1979.

of Earl Mountbatten, in Sligo, and of eighteen British soldiers near
Carlingford Lough, in Northern Ireland, the previous month.

At home, the Sile de Valera speech had a quite remarkable impact,
setting off a national debate on republicanism which filled the correspondence columns of the newspapers and led to endless debates on
radio and television. Inevitably, Lynch's authority as leader became an
issue in the debate. He blamed radio and television, and the press, not
without justification; but there were also problems deriving from his
elusive, relaxed style and his tendency to underestimate the attacks
against him.

There was clearly a leadership tussle in the making. Charles
Haughey's support was 'divided between two distinct groups – those
who support him as natural successor and those who would like to
precipitate his takeover of the leadership by putting pressure on Lynch
to stand down. This second group, numbering no more than ten deputies, is largely responsible for the heightening of every conflict within
the party to the level of "a leadership confrontation", and is ready to
interpret most things to the media in such colouring.'[1]

Lynch was upset. He could accept Sile de Valera's speech at face
value. But the distinct aura of orchestration and conspiracy made this
difficult. The party was being destabilized, virtually every issue traced
back to the leadership, and the possibility of recovery was becoming
increasingly remote.

Lynch had attended the Mountbatten funeral in London, on the
Wednesday before the Fermoy speech, and had then met Margaret
Thatcher for talks that embraced security. One of the changes agreed
between them was the introduction of an air corridor to facilitate better
Border surveillance. The story of this was leaked, first to Fianna Fáil
backbench politicians, then to the press; it was first published by
Michael Mills in the *Irish Press*. One of the Gang of Five, Thomas
McEllistrim, then tabled a motion for the parliamentary party meeting, on the grounds that Irish sovereignty was being infringed, and
this also appeared in the papers. On 7 November Lynch went to the
United States on an eight-day visit in his capacity as President of
the European Community. In his absence a further row developed,
this time involving another backbencher, William Loughnane, who

---

[1] Present writer, *Irish Independent*, Saturday, 29 September 1979, the day after the special
meeting of the Fianna Fáil Parliamentary Party. It was the day of John Paul II's visit to
Ireland.

described Lynch as a liar on the issue of air corridor assurances. George Colley, who, as deputy leader of the Government in Lynch's absence, was in charge, moved for his immediate expulsion.

It was a serious error of judgement. Admittedly, the Lynch faction – for so it had really become – was at the end of its tether and Colley had the support of all members of the Government with the exception of Haughey and Martin O'Donoghue. But the move was peremptory and handled in an autocratic fashion, provoking a much sharper reaction at the parliamentary meeting than had been anticipated. An attempt was made to postpone the consideration of the case against Loughnane until Lynch's return, since it was becoming increasingly apparent that Colley's motion would be defeated. In the end a compromise was reached, with Loughnane retracting his accusations against Lynch.

Charles Haughey lunched that Wednesday, 31 October 1979, in the Royal Hibernian Hotel. 'There he observed casually that Lynch and Colley had lost the party and it was only a matter of time before they were routed. He did a swift survey of his support within the parliamentary party and calculated that he had 35 certain votes and about 15 others leaning in his direction.'[1] He spoke with the confidence of a man who knew, not just the way things were going, but the way in which support had changed during the previous months. Quite how well informed he was about this, and from what stage in the progress of the conspiracy, has never been fully revealed. The contemporary view was that he did not become directly aware of the action being taken on his behalf until after the caucus meeting in July. With the benefit of hindsight a different view is entirely possible: that he knew and participated, though indirectly, through one or other of his supporters within the group. It is certain that immediately after that caucus meeting he discussed his own leadership prospects with members of the Gang of Five and, this being so, it is unlikely in the extreme that he did not then remain closely informed about everything that was done in pursuit of the leadership change he had been waiting for since 1966. It is splitting hairs to say that he was not part of the conspiracy, in the sense that he did not meet the Gang of Five, or involve himself in any of their debates or moves to gain support. He was the centre of it, the mainspring of action and the future guarantee of their positions within Fianna Fáil, for which they were risking a great deal.

That risk was at its greatest in the first half of November, when a

[1] Vincent Browne, op. cit., p. 36.

secret petition was drawn up and circulated among deputies who were judged to be hardline supporters of Haughey. It did not seek direct support for him, but was a commitment to support a motion for a change of leadership. Those approached were asked to sign not knowing who else had signed and more than twenty backed the petition. It greatly aggravated the distemper within Fianna Fáil.

Knowing by no means the whole story, but sensing the incipient climax in the matter of the party leadership (not helped, incidentally, by the fact that two by-elections in Cork were won by Fine Gael), I wrote an article in my newspaper that questioned Charles Haughey's suitability. I said that he lacked 'respect for citizenship and social order – that is, the capacity of a man to place the interests of the State before his own or his party's interests. . . . [he] is short on civility and maybe integrity as well. Led by [him] Fianna Fáil would lose the next election because effective and deep-seated reconciliation is not in his nature. There are too many question marks over Charles Haughey. He stalks the corridors of Leinster House, the silken predications of control and power emanating from his person. Yet nobody knows the nature of his republicanism and how it would manifest itself in terms of policy on Northern Ireland or a new attitude towards Britain. It would be more hardline than Jack Lynch's. But how? And to what purpose? And with what results? Nobody knows what the economic recipes would be. Nor whether they would work. As one writer has put it, "he prefers the attention of photographers to journalists." He has created an illusion and it is this: that, once the mantle of power falls upon his shoulders, he will then get it all together. But at what price?'[1]

The prophecy was accurate. Fianna Fáil did indeed lose the next election and in every general election after it they consistently failed to win an overall majority, let alone sustain the huge vote achieved by Lynch. But much more immediate was the understandably fierce reaction of Charles Haughey himself. It was, first, to threaten legal redress against the newspaper, and solicitor's letters were sent. Then he sought a retraction of the references to integrity. In order to achieve this, Dr John O'Connell,[2] acting as go-between, organized a lunch in the

---

[1] 'Politics and Politicians: Jack Lynch's Dilemma', *Irish Independent*, 17 November 1979.
[2] Dr John O'Connell (b. 1930) was a medical doctor and a Dáil deputy from 1965. A member of the Labour Party, he was a friend and admirer of Haughey's and was eventually persuaded by Haughey to join Fianna Fáil, though never made a minister by Haughey. Ironically, it was Albert Reynolds, after Haughey's resignation, who brought O'Connell into the Government and gave him the job he had sought since the early 1970s, the Department of Health.

Shelbourne Hotel for the three of us. It went extremely well until Haughey raised the issue of my article. I declined to withdraw anything, and O'Connell then intervened and suggested that discussion should be postponed to another date and the encounter ended.[1]

In the finely balanced situation which had developed after almost six months of secret moves to bring about the change from Lynch to Haughey, a direct attack of the kind I had mounted, which embraced the case against George Colley as leader, since he too would be divisive, needed urgent attention from Haughey. And the retraction was important.

When Lynch returned from the United States, Martin O'Donoghue advised him that a clear statement of his future intentions was needed, but that, if he decided to go, Colley would win the subsequent leadership contest. Lynch could not act immediately. There was a European Summit planned for 29 November, which he would have to host.

I pursued Lynch after his return from the United States for an interview. One of his close friends at the time was Gordon Lambert, the businessman and art collector, who had been giving Lynch press advice on how to combat the unpopularity surrounding him and the Government. I was granted the interview on the evening of Tuesday, 4 December, for forty-five minutes. Despite the pressures on him, and the fact that he was to broadcast for RTE immediately afterwards, he was relaxed, easy, confident. It was a background briefing, or discussion, not for publication. I expressed some of the misgivings that were the substance of articles I had been writing on Haughey, Colley, the uncertainty about the future and the generally disturbing sequence of events during the whole of 1979.

Lynch said it was his consistent practice not to attempt to promote or explain himself. He preferred his actions to be seen for themselves, without gloss. He felt that this placed him under a certain kind of handicap, but that this was his approach and he could not easily depart from it. He reminded me about Donogh O'Malley and his obsession with what the newspapers were saying, staying up until three o'clock in the morning to see what was being said about the Government and himself. He mentioned also 'meals which John Healy and Haughey used to have in the Shelbourne and Russell Hotels. I had to put a stop

---

[1] The solicitor's letters to the *Irish Independent* were withdrawn on 27 November. The editor, Aidan Pender, decided not to run an article on Haughey's republicanism, which I was then working on.

to that. I don't think John Healy has ever forgiven me.'[1] Referring to
the possibility of his deciding to resign, I suggested, as I had done in
an article the previous Saturday on the options facing him, that more
time was needed. He said he had read and absorbed my article. It was
the eve of the parliamentary party meeting. He thanked me for calling
on him and said: 'You're not to worry about tomorrow. I have decided
what I am going to do, and everything will be all right.'

The parliamentary party meeting was scheduled for the morning of
Wednesday, 5 December. An hour before it, after the Order of Business had been announced in the Dáil, with the customary and virtually
complete clearing of the whole chamber, I was sitting almost alone in
the press gallery. My eye caught that of Brian Lenihan, the only
member of the Government present at the time. He wrote a note and
sent it up with an usher: 'Jack is announcing retirement at party meeting 11.30. Brian.'

The statement that Lynch issued indicated that his decision to resign
midway through the Dáil term had been made before the 1977 general
election and reinforced after the local elections, in June, when he had
promised a reshuffle in the New Year, though not saying that he 'had
in mind of course that these Cabinet changes would involve my own
resignation'. Prompted by the results in the two Cork by-elections,
'associated with other recent events', and a feeling that doubts about
his intentions were creating public uncertainty, Lynch brought forward
his decision. He had spent thirty-two years in active politics, nine of
them as Taoiseach, thirteen as leader of Fianna Fáil.

[1] John Healy (1930–91) was a political journalist with *The Irish Times* and a former editor
of the *Sunday Review*. He wrote a well-informed weekly column under the name 'Backbencher', much of its inside information based on the relationship with Haughey and Donogh
O'Malley, until Lynch stopped the relaying of information.

CHAPTER XIV

PARTY LEADER AND
TAOISEACH

and then but now –
As if some planet had unwitted men –
Swords out, and tilting one at others' breasts
In opposition bloody.

AT HIS PRESS CONFERENCE on 5 December, Jack Lynch named
four possible contenders for the leadership, 'men whose shoulders were broad enough and whose minds were good enough'
to take on the task. They were George Colley, Charles Haughey,
Desmond O'Malley and Michael O'Kennedy. Later the same day Desmond O'Malley indicated that he would not be a candidate, but would
be supporting George Colley. It was the first mistake made by the
Colley faction. O'Malley allowed his loyalty to Colley to prevail,
despite a decided growth in support for his candidacy during the days
before Lynch's announcement and the possibility that his standing
would produce an important three-way split in the vote which would
then allow the position to be further examined. The reality was
that Michael O'Kennedy was very much an outsider and that no
one else would be likely to put their name forward, thus creating a
head-to-head contest between Colley and Haughey. The choice was,
therefore, between a new departure for the party and more of the same,
which simply brought the long-standing argument over the Colley–
Haughey confrontation to a climax. The party was set for a highly
divisive battle. With the injection of a third alternative, which would
also have been a new departure, a quite different outcome might have
resulted. But over-confidence on the part of Colley and his supporters
locked the two sides into a straight fight that distinctly favoured
Haughey.

It did so as a result of the skilful and protracted undermining of
Lynch which had gone on during the previous year. There emerged

lists of supporters of Colley and Haughey whose voting intentions were conceded by each side; these seemed to present an even matching between the two camps. This was all that was certain and served to conceal the intense rivalry which surrounded the remaining Dáil members of the parliamentary party who would decide the issue. An equally intense battle for their support then developed. The campaign was overshadowed by an atmosphere of unprecedented foreboding; the mood in Leinster House was laden with gloom. Haughey was greatly feared. Strange though it may seem, since he had been a central figure within the party for more than twenty years, he was feared as an unknown quantity. It was by no means clear what line he might adopt on Northern Ireland, but patently obvious that it would be different from Lynch's. There was the inescapable 'whiff of corruption', a leftover from Taca days, the 'kitchen cabinet' days of the 1960s, presided over by himself and Donogh O'Malley and evident in the aura of wealth and influence with which he surrounded himself. Most of all, there was the more recent fear deriving from the events of 1969–70: how exactly would his party and the country measure his respect for constitutional democracy in the event of his taking over as the country's leader? These were heavy fears to surround the candidacy of a potential leader in a contest now narrowing down to just two men.

On both sides the canvass for support was unevenly managed, and at times badly handled. It was not comprehensive and there was extraordinary complacency in both camps. Colley held the support of the overwhelming majority of the Government. Haughey did not even try to shift members who might otherwise have supported him and who were, in a sense, too senior, as full Government members, to be approached by anyone except Haughey. He sat much of the time in his office, believing that it was all over and that his victory was assured. His supporters were more cautious and continued campaigning to the end. Colley's mistake was to imagine that the solid support of the Government would sway many backbenchers towards him. He seemed unaware of the full extent of the backbench revolt which had been going on since mid-summer and which had generated levels of dissatisfaction and the desire for a major change of direction that were assuring Haughey of victory.

The following day journalists met Fianna Fáil deputies and tried to fathom the levels of support, the degree of honesty in the answers that were being given, and then compared notes. With many, the approach was straightforward enough: Ger Connolly, staunchly for Haughey; Ben Briscoe a Colley man; Michael Smith for Colley; Lorcan Allen for Haughey. Bit by bit a count was emerging.

Haughey claimed on the Thursday evening before the vote, which was scheduled for the morning of the following day, that he had 53 supporters. He asserted, 'My more conservative backers suggest 49.' He confidently annotated the lists which journalists carried around at the time, altering not just their claims, but his own as well. At one point, in the company of his closest supporters, Doherty, McEllistrim, Killilea and McCreevy, he was reported to have claimed 58 votes. 'Rubbing his hands, he had looked round the company for confirmation. . . . it was Doherty who, after a moment's mental arithmetic, laughingly commented on Haughey's estimate: "Do you know, you're the worst fucking judge of people I ever met".'[1]

Among Colley's supporters the prevalent feeling was one of exhaustion and defeat. Emerging from Leinster House Raphael Burke said he was still uncommitted. Then Ray McSharry came along. Always a stiff man and not given to idle chat, particularly not with the press, he paused and stood in front of the mixed group of people. He seemed tense and aloof, but clearly had something to say. After a pause, he spoke: 'I will be proposing Haughey for leader tomorrow.' And then he walked away. It was a statement which seemed to set the seal on the next day's vote.

The Friday election meeting in the Fianna Fáil Party rooms in Leinster House began mid-morning and attracted a strange medley of people, including figures from the Arms Crisis days, such as Captain James Kelly, John Kelly and Haughey's brother, Padraig. There were Fianna Fáil Party staff, the press secretary, Frank Dunlop, and a host of journalists. There were sharp contrasts in feeling; the predominant mood being a sense of doom.

Haughey won by 44 votes to 38. It was a remarkable victory. He had come back from the 1970 ruins of his political career, rehabilitating himself within Fianna Fáil and, with a wider public, recovering sufficient support and faith in his abilities for the early reactions to his victory to be generally favourable. It was no greater than that. 'The mandate given to Charles Haughey by the Fianna Fáil Party is a backbench mandate for change. . . . the force that gave him victory was one of dissatisfaction with the present team, with their policies, and

[1] Dick Walsh, op. cit., p. 141.

with the kind of determination they applied to them.... Charles Haughey is conscious of the extent to which ill is thought of him, and the extent of the expectation of bad things.'[1] The essential ingredient in this was self-interest. Beckbenchers worry about seats and about popularity. And it was their victory. At least, it appeared to be their victory. Within less than a month, as details of the leadership campaign were pieced together and then published, a rather different complexion was put on what had happened and what it would mean. 'For it was orchestrated by a handful of backbenchers who had schemed and connived for months previously to get rid of an administration which they believed would be routed at the polls in a few years' time.'[2]

Haughey was euphoric and at the same time bewildered as to what he should say about policy, and do about the construction of a new government. He gave an immediate press conference, surrounded by the backbenchers who had brought him to power. He assured the public of George Colley's 'total and fullest co-operation in my task', and said that he had been assured by Jack Lynch that all his vast experience as Taoiseach would be totally at Haughey's disposal. Colley subsequently denied that he had said anything of the sort. Haughey never once drew on the resources apparently offered by Lynch. Indeed, Lynch himself withdrew from Fianna Fáil affairs in a quite pointed way. He wrote to Haughey to tell him that he had asked Sean Browne, the Fianna Fáil Party chairman, not to arrange for any kind of presentation to him, on leaving office. The final paragraph of that letter read: 'As well as it being my own desire in this regard I am satisfied that it would be entirely inappropriate for the party to make such a presentation in the circumstances.' None was made. Lynch's departure as Taoiseach was clear-cut, an obvious severing of the normal ties of residual involvement. He felt betrayed, but he also felt guardedly sanguine about the future.

It was different for George Colley and the other members of the outgoing Government. The following Tuesday, Haughey was nominated as Taoiseach and announced his new Government. Four former ministers were dropped: Bobby Molloy, Martin O'Donoghue, James Gibbons and Denis Gallagher. Only one of the Gang of Five, Albert Reynolds, was given an appointment in the Government. The other members of the Gang of Five – Jackie Fahey, Thomas McEllistrim

[1] Present author, *Irish Independent*, 9 December 1979.
[2] Vincent Browne, op. cit., p. 22.

and Mark Killilea – were appointed as ministers of state.[1] It was not until the following March, when a further five junior ministers were appointed, that Sean Doherty was given office, as a junior minister in the Department of Justice. Colley remained deputy leader, but was moved from Finance to the Department of Tourism and Transport, an undoubted demotion, indicative of the need for a new start on the economy, with Michael O'Kennedy replacing him at the Department of Finance. Other new members of the Government included the first woman to be appointed to an Irish Government, Maire Geoghegan-Quinn, and Ray McSharry, Patrick Power and Michael Woods.

Haughey was severely constrained in what he did, or at least he felt himself to be so constrained, and he acted with a degree of caution which augured ill for the future. Colley asserted a triple veto over appointments. As a condition of serving in the Government, he insisted on being Tanaiste, or deputy to the Taoiseach; in addition he insisted on approving two key security appointments, those to the Departments of Justice and Defence. Haughey was genuinely worried about the past divisions in the party, despite the fact that he had been involved in the orchestration of those divisions, and he was worried about Fianna Fáil's capacity to hold together. He knew just how hard his supporters had worked to gain him the margin of votes required to become leader and was therefore more conscious of the evenly balanced forces for and against him. He was quite definitely there on approval, as it were, and would need to prove himself across the full range of policy and personal issues. He knew also, as the backbenchers did not, just how massive were the problems facing the country and how difficult it would be to turn the economy round and retain sufficient support nationally to win the next general election. In one sense, because of Haughey's previous history, the most difficult problem of all was Northern Ireland. A major factor in bringing him to power had been the resurgence of a republican conscience in the party. Yet he had no clear idea about how to construct a policy that would adequately satisfy the demands of the kind of wild idealism which had been expressed by Sile de Valera and was felt by many others. A week before the leadership election, on 27 November, John O'Connell reported asking Haughey what his new, positive policy would be on Northern Ireland, if he became leader after Lynch. 'Charlie said that he wasn't able to

---

[1] The title Parliamentary Secretary was replaced with that of Minister of State in November 1977.

put it into words. It was in his head [O'Connell pointed dramatically at his own skull] and he would only be able to voice it when he became Taoiseach.'[1]

George Colley was angered by the misrepresentation of his own position and more deeply distressed by the unfairness of what had happened in the months before Lynch's resignation. Growing evidence of a conspiracy suggested a serious decline within Fianna Fáil and reinforced him in his conviction that he had been right to impose the three conditions on his participation in office.

Up to the election, on Friday, 7 December, much of what had happened during the leadership battle had been experienced piecemeal and presented day by day in the newspapers. Though the atmosphere during those two days in Leinster House had a palpable sense of foreboding, and inspired much fear, there had been little or no public expression of this. The facts, as far as they could be ascertained, were reported from a campaign that swayed through party rooms, the bars in the Dáil, the offices occupied by the press, and the nooks and corners in which the vital business of lobbying and discussion took place. After Dáil business concluded on Thursday afternoon, the House seemed to be given over to Fianna Fáil and its inner workings, which were displayed in tense circumstances, and the two opposition parties departed to await the outcome. The following Tuesday, 11 December, it was their turn. Haughey came into the Dáil and was nominated Taoiseach. After the required formalities, he returned to the House to present his Government and faced there the full onslaught of Opposition criticism. It was a searing and unforgettable occasion. The public galleries were full, as were the Opposition benches. Every seat was taken in the press gallery. But the Government benches were entirely vacant, with the exception of Haughey himself. He had indicated to the party that the presence of any member, until the vote was called at the end of the day, would be unwelcome. And, entirely on his own, his face set in an inscrutable, blank expression, he listened to six hours of terrible comment: he was a politician of flawed pedigree; he had an overweening ambition; he was ambivalent about the IRA; he threatened to undermine the broad inter-party consensus on Northern Ireland; he was not fit to be the leader of the Government. In the public gallery his mother, his wife, his brothers and other relations sat witness to the seemingly inexhaustible catalogue of disapproval that flowed

[1] Private discussion with John O'Connell, Tuesday, 27 November 1979.

from one opponent or another. Sarah Haughey was reported to be 'greatly upset' at her son's ordeal.[1] It was an awful day for Irish parliamentary behaviour, painful and cruel, yet with many of the inevitabilities of a Greek tragedy. Haughey sat as though glued to his seat. Instead of it being the celebration of a victory, it was a spontaneous and relentless impeachment. Though the speeches were inevitably based on the past performance, his tormentors filled the air with forebodings about the future. For long enough he had waited in the wings, carrying his earlier ruin within him. Now, in power, he threatened to visit it upon the country which had previously rejected him and this generated powerful reactions among a very diverse group of politicians. The evening ended with a solid Fianna Fáil vote of 82, against the combined Opposition total of 62. But there was no jubilation. As with Pyrrhus, King of Epirus, the first battle had been so bloody that it had thrown a black shadow over Haughey's future fortunes which would never be successfully lifted. And the burden of that long day remained with him into the coming years.

George Colley's anger at Haughey's claim regarding a more comprehensive pledge of loyalty than in fact had been made was further reinforced by the very determined and outspoken reaction of the Opposition. He decided to go further and give a public dimension to the distance between himself and Haughey, and vent the widespread resentment which remained within the organization at the carefully orchestrated undermining of Lynch's position as leader during the summer and autumn. This, Colley claimed, had changed the basic rules about full loyalty and support for the elected leader. Colley's support was pledged only in respect of Haughey's efforts 'in the national interest' and to Colley's own role 'in his office as Tanaiste and as a member of the Government'. As far as party loyalty went, that was a different matter. 'We are in a new ball game ... The possibility of change at another time is always there.'

It was an extraordinary outburst and represented immediate grounds for Colley's dismissal from the Government, and his expulsion from the party. But the strategy for the issuing of this statement had been worked out in advance and depended not only on the support of other Government members – which had been obtained by Colley – but also on the fact that Colley, at a Government meeting held on Wednesday, 19 December, at 4 p.m., had told Haughey that he would be

---

[1] See 'The Haughey Years', *The Irish Times*, 31 January 1992, p. 12.

making his speech that night. 'Must you?' Haughey asked. And Colley replied, 'Yes.'

Haughey was pushed into a difficult corner by this. He was in no sense strong enough to take on the sizeable faction opposed to him. Moreover, there was considerable justification for what Colley had expressed. He had been misrepresented by Haughey; Haughey had been directly involved in disloyalty over a period of months and there was growing evidence – soon to be spelt out in extensive detail in *Magill* magazine – of a conspiracy which had directly undermined Lynch. Colley's own interpretation of loyalty – stuffy, perhaps, in the view of many commentators on his political style and its emphasis on high standards – was that the party required 'faithful adherence to one's promise, oath, word' to support the party leader up to and including the decision to resign. Colley had known of this decision two weeks before and had commenced his campaign then. Since Haughey had been campaigning, or supporting campaigns on his own behalf, for the previous five months, it was Haughey, not Colley, who had changed the rules about party loyalty within Fianna Fáil.

Haughey was the leader of a coalition. In some respects it was less cohesive than the National Coalition had been, since it had come about on a basis of disloyalty and it rested solely on a future eventuality: Haughey losing the next election. If he won, then Colley's vetoes would vanish, his claim to a position within Government would be reduced and Haughey's own strengths immeasurably enhanced for the future. If he lost, there would be a further leadership challenge, with everything once more on the table.

Colley could only make this clear at the outset. Once it had been stated, the collective will of the organization would demand that all members of the party, and in particular all Government ministers, pledge themselves to the work on behalf of the party that would lead to the winning of the next general election.

Under normal circumstances, the relatively even balance between the 44 votes achieved by Haughey and the 38 votes that went to Colley would have shifted, after Haughey's election, in his favour. But the intensity of the competition, the background of disloyalty and the misrepresentation of Colley's position, all worked against such a shift and left the balance hanging precariously over the party's future fortunes, like a clumsily balanced bucket over a partly open door. Haughey was in the unhappy position of having to retain his existing support by being the dynamic leader they expected him to be, and of having to win over, painfully, one by one, his opponents and critics in the party who felt that they had much to oppose and criticize.

Another's mistreatment that added to the sense of sourness and greatly distressed Lynch himself was the dropping of Martin O'Donoghue, who was himself shattered by Colley's defeat. He considered giving up politics altogether and immediately, but was dissuaded from this course of action on the simple advice, heard once before, that 'it's not over yet'. A pact had been agreed among certain of George Colley's supporters to the effect that, whatever the fate of individual ministers, those involved in the new Government would serve. And their motive was in part the belief that Haughey was 'dangerous, should have been blocked from the leadership, and should be got out as fast as possible'.[1]

[1] Notes from a meeting with George Colley, Wednesday, 19 December 1979.

CHAPTER XV

'A BETTER WAY
OF DOING THINGS'

Why, we have galls, and though we have some grace,
Yet have we some revenge.

AUGHEY BEGAN 1980, then, in the unhappy position of having to retain his existing support within the party, by being the dynamic leader his 44 supporters expected him to be, and of having to win over, painfully, one by one, the remaining 38, all of whom were his opponents and critics. He began well. His first target was the economy. On the evening of Wednesday, 9 January 1980, he addressed the nation on television and painted a bleak picture of its affairs. 'We are living away beyond our means. . . . we have been living at a rate which is simply not justified by the amount of goods and services we are producing. To make up the difference, we have been borrowing enormous amounts of money, borrowing at a rate which just cannot continue. A few simple figures will make this very clear.' He then proceeded with an excellent analysis of domestic income and expenditure, balance of payments, the appalling level of industrial unrest – 1979 had broken all records in Ireland in days lost through strikes and stoppages – and the measures that would be required to turn 1980 into 'the year in which we found a better way of doing things'. While the greater part of this address was directed at workers and employers, appealing for wage restraint and more co-operation, there were serious implications for economic strategy which would require a substantial change in direction by the Government itself. Most urgently it would mean major cuts in expenditure which would be in the Budget, now imminent, and which would have a fairly immediate impact.

It was a curious strategy to choose, even if correct in terms of the country's needs. It would have served Haughey well if he had been in a position to go early to the country, before the adverse effects had taken hold, and with the general approval for his actions which he received widely at the time. It would also have served if he had been given longer by Lynch before the next election. The course he set was undoubtedly the right one and in a better climate – which did not come until many years later – the kind of recovery programme on which he seemed to be embarking was a good long-term strategy. But it was only good after paying penalties in the present for prodigality in the recent past. And it soon became clear that Haughey was too nervous about his electoral prospects to risk the severity he was prescribing. He very quickly took fright. In fact he abandoned the 9 January strategy for Ireland's economy. And when the Budget was delivered at the end of that month, it was full of compromises. An innately generous streak in Haughey won through and he produced a number of popular provisions, among them almost prodigal taxation changes designed to win support from the PAYE sector, a favourable change in married couples' taxation law and a generous, across-the-board 25 per cent increase in social welfare. It was a blatant reversal of the January statement. It was only February and nothing had changed. We had been living beyond our means in January. We were living beyond our means in February. We are going to go on living beyond our means. That was Haughey's real message. He was engaged in a tussle between two options: being well-liked and being tough, ruthless, dynamic. The first option triumphed. Haughey was conceding that Budgets are about winning elections and in that light the 1980 Budget had a lot to recommend it. But if they are about the prudent, sober control of the nation's affairs in a period of widespread and growing instability, then a few items in it were not quite right.

Haughey, however, had by then already switched to something quite different – Northern Ireland. His speech to the Fianna Fáil annual conference, its Ard Fheis, took place on 16 February and was hammered out with great attention to detail in the weeks before delivery. Though the broad message was still to the effect that the country was living beyond its means, the remedies, which in January were harsh in their collective, unremitting severity, were softened in February into an either/or approach – *either* a cutting down in Government expenditure, *or* the increasing of tax revenue, *or* a balanced but selective combination of both; but not the full force of his original determined confrontation of the country's problems. Within a short month the decisions of January became the options and propositions of February. 'Hard decisions are called for, but because it is our duty to protect

and sustain the economy, and not to damage it, these decisions will
be taken on the basis of sound judgement and common sense.' Instead
of Government action on taxation, through budgetary strategy, the
Government instead set up a Commission on Taxation, thus deferring
the need for change.[1] As for public expenditure cuts, the expressed
need for this was in no way met. Nor indeed was any clear direction
defined for industrial relations, beyond the anodyne recipe of meetings
with employer and labour organizations to bring them closer together.
Essentially, Martin O'Donoghue's broad strategy remained in place.

But if this was the sorry outcome of Haughey's reconsideration of
the January rectitude, as far as the economy was concerned, quite a
different vitality was given to Northern Ireland policy at that first
Ard Fheis for Haughey as party leader. The revised approach on the
economy implied that he had already decided to work for his first
general election as leader and that his best chances would not be served
by the severe approach originally outlined. It was to be abandoned
and replaced with something more ambivalent and flexible. At the
same time he needed a high profile which would appeal to the people
and win him support. Those closest to him had used Northern Ireland
as a major factor in attacking Lynch's position and in bringing about
Haughey's victory. They had played the emotive republican card which
had been hidden up Haughey's mohair sleeve for many of his earlier
years. They could hardly take issue with his decision to place it now
on the table, even if some of them had reservations about the electoral
advantage of a 'solution' to the future of Northern Ireland, particularly
coming from a man about whom there were the deepest reservations
throughout the North, in both Unionist and Nationalist circles.

The 'solution' he offered was breath-taking in its political disdain
for the institutions of Northern Ireland – imperfect as they might have
been – and arrogant in its proposals. Northern Ireland had failed as a
political entity and a new beginning was needed. It could not be provided from within the Six Counties, largely because of this 'failure',
and would therefore have to come from Dublin and London. The two
sovereign powers, each with an interest in communities in the North,

---

[1] The commission, chaired by Miriam Hederman O'Brien, was appointed in March and
held its first meeting on 14 April. It worked prodigiously hard and produced five radical
reports on different aspects of taxation in as many years: Direct Taxation (July 1982); The
Role of Incentives (March 1984); Indirect Taxation (June 1984); Special Taxation (May
1985); and Tax Administration (October 1985). Very few of the recommendations were
implemented, either by Haughey or succeeding administrations.

each committed to an involvement, would come together 'to find a formula and lift the situation on to a new plane that will bring permanent peace and stability to the people of these islands'. The new plane was not defined, but the old recipe – of the British Government helping things to get started by a declaration 'of their interest in encouraging the unity of Ireland, by agreement and in peace' – was included in the speech. An old message was being deployed to herald a new departure.

It was immediately clear that necessity had governed this shift in policy. Lynch's relatively sound acceptability in Northern Ireland, itself inherited from Sean Lemass, had provided the foundation for the Sunningdale approach, which still lingered on, in a watered-down form which attempted to accommodate the fears of Unionists side-by-side with the aspirations of the Nationalist community. While Haughey was well able to sustain, and even to develop further, the ties between the Dublin Government and the main Opposition politicians in Northern Ireland – even if some of them were mistrustful of him – he had no chance of winning any kind of response other than utter rejection from the Unionist side. So he needed to go above the heads of the two opposed sides in Northern Ireland and come to an understanding with Margaret Thatcher.

They were a well-matched pair. In a curious way they were not unlike each other, and could even be said to have needed each other. Margaret Thatcher wanted solutions as much as Haughey. She was grappling with an economy just as perverse and difficult as the Irish one and with many of the same problems connected with industrial relations strife. Her political strategy included on its agenda the next general election and she badly needed a success in the kind of problem-solving which she presented as her own special strength. If that strength could be applied to the chronic and intractable problem of Northern Ireland, with the help of this new leader in the Republic, then she was not indisposed to co-operate, despite advice to exercise caution.

The summit meeting in May 1980, which was held in Downing Street, went well. Initially, Margaret Thatcher was guarded in her responses. In no sense did she reveal her own intentions on the North and, for this, her first meeting with Haughey, she steered much of the discussion away from details about the Six Counties and on to international questions, involving Europe, as well as defence and Irish neutrality. At least, Haughey implied that neutrality was involved because of the wide-ranging debate on international issues. He was disposed to put an expansive gloss on everything. He gave a press conference at the Irish Embassy in London immediately after the meeting which had little to do with the actual content of their talks and a great deal to do with his imaginative perception of what they might have implied or suggested. He expanded on his own aspirations and his willingness to meet whatever demands those aspirations required – a unique form of debate, but one which suited his nature. He emphasized that the Irish Government was prepared to go a long way in pursuit of a 'solution', though its nature had not been discussed. He responded to questions about security and defence with an expressed willingness to consider favourably an Irish commitment to NATO, or to some other kind of Western defence pact which would involve the abandonment of Ireland's neutrality. He even briefly considered, when the question was raised by one reporter, Ireland's return to the British Commonwealth, but then rejected it.

Privately, Haughey was both pleased and puzzled. He was pleased at the superficial success of the encounter. He and Mrs Thatcher had got on extremely well on a personal level. Haughey had brought with him an extravagant gift: an eighteenth-century Irish silver teapot. Their conversation had been intense but amicable. Department of Foreign Affairs officials confirmed the atmosphere of sustained energy; on previous occasions Irish heads of Government, going from Grosvenor Place to hold meetings in Downing Street, had often done so in a mood of gloom and 'frost', historical, psychological and social barriers often adding to the inevitable difficulties occasioned by the British never being as serious or well informed about Ireland as Ireland was about her powerful neighbour. In Haughey's case it was different. He had a great sense of himself as the central figure; he set higher store by atmosphere than by detail – though he always had an extremely good command of any brief prepared for him; and he was determined to ensure that the occasion remained warm, friendly and positive. He had, in fact, been close to despair in the run-up to the meeting, owing in part to Mrs Thatcher's hawkish answers in the House of Commons to questions about Anglo-Irish relations in respect of Northern Ireland. But he felt relief afterwards.

At the same time he was puzzled about what she might do about Northern Ireland in the future. He described Thatcher as 'a tough lady', who had gone over their joint communiqué word by word and had shown formidable grasp of detail. His own assessment was that she did not know what to do about the North and had no plans.[1] To a considerable extent this was to Haughey's advantage, since it gave him nothing to disagree with, and the warmth and success of the encounter clearly laid the foundations for a second summit and further moves forward.

Fianna Fáil were not too pleased. Haughey expected a certain amount of criticism on the republican side. In fact it was more broadly based than that. He had, in his press conference, indicated a number of possible policy changes which had in no sense been discussed by the Government and could well prove politically embarrassing. The most obvious of these was neutrality. Criticism was inconclusive; the general view was that the success of the talks, the undertakings by the two leaders to meet again and the wide range of options about Northern Ireland which might arise, precluded any strong reaction against the party leader. This stood to his advantage and he was quick to build on it through the summer, as the second summit, planned for December, approached. But in the meantime there was a problem.

Haughey was much more concerned about the forthcoming issue of *Magill* magazine, which was to contain a detailed examination of the 1970 Arms Crisis, based in part on the Berry Papers.[2] An earlier issue, in January, had given a careful and well-researched account of the conspiracy that had brought Haughey to power and this had been much more damaging to him than his supporters had reckoned when they agreed to divulge some of the details behind the events of June–November 1979. What was now promised seemed to threaten Haughey's position more seriously, since an exclusive 'inside story' was looming, centring on the private papers of a key civil servant at the time. As far as Vincent Browne, the editor of *Magill* and the author of the articles, was concerned, it was probably the most important piece of journalism he had so far undertaken and it ran into severe problems over printing and distribution. The Arms Crisis sections in the magazine had to be printed outside the country and there were serious threats of these being impounded. He also had to contend with problems within his own editorial board. Among its members was

---

[1] Interview with the author the day following the summit, 22 May 1980.
[2] The issues of *Magill* for May, June and July extensively detailed the events of June 1970 and led to a debate in the Dáil. They are referred to in the relevant earlier chapters dealing with that period.

Cecil King,[1] the former British newspaper editor and publisher who had retired to Ireland. He felt that Browne was not taking sufficient notice of libel risks in what he was publishing. He also felt unwilling to be directly involved in the deliberate antagonizing of Haughey.[2] There were some indications that Haughey considered using the Official Secrets Act, but it was not in his nature, and he was advised against so doing. There was even the suggestion – also rejected – that Haughey should himself give an extensive interview about the Arms Crisis 'and his place in it', in order to clear the air and remove residual suspicions.

Haughey misjudged the impact of the *Magill* articles, which was immense, and badly handled the issue in the Dáil. A short, sharp debate, offered by the Government and controlled by the Government – as had been Lynch's method of handling the Opposition at the time of the Arms Crisis itself – would have allowed Haughey to deal with his opponents, who sought to raise the matter and use it against him, and also his own party, whose covert opposition was part of the grinding mill of general suspicion which surrounded him during the summer of 1980. But he chose to block that option. The debate itself, which Dr Noel Browne[3] had pursued most strongly, was agreed, but was then scheduled for October.[4] There was every indication that Haughey would remain silent, that Gibbons would repeat his basic Arms Trial argument and that Lynch and O'Malley would reiterate their statements of the time, reinforcing their positions and actions. And if they had done so, all well and good – it would have been an end to the matter, even though it would not have resolved it. Everything would have remained as before. But putting it off had two bad outcomes: it led to dismal expectations, sustained through the summer; and it also meant that the Dáil debate, when it eventually took place during

---

[1] Cecil King (1901–88), whose mother was a Harmsworth, was a newspaperman throughout his life and the former chairman of the International Publishing Corporation and the Reed Paper Group.

[2] King resigned in late May. I was also on the board of *Magill* and, though for rather different reasons, also resigned.

[3] Noel Browne (b. 1915) was first elected to the Dáil in 1948, when he became Minister for Health on his first day as a deputy. He had a chequered career after that, spending some years as a member of Fianna Fáil in the 1950s, then joining the Labour Party. He was a member of the tiny Socialist Labour Party from 1977 until he retired from politics at the end of 1982.

[4] It eventually took place at the end of November, just over two weeks before the second Haughey–Thatcher summit meeting.

the final week of November, overshadowed the second Haughey–Thatcher summit.

The shadow so cast extended beyond the material issue of the Arms Crisis, which after all was history, and into the territory of answerability. And the Opposition parties, together with Dr Noel Browne, who had been the prime mover of the debate, performed well, and used the occasion to demonstrate a high degree of solidarity and a high Dáil profile, with many participating and with the unusual spectacle of well-filled benches. There was a moderately good turnout on the Fianna Fáil side of the House, not so much to pick up answers from the principals – Lynch, O'Malley and Gibbons kept their counsel – but to demonstrate personal independence from the attempted orchestration of the occasion by Haughey. He had the Government side represented by the Minister for Justice, Gerard Collins. But Haughey himself did not speak.

The Opposition were grappling with Haughey's elusiveness. Their interpretation of democratic answerability centred on the Dáil. That was where challenges and questions were at the heart of political life. His interpretation was that democracy was a pact between himself and the people of Ireland. All he needed to do was to win *their* approval and he could ignore his political opponents. They were acutely aware of this strange formula and pressed for its reversal. A nursery jingle provided an epitaph to the Arms Crisis debate:

> The other day upon the stair
> I met a man who wasn't there;
> He wasn't there again today;
> I wish that man would go away.
>
> It's no good wishing, on the stair,
> About the man who wasn't there,
> That, if you wished he'd go away,
> He'd go. My friends, he's there to stay![1]

Through that summer the prospect of this debate had hung over Haughey, and with it the clear and depressing picture of a party

---

[1] I quoted the jingle, adding a second stanza of my own for good measure, *Irish Independent*, 29 November 1980.

divided, unable to grapple firmly with a growing crisis in public confidence as the various key problems remained unsolved.

Those problems grew in magnitude and proliferated in number during the remaining months of 1980. It was as if Haughey had on his fingers a pernicious kind of glue, so that everything he touched, with the intention of resolving it and handing it on, became stuck. He had responded in his choice of ministers, on his election, to the balanced division of the party between himself and George Colley. But he had, in several important areas, chosen badly. In dropping Martin O'Donoghue he had signalled an end to serious planning. At the same time, he was personally committed to planning – of a broad, imprecise kind – and determined to construct it himself. He had retained as Minister for Labour Gene Fitzgerald, a Cork deputy who had held the position through the appalling industrial relations experiences of 1979, but then did not hesitate to usurp the latter's role when the issue was major, as in the case of the National Understanding hammered out between Government, trade unions and employers. He made a habit of intruding on ministerial territory, more or less at will, though usually when the issue was either big or attractive, and this was undoubtedly disruptive. Of course, as Taoiseach, he had the right and duty to help to determine and indeed to interpret the major direction of Government policy, but he was not a particularly good judge of men, or of women – as Sean Doherty had pointed out in colourful language a year earlier – and his ability to forge a team and deliver the dynamism so urgently required by his supporters was beginning to look threadbare.

He was committed to a reshuffle. Ireland's European commissionership, held by Richard Burke of Fine Gael, was due to end on 1 January 1981, and Michael O'Kennedy was to succeed. But this was poor timing for Haughey. The need to keep open the option of an election in the spring or summer of that year (though it was not constitutionally necessary until the summer of 1982) meant that sweeping social and economic changes – which might just have been possible in mid-1980 – were ruled out. Instead, he sought short-term and attractive solutions or 'strokes', such as his dramatic descent on the Federated Union of Employers, in their offices in Baggot Street, to conclude the National Understanding, in late September.

But his big triumph was the December Summit, in Dublin Castle, with Margaret Thatcher. Building on his successful May meeting in Downing Street, Haughey set enormous store by this follow-up event, the drama of which was heightened and overshadowed by the first of the H-Block hunger strikes. The two leaders were accompanied by teams in the talks.[1] But from Haughey's point of view the most crucial moments were those he spent alone with Margaret Thatcher. He over-sold the encounter. Out of it he constructed a picture of private agreement which he presented later as involving 'constitutional' change. He did this with great subtlety, never actually using the word, but inferring it by gesture, so that journalists attending the briefing, which took place after the main press conference, wrote to the effect that constitutional change in the status of Northern Ireland had been discussed. It had not.[2]

The communiqué did, however, indicate some important achievements, with commitments for closer collaboration between Dublin and London, in respect of the North, giving Haughey exactly the kind of platform he relished. There was an inner, secret core to the Summit, which neither leader, for obvious reasons, sought to lay bare. From it Haughey extrapolated exciting suggestions. There had been agreement that there existed a 'unique relationship between the two countries'; the two leaders had expressed themselves willing to examine 'the totality of relationships within these islands'; there were to be 'joint studies'; 'institutional structures' were going to be examined; there would be 'measures to encourage mutual understanding'.

Haughey made a feast of this unexceptional but emotive fare. He claimed that the joint studies were not only new, but would be pursued 'on a different plane than [sic] anything that has gone on so far'. No limit was set on the institutions which might be established. There was some justification, as there always is, for claiming that the encounter had been 'historic' – all such encounters, by their very definition, are the stuff of history – and that the Northern Ireland problem, in the eyes of the two sovereign Governments, 'is now firmly on a new plane'. He concluded the press conference with very positive claims: 'I would first take today's meeting on its own merits, as a very successful

[1] Margaret Thatcher had Lord Carrington (Foreign Secretary), Geoffrey Howe (Chancellor of the Exchequer) and Humphrey Atkins (Northern Ireland Secretary) with her; Haughey was accompanied by Brian Lenihan (Foreign Affairs) and Michael O'Kennedy (Finance).

[2] Haughey gave a general press conference, attended by Irish and international journalists. He followed it with separate interviews and briefings. One of these was for political correspondents. I was a commentator and had been excluded by my colleagues from these briefings. My own information, partly from the British side in the talks, indicated that constitutional matters had not been raised and I wrote an article challenging this perception.

meeting, a significant meeting, a constructive meeting, a meeting which in my view had brought very considerable political movement, forward political movement, into this type of situation of Northern Ireland.'[1]

But what stuck in people's minds, in the following days, were the hints and suggestions, fostered by Haughey himself, that 'constitutional' change was discussed. This could only mean one thing: that the issue of some kind of movement by the British on the future constitutional status of Northern Ireland had been raised. Such a development, if true, would serve Haughey as an invaluable answer to his party. But was it true? If it proved so, then it might even provide him with a central plank in an election platform. He certainly needed one and it had to be something other than the economy, in which he had already made a much-criticized U-turn. Though any pundit worth his salt would have said that Northern Ireland was not serious enough, or central enough, to serve throughout the running of a three-week campaign, it could well have served in Haughey's unique situation.

It was not to be. The Dáil descended on the issue of 'institutional' versus 'constitutional' change on the following Tuesday, 11 December, when it debated the outcome of the Summit, and there was a sufficient measure of outrage among senior political commentators to force Haughey into denials of what he had originally claimed. The ebullient atmosphere which had immediately followed the talks was replaced by a very negative, and at times acrimonious, debate about details, with Haughey himself retreating into an almost exclusively negative mode. He denied that he had used the word 'constitutional'; he ruled out the possibilities of federal or confederal solutions for the North. He repudiated any idea that the word 'breakthrough' had been used to describe what he and Margaret Thatcher had achieved. And he concluded by referring people rather curtly to the communiqué, which, he said, was 'precise and meticulous'. Yet again, he was indulging his own unerring capacity to overstate his case. As on previous occasions, it was forcing him to spend energy in retracting and rephrasing his claims about what had happened, what had been going on and what it meant. And this, in his own mind, had started out as a central support for the election he was planning for early 1981.

[1] Verbatim statement from press conference, Dublin Castle, 8 December 1980.

CHAPTER XVI

THE STARDUST FIRE

It makes us, or it mars us; think on that,
And fix most firm thy resolution.

HAUGHEY WAS an unlucky man. Throughout 1980 he had been setting in place the dominoes which, with just one little push, would all fall into place and give him victory in the vital general election which would confirm him in power, and unshackle him from the constraints under which he had been operating as a leader, still in debt to Jack Lynch for the comfortable majority of twenty. Those dominoes included the economy, generous budgetary provisions and the elusive but seemingly impressive relationship forged between himself and Margaret Thatcher. Early in 1981 the Government produced a curious document called 'Investment Plan, 1981'. In reality it was simply the capital expenditure programme for the year, usually brought out in advance of the Budget, and one of the final documents governing the traditional financial resolutions, the Budget Speech and then the Finance Bill. On this occasion it was dressed up in manifesto clothing and announced with great publicity. And when the Budget followed, on 28 January, it bore virtually no relationship at all to the economic situation which had been so perceptively analysed exactly one year earlier. Haughey gave a confident, positive speech in the debate that followed, laying down a broad and comparatively painless strategy of using economic growth to bring the nation's economy 'through this current deep recession as safely as possible'. To do so required 'productive investment' – hence the 'Investment Plan, 1981'. A secondary target was the protection of the living standards of the under-privileged. Thirdly, and least clearly explained, there was to be a restructuring of public finances. The country had certainly come a very long way since the brief agony flashed before its eyes the previous year.

It was Haughey's intention to use the Fianna Fáil Ard Fheis in

the Royal Dublin Society's largest hall, in Ballsbridge, as a launching
platform for a general election. And he threw everything into it. The
normal allocation of ten conference tickets, issued from party headquarters in Mount Street to each deputy and senator, was augmented,
in 1981, by a further *thirty* tickets from the Taoiseach's own office
'and who can say how many more have gone elsewhere from that busy,
swollen hive of activity?'[1] Haughey had left all options open, but had
created a climate favourable to an early poll.

This, the fiftieth Ard Fheis in the party's history, was going to be
the biggest and the best. And a mood of excited anticipation heralded
this annual hosting of the organization, as delegates poured into Dublin
on the evening of Friday, 13 February. It was an inauspicious date,
arguably of greater significance in Haughey's fortunes than any other.
For that night a dance was held in the Stardust Ballroom, in his own
constituency of Dublin North-Central. It ended in an inferno in which
forty-eight young people died. And when Fianna Fáil delegates gathered on the morning of St Valentine's Day in the Royal Dublin
Society, after two postponements, it became clear that the whole conference would have to be cancelled. With it went an early election
and, with the whole carefully crocheted texture of planning to that
end coming unravelled, Haughey's political prospects seemed daily
more bleak.

Worse was to follow. Not only did the Stardust Tragedy produce a
great deal of heartbreak, linked with unwelcome criticism of fire-safety
lapses; it also provoked in Haughey reactions which disturbed the
Opposition. He handled the Dáil responses to the fire badly. In a sense
this was understandable. The event had been responsible for wrecking
his chances of an early election, on which he had planned for so long
and with such care. In the process, of course, he had prejudiced his
chances on the longer-term options. Moreover, the more that came
out about the fire the worse it all looked.

Much more was to go wrong. Opposition pressures rapidly built up
as the perception of a still-imminent early election sank in. Garret
FitzGerald and Frank Cluskey, despite marked differences in their
political styles, worked well together, so that Haughey was forever
looking from one to the other, like a spectator on the centre court at
Wimbledon, trying to anticipate the source of the more aggressive
shots – being directed not at each other but at him. They came on all

[1] Present author, *Irish Independent*, 14 February 1981.

fronts: the Budget, Northern Ireland, internal Fianna Fáil divisions, Dáil performance, answerability, even the prospect of a new 'Farmers' Party' as a result of the drop, by 50 per cent, in farm incomes. Frank Cluskey, a tough Dublin trade union official before becoming leader of the Labour Party, identified the heart of the matter, and the main source of public suspicion, in his speech on the adjournment of the Dáil for Easter: 'He regards the Dáil as something to be at best tolerated. If he can avoid having to come in here and face up to the normal responsibilities of a Taoiseach in a parliamentary democracy he will take every opportunity to do so . . . The Taoiseach's term of office has been distinguished by one thing more than any other, his evasiveness. Everything has come under the heading of confidentiality and secrecy. We have this with Mrs Thatcher, and we now have it with the Stardust people. Every time a legitimate question was asked in the House and it was politically difficult and embarrassing, the Taoiseach used one of two tactics. He jumped behind procedure, or he said the matter was confidential. The confidentiality is over, and the bit in the bunker is over, because whether the Taoiseach likes it or not, the time has come when he will have to face the Irish electorate. He certainly will not escape the wrath of the Irish electorate.'[1]

Stardust had been particularly difficult for Haughey, partly because of it being in his own constituency, but largely as a result of it throwing out the most carefully laid plans for the general election. But Haughey then made it far worse by indulging in precisely the kind of secrecy to which Cluskey had referred, and doing so in circumstances that were extremely ill-judged. He took direct charge of the negotiations with the Stardust Relatives' Committee and gave them undertakings which he refused to divulge to the Dáil. He claimed that this secrecy was part of an agreement between the committee and either himself or the Government (he was generally speaking, at this stage, as though the two were synonymous). There was no such agreement. Haughey claimed in the Dáil, 'I gave an undertaking . . . I would not publicly discuss any of the other matters which were discussed at that meeting.' A detailed record had been kept, however, and contained no such reference. Nor did the committee want it. The fact was revealed by Dr Noel Browne and was pursued energetically in the Dáil by him and by John Kelly, the former Fine Gael Attorney General. What came out was increasingly embarrassing. Haughey had given lavish

[1] *Dáil Report*, 9 April 1981, col. 277.

undertakings to the relatives about distress and compensation payments, about their legal costs in any inquiry. He had promised a memorial and a youth or community centre. And he had wanted to keep it all secret. The comparison was drawn between secrecy over Stardust and secrecy about what was discussed at the December Summit; either too much, or too little, had been said, and in either case the concealment of the truth had a political motivation that was suspect.

Then came a more direct challenge to Haughey's supposedly magical touch. On 1 March, in the Maze Prison, a second and much more determined hunger strike was started by Provisional IRA prisoners. If the 'unique relationship' between Britain and Ireland, and the special bond between Haughey and Margaret Thatcher, meant anything at all, it would provide a solution to the issues on which the H-Block hunger strike was based. These were complex, but in essence amounted to a set of five conditions which would give the hunger strikers noncriminal status. They already had it, in the sense of being known members of a para-military organization and being under special security control. But they were seeking the right to wear their own clothing, associate together and operate as 'prisoners-of-war'. There were no circumstances in which the British could allow this; there were no concessions which Haughey was in a position to obtain; and the limited scope of his Northern Ireland achievement was further exposed.

But it was worse than that. A legitimate admiration for the remarkable personal courage of the hunger strikers, in going, one by one, to their deaths in horrifying circumstances, was countered by memories of other deaths and by very serious reservations about how far sympathy could and should extend. This was particularly the case within Fianna Fáil and, when Bobby Sands died, his funeral, on 13 May, provoked legitimate questions: should there be votes of sympathy at county council or local government meetings?; should people be advised to close premises? The Fine Gael and Labour Parties were unequivocally opposed to such partiality in the face of so many other deaths. But Fianna Fáil was more deeply divided than it had been in ten years. Perhaps as many as twenty-five members were what is called 'staunch republicans'. At the time they would have looked towards Sile de Valera as their 'voice' and they wanted a strong stance to be taken by Haughey, in fulfilment of the view they had of his equally strong republican sympathies. About the same number were of the opposite persuasion. One deputy seemed to express the dilemma better than the rest. He was Joe Farrell, the oldest sitting member, who had been ten years old at the time of the Easter Rising and who came from the Border constituency of Louth. He told the Fianna Fáil parliamentary party meeting that the party had been founded 'by men who stood up for things'. The party should not be afraid of the Bobby Sands situation. People had come to him looking for support for republican prisoners in the North. But he had told them: 'Fianna Fáil has nothing in common with what is being done in the name of republicanism today in Northern Ireland.'[1]

The sombre tone of Stardust and the Maze Prison hunger strikes was not unrelieved by lighter moments, even if the leitmotif seemed always to be the same, that of pursuing Haughey in order to get answers out of him. When Haughey was successfully pinned down, the revelations tended to be embarrassing and his claims to seem almost humorously inadequate. One such cross-examination resulted from the issue of neutrality. When it had first surfaced, in May 1980, after the Downing Street Summit, that Haughey had more or less put all matters on the table with Margaret Thatcher, including Western defences and Ireland's possible participation, there had been rumblings within Fianna Fáil, as well as the other parties. With Haughey continuing to vaunt the second summit in Dublin Castle beyond levels that could be regarded as realistic, the Opposition pushed for clarity with a debate on neutrality. The auspices were not good. The Labour Party put down a motion which was then replaced by a Government motion confirming 'the principles which have guided the defence policy of the Government'. To this Fine Gael put down an amendment calling on the Dáil to confirm that there was no defence pact within the current Anglo-Irish discussions, to which the Labour Party then added a reaffirmation of Ireland's neutrality.

Again, Haughey had not fully informed the Government of what had taken place between himself and Margaret Thatcher. If other ministers were to defend what they did not understand, then there was only one way out of the chaos and that was to introduce more chaos. This was admirably achieved by the Minister for Foreign Affairs, Brian Lenihan, who, in a brilliant piece of knockabout music-hall virtuosity, at the very end of the debate, managed to confuse and block discussion, and even to block the division at the end. There was this visible purpose, and a hidden purpose as well – namely, to warn Haughey, on

---

[1] Present author, Politics and Politicians: 'Special Irish Answer: Silent Leadership', *Irish Independent*, 9 May 1981.

behalf of the Fianna Fáil Party, that he was moving too fast and committing himself and them to too much. Lenihan, who had himself been closer to the talks than anyone, came as near as he could to contradicting Haughey's claim that defence issues had formed part of his second summit meeting with Thatcher. 'Defence arrangements would be the last matter to be discussed,' Lenihan said, and Anglo-Irish relations were a long way from that.

The country went into the 1981 general election in a state of confusion about almost everything. From Haughey's point of view the most damaging of his actions was to confuse his own party. He had been playing his cards so close to his chest for so long that he had forgotten what they were. And of course no one else knew. He confidently placed Northern Ireland at the top of his list of priorities. But when deputies and aspiring candidates went out to campaign, they found a quite different set of priorities on the doorsteps around the country. Unemployment was up. Inflation was running at 21 per cent. The balance of payments crisis had deepened. None of Haughey's economic targets had been achieved. And the economists for whom he had such disdain were united in their condemnation of the mismanagement that had caused the country's plight. Frank Cluskey and Garret FitzGerald led the Opposition into the campaign on these issues, which were essentially the doorstep issues, and they made no specific pre-election pact on coalition. The main difficulty for them was defining what it was that they were attacking. Was it the old Fianna Fáil economic policy, under Jack Lynch, between 1977 and 1979? Was it the policy which had replaced that one, in January 1980? Or was it the later and much-altered 'Investment Plan, 1981', which constituted Haughey's electoral platform?

Both FitzGerald and Cluskey ran good campaigns, which, while emphasizing economic issues, managed also to dismiss Haughey's attempt to use the Northern Ireland problem for electoral purposes. Fine Gael did much better than Labour.

The election had its lighter moments. Among them was the Frank Kelly song, 'Learnin' to Dance for Fianna Fáil':

> Four long years they spent in government,
> Four long years doin' nothin' at all;
> Four long years they spent in government,
> Learnin' to dance for Fianna Fáil . . .

Another song made popular during the campaign was a ballad to a less traditional tune, with the refrain 'Arise and Follow Charlie'.

There was no direct television debate between Haughey and Fitz-Gerald. Instead, a panel of journalists interrogated all three party leaders in a studio discussion. And all three did better than their interrogators.[1] The journalists were agreed about the relative merits of the political leaders, and in respect of Haughey this amounted to a judgement of his considerable ability, flawed by an innate distrust of the media, which was quite absent in both Cluskey's and FitzGerald's relationships, the latter in particular getting on extremely well with radio and television interviewers and with the press. Haughey's problems with journalists were inextricably mixed up with his desire to orchestrate their reactions to him and an apparently inexhaustible capacity to change and reorganize his views. It was summed up by Vincent Browne, commenting on the debate: 'Straight away Mr Haughey told a whopper – stating that the reason he changed tack on economic priorities in the middle of 1980 was the 80 per cent increase in the price of oil. . . . the increase had taken place the previous year . . . I let him get away with this . . . I could never nail him down on the astonishing about-turn on economic policy he made within six months of taking office.'[2] The panel was agreed on the confidence, even enthusiasm, of Haughey and his coolness. Browne described this as 'a marvellous example of self-discipline, which is a central feature of his character'. Paul Tansey wondered if he was as relaxed as he looked. Haughey, leaving the RTE studios, remarked on the fact that he had not lost his temper.

In that same election there emerged a figure who was to assume some prominence in Haughey's future political career. This was P. J. Mara, a businessman, who had been actively involved in political affairs in Haughey's own constituency since 1964. He was intensely loyal to Haughey, and Haughey valued loyalty above all else in those around him. Mara's strength within Fianna Fáil had been extended by his appointment to a key organization committee of the national executive in 1978 and he had been involved in Haughey's moves to take over the party leadership the following year. He became vice-chairman of

[1] The four journalists were Vincent Browne, Michael Mills, Paul Tansey and the present author. Brian Farrell, of RTE, chaired each session.
[2] 'How We Bored the Nation', *Magill*, 14 June 1981. The four journalists involved all commented briefly on the debates.

the committee after Haughey succeeded Lynch, and this gave him a controlling influence in constituency affairs.

Haughey was defeated by his own obsession with power. His timing, which should have directed a measure of concern towards resolving real problems faced by the economy, or bringing about real change in Anglo-Irish relations over the North, was directed exclusively towards electoral advantage. He exerted no real discipline within his party. He defined nothing for them, in policy terms, and left them puzzled and bewildered. He tolerated indifferent levels of loyalty. He operated as though he was the Government, taking decisions and making agreements without prior consultation, which was bad, and then without subsequently informing his colleagues, which was much worse. He analysed the economy correctly, at the outset, from the country's viewpoint, and adopted correct solutions. But when he saw that these were less attractive from the point of view of electoral success, he abandoned them and substituted more ameliorative measures and targets. Once he had done this he allowed himself to make matters far worse, and the summer of 1980 became what Vincent Browne described as 'the nadir of his brief tenure in office': 'He engaged in a breathless series of public relations gimmicks, culminating in his unveiling a plaque to himself in Castlebar, a gesture which made even his most ardent and closest political colleagues cringe.'[1]

Browne regarded Haughey's achievement on Northern Ireland, in getting from Margaret Thatcher concessions in dealing with 'the totality of relationships', as considerable. Conor Cruise O'Brien was less enthusiastic. He pointed out that Haughey had brought Northern Ireland 'down here', dismaying ordinary people, and that the awfulness of the hunger strikes had substantially altered perceptions in the South: 'We are getting a whiff now – only a whiff but a real one – of a Northern tragedy which we helped to create. I don't know whether these experiences will tend to discredit the politicians of illusion in the Republic: to give a salutory warning against all the childish playing with the fire of "unification". I very much hope it will have some such effect.'[2]

If it did, that effect was marginal. There was no definite turning

---

[1] Vincent Browne, 'A Mandate of His Own: Haughey's Record in Office', *Magill*, 6 June 1981. During the general election, *Magill* became weekly. Castlebar was Haughey's birthplace (see Chapter One).
[2] Conor Cruise O'Brien, 'Charlie on the Stroke of Midnight', *Magill*, 6 June 1981, p. 47.

away from Haughey and all he stood for; there was no warm embrace offered to the implicit coalition between Garret FitzGerald and Frank Cluskey. The electorate were undecided, the result inconclusive. Haughey was undoubtedly exposed as a result of the Stardust delay and the new scheduling of the poll in the mid-summer, and this had several precise results. Firstly, the economy came in for exposure and punishment: it was revealed to be in more dubious health than the January Budget had led people to believe. Secondly, the 'special relationship' between Haughey and Margaret Thatcher, which had been acclaimed to be close enough to lead the Irish people 'down the road to unity', was exposed to sustained examination which undermined its seriousness. Furthermore, when the Maze hunger strike, which began on 1 March, produced the grim reality of sacrificial starvation, that 'special relationship' failed to come up with any answers. Thirdly, Fine Gael and Labour, with ample warning that an election was in the offing, had plenty of time to prepare reasonably convincing campaigns. Finally, deprived of the element of surprise, the greatest electoral asset of any leader when calling an election, Haughey was lured into making extravagant last-minute decisions which discredited him going into the campaign.

More seriously still, in terms of the campaigning itself, Haughey declared at the outset that his priority in calling the election was on account of 'the grave and tragic situation in Northern Ireland'. He did this because of all the work he had done with Margaret Thatcher in creating a new and different climate for Northern Ireland progress. On other electoral issues – notably the economy – a certain confusion surrounded what he stood for. At least on the North, his talks with Thatcher were shrouded in a compelling secrecy which gave them presentiments of major change. The opposition parties, however, were simply not having this. They condemned the paucity of Northern Ireland policy proposals and declared that the interests of the electorate lay predominantly in the economy. This proved entirely correct. By the end of the first week of campaigning, economic issues dominated debate everywhere and were exclusively the issue on the door-to-door canvass. In percentage terms the North, as an issue, hardly rated mention at all.

The two opposition parties were at odds over which economic issues were more important: inflation, taxation or jobs. And if Haughey had focused on the economy instead of Northern Ireland, he might well have driven an effective wedge between FitzGerald and Cluskey. As it was, they dictated the way the campaign went, despite the fact that they had no clear joint platform for coalition.

The election took place on 11 June 1981. All the care and political shrewdness which had gone into Haughey's speeches, his summits, his press conferences, failed to produce the vital overall majority on which he had set his sights. Support, at 45 per cent, represented a drop of more than five per cent from Lynch's 1977 vote. Fianna Fáil won 78 seats, Fine Gael got 65, and the Labour Party won 15, making a coalition deal possible, but by no means stable, since there were eight independents. Michael O'Leary was Garret FitzGerald's coalition partner, since Frank Cluskey lost his seat and was succeeded by O'Leary as leader of the Labour Party. The coalition needed the support of independents, of whom there were rather too many for comfort or stability, in that twenty-second Dáil. There had been two successful H-Block candidates, Paddy Agnew in Louth and Kieran Doherty in Cavan-Monaghan. They did not take their seats. Indeed, they were too weak and emaciated and Doherty was to die later, causing a by-election in an inherently unstable parliament. The five independents who did matter, however, included Dr Noel Browne, by far the most experienced; indeed, his Dáil career, dating back to 1948, when he had been appointed a member of the Government on his first day as a deputy, gave him greater parliamentary experience than anyone. His sympathies were with Labour and his commitment went to FitzGerald, whom he admired while at the same time having reservations about his political ability. Jim Kemmy also supported FitzGerald. Sean Loftus and Joe Sherlock, the only Sinn Fein–Workers' Party deputy in that Dáil, abstained. Neil Blaney, now independent, spoke as a true republican – of a choice between bad and worse – but voted for Haughey.

It was poor consolation for a man who, eighteen months before, had achieved a lifelong ambition by replacing Lynch as leader of Fianna Fáil and on whom the party had placed so great a reliance in maintaining their hold on power. He had lost it all. The regular collapse of his political fortunes had occurred once more. Like the counter in a game of snakes-and-ladders, he had slithered down to the bottom of the board and had to start up again, from a defeat made all the more difficult to bear because it was so narrow.

CHAPTER XVII

INTO OPPOSITION

You must therefore be content to slubber the gloss of your new fortunes with this more stubborn and boisterous expedition.

AUGHEY HAD BEEN elected leader of Fianna Fáil to sustain the party in power and to win the next general election. He had failed on both counts. This did not mean an immediate challenge to his leadership; but he had been put there in acrimonious circumstances which carried with them high expectation by his followers and the threat of severe penalties if he failed. What now helped him was the narrowness of the defeat and the quirkiness of certain components, such as the two seats won by Sinn Fein hunger-strike candidates which had both been at Fianna Fáil's expense. He rejected much of the criticism of his handling of the election and all suggestion that changes were needed in policy or party organization. Instead, he claimed repeatedly that he had lost the Fianna Fáil twenty-seat majority by an electoral 'quirk', that the Coalition would neither hold together nor survive (in this he was partly right, partly wrong), and that his own economic recipes had been the correct ones for the country.

The only thing that could be argued in favour of this approach to his first electoral defeat was that it was protective of Haughey himself. The Coalition *was* in danger of falling apart, not because of any lack of cohesion between the two principal partners – Fine Gael and Labour – but because they, in turn, were dependent on the additional support of less reliable individual deputies. These deputies, in the end, brought about its downfall. But fear of that collapse, greatly aggravated by Haughey's noisy prediction of it, meant that Fianna Fáil was reluctant to ditch the leader who had let them down so badly. What was more worrying was the fact that, if the party had been defeated by an electoral quirk and the economic policies it had pursued were 'correct', then what changes in emphasis or personnel were necessary? Haughey had really prescribed a 'stay as you were' stance and, in the event of a return to power, a repeat performance. He did, however, make a number of significant changes, one at least of which was a substantial concession to his opponents in the party and a *de facto* recognition that things had not been entirely right, either under Haughey's first appointment to the Department of Finance, Michael O'Kennedy, who went in January 1981 as Commissioner to Brussels, or under his successor, the Cork deputy, Gene Fitzgerald. This concession was the re-appointment of Martin O'Donoghue, who had previously held an economic planning portfolio, to the key responsibility of Finance. Into his Opposition front bench crept two more members of the Gang of Five – Mark Killilea and Sean Doherty.

During the autumn and winter of that year, Haughey's economic mismanagement and of his misrepresentation of Anglo-Irish relations in respect of Northern Ireland during the two summit meetings with Margaret Thatcher in 1980 were increasingly and relentlessly exposed. Garret FitzGerald developed his own relationship with her cautiously, and kept it businesslike and formal. He was comparatively open about what he wanted to achieve – which was to strengthen the hand of democratic nationalists in Northern Ireland at the expense of Provisional Sinn Fein and the Provisional IRA – and his objectives were shared by civil servants in his own Department and in the Department of Foreign Affairs. He promoted 'joint studies', but otherwise moved cautiously. It rapidly became quite clear that much of the achievement claimed by Haughey, the 'new plane', the 'unique relationship', the 'forward political movement', was illusory and exaggerated.

Haughey, from being deliberately secretive, became quite expansive and demanding. He wanted from FitzGerald rapid progress on all fronts. He wanted his own initiatives fulfilled and, if these, which had been shrouded in obscurity while he himself was in power, suddenly became the subject of inspired leaks and rumours, so much the better; this allowed him to debate what FitzGerald was attempting and set it in the context of his own earlier efforts.

It was a cynical approach. It paid little or no attention to the delicacy of the Northern Ireland situation, which had become bitter and more divisive as a result of the hunger strikes. It had little to do with the real progress between Haughey and Thatcher, which had been modest enough. And it was less than fair to the minority party in Northern Ireland, led by John Hume, which was losing support to Sinn Fein. None of this really mattered to Haughey. His target was FitzGerald;

his motive to destabilize and undermine the shaky coalition. It did not really work. But it did reveal a curious failing in Haughey, his inability to cope with complex detail in a sustained and constructive way. And this was precisely FitzGerald's strength. The joint studies, which became the main Northern Ireland initiative that autumn and which were to represent in the future the groundwork leading eventually to the Anglo-Irish Agreement, were complicated and also embarrassing for Haughey, because they had been initiated while he was still in power and in theory anyway should have inspired his interest and support. Instead, he took issue with the priorities, extracting the proposed three-tier Anglo-Irish Council for special attention, when in fact it was something to be brought on later.

What in fact was happening during those crucial months was the exposure of Haughey's Northern Ireland policy for the unworkable sham that it was, and the substitution by FitzGerald of a more logical sequence of actions by the Republic, aimed at reinforcing the democratic strength of the minority in Northern Ireland and confronting the pernicious alternative: Sinn Fein and the Provisional IRA. It was an attempt to restore something of the continuity in policy which had existed throughout the Lynch–Cosgrave era, from 1969 to 1979, and which had been abandoned by Haughey in favour of a policy which treated Northern Ireland as 'a failed entity'.

The gap widened between Fianna Fáil and the FitzGerald-led administration. On Tuesday, 10 November, in a Dáil debate that followed a FitzGerald–Thatcher meeting in London the previous Friday, Haughey criticized the Taoiseach for his failure to bring any closer 'a peaceful solution to the problem of Northern Ireland', his chosen criterion of judging everything that was being done and one that allowed him almost unlimited scope for disappointment. Late in the speech, referring to his own December 1980 summit with Margaret Thatcher, he said: 'The British Government then agreed to my proposal that the British and Irish Governments had joint responsibility for the resolution of the Northern Ireland problem and for bringing forward policies and proposals to achieve peace, reconciliation and stability.' If this had been true, it would undoubtedly have been in the joint communiqué, since it would have represented a substantial movement forward in co-operation. There were quite serious reservations within Fianna Fáil about the line Haughey was taking. His alternative option was to be supportive of FitzGerald, while at the same time claiming a not inconsiderable slice of the credit for being the initiator of what was now being done. And this was favoured, not just by Haughey's opponents, but more generally by politicians in the party who felt that the consistently negative line was damaging Fianna Fáil's authority.

One of Haughey's party colleagues spoke out. Charles McCreevy,[1] one of those within Fianna Fáil who had attended the caucus meeting in July 1979 and had been strongly in favour of Haughey replacing Lynch as party leader, now expressed criticisms of the direction in which Fianna Fáil was moving. 'We seem to be against everything and for nothing', he said. 'There is a considerable number of the Fianna Fáil parliamentary party, representing the views of the organization throughout the country, who are less than satisfied with Fianna Fáil in Opposition.'

Haughey was just then completing a reshuffle of his front bench which seemed to have been going on for weeks, if not months, almost to the point of public boredom as everyone waited for the announcement: 'So mesmerizing has been the impact of McCreevy over the past week or so that it has made the reshuffling of the Fianna Fáil front bench almost an incidental matter. The question should be: "Have you seen Charles Haughey? What did you get?" The question is: "When did you last see Charlie McCreevy? Who was he with?"'[2]

Haughey's eventual tally of spokespersons, in one area or another, reached an absurdly large number – 53 out of a Dáil strength of 78, and a Senate representation of 19. McCreevy had somehow been overlooked. He was still a backbencher, quite a rare Fianna Fáil person to meet in the corridors, and felt free to deliver his views. Nor was it the first time he had done so, making the oversight more careless. Back in early 1981, before the election, he had deplored what he saw as 'an auction in vote-buying' by Haughey and had been critical of the give-away economic strategy which had replaced the January 1980 rectitude. This, in his view, was the reason for putting Haughey into

[1] Charles McCreevy (b. 1949) was a chartered accountant who only entered the Dáil in 1977 and whose main interest was in business. He gave the interview (27 December 1981) to Geraldine Kennedy, who was then political correspondent with the *Sunday Tribune*. She was later to have her telephone tapped and, with the present author, to take an action against the State. McCreevy received no promotion under Charles Haughey, but was made Minister for Social Welfare by Albert Reynolds in February 1992 and retained his position in the Government in the 1993 coalition as Minister for Tourism and Trade.
[2] Present author, 'Where have all the leaders gone?', Politics & Politicians, *Irish Independent*, 9 January 1982.

the leadership of the party in the first place. It was now a reason for taking issue with that leadership.

Haughey saw it in precisely those terms, an indication of his sensitivities about how vulnerable he was within the party. He sought McCreevy's expulsion. His own front bench thought differently. For the very reasons which he had been promoting in defence of his own position – namely, that the Coalition was unstable and would soon break up – members of the front bench felt that censure would be better than expulsion. Haughey then asked those who dissented from the expulsion course to abstain at the parliamentary party meeting. All of this, of course, was discussed in confidence. But it was leaked and the internal divisions and arguments became public knowledge.

McCreevy, an intelligent, entertaining and courageous individual, became a celebrity overnight and handled his criticisms of the party well. He let his outspoken challenge come to a parliamentary party meeting and then used the occasion to repeat his criticisms, confining them to party uncertainty and lack of direction, caused principally by the failure to discuss issues. Then he resigned the party whip and left the meeting, pledging his continued loyalty to Fianna Fáil. Haughey was cheated of any show of strength. Nor could he risk the alienation for too long of so powerful a vote-getter in Kildare – one of the country's marginal constituencies – as McCreevy. The party leader announced almost immediately that he could 'apply to rejoin at any time', or 'be invited to rejoin', an obvious reference to the will of the constituency organization. McCreevy himself spoke even more freely, suggesting that 'the leader of Fianna Fáil is there for the time being', and 'I remain to be convinced that there is someone better than Charles Haughey'. No one laid claim to that position. But it brought out into the open widespread dissatisfaction.

McCreevy was in fact invited to rejoin rather sooner than anyone had anticipated. Garret FitzGerald's wrestling match with the Irish economy had reached conclusions of sorts and his Minister for Finance, John Bruton, brought in a Budget on 27 January which attempted to address collectively borrowing, inflation, growth and tax reform. It was a sound package of measures, appropriate to the country's needs and agreed between Fine Gael and Labour. But it had a fatal flaw: the imposition of value added tax on children's shoes. The Coalition partners needed the additional support of two independents. They got one – Dr Noel Browne. Even then they could have survived with the abstention of one other. But the rest voted with Fianna Fáil and the Government fell.

The first vote on the series of resolutions that followed the Budget speech by John Bruton took place at around six o'clock. It was an 82–81 defeat for the Government. Garret FitzGerald claims that he felt 'total exhilaration'. He had confidence in the overall strategy of the Budget and believed in its ultimate appeal to the electorate. His colleagues in Government were not so sanguine and the press found it difficult to believe his mood of excitement. For a number of reasons his departure for the President's residence in the Phoenix Park was delayed and he did not arrive there until after ten o'clock. In the meantime, at 8.25 p.m., Haughey had issued a statement: 'It is a matter for the President to consider the situation which has arisen now that the Taoiseach has ceased to retain the support of a majority in Dáil Eireann. I am available for consultation by the President should he so wish.' This apparently neutral position was very much at odds with intense behind-the-scenes activity designed to avert an election. Seven phone calls had been made to the President's official residence by members of the Fianna Fáil front bench, in an effort to persuade Patrick Hillery to exercise his constitutional prerogative, refuse Garret FitzGerald a dissolution and call on Charles Haughey to form a government.

Haughey was understandably anxious to avoid a general election. He had used the prophecy of an early collapse of the FitzGerald administration for his own internal party purposes and had not really anticipated the event at all. The long-delayed reshuffle, which was not completed until well into the New Year, was evidence of this. And on top of it there had been the McCreevy challenge.

Under the Irish Constitution a prime minister who loses majority support in the Dáil can be refused a dissolution by the President. It is one of the few overtly political powers enjoyed by the Irish Head of State; but it has never been exercised, in part because of a widely recognized perception that it might possibly result in an inconclusive outcome in the Dáil, with no provision in the Constitution for resolving any stalemate where no one emerges with a majority.

Hillery, who had been a Government minister since 1959, two years before Haughey's own first ministerial appointment, and who had worked quite amicably with him until the Arms Crisis, was disturbed and angered by what he regarded as quite unwarranted efforts, repeatedly made, to interfere with his office. In addition, one of the calls, received by the President's aide-de-camp, an officer of the Defence Forces, included threatening language concerning that officer's future, if he did not put the caller through to the Head of State. It has never been confirmed that any of the seven calls came directly from Haughey. Hillery's distress was such that he delayed FitzGerald for three-quarters of an hour, leaving politicians and journalists in Leinster House to become increasingly convinced that the unused constitutional prerogative had indeed been invoked. Hillery granted FitzGerald a dissolution of the Dáil. The poll was fixed for 18 February.

In the 1981 general election, Haughey was defeated by his own obsession with power. It had surfaced again, within hours of the Dáil defeat, in the sustained and constitutionally inappropriate telephoning of Aras an Uachtarain. And this hunger for power largely coloured the Fianna Fáil campaign. Haughey was frantic to get back and this had the immediate effect of distorting his judgements about what had happened and what it all meant. Fianna Fáil, in fact, had made no advance on their position of June 1981. Their standing in the opinion polls was virtually unchanged, except that the ending of the Maze hunger strike had reverted a tiny Sinn Fein support to them. The element of secrecy and vague promise about Northern Ireland had been stripped away by FitzGerald's quite real and mainly open progress with Margaret Thatcher. And on the economy the basic correctness of FitzGerald's budgetary strategy, even if it was insufficient to carry the motley aspirations of independent deputies, was judged widely to be the correct and necessary course for the country.

Haughey made a lamentable start to the campaign. He was torn between a high-spending approach and a campaign based on restraint, and he lurched first towards the easy option. His opening press conference, which was uncertain and unconvincing, ran so much in the teeth of economic reality that Martin O'Donoghue threatened to have nothing to do with the national progress of the election unless the basic arguments were changed.

Reluctantly, Haughey agreed. He passed over much of the control of the detail to O'Donoghue, who, with George Colley and Desmond O'Malley, took over the serious campaigning. Haughey seemed to find this acceptable. Indeed, if his enemies in the party could win him power, so much the better; they would be serving a purpose in the end.

The campaign became locked in economic argument. Essentially, the Budget was at the centre of this and, with minor adjustments, was the joint manifesto of Fine Gael and Labour. There was a relentless, obsessive concentration on the economy. Uniquely, since the election had come about through the defeat of the Government on Budget night, its contents became the detailed matter of day-to-day debate during the campaign and when Haughey, advised by O'Donoghue, proposed alternatives, but jibbed at the idea of delivering details on these, FitzGerald opened the doors of the Department of Finance and offered him civil service co-operation in costing whatever ideas he had. The differences between the two sides became marginal rather than central, with Haughey being forced to compete entirely according to FitzGerald's rules and having to fall back on a much-pressed Martin O'Donoghue – who was fighting his own campaign for a seat – to fill in the details. Somewhat later, racier material was injected, in the form of a proposal by Haughey to honour a pledge given to the Pro-Life lobby and bring in a constitutional ban on abortion. Both Haughey and, in a moment he later much regretted, FitzGerald had given undertakings on this. Haughey's motive in bringing it forward was entirely political. It stood a good chance of embarrassing FitzGerald, whose image was much more liberal, and would recruit the backing of right-wing Roman Catholics and probably the more militant republicans, since their thinking, on social issues, tended to be conservative. But it failed to 'cut the mustard', as an issue.

For the first time, Haughey and FitzGerald met for a live television debate. This was on Tuesday, 16 February, two days before the poll. Haughey was cooler, more assured. There was an admirable sang-froid in his attitude; genuinely he seemed to have nerves of steel. But he was not in command of the facts. And facts were essentially what this election of 1982 was about. On key points, with the details and the evidence before him, FitzGerald was able to expose and defeat Haughey in the presentation of a picture of past misrepresentation of the country's problems and failure to address the issues correctly. Though Haughey debated his way through these points in the encounter with considerable skill, he did not convince the audience of his credibility, honesty and reliability. On these, and on the general impact of their very different approaches to leadership, FitzGerald – on the evidence of a 'spot' survey conducted later that night – was ahead by a margin of over three to one.

On polling day itself, Haughey's friend and election agent, Pat O'Connor, a solicitor, was recorded by those monitoring voters at the polls as attempting to vote in two polling stations in each of which he had been registered. He was charged with personation, a charge which later failed on the grounds that it could not be proved that he had actually voted on the second ballot paper.

The election result was inconclusive. When the Dáil met, on 9 March, Haughey was nominated Taoiseach by 86 votes to 76, a convincing enough margin. But three of these votes were from Sinn Fein –Workers' Party (not to be confused with Provisional Sinn Fein) and a further two came from Neil Blaney and Tony Gregory. It was not a stable situation. Given the quite remarkable circumstance, of an election being called and fought over a stern Budget, the fact that Fine Gael had actually gained a point in the overall vote was a phenomenal achievement for FitzGerald and a sobering outcome for Haughey. But both had failed to win an overall majority. The country was faced with a hung Dáil.

In Britain, administrations change immediately, with prime ministers departing from Downing Street on the night of their defeat and the new government coming in the next day. In Ireland, the matter is governed by the Constitution and the changeover effected by the Dáil and the President. The resumption of the Dáil was fixed for 9 March, almost three weeks after the poll. FitzGerald remained as Taoiseach and in any case had not conceded defeat, though the odds were now in Haughey's favour. Fianna Fáil, though still in a minority, had three more seats than the combined Fine Gael–Labour total and it was clear that, for either side to come to power, deals would need to be done with the independents.

But other deals were being contemplated within the Fianna Fáil Party. In the space of one month, Haughey had reshuffled his Opposition team, attempted to discipline his maverick backbencher, Charles McCreevy, sought a constitutional invitation to form an administration without an election, fought and failed to win a real general election, and was now preparing to canvass support for himself as the leader of a minority government. At the time of his inconclusive confrontation with Charles McCreevy he had emphasized the seriousness with which he viewed the challenge by referring to his leadership of the party and the circumstances in which he might hand over to another leader. This would be when he no longer considered himself an asset to Fianna Fáil. But he was an asset, he told the party, and therefore there would be no resignation.[1] Despite more or less open conflict within the party

---

[1] Fianna Fáil Front Bench meeting, 19 January 1982.

between pro- and anti-Haughey factions, it was hard to challenge a
man who relied on this self-assessment approach to asset values. The
election cast a different light on things. Public reaction, opinion polls,
the door-to-door canvass, the outcome of the head-to-head television
debate, and the inconclusive election result itself, made the argument
about Haughey's asset value – and therefore his continued leadership
of the party – an urgent and pressing one. There were even politicians
who considered that a change of leader, midway through the election
campaign, might well have secured victory. Now, in the frozen period
between the poll and the meeting of the Dáil on 9 March, Desmond
O'Malley challenged for the leadership, provoking an intense and
threatening battle, and involving a 'numbers game' not unlike that
which had so strongly characterized the leadership struggle in
December 1979.

It was bitter and destructive of Fianna Fáil unity. Haughey, always at
his most resourceful under threat, was once again fighting for political
survival and he, with his supporters inside Fianna Fáil, engaged in an
intense and vigorous campaign to marshal a majority for the crucial
party meeting. He knew that a key element would be the credibility
of his claim that he would form the next government. He therefore
combined the internal party fight with efforts to get commitments
of support from among the newly elected deputies, concentrating in
particular on Tony Gregory, an independent deputy from a Dublin
inner-city constituency. Gregory set a high price on his support. He
represented poverty and deprivation, and he wanted things done about
these issues for his own supporters. That was how he saw his role as
a public representative and, though he did not at the time reveal details
of the talks, he handled them with a commendable coolness. Emerging
from his first session with Haughey he said: 'I spelt out my recommendations to him. He agreed with some and is to come back to me with
his reaction on the others. I suppose some are so obvious nobody could
refuse them.' They were obvious, but costly, too. One estimate made
after details had been revealed put the price of Gregory's support at
£94 million. This was followed by an apparent decision by the
Workers' Party – now in command of three seats – to support
Haughey. This was not the kind of horse-trading which FitzGerald
could countenance. Together with the pressures put on individual
Fianna Fáil deputies, the growing indication that Haughey would
be able to patch together sufficient support to allow him to take
over government meant that he would hold the key to numerous

appointments in the new administration. It weighed significantly in the leadership battle, which came to an ignominious conclusion on 25 February, when Martin O'Donoghue, who had been a key supporter of Desmond O'Malley, distanced himself from him and suggested to the party that a contest was 'ill advised'. O'Malley withdrew his challenge.

Up until the time of the Dáil vote itself, exhaustive attempts were made by FitzGerald to prevent Haughey coming to power, one of them being an effort to persuade John O'Connell, the Ceann Comhairle (speaker), to return to his party and force Fianna Fáil to elect to the office from their own number, thus diminishing their vote. But with Tony Gregory, the three Workers' Party deputies, and Neil Blaney all declaring for Haughey, he was duly nominated as Taoiseach. In the Dáil speeches that preceded that nomination, by far the most extraordinary was that made by Tony Gregory. Mindful of the achievement of his deal with Haughey, mindful too of the fragility of the administration he was supporting, he decided to put on record before the House not just what he had been promised, but some of the circumstances in which the promises had been agreed.

A form of written contract, witnessed by the General Secretary of the Irish Transport and General Workers Union, gave details of a new inner-city community school, a new national community development agency, the nationalization of the threatened Clondalkin Paper Mills, and environmental and housing schemes which, on assessment, were to cost a total sum that exceeded the earlier estimates of £94 million by at least a further £50 million.

When the vote for Taoiseach was called, there was sudden and extreme consternation. As the division bells rang on and on, the three Workers' Party deputies remained absent. A frantic search discovered them in their offices; a malfunction of the bell, or possibly a misunderstanding of what it was for, had produced near-disaster for Fianna Fáil. Even running through the corridors brought them too late to the main entrance to the Chamber. They ran round through the press gallery, tumbled over the barriers into the Distinguished Visitors' Gallery, and on into the Chamber itself, in order to pass through the lobbies and vote for Haughey's nomination as Taoiseach. Like so much else that happened then, and continued to happen in the early days of the administration, it reeked of ineptitude.

Haughey formed a government which did not include George

Colley, but he did appoint both Martin O'Donoghue and Desmond O'Malley.[1] The other significant appointment was that of Sean Doherty to the Department of Justice.

[1] O'Donoghue was given Education; O'Malley went into Trade, Commerce and Tourism. Colley's exclusion resulted from Haughey's unwillingness, this time, to make him Tanaiste (deputy leader of the Government). This role went to Ray McSharry, who also took over the Finance portfolio.

CHAPTER XVIII

THE YEAR OF GUBU

To mourn a mischief that is past and gone
Is the next way to draw new mischief on.

AUGHEY, now back in power, attempted an extraordinary gambit. Michael O'Kennedy, after only one year in the job as Ireland's Commissioner in Europe, had returned, won back his North Tipperary seat and resigned as Commissioner. This position obviously had to be filled. Haughey, to everyone's amazement, tried to persuade Richard Burke,[1] a member of Fine Gael who had already served one term as Brussels Commissioner before O'Kennedy, to go back there. Haughey's motive was simply to precipitate a by-election which he was confident he would win, thereby further depleting Fine Gael strength in a tightly balanced Dáil and lessening the precariousness of his own minority strength.

Burke accepted, then changed his mind, then accepted again. The by-election was called. The Fianna Fáil candidate was Eileen Lemass, the widow of Haughey's brother-in-law, who had lost her seat in the same constituency – Dublin West – during the election, having held it since 1977. She was a good candidate, known in the area and committed to its many 'new town' problems. Fine Gael, on the advice of the sitting deputy Jim Mitchell, took on as its by-election candidate an unknown and inexperienced politician, but also from within the constituency and committed to it. It looked unpromising. But a highly organized Opposition campaign, and a widespread feeling of repugnance at the manipulation involved, gave victory to Fine Gael's Liam Skelly.

[1] Richard Burke (b. 1932) was a teacher. First elected in 1969, he had been appointed Minister for Education by Liam Cosgrave in the 1973–77 administration. He was close to Cosgrave and the only other government minister to vote against that Government's contraception legislation, thus ensuring its defeat. FitzGerald, then in Foreign Affairs, had opposed Burke's appointment to Brussels and had not appointed him to the 1981 Government.

'This by-election,' wrote Garret FitzGerald, 'was one of the most significant in recent times. It severely damaged Fianna Fáil morale, and weakened Charles Haughey's position in the party, which was already under challenge. His attempted stroke with Dick Burke had backfired, with the result that we still held three of the five seats in Dublin West as well as the Commissionership – even if many in our party refused to look on Dick Burke as Fine Gael! The Workers' Party learned that its support for Fianna Fáil was extremely unpopular with the voters, and this encouraged it to "ditch" the Fianna Fáil Government at the first opportunity six months later.'[1]

The year had got off to a bad start. It rapidly became worse. Haughey made several serious misjudgements on important foreign policy issues. On Northern Ireland, now dealing with James Prior as Britain's Secretary of State for the province, he made claims about the state of Anglo-Irish relations that were confused, contradictory and unconvincing. In Brussels, where he was attending a celebration of the Community's twenty-fifth anniversary, a Haughey–Thatcher meeting took place. Northern Ireland was discussed, according to Haughey; it was not, according to British officials speaking for Margaret Thatcher. On a St Patrick's Day visit to the United States, there were statements which were decidedly at odds with what was being said in the Dáil. Nor was Haughey much helped by his Minister for Foreign Affairs, Gerard Collins, who had taken Brian Lenihan's place. Collins was equally at odds with James Prior, their differences of recall about discussions on Prior's 'devolution' proposals for the North being the subject of public contradiction in early April.

A not dissimilar divergence of policy presentation developed between Haughey and his Minister for Defence, Paddy Power, over the highly sensitive Falklands crisis, which Haughey handled ineptly. Ireland's international interests do not extend to the South Atlantic to any great degree. The country's defences were not threatened by Argentinian aggression and it did not need to defend trade links with the Falkland Islanders, having enough sheep of its own. But the country suddenly took a passionate interest, invoked in one of the slogans that became current at the time: 'The Malvinas unfree will never be at peace!' It meant, of course, like the north-east counties of Ireland, unfree from Margaret Thatcher's rule. This anti-British stance over their Falklands campaign was noisily expressed by Paddy Power in his

---

[1] Garret FitzGerald, op. cit., p. 407.

own constituency. It may have had some objective validity, but was out of step with Ireland's European partners, whose support Thatcher managed to engage, and was distinctly unwise in terms of the much more real problem facing Haughey – that of getting his Northern Ireland agenda back on the rails. In fact there was no possibility of this. It seemed illogical and perverse to be undertaking an independent, international role on the Falklands, invoking such issues as Irish neutrality – which had ill served Haughey only a year before – and the quite absurd prospect of this stance on the Falklands being traded in some way for a British declaration of intent to withdraw. This was Paddy Power's position.[1] It was softened subsequently by Government statements, but there remained a confused and ambivalent atmosphere over the Falklands crisis, despite strenuous efforts by Ireland's permanent representatives, Noel Dore at the United Nations, and Sean Donlon, who was then Ambassador to Washington.

We were clearly witnessing an increasingly unstable administration, whose nerve was severely tested on 24 June with the first vital division on the committee stage of a Finance Bill. By this stage the continued support for Haughey's Government of the three Workers' Party deputies was in doubt. They in fact voted against the measure, signalling their autumn withdrawal of support, and a tie resulted in the Dáil, with Haughey dependent on Neil Blaney and Tony Gregory, and then ultimately on the casting vote of the Chair. The familiar prelude to an election, as deputies hurried to their cars from Leinster House with large cardboard boxes filled with franked envelopes and election literature, raised the political temperature.

Haughey had struggled through the usual honeymoon period, with almost everyone thinking that the marriage that had taken place, whatever its precise nature, was a disaster. In fact what did happen, at the '100-day point', constituted an unsavoury whiff of scandal and abuse which in retrospect invites a rather different interpretation from that given at the time. Jim Mitchell, the Fine Gael spokesman on Posts and Telecommunications, caused a Dáil sensation on 23 June, when he revealed that certain telephones within the Leinster House system, including the telephone on Charles Haughey's desk, contained an override capacity by which, through a simple operation, any calls could be secretly intercepted and heard. The facility, as Mitchell explained, was

---

[1] Paddy Power made a constituency speech to this effect in Edenderry, on Monday, 3 May 1982.

apparently quite normal for senior executives in large corporations and had been included with telephones installed in 1980, after Haughey had come to power. A year previously, the former General Secretary of the Fine Gael Party, Peter Prendergast, had suspected surveillance of his phone in the Dáil and went on record with these suspicions.

The investigation of Mitchell's allegations was handled by John Wilson, the minister responsible, and led to no clear explanation. Haughey did not respond directly to the House, but made certain points to Wilson which were included in Wilson's statement. (Haughey did not appear in the House for the explanation or subsequent exchanges.) Wilson asserted that the Taoiseach in 1980 'never asked for the override facility', that he 'never knew such a facility was available . . . and he never used it'. Yet at the time when Haughey fell from power, in June 1981, identical phone sets, with the override facility, were then installed in his new offices as leader of the Opposition. Clearly an inquiry was needed.

Secretly, the Minister for Justice, Sean Doherty, was already engaged in illegal phone-tapping. On 10 May he had signed a warrant for the tapping of the present writer's telephone and that surveillance was going on at the time of the Dáil exchanges provoked by Jim Mitchell's statement and John Wilson's reply. Also, Doherty, according to his press announcement in early 1992, was passing the transcripts of those telephone interceptions directly and immediately to Charles Haughey. Haughey strenuously denied this version of events, but was widely disbelieved.

Nothing came of the Mitchell allegations. The Committee on Procedures and Privilege considered the matter, but inconclusively. No instruction concerning the installation of the phones with the override facility could be traced to Haughey.

The mid-summer situation was a stalemate, electorally speaking. So long as everybody in Dáil Eireann remained healthy and in their right minds, and so long as Tony Gregory and the Workers' Party continued in their support for Haughey, he could just survive.[1] It was difficult to foresee change, even with the defection of the Workers' Party, unless electoral numbers changed through death or incapacity. And

[1] Fine Gael had 63 seats, Labour 15, against Fianna Fáil's 80. The Workers' Party, with three, Jim Kemmy and Noel Browne, generally supportive of FitzGerald, and Neil Blaney and Tony Gregory, supportive of Haughey, completed the numbers, with John O'Connell in the chair.

the Fianna Fáil victory in the East Galway by-election, on 21 July, ensured short-term stability.

This stability took a severe battering, however, with the McArthur Affair. On Friday, 13 August, another unlucky Friday for Haughey,[1] Malcolm Edward McArthur was arrested in the flat of the Attorney General, Patrick Connolly, and charged with the murder of Bridie Gargan, a nurse, in the Phoenix Park three weeks earlier. The Attorney General was not involved, but did misjudge the situation badly, as did Haughey. The two men had a conversation on the Friday night of the arrest, after which Connolly, with Haughey's knowledge, left for London and from there went on to New York. Only after his departure was the question raised of his need to be back in Ireland, rather than on holiday, given the somewhat unusual circumstances. Initially, Connolly told Haughey that he would prefer to discuss the matter from New York, and only after his arrival in New York did the Attorney General decide that perhaps, with an alleged murderer having been found living in his flat, he should be back in Dublin. The embarrassment to the Government deepened. Connolly resigned. Haughey described the events,[2] not without adequate justification, as 'grotesque, unbelievable', a 'bizarre happening', an 'unprecedented situation'. The press took up these dramatic words in reports and headlines, and out of the initial letters Conor Cruise O'Brien, lest anyone forget, constructed the acronym and mnemonic GUBU. No one did forget and the name attached itself thereafter to every subsequent crisis undergone and mistake made by Haughey.

Haughey was as aware as everyone else that this kind of accident-prone Dáil simply could not be sustained indefinitely. His Minister for Finance, Ray McSharry, having watched the party fight the election on a set of economic compromises, and deliver a Budget which matched in most respects the one on which FitzGerald had fallen, determined to tighten the economic reins. If this led to defections, notably by the Workers' Party deputies, then so be it – they would go to the country on the basis of a 'new deal'. This was the comprehensive plan for Ireland's future which was worked out through the summer months. It was scheduled for presentation before the Dáil resumed in late October and it had all the hallmarks of the kind of planning proposal which Haughey favoured in the run-up to an election and

---

[1] The Stardust Fire took place on the night of 13–14 February 1981; the 13th was a Friday.
[2] At a press conference, on 16 August 1982.

which he had used, rather more loosely, in 1981. But this time it had a backbone of much-needed stringency. Eighteen months on, and McSharry seemed to be exercising a tighter grip on his leader.

But the strategy was overtaken by events. Fianna Fáil was in serious revolt and the growing conviction that Haughey would never deliver an overall majority was now greatly augmented by embarrassment at his perpetually accident-prone political existence and his inability to judge situations even tolerably well. In the minds of many within Fianna Fáil, including, it must be said, his stoutest activists in bringing him to power in 1979, he was a disaster. What he could do, however, was run a tough internal party campaign when the need arose. The need arose when backbencher Charles McCreevy, still a party maverick, still outspoken and unrepentant about his challenge to Haughey ten months earlier, tabled a motion of no confidence in Charles Haughey's leadership for debate at the parliamentary party meeting on 6 October. It was not a pre-planned challenge. He consulted very few members of the party.

Haughey was fairly shattered by it and reacted badly in public. His usual head-on response to such events – now a predictable part of his life – led him to outline his terms for the meeting in a radio interview the preceding Sunday, 3 October. He wanted an open, roll-call vote, with each deputy standing up, in alphabetical order, and declaring his or her position. He wanted a full prior commitment of support by members of the Government. He wanted the Fianna Fáil Party's national executive to declare support in advance. And he wanted constituency organizations around the country to exercise a mandate over their elected representatives, dictating how they should vote.

The listing of these demands, and their delivery, nationwide, on radio, outraged many within Fianna Fáil and proved counterproductive. Desmond O'Malley and Martin O'Donoghue resigned from the Government rather than give the undertaking of support. Haughey did no better with the party's national executive. A senior and highly respected senator, Eoin Ryan, who was the son of de Valera's and Lemass's finance minister, James Ryan, not only refused to support Haughey but announced that he was an electoral liability and should resign.

The challenge had been seriously underestimated by Haughey and his advisers. Here was a leader and head of Government under the very real threat of a collapse in the essential Dáil support needed for survival, facing an internal challenge of the utmost gravity. It was painful and humiliating for deputies to be subjected, by newly invented electoral rules, to a kind of 'pocket borough' approach to voting and to the exercise of a constituency mandate which was open to abuse and intimidation.

The pressures put on individual deputies were even more intimidatory. Constituency organizations were persuaded to 'instruct' their deputies to vote for Haughey, using the threat of no re-selection if they failed. Thousands of messages were allegedly received at party headquarters in support of Haughey; none were received against him. And telephone calls, some of them threatening, were made at all hours of the day and night to the known dissidents who intended to vote for Haughey's removal as party leader. There were obscene phone calls made to the families of Seamus Brennan and George Colley; Mary Harney was accused of spending her time in Leinster House 'in unorthodox ways'.[1] Despite all the intimidation, and in part because of the successful pressure used against them in February, those opposed to Haughey were more determined this time and went public, issuing statements to the effect that they had been threatened.

During the meeting itself, there was widespread and open criticism of the party leader. It was unprecedented. This was the first time the suitability and fitness of the Fianna Fáil leader's continuation in office had been debated in so public a way – at least as far as the party was concerned – and it loosened tongues on every side. There was severe criticism from Pádraig Flynn of what members were doing to themselves: they were playing 'into the hands of Fine Gael, the British and their "media collaborators". Asking rhetorically who was pressing for this motion, he named three journalists – Bruce Arnold, Geraldine Kennedy and John Feeney, the *Evening Herald*'s main columnist. They were trying to be divisive and, he asked, was the party going to be divisive for them?'[2]

After a day-long party debate, filled with rancour and widespread criticism, 22 voted in support of McCreevy, 58 supported Haughey.

---

[1] See Peter Murtagh and Joe Joyce, *The Boss: Charles J. Haughey in Government*, Dublin, 1983, pp. 256–7. Seamus Brennan (b. 1948) had been general secretary of the Fianna Fáil Party before taking a Dáil seat in the 1981 general election. He became Minister for Tourism and Transport in 1989, having served as a junior minister in the 1987–9 administration. He was later made Minister for Education. When the 1993 Coalition between Fianna Fáil and Labour was agreed he was a casualty, losing full Government rank. Mary Harney (b. 1953) was also first elected to the Dáil in 1981. She was a co-founder of the Progressive Democrats and in 1989 was a junior minister in the Fianna Fáil–PD Coalition.
[2] Ibid, p 263.

The 22 were triumphant, behaving as though they had won. The majority were furious at the damage inflicted by the exposure of this deep and irremediable fissure through the party, in both Dáil and country. Haughey was, once again, shattered by it. He cancelled a pre-planned press conference, made a brief statement and then withdrew. Bitter scenes followed the meeting. Jim Gibbons was struck by Haughey supporters, Mary Harney was jostled, Charlie McCreevy was advised to leave Leinster House by the back entrance, declined and, under heavy police escort, he went out to cries of 'Judas!' and 'Blueshirt!' Both Geraldine Kennedy and myself were threatened, after the meeting and later, in a series of anonymous telephone calls. He was in a disastrous situation. Under McSharry's urgings he had initiated stringent economic measures during the summer, in the full knowledge that this would lose him Workers' Party support and precipitate an election. He intended that. Now he was faced with major difficulties in easing back on the strategy and buying time in which he could once again attempt to restore the confidence which the vote supporting him was meant to represent.

Yet again, luck was against him. On 18 October, William Loughnane, a backbench deputy from Clare, died. Loughnane, a colourful, fiddle-playing country doctor with a puckish sense of humour, whose accusation of lying, made against Lynch late in 1979, helped to precipitate Lynch's departure, would have relished the quandary into which his death threw Fianna Fáil. If he was unable to be a witness, the same did not apply to James Gibbons, whose health, threatened by a heart complaint, made it necessary for him to be absent from the Dáil and to watch from the sidelines as the situation steadily worsened.

It seemed that some factors at least were in Haughey's favour when, at the annual Labour Party conference in Galway, the party leader, Michael O'Leary, sought to alter the terms for approaching the forthcoming general election and get a commitment to a pre-election pact with Fine Gael. The move failed. O'Leary resigned and his place as leader was taken by Dick Spring, a relatively inexperienced politician, but one committed to Labour independence from pre-election 'deals'.

Haughey's declared intention, earlier in the summer, had been to bring before the Dáil the economic package, which was called 'The Way Forward', and put it to a vote. It was future Government policy and would be ratified as a blueprint for economic advance. Whether it had been amended or not, rewritten in the light of events, or was simply defective from the start, the document failed to address key economic problems. It ignored the work of the Commission on Taxation, making no in-roads into reform; it ignored the complex but dynamic Telesis Report on industrial strategy; it ignored the recommendations of the Commission on Industrial Relations. It was, in fact, deeply flawed.

When it came before the Dáil, in early November, the tactics had changed. Haughey sought to have the document 'noted'; then he tried to have it passed to a select committee – a highly unusual approach in any event, but particularly so from a man who set small store by such parliamentary devices as committees; finally he tried a filibuster. Garret FitzGerald threatened a no-confidence motion, forcing Haughey to table a motion of confidence in the Government.

The no-confidence debate took place on 4 November. Haughey continued to try to avoid an election. He offered talks with the Labour Party, which were rejected. So was any further support from the three Workers' Party deputies. Tony Gregory politely informed him that he would be abstaining. Only Neil Blaney was left and sitting on the bench at the foot of the main stairway in Leinster House, the previous night, he rather forlornly speculated on the possibility of 'something turning up' for Haughey, though what this might have been was not revealed. Haughey lost the vote of confidence and sought the dissolution of the Dáil from President Hillery, who nine months earlier had been invaded by calls trying to stop a similar request from Garret FitzGerald. The general election was fixed for 24 November.

'Conceived by accident, born in confusion, nourished amid epidemics which regularly threatened it with extinction, the 23rd Dáil was doomed from the start to a short life. And it was a short life without being a merry one. The sickly creature wailed its way from one affliction to the next. Artificially supported, and nursed by eccentric political midwives, it hobbled from vote to vote, challenge to challenge, issue to issue. In its way it evolved a life of its own, a life of sorts, just as the survival of a sickly child generates a form of immunisation all its own. But, permanently under threat from inside its own frail body, it could not last. In the end it succumbed to its primary ailment: instability ... and was buried without much grief, its last hours having been speculated on at great length ...'[1]

As for Charles Haughey, he fought from his beleaguered corner

[1] Present author, 'The Short, Unhappy Life of the 23rd Dáil', *Irish Independent*, 5 November 1982.

with quite remarkable resilience. Few leaders could possibly have lost
the support of Parliament and been forced to go to the country in
worse circumstances. His party was divided. Two key ministers had
resigned from the Government only a short time before it fell. A
quarter of the outgoing deputies had registered no confidence in him
as their leader. His whole period in power, during 1982, had been
punctuated by crisis and disaster. And just when he had managed to
get some imperfect semblance of order and direction into economic
planning, he was required to turn the programme into an election
manifesto.

Watching him at that time was a remarkable experience. The Fianna
Fáil Party took the unique step of using an upstairs room in a mews
building behind its Mount Street headquarters for press conferences
and briefings, which Haughey often took, unaccompanied by other
ministers and in the presence of close aides only. These occasions were
undoubtedly confrontational. The press had experienced his blandishments, they had experienced his grand occasions for the launch of
policies and programmes. Now they were confronted by a fighter, with
little to offer beyond his invective and disdain. And they experienced
him at close quarters, in a room in which space was cramped for twenty
people. It was a cockpit for pent-up fury; pent-up because, even under
the extreme pressure induced by the situation, Haughey still showed
a remarkable capacity for self-control.

He believed himself the victim of vilification. He frequently mentioned 'personal attacks', both from politicians and from the media. He
seemed both beleaguered and bewildered by the fall in his popularity. It
had slumped into a moody resentment and suspicion, and he fought
back against this with accusations of personal vindictiveness. Anthony
Cronin, a close friend for many years and his cultural and artistic
adviser since the beginning of 1980, attempted to assess the reasons,
putting the supposed resentment down to envy of Haughey's wealth
and antagonisms toward his Northern Ireland views.[1] Cronin saw
Haughey in epic, mythic terms. 'I became aware of his truly extraordinary myth-making powers. There are personages in ancient Irish sagas
who have this characteristic. They can be in two places at the one time.
They can assume physical traits which are apparent to one observer but
not to another, "basilisk eyes" perhaps. They are credited with curious

[1] Anthony Cronin, 'Haughey: the Man and the Legend', *Irish Independent*, 17 November
1982.

abilities, fantastic capacities, extraordinary deeds, superhuman appe-
tites. Now I must confess I don't know why legend should attach itself
to Charlie Haughey in quite this way. I know of course that he is a
remarkable man; and that he has had in many ways a remarkable career;
but the mere facts do not account for the phenomenon, so one must
assume some singling out process, to do with the wishes and fears of
our society.' Whatever these qualities and the powers that went with
them were, they were not working.

Haughey accused Garret FitzGerald of collusion with the British
over Northern Ireland. He used a luncheon meeting which FitzGerald
had had with the Duke of Norfolk – a former head of British Intelligence – as justification for casting on the Fine Gael leader the supposed
enormity of collaboration, apparently endorsed by the fact that the
Northern Ireland Secretary of State, James Prior, was briefed in
advance about a speech which FitzGerald made on the North, proposing what seemed to be an all-Ireland court and police force. Haughey
also delivered in this cockpit what appeared to be threats to individual
journalists. There was a gritty, intense atmosphere, remembered to
this day by those who experienced it in much the same way as the
1979 leadership campaign in Leinster House is remembered.

More broadly, Haughey's position was that the election was unnecessary and unwanted, damaging to the economy and forced on the Irish
people by a small group of power-brokers in the Fine Gael and Labour
parties. They had brought down a Government which had 'a detailed
and well-considered plan for national recovery', supported by farming
and employer organizations, though not, significantly, by the unions,
which at the stage when the Dáil was being dissolved were studying
the proposals. The objectives and strategies, Haughey claimed, were
endorsed by the European Community.

The plan was a comparatively convincing document, as far as it
went, and it certainly went further than anything on offer from the
other parties, which had problems of their own, including the very
recent Labour leadership tussle. Haughey sought to add to these problems by putting forward the wording for a Pro-Life amendment to
the Constitution, outlawing abortion. The wording was contentious,
but the commitment was a shrewd addition to the political debate.
Combined with the tide of allegations about hidden moves on Northern Ireland on the part of Garret FitzGerald, it added up to a coherent
and dynamic indictment of the Opposition.

Unfortunately, Haughey had burned up a good deal of the goodwill which he might have been able to demand in other circumstances. In the whole field of Anglo-Irish relations, his intemperate behaviour over the Falklands, his failure to sustain any kind of relationship with Margaret Thatcher, his inability to achieve even rudimentary concessions for the Republic in monitoring the affairs of Northern Ireland, made his whole policy on the North look threadbare. Put succinctly, which in a rare moment of economy Garret FitzGerald did, in respect of the period preceding this election, 'It had been an appalling six months for Anglo-Irish relations.'[1] The playing of the 'Green Card', with innuendoes of collusion and treachery in FitzGerald's meetings with the Duke of Norfolk and his close identity of thought with James Prior, simply did not work.

At the end of the campaign the two leaders debated the issues on television. FitzGerald, who had been under fairly tight management control by his 'handlers', was aware of RTE's plan to have the two leaders meet before the debate, shake hands and be photographed. He turned down the proposal and arrived just in time to go straight into the studio. At his best, FitzGerald is a powerful performer in debate and he was well briefed. He demolished claims about the economic document and when Northern Ireland was discussed, including the issue of the all-Ireland police force, he delivered a simple but devastating 'stroke' by handing Haughey a copy of the relevant speech and asking him to point out the proposal. Haughey came out of the encounter the loser. He lost the national vote as well. Fine Gael, with 39 per cent of the vote, won 70 seats, only 5 behind Fianna Fáil. With the Labour Party, the prospective coalition had an overall majority of 6. By 85 votes to 79, Garret FitzGerald was elected Taoiseach for the second time. And Charles Haughey, his dreams of power once more shattered, was again in Opposition.

The year's events, sorry, tangled and in some respects shaming, still needed some clearing up. In the election aftermath a page-one story appeared in *The Irish Times* revealing that the telephones of two journalists had been tapped.[2] The article's author, Peter Murtagh, who was security correspondent for the paper, had been aware of the facts for some time, but had wisely held back on the story during the final stages of the election in order to confirm certain points. The story was confirmed by the Government. They sought the permission of

[1] Garret FitzGerald, op. cit., p. 412.
[2] *The Irish Times*, 18 December 1982.

Geraldine Kennedy and myself to investigate the matter fully. In January, the Commissioner for the country's police force, Patrick McGloughlin, and the Deputy Commissioner, Joe Ainsworth, resigned. Full details of the phone-tapping were revealed by the new Fine Gael Minister for Justice, Michael Noonan, together with details of the supply of a tape-recorder, on the instructions of the Minister for Justice, to the Minister for Finance, Ray McSharry, who then used it covertly to record a conversation between himself and Martin O'Donoghue.

My phone had been tapped from 10 May to 12 July; Geraldine Kennedy's phone had been tapped from 28 July to 16 November. On 27 October, when the warrant on her phone had come up for quarterly review, a certificate had been issued to the effect that the surveillance 'was yielding results'.[1]

The official reasons for surveillance in each of our cases were couched in different terms. In the case of Geraldine Kennedy the reason was 'national security' – in effect because of alleged leaks from the Government. This was a departure from the usual wording, 'security' being the standard for two – and only two – justifications for telephone-tapping in the State. These two relate to serious crime and to subversive activity. And, in the context of the second justification, this in part may explain the tapping of the phones of other journalists, notably those whose work involves legitimate contact with members of para-military organizations.[2]

It provided no justification in the two cases which came to light at the end of 1982. In the case of Geraldine Kennedy's warrant, the Department of Justice objected to the change of reference to 'national security' and recommended to the Minister for Justice, Sean Doherty, that the certificate should not be accepted. It was, however.[3]

In my own case the justifications given had much more serious implications and went far beyond the matter of Government leaks,

[1] Ministerial statement, 20 January 1983. There were three statements in all issued on the evening of that day to a crowded press conference. One dealt with the resignations of the country's two most senior police officers and a third dealt with the other example of surveillance.

[2] At least two journalists, Tim Pat Coogan, former editor of the *Irish Press* and the author of a number of books, including one about the IRA, and Vincent Browne, who wrote extensively about the IRA during the 1970s, are thought to have had their phones tapped.

[3] There was a further complication, in respect of Geraldine Kennedy, in that she was living in an apartment where the telephone was registered in another name, meaning that the warrant had the number only on it.

stigmatizing me in terms which, particularly in 1982, were both damaging and hard to refute: 'Mr Arnold was anti-national in his outlook and might be obtaining information from sources of a similar disposition.'[1]

The tapping of both phones was allegedly to track down 'leaks' from the Government, which Sean Doherty was said by the Deputy Commissioner to have offered as the main justification. This made no sense. Doherty offered no actual information on such leaks, nor was there any. Nor had there been any publication of Government discussions or decisions by either of us in our respective newspapers. Our articles at the time were well-informed as to what was going on, but in no sense did they invade the strict territory of 'Government or cabinet secrecy'. They were about political disagreements, party differences and divisions and reservations about Haughey's leadership. Given this, the action by the Minister for Justice was unquestionably illegal.

The reason, in both cases, was to track down the sources for well-informed articles about the future plans of the dissidents within the Fianna Fáil Party – what they were saying and what their strategies might be. This was an essentially futile pursuit. In my own case, I had already expressed, in the course of a tapped conversation, my reservations about speaking too freely on the telephone. I had been alerted by the Jim Mitchell allegations in the Dáil, in the summer, and by certain oblique references in conversations with politicians. Most such conversations, in any case, took place in Leinster House.

But there was one phone conversation, with George Colley, who stood in high esteem in the country, and this alarmed and offended those engaged in the surveillance. There were Department of Justice protests about the Colley surveillance and when they went unheeded, Opposition politicians were alerted about the improper surveillance.

Once set in train, the illegal acts became institutionalized. Those engaged in the day-to-day tapping of the two telephones 'took it for granted from the identity of the two journalists concerned that what

[1] Statement by the Minister for Justice, 20 January 1982. When Deputy Commissioner Ainsworth was informed of this reason he gave the morally rather crumpled response that 'he would wish it to be known, in fairness to Mr Arnold and himself, that any comment on those lines would have been intended as a reference to a view that some might hold about some of Mr Arnold's published opinions and intended also as confirmation that there was no suggestion of any kind that Mr Arnold had any association or contact with para-military organizations.' In other words I was not trying to import arms illegally or consorting with members of the IRA; I was only writing in an anti-national way. And for this my phone was tapped.

they in the Garda Siochana were expected to look out for was material of party political interest. Apart from the fact that some of them have said so explicitly, the proof is in the fact that the excerpts that were transcribed by them were for all practical purposes exclusively concerned with party political matters.'[1]

'Security' became 'national security'; then it became 'Government leaks'; finally it became the tracking down of alleged party 'disloyalty'. And this shabby and illegal abuse of power was discussed in these totally unacceptable terms by the Minister for Justice, the Commissioner and Deputy Commissioner of the country's police force, and by others, both in the Department of Justice and the police. And it was discussed between Doherty and Haughey.

Haughey strenuously denied any knowledge at all of the phone-tapping. In a radio interview he said that neither he nor the Government knew anything about the telephone-tapping. Asked directly, 'Did you know about any of these affairs disclosed in the Department of Justice?', Haughey replied: 'Not at all. No. But then, again, I wouldn't know about them. As Taoiseach you wouldn't know about these things. This is a very secret, confidential area of Government activity and it is normally confined to the Minister for Justice, the Department of Justice, the Garda Siochana.' He later added: 'I want to make it crystal clear that the Government as such, and I as Taoiseach, knew absolutely nothing of activities of this sort, and would not countenance any such abuse.'[2] In a statement issued the day after the Noonan press conference, Haughey said: 'Before leaving office as Taoiseach I had taken preliminary steps to establish such an inquiry as I considered that the many allegations made about political interference with the Garda Siochana should be fully investigated.' He also established 'a special inquiry team' within Fianna Fáil.

Sean Doherty accepted the Noonan interpretation of the events at the time and this led to his departure from the Fianna Fáil front bench and his effective disgrace within the organization for many years. It also contributed to the loss of his Roscommon seat in the 1989 general election, his failure to win a European seat that year and the continued public perception of him as the unacceptable face of the Fianna Fáil Party.

The statements made by Charles Haughey, immediately after the

[1] Statement by Michael Noonan, 20 January 1983.
[2] RTE interview, February 1983.

phone-tapping was officially made public, placed Doherty in an impossible position. And this was further reinforced by the Fianna Fáil Party statement, which followed, calling for a full judicial inquiry. The collective weight of this gave Sean Doherty only two options. He could go along with and endorse the position adopted by his leader and the party; or he could confront Haughey, there and then, with the truth. In all this he was under massive pressure, both within the party and in the public eye. Many people will understand why he took the dishonourable course.

CHAPTER XIX

OUT OF POWER

I do agnize
A natural and prompt alacrity
I find in hardness.

MANY PEOPLE HAVE SAID that the incoming Government led by Garret FitzGerald devoted too much of its time and energy to Northern Ireland, and not enough to the economy. Yet that Government did achieve the present permanent settlement whereby the British and Irish administrations, through formal treaty, play a joint part in the administration of Northern Ireland and, until some better solution emerges, this represents a set of safeguards breached only by the violence associated with terrorism. As regards the economy, there was from the start recognition of its dire circumstances and a consistent effort was made to put them into some kind of order. Despite its later instabilities, this represented a very considerable achievement.

Haughey supported neither of these two main initiatives. He adopted from the start a negative approach to the Government's programme for Northern Ireland and he then advocated a *reflation* of the economy, by borrowing, a reversal of McSharry's policies of the second half of 1982. And this at a time when exchequer borrowing was running at 14 per cent of GNP.

But before embarking upon this particular line of opposition, which he sustained during much of the period under Garret FitzGerald, he first had to deal with internal revolt. To most people, at the end of January, Haughey's survival prospects looked bleak. On three successive occasions he had failed to lead his party to a convincing victory. When he had managed to scramble into power, after the February 1982 election, it had led to one of the most disreputable administrations in modern Irish political history. Fianna Fáil had sunk terribly in public esteem. Haughey had managed to sever himself from direct personal involvement in the disgrace of Doherty, who resigned the party whip, and McSharry, who moved from the front bench to backbench status after the scandal concerning the tape-recording of a conversation with a colleague had come to light. But Haughey was seen by more people than ever before as the inspiration for such declining standards.

The challenge to Haughey's leadership, when it came, produced several contenders, including Michael O'Kennedy and Gerard Collins. It was thought that John Wilson might also stand for the leadership. Newspapers became convinced that Haughey was on the point of resigning. The *Irish Press*, on Thursday, 27 January 1983, ran a two-page political profile of Haughey, covering his whole career, the *Irish Independent* ran a front-page story headed 'Haughey may quit', and *The Irish Times* claimed 'Haughey resignation thought imminent as support crumbles'. The party meeting was set for 2 February, but then Clement Coughlan, a deputy from Donegal travelling to Dublin for the meeting, was killed in a car crash and, in controversial circumstances, the meeting was put off until the following week. On the day of the Coughlan funeral, Haughey issued a statement to all members of the Fianna Fáil organization throughout the country, calling on them for their support: 'Are its policies and its leader in future to be decided for it by the media, by alien influences, by political opponents or, worst of all, by business interests pursuing their own ends?'[1] There were alarmed reactions to the statement. Haughey was seen as pre-empting the democratic right of the parliamentary party to call for his resignation and choose a successor. One deputy, Ben Briscoe, said in a radio interview that the statement 'smacked of dictatorship' and he tabled a motion calling for resignation 'now'.

With his usual resourcefulness and a stubborn determination not to relinquish his hold on power – at least within his own party – Haughey mustered his forces and fought on what was by now familiar territory. In an interview the day before the party meeting he claimed that an overwhelming majority of members and supporters of Fianna Fáil wanted him to stay on. 'Politics are my life. I fight battles, I try and move things forward, do what I can, achieve progress, achieve reforms, achieve improvements, look after the old people, look after the disadvantaged.'[2]

---

[1] Public press statement made on his behalf.
[2] RTE interview, 'This Week' programme, 6 February 1983.

An issue central to the party meeting was the phone-tapping. Though not unanimous, the committee chaired by Jim Tunney discovered the unknowable: that Haughey had not known of the phone-tapping. An extensive debate on this was followed by Haughey seeking to remove the party whip from Sean Doherty and Martin O'Donoghue. The substantive issue of his resignation came next. Once again, by 40 votes to 33, Haughey retained leadership of the party. It was an astonishing outcome. Commentators had run out of comment. The press corps was punch-drunk. Prediction was a futile exercise. Logic seemed an entirely un-Irish pursuit. Chaos was the political order of things.

The scenes that night inside and outside Leinster House were as extraordinary and as frightening as they had been the previous autumn. After receiving details of the vote and filing a story, I left the press gallery and went down the stairs with two colleagues – who expressed diffidence about walking with me – into the crowded hallway. Angry supporters there included Haughey's brother 'Jock', who launched himself towards me, but was intercepted by two ministerial police drivers and held back by them. The Leinster House superintendent then suggested that the group of journalists who had gathered round me should leave by the back entrance through Leinster Lawns. He reached for the handle of the door, but for some reason it was being held on the other side and he called for the assistance of ushers. As we stood around waiting I tried in turn to open the door. By this stage the handle was free again and it swung open easily. As we passed through it, Vincent Browne pointed at me and turned to the superintendent. 'He can walk on water, too,' he said and we left.

As if in keeping with this prescription, it was Brian Lenihan who wrote in the *Irish Independent* after the contest: 'We have had three such leadership meetings within twelve months and the almost unanimous view now is that we do not want any more. It is essential that we should get on with our business in Opposition and as the alternative Government under the leadership of Charles Haughey. It is my belief that there will not be a residue of lasting bitterness after the third challenge to Mr Haughey's leadership. In fact, psychologically, it is quite the reverse. Everybody in the Parliamentary Party now recognizes that we simply cannot afford to go along this path of frequent challenges to the leadership.'[1] When the press had regained its breath and recovered its equilibrium, it came to much the same conclusion.

[1] Brian Lenihan, 'FF – Time to heal the ugly wounds', *Irish Independent*, 9 February 1983.

When Haughey announced a new front bench, two weeks later, with Dessie O'Malley prominent on it and with Denis Gallagher and Bobby Molloy restored to it, the last thing anyone wanted to pursue was the idea of disunity or dissaffection. Haughey, 'true to his political character . . . virtually ignored even the possibility of there being differences, splits or divisions in Fianna Fáil; therefore, of course, there was no reconciling to be done. The illusion of opposition to himself was a thing of the past. Personality was to be played down. All of that represented backward thinking. Fianna Fáil, as exemplified in the Front Bench presented to a very minor key press corps yesterday afternoon, was unified, determined, purposeful, as it looked keenly towards the back of the room and played down personality with throbbing conviction.'[1] George Colley was the major absentee. He had not been approached and had made a fairly dignified retreat to the back benches.

With the party endorsement of his leadership now clearly established, Haughey undertook the challenge of opposition with a vengeance. It has frequently been said of this period that he opposed for opposition's sake, without proper regard for the interests of the country. Garret FitzGerald certainly anticipated no assistance. 'I knew that they would oppose ruthlessly and opportunistically all the unpleasant measures that their past actions in government would now force us to take.'[2] And though this judgement applied primarily to the economy, FitzGerald was also gloomy about any initiatives that he might take on Northern Ireland.

Yet Haughey himself was in a difficult position. Fianna Fáil has never been a party of policies. It prides itself on pragmatism and historically its instincts were remarkably sound, at least under its first three leaders. They had all fostered a reasonably democratic balance and had all brought on successors, even if the first transition – from de Valera to Lemass – had perhaps been over-delayed. Haughey, in changing this, had centralized decision-making to an extreme degree and now, totally in control, had to dictate what attitudes were adopted, what statements made. He both set the tone and delivered the message. And he felt that he was under pressure to make it aggressive. Any other approach would require quite substantial concessions, since the main direction of FitzGerald's policies indicated sharp disagreement with what Haughey had done before.

[1] Present author, 'FF's front bench – The best or a compromise?' *Irish Independent*, 22 February 1983.
[2] Garret FitzGerald, op. cit., p. 428.

When he went before the party's annual conference, just a fortnight after the third leadership challenge, it was a triumphant and triumphalist occasion. Power, authority, discipline, direction inspired his every word. Peter Murtagh and Joe Joyce describe the occasion: 'Brian Lenihan whipped up the crowd just before Haughey once again stepped on to the platform to make his presidential address. It was timed to last slightly less than the normal one and a half hours. The bit over was to allow time for the extra cheering and applause. The crowd went wild when Haughey appeared and it was several minutes before he could begin his address. He told them he would do everything in his power to prove worthy of the trust they placed in him. "The difficulties we have had are now behind us. We are again on the high road as a great unified party: there will be no turning back. We face the future eager and determined ... Looking around me here tonight I know one thing for sure. Those who sought to weaken and confuse us have failed." On a balcony, Haughey's brother Jock screamed: "Name them, name them." His words were drowned in the general tumult of applause. With him were most of Haughey's close friends. As Haughey's voice rose and fell during the speech, some of them paced up and down the balcony, identifying several of his enemies in the crowd below ... Haughey was given an eight-minute standing ovation by the 7,000 delegates and observers in the hall ... "It was", Haughey said later, "the greatest, the best, the most wonderful Ard Fheis of all time."'[1]

The most serious purpose of his speech was to make Northern Ireland a central policy issue for the party and to bring neutrality to the forefront. The message was hardline; it called for a constitutional conference as 'a prelude to a final withdrawal of Britain from Ireland within a stipulated period of time, enabling the Irish people North and South to come together and freely determine their future. Such a multi-representative constitutional conference would work out the conditions for the transfer of power to new political structures for the whole island.' It was not a promising message and cut no ice either north of the Border or in Britain. But then, was this the intention? Its real focus was FitzGerald and his quite different set of perceptions about the way forward. Both he and Haughey did share concern about the threat which the IRA represented, as it seemed to gain support at that time. But FitzGerald's answer was

[1] Peter Murtagh and Joe Joyce, op. cit., pp. 353–4.

an All-Ireland Forum designed to achieve peace and stability through democratic processes.

The story of the Forum for a New Ireland, to give it its full title, leading as it did to the Anglo-Irish Agreement, is a monument to Garret FitzGerald's ability and determination to achieve change in not very promising circumstances. He had to deal with a tough lady in Margaret Thatcher, who took a great deal of persuading. He had to keep the SDLP party fully in support of what he was attempting. He had to win over the Unionists. He had to satisfy the Church on certain issues. And he had to work out some kind of operating procedure for debates which would involve Haughey. He could not expect support, but if Haughey walked away from the Forum it would probably collapse.

As far as Garret FitzGerald was concerned, the Forum for a New Ireland was conceived in order to provide him with a mandate for an Anglo-Irish agreement. It was his very strong wish that the Unionists should use this opportunity to present their point of view in the Republic. Unhappily, they were overlooked. Nor was FitzGerald's relationship with the SDLP entirely plain sailing. Between Fianna Fáil and Fine Gael there had always been competition for the loyalty and involvement of the Northern Ireland nationalist party and Haughey's initial bid for this, made at the party conference in February, involved pressing for John Hume's current idea, favouring a 'Council' for a new Ireland, which would bring together the nationalist parties without *all* the other parties becoming involved. FitzGerald completely misread the attitude of his own Government and had to use a good deal of pressure to persuade them to adopt his scheme in advance of Haughey plumping for the Hume proposal. He also had his work cut out persuading John Hume. Hume's commitment became the deciding factor for Haughey and, with minor amendments, the Forum was agreed. But it was something of a botched job. The Alliance Party in Northern Ireland was by no means treated as conscientiously as the SDLP. Nor were the two Unionist parties. And even FitzGerald's own Government was not handled well. His own description of this period reveals considerable anxiety about how to handle Haughey. There was the need to 'outmanoeuvre', to 'persuade', even to allow Haughey to claim, without justification, that the Forum would lead to his 'all-round constitutional conference' and on from that to a 'final constitutional settlement'.

The Forum debates did not go all that smoothly, but did progress.

Haughey, never a great debater, was nevertheless shrewd in his handling of certain episodes and quick to take advantage of situations.
Notably, on one occasion, in respect of submissions made by two
economists, Sir Charles Carter and Louden Ryan, who showed convincingly that Northern Ireland, deprived of United Kingdom sub-
sidies, would be far worse off and the Republic would be faced with a
heavy burden. Haughey, in a scripted statement 'apparently prepared
by Martin Mansergh',[1] insisted that Britain would have to provide the
finance for a united Ireland. Though the deliberations were confidential and only reported to the press in briefings, there were many leaks.
On one occasion, when both FitzGerald and Haughey had voiced their
anger at these disclosures, Dick Spring asserted that at least some of
them were emanating from Fianna Fáil sources. According to Fitz-
Gerald, whose account is the only extensive one so far published,
Haughey was outraged and threatened to withdraw unless Spring
retracted, which Spring refused to do. Then Haughey appealed to the
Forum as a whole, claiming that he had never betrayed confidences
and that 'No one has suffered more than I have from journalists', and
then broke down. Though FitzGerald at first thought it an act, it
turned out that Haughey was truly shaken. The previous day, a book
by Peter Murtagh and Joe Joyce, *The Boss*, which dealt with Haughey's
political career generally, but concentrated in particular on the events
of 1982, the GUBU crises and the phone-tapping, had been published.
It had caused Haughey and his family considerable distress and he was
absent for about an hour before the leaders sat down to lunch. It was
only after this, and after Spring and Haughey had become reconciled,
that the combination of causes emerged. To the dismay of both Spring
and FitzGerald, they realized, on discussing the matter later, that they
had both listed *The Boss* for their Christmas reading in reply to a survey
which was to be published the following Sunday by Vincent Browne.[2]
Though it was something of a confirmation of their fears, FitzGerald
discovered, when he rang Browne to ask him to delete the references
to the book, that Browne already knew of Haughey's breakdown!

Haughey was shrewd enough to know that the underlying strategy
of the Forum was to obtain an agreed position between the participating parties on a set of options, even on a preferred option, which would
then allow the Government to go forward with negotiations leading

[1] Ibid., p. 479.
[2] Vincent Browne was now editor of the *Sunday Tribune*.

to an agreement. Once the forum process was over it would be a matter for negotiators. Indeed, side-by-side with the Forum discussions, this negotiating process was already going on. It was therefore necessary for Haughey to make his mark during the weeks of debate, and above all in drawing up the final conclusions. Disagreement turned on the options, three in number, which were to be included in the final report: that the 'new Ireland' envisaged in their deliberations would be either a unitary state, or some kind of federal/confederal structure, or governed by a 'joint authority' exercised by the British and Irish Governments. The Fianna Fáil delegation favoured 'the unitary state', and wanted a general commitment to it as 'the best and the only constitutional model for a new Ireland'. Both Spring and FitzGerald reckoned that this would be counter-productive; so did John Hume. There was some disagreement between Hume and Seamus Mallon, who sided more strongly with the Fianna Fáil position, inherently more republican.

For Haughey the Forum had been something of an ordeal, testing in the most real and fundamental ways his beliefs about Ireland's future, his capacity to handle very complex debating situations, his command over his party's loyalty on issues that were central to what it thought of as its 'core values', and his own personal difficulties in contributing to a process that was very much the initiative of his main political rival. He consented to the range of options. FitzGerald obtained his grounds for the start of major negotiations. 'It had been an unprecedented episode in Irish political history. In the course of eleven months the three main political parties in the Irish state, together with the constitutional nationalist party of Northern Ireland, had met on almost a hundred occasions, including over fifty leaders' meetings, to establish a considerable measure of common ground on the most divisive national issue.'[1]

It did not quite end there. When the Forum completed its deliberations and the party leaders gave press conferences, Haughey took a narrow and hawkish public line: 'The only solution is as stated in the report: a unitary state with a new constitution'. This damaged the value of the final report, since it undermined the reality, which was that the actual written text represented an agreed, four-party position. Public perceptions, as a result of the way Fianna Fáil had briefed the

[1] Ibid., p. 491. The lengthy account in the book is, perhaps for obvious reasons, by far the best published record of the background to this historic event.

press and the way Haughey himself presented its conclusions, were and remained confused. Politically, the report allowed Haughey to imply that he and the others had agreed to differ and therefore restored to him the remnants of his earlier Northern Ireland policy.

But he paid a price. The Forum delegation had included Ray McSharry, despite the fact that the phone-tapping revelations concerning his bugging of a conversation with Martin O'Donoghue had forced him on to the back benches. McSharry had been a significant hardliner in presenting the Fianna Fáil point of view. Not only that; he had, on the questionable basis of being part of the Fianna Fáil delegation, chosen to speak out on Northern Ireland, something which Haughey did not allow. The outcome, despite Haughey's earlier success against the third leadership challenge and the supremacy this supposedly gave him, offended some within the party.[1] Senator Eoin Ryan called for a proper debate on the line taken at the Forum. This was held and Haughey got the support of the party, but Desmond O'Malley publicly criticized the way in which real discussion had been stifled. Haughey moved against him immediately. The party whip was withdrawn on a 56–16 vote, an event which occasioned the brief and cryptic characterization of the Fianna Fáil Party by its new press officer, P. J. Mara, as 'uno duce, una voce'. This slogan of the Italian *Fascisti*, glossed in more human terms by Mara when he added 'There'll be no more nibbling at my leader's bum', was typical of the more printable epithets and epigrams which derived from the new party press officer. But it also emphasized McSharry's special position; he was free to speak, O'Malley was not.

When the 'uno duce, una voce' remark was quoted by Geraldine Kennedy, in the *Sunday Tribune*, Haughey was furious. Mara recovered his equilibrium, but switched to calling his boss by a different name. Instead of 'Duce' he became 'the Caudillo'.

Mara's closeness to Haughey, his inexhaustible store of stories and the apparently intimate detail he was prepared to divulge, gave him a unique position as a 'source'. 'He kept the political journalists entertained with anecdotes and impersonations of the leading lights in the party, including his boss. His indiscretions soon became legendary but they were often so scabrous or libellous that they were unprintable.

---

[1] Gemma Hussey, *At the Cutting Edge: Cabinet Diaries 1982–1987*, Dublin, 1990. Entry for 15 February 1984 says, 'Had a little chat with Martin O'Donoghue, who says that Charlie Haughey is under threat again.'

While they didn't do any harm to his boss they conveyed the impression that Mara was telling all there was to know. As a result journalists believed they were getting the inside track on what was happening in government but at the same time they never got much usable information.'[1] At this time, of course, Mara was speaking on behalf of a party in Opposition.

In the Forum, FitzGerald had achieved his objective: 'Only in one respect did it fall short of what I had wanted: its preparation had taken four months more than I had allowed for.'[2] It was a problem central to Garret FitzGerald's period in power. Gargantuan in his appetite for work and in the unique digestive system he seemed able to apply to documents, ideas, proposals and reports, his actual planning for his own and Government business never took sufficient note of possible setbacks or of unforeseen developments. And the physical strain of this was obvious: 'Garret was looking grey and worn out at Cabinet on Thursday and also on Friday' was how Gemma Hussey described him in her diary.[3]

One of the setbacks, which had taken up time at the outset of this period, was the abortion referendum, on which Haughey achieved a political victory. From the late 1970s Roman Catholic anti-abortion organizations, aware of the growing permissiveness which had allowed abortion on demand in many democracies, became alarmed at the possibility of legalized abortion in Ireland and started to campaign for an absolute ban to be written into the Irish Constitution. The Society for the Protection of the Unborn Child and the Pro-Life Campaign began to lobby political leaders and politicians generally from the beginning of the 1980s. In fulfilment of his own promises made to the Pro-Life organization, Haughey had published a wording for the amendment of the Constitution just before the general election in November 1982. FitzGerald had found nothing wrong with it and, in the interests of keeping it out of the campaign – since it was potentially divisive – had agreed to it. Early in 1983 Peter Sutherland, the Attorney General, found fault with the wording – correctly, as it turned out – and proposed an alternative. This led to general division on this issue and generated a public debate that was totally at odds with the spirit and intent of the whole Forum discussions, based as they were on

[1] Stephen Collins, *The Haughey File*, Dublin, 1992, p. 69.
[2] Garret FitzGerald, op. cit., p. 491.
[3] Gemma Hussey, op. cit., entry for 20 May 1984.

an attempt to achieve consensus. A modest victory for Haughey ensued when the Fianna Fáil wording was adopted in the Dáil, rather than the revised wording which Peter Sutherland had proposed. But it was to have far-reaching implications. Once adopted, the country went ahead with a painfully contentious campaign which resulted in approval for what was seen as a cast-iron constitutional ban on abortion. The constitutional amendment was put to the people on 7 September. In a turnout of 54 per cent, it was carried by a two-to-one majority. In one sense the Forum debate healed some of the breaches. By the time the abortion referendum was passed, in September 1983, the issue seemed to belong very much to the past – an unfortunate episode, but possibly a mere verbal formula, unlikely to materialize in any of the sorry outcomes of which opponents of the wording had warned.

The Forum, on the other hand, was forward-looking and rep-resented a staging for the more important inter-governmental negoti-ations which FitzGerald had set in train early in 1983, bringing together a powerful team of civil servants to work towards an agree-ment. His preoccupations from 1983 on were to be principally the economy and Northern Ireland. Haughey's own preoccupations, apart from the Forum involvement, were far from any such constructive contributions to economic and related social issues. He was still con-cerned with internal party unity and the growing impression that he was failing to unite the party behind him. He was also failing to gain any electoral advantage out of the increasingly rocky time the Fitz-Gerald-led coalition was experiencing. In the European elections, in the summer of 1984, despite an increase in the number of seats, cor-recting the near-disaster which the party had faced in 1979, Fianna Fáil's vote was clearly not sufficient to offer the party any positive prospect of an overall majority in a general election. It really rep-resented a *fourth* electoral defeat for Haughey and was seen in this light by many in the party.

With George Colley's sudden death, in September 1983, Haughey's anxiety about further challenges to his authority focused almost exclu-sively on Desmond O'Malley. Other courageous backbenchers, notably Mary Harney, stood up against him on certain issues, but O'Malley was a real force, commanding deserved national admiration for his political ability and judgement. The removal of the whip from him, over Northern Ireland policy, set in train his departure from Fianna Fáil. It also turned him into one of the most powerful figures in the country, in due course to become the maker of governments, the

breaker of reputations other than his own. For the present, he was set
on a collision-course with Haughey, which came to a head in the
family planning legislation introduced by FitzGerald's Government in
February 1985.

O'Malley had had enough of the pusillanimous subservience of
Fianna Fáil to the Roman Catholic Church and self-interest, in whatever order these powerful motivations for politics in Ireland chose to
arrange themselves. He took a stand on the legislation brought forward
by the Coalition, gave a brilliant speech, supportive of the Bill which
greatly modernized and liberalized the image of the Republic in the
eyes of the world and particularly in the eyes of the people of Northern
Ireland, and then abstained. Barry Desmond, Minister for Health and
therefore responsible for the legislation, described the speech as the
best he had heard in thirteen years in the Dáil and the measure was
passed. It was a moment of deep humiliation for Haughey and for the
Fianna Fáil Party. Their attitude towards the Bill had been callously
political. They had sought only to shame and defeat the moves to
give freer access to contraception and to advice. They had aligned
themselves with the most entrenched conservatism of Roman Catholic
Church teaching.

O'Malley's abstention was a symbolic act. It did not decide the issue.
The measure was carried by 83 votes to 80. 'Today we defeated the
bishops and Fianna Fáil and Oliver J. Flanagan!' wrote a jubilant Minister for Education, Gemma Hussey, in her diary entry for Wednesday,
20 February 1985.[1] O'Malley had shamed his party, quite rightly. But
the party sought its revenge. His expulsion from the organization, as
opposed to his loss of the whip in the Dáil, was proposed and he was
summoned to party headquarters in Mount Street to face a motion
against him almost a week after the vote, on the night of 26 February.

O'Malley correctly asked for a secret ballot. This was in accordance
with party rules which required all votes to be secret. It was quite
clear that there was no possibility of a unanimous vote, but Haughey
countered by demanding an open, roll-call vote and no one opposed
him. The motion to expel O'Malley was passed by 73 votes to 9.

To many people, heroic though O'Malley's stand against Haughey
had been and dignified though his acceptance of this parting of the
ways was, it did look like the end of a career. But the gap he left behind

---

[1] Ibid., p. 143. Oliver J. Flanagan was a conservative Fine Gael backbencher who had been
Minister for Defence under Cosgrave, in the latter period of the 1973–77 coalition.

him did not close up. He had left a gaping hole in the Fianna Fáil Party's ideology, taking with him an irreplaceable set of principles. He had stood up for an older version of Fianna Fáil. The real divide in the party went back to the 1960s. It came to a climax in 1970, with the Arms Crisis, and was essentially a division between Haughey and Lynch. In the period of just over five years since Haughey had taken over, he had increasingly acted as though the party had become his possession. His style had become more and more dictatorial. He saw himself as the Government, his ministers as advisers and executives, bringing their ideas to him, being told what to do and being sent on their mission to fulfil the brooding, solitary, visionary concepts which issued from his threatening presence. The fact that the concepts themselves were usually ill-conceived, and often wrong for the country and for the party, may have distressed a growing number of its members, but had signally failed to bring about change.

O'Malley was interested in change. He wanted the vacuum filled. He wanted the kind of beliefs which Lynch had represented restored to Irish politics, not because they were Lynch's – they went a good deal further than that – but because they were also O'Malley's and they were clearly not forthcoming from any other source. To some extent FitzGerald, who – with reservations – admired Lynch, had tried to attract some of those elements from Fianna Fáil, but with indifferent success. Nor was it just a question of alternative attitudes within Fianna Fáil being suppressed in an increasingly undemocratic manner. O'Malley's reservations about Haughey went much deeper than that. In the heat of his anger and dismay, O'Malley declared that he had reservations about Haughey's fitness for public office, his judgement, the specific presentation, in power, of economic data – particularly the presentation of the 1981 estimates, which was 'not as it should have been' – and he summarized his views by stating that 'the Fianna Fáil Party, under Charles Haughey, [was] authoritarian and undemocratic, a party in which differences of opinion, however slight, were seen as disloyalty or treachery.' This was grim, irreversible and caustic criticism made by O'Malley in the immediate aftermath of his expulsion from the Fianna Fáil Party, on Wednesday 27 February 1985. He later sought to moderate the stark criticisms of his former leader. But O'Malley's departure from Fianna Fáil in such circumstances raised straight away the prospect of a new political party. O'Malley had served fourteen highly eventful years as a dynamic part of the leadership of Fianna Fáil and was forty-six years old. Opinion polls at the time

demonstrated that there was, in the country, considerable support for
the idea of a new political party representing a similar set of views to
those expressed by O'Malley and traceable back to the Fianna Fáil of
Lynch, Lemass and de Valera.

O'Malley had no choice but to follow the consequences of this final
breach with Haughey. He would have to establish a new party, since
there was no future for him as an independent. Not many commentators interpreted his situation in these terms. But opinion polls
consistently endorsed public demand for or expectation of a new,
O'Malley-led party. They also registered a sizeable drop in support
for Haughey as a result of the expulsion. The biggest problem of all
was the hold which the Fianna Fáil organization had over so many of
its supporters. The party is a way of life to its members and from this
it derives both its strengths and its weaknesses. Instinct and loyalty
play an inordinate part in the way it manages and directs itself, which
largely removes the need for carefully wrought policies. And this same
instinctive sense of what the party believes has a powerful hold on its
members.

From the ordinary constituency workers in O'Malley's home base
of Limerick to fellow deputies in the Dáil who were deeply dissatisfied
with Haughey's leadership, there was resistance to the idea of a new
party, despite the strong backing which the opinion polls accorded it.
O'Malley himself was in doubt for much of the summer of 1985.
Earlier in the year, Michael McDowell[1] had welcomed the idea of a
new party and had expressed his interest in co-writing a letter to
O'Malley, following O'Malley's expulsion. McDowell was in Fine Gael
and was chairman of the party organization in Garret FitzGerald's
own constituency. But he was disillusioned with the performance of
the Coalition and the direction being taken by Fine Gael and had
actually expressed this disillusionment, a pledge never to vote again
for the Fine Gael–Labour Coalition, in a speech to the constituency
organization. It had greatly irritated the party leader.

Haughey played a significant part himself in bringing O'Malley's
new party into existence. Much of 1985 had been concerned with
negotiations between the British and Irish Governments on Northern

---

[1] Michael McDowell (b. 1951) is a Senior Counsel, and was active with Fine Gael, being
chairman of the branch to which Garret FitzGerald belonged until 1986. He then became
a founder-member of the Progressive Democrats and its chairman. He was elected to the
Dáil in 1987, lost his seat in 1989 and regained it in 1992. He is a grandson of Eoin McNeill,
leader of the Irish Volunteers, the man who attempted to call off the 1916 Rising.

Ireland and on 15 November the Anglo-Irish Agreement was signed. Haughey had earlier sent Brian Lenihan to the United States to lobby against the Agreement, to the consternation and dismay of leading Irish-Americans, including Tip O'Neill, speaker of the House of Representatives and a solid supporter of a moderate line on Ireland in the States. At home, Haughey denounced it and in the Dáil, when it came forward for ratification, opposed it. Such was the climate prevailing between Haughey and the Fine Gael leader, such the general expectation raised by the Agreement, that, in writing about it later, Garret FitzGerald displays a kind of world-weariness about Haughey: 'The negative character of that party's opposition during the 1982–87 Government on so many issues, and Charles Haughey's handling of the situation at the ending of the New Ireland Forum, had led me to expect that Fianna Fáil would vote against the agreement – although in view of the remarkable scale of public support for it this was, I think, a political mistake on their part. I calculated, however, that if, as I intended, we remained in power until early 1987, sufficient time would by then have elapsed for him to effect, as public opinion demanded, the necessary U-turn on the issue that would secure the survival of the agreement if, as seemed likely, the Government changed at that point.'[1] The Agreement was widely welcomed elsewhere, and certainly by O'Malley and Jack Lynch. Mary Harney, still at this stage within Fianna Fáil, issued a statement in support of the Agreement and said that she would vote for it, and did so, in company with Desmond O'Malley. A week later she was expelled. On 21 December the Progressive Democrats were formed. Haughey had helped create another party to oppose what he was doing and what he stood for. He made little of it. It would hurt the others, not Fianna Fáil. But, as in so many other things, his judgement was to be proved wrong.

[1] Garret FitzGerald, op. cit., p. 569. On most issues, by mid-1985, FitzGerald had written into all his political calculations the inevitability of Fianna Fáil obstruction. It was the hallmark of Haughey in opposition.

CHAPTER XX

THE FALL OF
GARRET FITZGERALD

For I do know the state,
However this may gall him with some check,
Cannot with safety cast him.

E ARLY IN 1986 Garret FitzGerald reshuffled his Government. The move was a disaster and set in train the gradual break-up of the Fine Gael–Labour pact. As in so much that he did, the reshuffle was rushed. Unlike so much that he did, it lacked motive and purpose. The broadly benign changes, aimed at adding experience to his senior ministerial team, had been previously announced for 'the second half of our term of office'. But, in spite of his worthy intentions, he failed to discuss them sufficiently with individual ministers. And, given the pressures under which they were working – in remarkable harmony, it must be said – the changes were inevitably misunderstood as a severe criticism for the failure of individuals. FitzGerald also totally misconceived the prospective and quite inappropriate splitting in two of the Department of Foreign Affairs. He only knew that he had made a mess of this on the very morning of the announcement.

Additionally, Barry Desmond refused to leave the Department of Health. He simply declined to be part of the reshuffle; others, of course, should have done the same, forcing FitzGerald to get back to normal business. It was so badly handled that Dick Spring threatened to resign and lead the Labour Party out of coalition. Gemma Hussey first learned of the offer of the new ministry for European affairs, which was to be constructed out of Foreign Affairs, on the evening of Wednesday, 14 February. 'I'm a bit stunned', she wrote in her diary. She expressed her worry that it would 'look like a souped-up junior ministry . . . Garret is adamant that it's a full ministry, but then he's not me . . . the Parliamentary Party is in a fit and now Garret has set his reshuffle in train. It may, however, be too late to save us and who

Sean Doherty and his wife, Maura, at his press conference, claiming that Charles Haughey knew about and saw the phone-tapping transcripts, 21 January 1992

Cartoon following phone-tapping revelations in 1992

At his January 1992 press
conference, denying
knowledge of the 1982
phone-tapping

Haughey's hands at
the press conference

Campaigning on behalf of his son, Sean, at St Brendan's Church, Coolock, in
Dublin North Central on the first Sunday of the 1992 general election

will he have to blame? I am desperately trying to protect myself and I hope I succeed.' On Friday, the morning of the announcement, she was then told that she would be getting Social Welfare instead. 'I am in black depression. Garret has made the most appalling mess of the reshuffle and I . . . have spent some of the time in tears and had seriously considered resignation . . . If Garret had thought I was a bad Minister for Education, surely he would have had the guts to tell me?'[1]

Haughey moved quickly, tabling a motion of no confidence in the Government. It was more than justified, not simply because of the botched reshuffle, but also because of the evidence this provided of growing strains within the partnership occasioned by the mounting tide of problems. Government meetings were going on until three and four in the morning. There were critical public service and teacher pay talks, there was the closure of Carysfort Training College, news of which was leaked, but the overriding problem was the Budget.

Over everything there hung the shadow of Desmond O'Malley's highly successful launch of his new party, the Progressive Democrats. The announcement of this, just four days before Christmas, had seemed an odd piece of timing. But in fact it coincided with the predictable shortage of hard news for newspapers during the Christmas holiday period and great attention was paid to every detail and each new development. When O'Malley called for £150,000 to get the party started, it was news. When crowds rolled in to the initial meetings, they were photographed and interviewed, and that was news. And when Haughey expressed the view that the Progressive Democrats were not acting in the public interest, it was taken as decisive endorsement of the wisdom and justice of O'Malley's decision. The party sustained its high standing in the opinion polls; in mid-January they were at 19 per cent, compared with Fine Gael at 22 per cent. Rather ruefully, Gemma Hussey summarized: 'O'Malley is really a rolling force; he has caught the people's imaginations without actually saying what he is going to do. How very frustrating when we're in there grappling with the impossible.'

Pearse Wyse, an experienced deputy from Cork, left Fianna Fáil to join the Progressive Democrats on 20 January. Three days later, in the biggest bombshell of all, Bobby Molloy resigned from the party and joined O'Malley at a Progressive Democrat rally in the huge

[1] Gemma Hussey, op. cit., p. 196-7

Leisureland complex in Galway. Molloy had been a party member and deputy for twenty years, and a Government colleague of O'Malley's under both Lynch and Haughey. He was a great vote-getter in the huge West Galway constituency, stretching into Connemara, and the shock of his departure, within Fianna Fáil, was enormous.

It was the last such shock. Despite other notable new members, no other Fianna Fáil deputies crossed over. There had been some expectation that Seamus Brennan or David Andrews might join the new party, but in the event they stayed put.

The damage had been done, however. O'Malley, in many respects a prickly political figure whose relationship with journalists, interviewers and commentators had never been particularly smooth, seemed to have brought off a near-perfect party launch. No public relations expert could possibly have wished for better. It was clear to Haughey that dismissiveness – his usual ploy when challenged, particularly by unforeseen developments – was not going to work. His old rival within Fianna Fáil had been transformed into a sparkling new kind of rival, instantly equipped with supporters, a team of fellow politicians, an impressive range of policies and, for an entirely new political party, unprecedented public approval.

Inevitably, Haughey mounted a strong attack on the FitzGerald-led Government, in a two-day confidence debate which had commentators questioning the value to Fine Gael, and therefore to the Coalition, of going into the next electoral contest under the leadership of Garret FitzGerald. That was the extent of the self-inflicted damage.

He had lost confidence within his own party to an unprecedented degree. He was now dominated by growing, and increasingly intractable, economic problems. The Anglo-Irish Agreement had provoked a substantial Unionist backlash which, while it did not threaten the accord, certainly indicated the errors they had made in ignoring the majority in Northern Ireland when negotiating the Agreement. He survived the motion; but the year continued to deteriorate for him. He lost another major battle over divorce. Its introduction required a referendum. FitzGerald prudently sought the prior agreement of the Churches and obtained from the Roman Catholic hierarchy a commitment 'not to tell people how to vote but to confine themselves to stating the Catholic moral position'.[1] The hierarchy did not adhere to this, however. Instead, there was a fierce pulpit campaign against

[1] Garret FitzGerald, op. cit., p. 631.

divorce. Though Fianna Fáil's stated position was neutral, there was in fact equally fierce party opposition throughout the country, not greatly motivated by concern for the victims of marriage breakdown, still less by moral dismay, but by the political advantage they might gain once the move looked as though it might fail. This perception was reinforced by the complicated presentation of the terms for the referendum, which made people fearful about property rights. It could more easily have been achieved if a simpler form of 'divorce by consent' had been proposed in order to amend the constitutional ban, thus leaving to later legislation whatever further necessary development seemed appropriate. In Gemma Hussey's opinion the campaign had been grossly mishandled, but 'Fianna Fáil have behaved utterly disgracefully and without principle all during this campaign and will come out unscathed.'[1] Haughey was magisterial in the way he presented the Fianna Fáil position, 'accepting, in a non-political way, the Government's decision to hold a Referendum and put the issue before the people. We have consistently maintained, over the years, that it was the duty of the Government to put forward proposals. The Government have now done that. In keeping with what we have been saying, it is now our duty to look calmly and objectively at what the Government has proposed, not to make a divisive political issue out of it, to examine every aspect and all the implications and then to leave it to the people to decide.'[2] He went on to blame Coalition deputies for attempting to politicize the campaign and stated that, in the Dáil and Senate at least, the party would not oppose. But the statement, a personal one from the party leader, contained a hidden agenda, part of which was a pious homily about the family. 'I have an unshakeable belief in the importance of having the family as a basic unity of our society. My experience of life tells me that this is the best way in which to organize society . . . Of course, it [divorce] has an appeal for some individuals, the attraction of superficial freedom. But in my view, the family is a great buttress for the individual. The family is a support system. The family is a natural grouping, and it seems to me that it is the best background against which to bring up children, prepare them for life and help them to meet the challenge of growing up and to cope with the difficulties and pressures. The family is an anchor for the individual, a haven of security and support. I give that as my purely

[1] Gemma Hussey, op. cit., entry for Tuesday, 24 June 1986, p. 222.
[2] Ed. Martin Mansergh, op. cit., Statement on the Amendment, 20 May 1986, p. 1120.

personal view.'[1] The statement went out to the party faithful as though it were an electoral manifesto and they responded accordingly.

Any comparison of speeches on the economy, throughout 1986, would suggest that the Coalition parties and Fianna Fáil were discussing the problems of different countries, or of Ireland in entirely different historical periods. While the Government grappled with the hard facts, Haughey developed glowing ideas about taxation reform and offered a future climate sympathetic to investment. There would be a host of job-creating initiatives, better industrial relations, a surge forward for building and construction, and better use of natural resources. The multiple recipes, broadly summarized in advance of the Budget at the beginning of the year and reinforced after its grim realities had been announced, became the basis for a series of relentless attacks.

In the autumn, actual Dáil support fell away from FitzGerald. He was threatened with defections from Fine Gael and Labour. A situation developed in which individual deputies could effectively hold the Government to ransom over constituency issues. Liam Skelly, who had been elected for Dublin West in the crucial by-election that followed Haughey's appointment of Richard Burke as European Commissioner, signalled he was contemplating defection. Alice Glenn, who was strongly opposed to FitzGerald's liberalism on social issues, failed to win re-selection in her own constituency and resigned the Fine Gael whip. And, in the Labour Party, several deputies, including the former party leader, Frank Cluskey, also threatened a withdrawal of support.

By mid-December it was clear that the Coalition would not be able to reach agreement on the 1987 Budget and that it would break up, precipitating an election. The event was amicable. Labour simply could not support the social welfare and health cuts which were required, and Dick Spring and his ministers resigned on 20 January.

'We had soldiered together in this Government for over four years, restoring confidence in the political independence of the Gardai and in the integrity of public life and introducing many social and tax reforms despite the financial pressures under which we operated. We had initiated the New Ireland Forum and had negotiated the Anglo-Irish Agreement . . . Although our two parties responded to somewhat different economic constituencies, we shared a deep concern for social justice, liberal values, and integrity in public life.'[2]

[1] Ibid., p. 1122
[2] Garret FitzGerald, op. cit., p. 640.

FitzGerald set the longest possible period for the election campaign. His purpose, as far as Haughey and Fianna Fáil were concerned, was to lock them into a debate about the economic measures already taken and block any exploitation of the fairy-tale world of optimism which Haughey had been presenting in so many of his speeches. FitzGerald also wanted the maximum amount of time in order to ensure the fullest possible debate on the economy. Fianna Fáil would have to account for the expenditure involved in fulfilling their promises and would also have to respond to the Government's budgetary intentions. And the predictable result was that support for Fianna Fáil declined as the campaign progressed. Haughey did not really help the situation in a television debate with FitzGerald, who taxed him with a remark made the previous day about renegotiating part of the Anglo-Irish Agreement. At this stage in FitzGerald's political fortunes, the Agreement was widely – if perhaps mistakenly – regarded as his principal achievement in ten years as leader of Fine Gael and after more than four years of gruelling political leadership. But he was greatly admired for it and attention quickened as it had failed to do during the earlier exchanges on the economy. Haughey made the mistake of denying that what he had said had referred to the Agreement at all, claiming that it had related to emigration. In one of those telling moments which can neither be predicted nor ever unravelled, FitzGerald was able to prove the point that it *was* the Agreement. The document was visible, the cameras zoomed in on the relevant sentence, reinforcing its validity; Haughey was exposed as misleading the viewers and the country.

Despite their high showing in the opinion polls, no one could have foreseen the actual impact of the Progressive Democrats in the election. They were the real winners, taking 14 seats in their first electoral battle and firmly ensuring that Haughey would not win. Fianna Fáil won 81 seats, three short of an overall majority. For the fourth successive time, Haughey had failed, in apparently perfect circumstances, to record the victory his party so desperately wanted. It was a bitter outcome. It was precisely what FitzGerald – who knew full well that Haughey would almost certainly lead the new administration – had hoped and fought for. He wanted the Fianna Fáil leader to be dependent in coming to power and not to have and use that dangerous commodity absolutely. He could then be forced to address the problems as they really were and finally to abandon the policy of unremitting largesse which had so crippled Ireland in the past.

The situation remained tense right up to the Dáil nomination of a new Taoiseach. Committed against Haughey were all the Opposition parties. After all these elections, Neil Blaney was still there, still prepared to give him his support. Tony Gregory was by now an uncertain force. He had assuredly not received at Haughey's hands the fulfilment of the extensive deal negotiated in 1982 and had every reason therefore to vote against him. And this Haughey fully expected. His own line, since the election count, had been to insist that he would win the necessary support in the Dáil and that if he did not the country would face another immediate election. There would be no deals this time. And he was supported in this by the Fianna Fáil Party. In a predictable, but nonetheless bizarre, departure from previous reactions to his indifferent electoral performance, it seemed to have made a collective decision *not* to challenge Haughey's leadership, although any other leader offered from within Fianna Fáil would probably have gained sufficient support for easy election by the Dáil.

There was justification enough for believing that the country might have to have another, immediate election for FitzGerald to make provision for the crisis. He sought the advice of President Hillery about what he should do in the event of an impasse. The response is interesting: 'Under no circumstances, the President advised, should I suggest that in the event of a deadlock I would seek a dissolution, although I would of course have to resign following the defeat of my nomination as Taoiseach. Then, after visiting him, I was to go back to the Dáil and attempt, by knocking heads together, to get a resolution of the deadlock. If I failed in this attempt I was to return to the President once again, at which point he would publicly instruct me to make a further effort, acting on his authority. We both hoped that the mounting pressure thus created would resolve the problem, should it arise.'[1] While FitzGerald speculated on the possibility of a crisis bringing about a leadership change in Fianna Fáil, he discounted it. In the event Tony Gregory abstained, Blaney supported Haughey, giving him 82 votes against the Opposition's 82, and on the casting vote of Sean Treacy, newly elected to the chair, Haughey became Taoiseach for the third time.

It could hardly have been a less auspicious beginning for any administration and its life expectancy was measured in months, if not weeks. Yet that shrewd old Labour Party campaigner, Frank Cluskey, told a

[1] Ibid., p. 644–5.

group of politicians of all parties and journalists that this was a mis-reading of the situation. 'All Charlie has to do is to be twice as tough as Fine Gael and the PDs and they won't be able to touch him. If he keeps his nerve he can govern as long as he likes.'[1] Haughey did just that.

---

[1] Quoted by Stephen Collins, op. cit., p. 94.

CHAPTER XXI

CONVERTED TO RECTITUDE

For when my outward action doth demonstrate
The native act and figure of my heart
In compliment extern, 'tis not long after,
But I will wear my heart upon my sleeve
For daws to peck at – I am not what I am.

AUGHEY ACCEPTED CONVERSION to rectitude with the
humility and passion of Saul. He was a new man, committed
to order and discipline in economic affairs. And the impact
was remarkable. FitzGerald, in conceding electoral defeat, had given
an undertaking that Fine Gael would support the new administration
if it took a correct course on the economy. He then resigned as leader
and was replaced by Alan Dukes. This supportive approach was then
endorsed by Dukes in what became known as the Tallaght speech or
strategy, since it was first enunciated at a political meeting in that city
suburb to the west of Dublin. It was a highly appropriate place to
choose: large, new, sprawling, with few facilities and filled with young
families impoverished by unemployment.

The doubts over Haughey's conversion were numerous. How deep
was it, and how lasting? What direction would it take, and to what
extent would it involve the other parties? How soon would he modify
it in anticipation of a further attempt to win an overall majority? Or
was the search for that objective set aside in favour of the more urgent
needs of the country? After all, the Cluskey prediction, that he could
govern for as long as he liked if he followed tough economic policies,
was now underpinned by the leader of the largest Opposition
party.

The answers are not as straightforward as one might imagine.
Haughey had certainly listened to economists with greater care than
he had done previously, during the last and least happy phase of the
FitzGerald–Spring coalition of the summer and autumn of 1986. And,
while still pouring scorn on that administration's so-called monetarism,

he was apparently trying to evolve a less reckless answer than his views implied.

He had appreciated the obvious reality that the interests of the two parties, under the deep and abiding distress which heavy cutbacks imposed, were bound to pull them apart, which was not the case with Fianna Fáil. Wherever he chose to lead his own party, it would follow. But when he came to power and established the new administration, he was not prepared to go far enough in terms of the country's deep-seated problems of legislative reform, particularly in taxation and the longer-term strategies which might bring employment. He reputedly addressed one meeting with economists by saying, 'So we're all monetarists now', embracing, somewhat sardonically, a term which he had disdainfully and repeatedly used from the Opposition benches against FitzGerald and his leading ministers.

And he certainly showed monetarist tendencies. That he meant business, at least at the outset, was indicated by his appointment of Ray McSharry to the Department of Finance. And it was confirmed by the shape of his first Budget. But nothing much followed. Deep down, he was afraid. His nature would not let him sustain hard strategies so long as his remaining in power depended on others. He lacked the iron resolve of his father-in-law, Sean Lemass, who had governed well in a minority situation. He was vulnerable and still yearned for that elusive overall majority.

But soon enough he signalled his dissatisfaction and general sense of frustration with a political stroke aimed at his most trenchant critic and the man who had cost him an overall majority in the February–March election: Desmond O'Malley. O'Malley, unlike Dukes, had made no underpinning commitment to Haughey's policies. His own much greater experience made him sceptical of Haughey's sticking-power and it was ironic that evidence of this should have been delivered on the eve of the autumn conference of the Progressive Democrats. Haughey's stroke was to publish his National Economic Plan in order that it should take the limelight from the Opposition party's conference and wrong-foot O'Malley. It only partly worked. It certainly attracted widespread media coverage and dutiful admiration for some of its aspirations. It also meant that O'Malley and other conference speakers had to alter their well-honed texts and re-address themselves to the new material. But at the same time it offered them a soft under-belly of concession and orchestration on Haughey's part, which showed that he was slipping out of the very temporary control of monetarist theories and into the kind of pre-planning phase for an election which demanded hope and optimism, however misplaced at the time these qualities might be.

The National Plan was the product of Haughey's illusionism, his belief that setting in place the easy kind of agreement that it is possible to negotiate with organized labour and employers and then basing on that a set of targets which are highly optional, would actually work. He had always been good at offering the Irish people the option of wealth from the country's own natural resources, like the fish in the sea, and from the talent of intelligent, well-educated young people who were available to take up the new kind of employment which off-shoots of Silicone Valley seemed to be offering. But this was a passive, static, conservative response. In monetarist Britain, Margaret Thatcher had at least recognized the need to reduce taxation and had gambled on this being an incentive to private and business enterprise. Ireland badly needed the same kind of tonic, the same kind of low-tax industrial and commercial incentive thinking. One of the strengths of the Progressive Democrats was their policy of fundamental reform in this area, which recognized that rectitude on its own, as practised by the FitzGerald–Spring coalition, was too hard, too depressing. It needed the lift of deep-seated reforms which would encourage job-creation. The National Plan was weak on this and gave O'Malley a surprising but welcome justification for the very existence of his party on the occasion of that weekend party conference.

But the National Programme for Recovery was weak in a far deeper sense, which soon emerged on the issue of public sector pay and quickly demonstrated the inherent weakness, in a monetarist epoch, of the kind of broad, national agreement which was central to Haughey's thinking. He had achieved general consensus from the unions on cost-cutting, either through pay restraint or redundancies or other changes. But none of this had been specified. National programmes, by their very nature, preclude such detail. Haughey was faced with three broad areas for public sector savings – health, education and social welfare. He had little scope for savings in the social welfare regime. Health had been a principal area for cost-cutting in the final year of the Coalition. There remained education. But the teacher unions were in no mood to honour the generalized undertakings in the National Programme if confined to themselves. They confronted Haughey and his education minister, Mary O'Rourke, and they won. There would be no reductions in class sizes; there would be no voluntary redundancies. With unemployment still rising and with public-sector borrowing scheduled to be brought down in order to honour the new, reborn monetarist leader, thoughts inevitably turned to the only remaining solution: increased taxation.

Haughey had benefited considerably from the punishing time which the Coalition had endured and from his own conversion. He had inherited public finances in a healthy condition and had sustained that buoyancy with his own short-term bout of courage. The prospects, by mid-1987, were that the seemingly irreversible rise in the country's burden of debt would be arrested and reversed by 1990 and all without Haughey having an overall majority. But by the end of the year the picture had already become confused. The opinion polls indicated that he was popular and that what he was doing was judged to be correct for the country. But this popularity, in which there were reservations, was bought at the price of style and content in his leadership, the two enmeshed. He no longer dictated the direction and purpose of events. However enthusiastically he appeared to have embraced rectitude, it made him the creature of circumstance rather than its architect. And Ray McSharry became a more significant force. In more constructive activities, other ministers also emerged and Haughey's role, when not deliberately and dramatically intrusive – as it became, for example, in the ill-judged announcement of the reorganization and expansion of the Irish beef industry under the guidance and leadership of Larry Goodman – reverted to a more conventional 'chairmanship of Government' approach. On Northern Ireland there was no prospect of Haughey exercising any kind of imaginative input. His first summit with Margaret Thatcher produced a chilly definition of how things were between the two leaders when she publicly revealed the state of the relationship in a rhetorical question to her press secretary, Bernard Ingham: 'What does it say in the communiqué?' she asked. 'I think we worked it up to cordial, didn't we, Bernard?' And in his own press relations, which had improved immeasurably, Haughey was quite clearly seen to be in the hands of his shrewd, able and by now quite experienced press secretary, P. J. Mara, who was responsible for suppressing all the instincts of hatred and frustration with journalists that had made Haughey's public relations ride so rocky in the past. All this pointed him in the direction of passive leadership and superficially it suited his situation. It meant that he would survive, if he so chose, for the full term. But it deprived him of the capacity to demonstrate any kind of vision. He was increasingly the victim of circumstance, increasingly passive on policy initiatives. Whether it was the economy, Northern Ireland, the development of special pet enterprises, such as mariculture, or the promotion of the arts, he was constrained from delivering a vision of the future and he ceased to talk in such terms.

It was a relief. His visionary concepts of Ireland had never worked out in the past. And the new, more passive leader seemed less dangerous, less threatening, less demonic. His illusionism took a different path. He developed a form of statesmanlike brooding, a Father-of-the-Nation image, which he handled surprisingly well. Always a consummate actor, with a mercurial ability to assume roles and drop them with remarkable rapidity, he seemed at times to be waltzing through a harlequinade, surrounded by a *commedia dell'arte* team of players, all of whom were responding to the circumstances imposed by their large audience, its participants no less than the total population of the Irish Republic.

Political commentators became theatre critics. The drama lay in a simple enough question: what would he do next? When the Budget of 1987 had been presented, Michael Noonan, the principal Opposition finance spokesman, said with a touch of asperity, 'I have great pleasure today in welcoming Fianna Fáil's acceptance of the Fine Gael analysis of the problem and of the targets which we have set down. This is grand larceny of our policy as put before the electorate.' And this was entirely true. Fianna Fáil had taken up what had caused the Coalition to fall and in delivering it had split the Opposition parties in such a way that the unprecedented spectacle emerged of a Budget going through the Dáil with two parties – Fine Gael and the Progressive Democrats – abstaining and only the parties of the Left voting against.

Everything about Haughey's career contains elements of the bizarre, none more so than the sudden rise in his popularity during 1987 and 1988, for the most unexpected of reasons. Here he was, being far tougher on people than any other leader and being supported in this by at least some of the other leaders. He introduced departmental cuts which were more punishing than any contemplated by his predecessors and they were publicly welcomed. He tried no new initatives on the North and this was approved of. He allowed himself to be forced into a compromise over extradition and this also was welcomed. Overall, the situation that developed was unprecedented.

Although the Tallaght strategy was central to Haughey's success, there were other contributing circumstances. The decision by Alan Dukes certainly introduced a major shift in Irish politics. But the situation facing all the Opposition parties was unique. The towering figure of Garret FitzGerald had provided a single focus in the past. What now presented itself was the spectacle of four quite different personalities at the head of the four Opposition parties, with their experience and numerical strength creating unevenness of performance and impact. Dick Spring, for example, though he was leader of the second-largest opposition party, was less experienced as a politician than O'Malley and had to learn the business of leadership in Opposition. Dukes had to do the same. The approaches were different. And Haughey himself had quite different responses to each of them, rarely concealing his dislike for the Progressive Democrats and their leader, while accommodating himself to the Dukes strategy and to the quite new prospect of co-operation between the two main parties.

This represented an historic change. Here were the two Civil War parties, politically opposed since the formation of the State, responsible, turn and turn about, for the leadership of every administration since 1922 and atavistic in the entrenched bitterness with which they had viewed each other, now working in a harmonious and positive way. No one knew where it would lead; no one really knew how to handle it, least of all Haughey himself. The members of his party were suspicious. From an initial position of instability, following the election, they were being led into the unprecedented calmness of votes which often had more than a hundred deputies opting in favour of measures which ultimately were the fulfilment of Haughey's wishes. And it looked very much as though Frank Cluskey's prophecies were being fulfilled, beyond Haughey's own wildest dreams. He was being tougher than his predecessor could ever have dared. He was building a record of probity over public finances which seemed daily to improve his standing in the country. And he was popular. He remained firmly in control, largely on account of this remarkable tide of public approval. So long as it prevailed his party could not fault him. Not since his days as Minister for Finance in the 1960s had he enjoyed such broad and uncritical public admiration.

There were occasions when his position was threatened and he was reminded of the fact that he was leading a minority administration. The teachers' dispute with the Government, at the end of 1987, was the first of these. But these events were mere hiccoughs along the way. In his fundamental strategy there seemed to be a grand sense of design. The economic figures implied so. And for a time luck ran with him.

Still it was not enough. He could not bear the uncertainty, the feeling of vulnerability, the indebtedness to other politicians and their parties. He could not take the accountability which his minority position imposed. Generous though Alan Dukes' Tallaght strategy was to him, he found it too irksome. He wanted what dictators want: absolute power. And it led to the worst mistake of his political career.

In the spring of 1989, his hand apparently full of aces, Haughey decided to gamble on another general election and seek the elusive overall majority. The decision was triggered by another Dáil defeat. It was not one of earth-shattering importance; much more a matter of human sympathy. A motion down in private members' time – an essentially marginal parliamentary occasion, designed to give the Opposition parties, in turn, the chance to bring forward issues – had achieved broad Opposition support and was certain to be carried. It called for a Government allocation of £400,000 to help sufferers from haemophilia who had AIDS. Haughey had instructed his Minister for Health, Rory O'Hanlon, to sort out the problem and had then gone to Japan on a visit designed to bring new industrial investment to Ireland. He returned to face the impending defeat and lost his temper. His vehement onslaught on Government colleagues, including the Government Chief Whip, was delivered in the presence of the Fine Gael Whip, James Higgins, who had never witnessed such an attack. And Haughey went on to threaten his own party with an election if the Government were defeated.

The combined Opposition parties voted 72 to Fianna Fáil's 69. It was the sixth defeat for the administration. It meant little beyond the embarrassment of losing a vote. The only element of crisis was in Haughey's own reaction. He had decided on drama and had almost closed the loopholes that had allowed him to govern so effectively. He was pulled back from the brink of an immediate election by Albert Reynolds, who persuaded him to put off any decision until he had slept on it. And Reynolds represented a majority in the Government totally opposed to an unnecessary general election when things were going so well. But Padraig Flynn and Raphael Burke were of the opposite view. They came from very different backgrounds: the former was a Mayo deputy and a staunchly loyal supporter of Haughey's; the latter, a Dubliner who had voted against Haughey as leader and had also voted against him after the phone-tapping revelations in 1983. At this stage they both enjoyed Haughey's confidence and he listened to their advice. In summary the advice was based on the high opinion-poll standing of the party, around 51 per cent in private Fianna Fáil polls, and the vulnerability of the Opposition, divided on strategy and economic solutions. How could Haughey fail?

The question seems to contain within itself the fatal flaw. Put a general election in front of Haughey and he had an absolutely cast-iron capacity to lose it. The facts proved this as conclusively as such matters can ever be proved. But he did not see it, nor did his closest advisers. He began losing it straight away, by making absolutely clear to political commentators that he would not rule out an election. This immediately fuelled anxiety in all the other parties and set them all on a war footing. They had weeks in which to prepare and they did so with calm, measured deliberation. Haughey had returned from Japan on 27 April. There was speculation about an election, tied in with the European elections which were scheduled anyway for 15 June, throughout May, so that when Haughey sought the dissolution of the Dáil on the evening of 25 May, no one was surprised.

Haughey thus gave an extensive warning of his intentions to the Opposition parties. But he neglected to tell his own party to prepare for an election and its situation, when the election was actually called, was more confused and uncertain than that of any of the others. It had no election manifesto ready. Its National Programme for Economic Recovery was two years old and in several respects out of date. It was divided on the advisability of holding the election at all. In fact, it was simply intending to fight the election on its record of the previous two-and-a-bit years. Not having been forced to the country placed a heavy emphasis on the lack of necessity for having an election and consequently Haughey's opportunism became an issue. After a period of exemplary government, resulting in unprecedented but broadly deserved popularity, he was suddenly an object of suspicion and doubt all over again. And in no sense had he sufficiently laundered his reputation. Older, darker doubts prevailed and the campaign, from the start, went against him. He started strongly, with opinion polls showing support for Fianna Fáil at 51 per cent, but a steady erosion of that lead set in almost immediately and continued throughout the campaign, which came to be dominated by Opposition criticisms. The poll turnout was low by Irish standards, just 68.5 per cent of the electorate, reflecting a dismissive reaction against the calling of the election. It also reflected against Fianna Fáil. Their 51 per cent lead at the beginning of the campaign had dropped to 44 per cent by the end. The party lost four seats, returning just 77 deputies to the twenty-sixth Dáil.

This was the worst piece of political misjudgement of Haughey's career, unparalleled since the Arms Crisis. Unlike previous election failures it set in train the events that were to bring about his fall. He had lost the trust and forbearance of the main Opposition party, whose underpinning of his strategy had made possible the first Government success of his leadership of Fianna Fáil. He had thrown away virtually all his own party's support and faith in him. Members of Fianna Fáil were enraged at the wilful, intemperate and unnecessary abandonment of their settled and praiseworthy use of power. For the first time in ten years they had been getting things right and both the administration generally and individual ministers had been as popular as their difficult decisions would allow. Nor was there any reason to envisage a change in this. The only possible change was that which Haughey had initiated and it had gone terribly wrong. Worst of all, in order to remain in power, Haughey was now forced into an entirely different bargaining position from the one he had enjoyed in 1987. No one was in the mood to offer him favours or help him towards any kind of deal. He faced a monumental challenge in arriving at a government with himself as its head and it is characteristic of his supremely audacious nature that he approached the whole problem in a calm and confident way, never giving the slightest impression that he would not succeed. Yet even his success involved a further humiliation, that of going into coalition, and a coalition with his political enemy, Desmond O'Malley.

Haughey's confidence again outstripped his judgement. His instincts favoured minority government and he firmly rejected any arrangement other than support from one or more of the Opposition parties, but without their participation in the administration. Once this was achieved, he would be back in his pre-election position; everything would continue along the rosy path of rectitude. He met with Desmond O'Malley on 20 June and Alan Dukes the day after.

The Progressive Democrats had dropped from 14 seats to 6 in the election. This was sufficient to put Haughey back in power and Mary Harney, one of the party's founders and a former member of Fianna Fáil, suggested that, in order to give the country a government, they should support him for Taoiseach. The party's reaction to this was very negative and its deputies were divided. It soon emerged that they could not accept Haughey as Taoiseach and would not be voting for him when the Dáil met.

The Fine Gael leader, Alan Dukes, set a high price on his support: seven of the fifteen Government positions and, on the Israeli model, a turn-and-turn-about sharing of the top job. It was obvious that this would be rejected. The parties of the Left were opposed to Haughey. When the Dáil met he was rejected and no other candidate succeeded in getting a nomination. Haughey then made a further and damaging mistake in not going directly to the President to tender his resignation. He was challenged on this by Dick Spring. The situation was unprecedented, but whatever the constitutional niceties – and there were legal arguments to the effect that the resignation need not be immediate – the political demands were overwhelming: if Haughey wanted to move forward and start real negotiations he needed to place himself in the hands of Parliament and not continue to act outside its remit. This was recognized clearly by his own party and particularly by members of the outgoing Government, who were increasingly dismayed at the way matters were being handled. Even so, it took a great deal of argument in the Government meeting, which Haughey called during an adjournment of the Dáil, before he eventually conceded. He then returned to announce that he would be resigning and drove to the Phoenix Park to present a written note of resignation to President Hillery.

The seriousness of Haughey's position was finally getting through to him. Constitutionally, it seemed doubtful whether he actually had the power to call a general election, if it came to that. The President had the power to refuse him a dissolution and some aspects of this had been envisaged and explored only two years earlier, by Garret FitzGerald, in consultation with Hillery. Hillery himself was circumspect in his views of Haughey, having experienced, back in January 1982, the intense pressures from him not to dissolve the Dáil after FitzGerald's Budget defeat. Collectively, therefore, Haughey's initial refusal to resign had reactivated on all sides anxiety about him and a wish to enforce and maintain a measure of parliamentary and constitutional discipline. He was to be placed firmly and demonstrably in the position of being a caretaker Taoiseach leading an interim government. Only the proper constitutional procedures would resolve his dilemma. Only the Dáil would confirm his nomination and allow the formation of a new government.

The key to this was O'Malley. He needed to present his party with a coherent argument for coalition in order to unite it behind the difficult negotiations which everyone now faced. He presented coalition less as a partnership than as a watching brief involving direct participation. It was clear to the people generally that Haughey needed surveillance and control. It was also clear that his party was incapable

of exercising such control. The Progressive Democrats would therefore have to be represented in government as the people's watchdog.
It would be anything but a friendly partnership. The deal would be
with the public on whose behalf the Progressive Democrats would
contribute to the formation of a government and the reactivation of
the prudent and restrictive economic policies which had been pursued
during the previous two years.

This was the approach that O'Malley offered his colleagues and it
was acceptable. Robert Molloy and Pat Cox formed the negotiating
team on behalf of the party and met on the last day of June with
the Fianna Fáil team, comprising Albert Reynolds and Bertie Ahern.
Without the very clear objective of insisting on direct participation in
government, there was the danger that broad policy objectives would
be agreed and that the Fianna Fáil Party would then be able to insist
on support with a coalition arrangement, blaming O'Malley's team for
wrecking the chances of a government. For this reason they placed
emphasis on the basic coalition arrangement.

It blocked any early progress. Haughey, weakened within his own
party, was more aware than anyone else that, if he did not concede on
coalition, he would be under threat from Fianna Fáil, since the choice
would then become one between another general election and another
leader trying to form an administration. It was defensive talk that led
him to rule out coalition and invent a quite untruthful argument to
the effect that the party had gone before the electorate on the basis
that it would not form a coalition and that if it did not win a majority,
it would form a minority administration. Haughey's objective was survival as Fianna Fáil leader and therefore as Taoiseach. He had already
decided to concede on coalition when the Dáil met on 3 July and again
adjourned, having failed to resolve the impasse. It endorsed Haughey
in further efforts to break this.

The interim, caretaker Government was divided. Its more experienced members saw the inevitability of coalition and knew that their
party, renowned in the past for its pragmatism, would absorb and
survive this indignity in order to retain power. It was Haughey's more
fiery past supporters, including the only remaining member of the
Gang of Five to be a serving Government minister, Albert Reynolds,
who were so strongly opposed to coalition that Haughey simply
decided he would sidestep them and make the decision on his own.
They did lead a majority within the Government and, if they had so
wished, they could have brought him down and proceeded under a

new leader more welcome to the Dáil and probably in a minority rather than in a coalition arrangement. But they baulked at this, essentially out of cowardice, and despite clear statements – from Padraig Flynn among others – that refusal to enter coalition was a so-called 'core value' in the party, Haughey steered them towards the surrender of what they allegedly held too dear for bargaining.

Haughey conceded a coalition deal with O'Malley, Molloy and Cox, and without asking his own negotiators to be present. He then returned to tell the members of the Government. Their anger was a mark of their impotence. He treated them with a disdain in which he was well practised and which he now knew would not be challenged, ever. He held them in no regard. He knew they would do nothing and that in fact they did not even know what to do, in the unusual circumstances. The very progression of the talks had created a momentum of power and when it was announced, late on Wednesday, 5 July, that the principle of coalition had been conceded by Haughey, speaking for Fianna Fáil, the 'core value' simply ceased to be a core value. Whatever was meant, at the time, by people being strongly opposed – and Albert Reynolds, Padraig Flynn, Maire Geoghegan-Quinn and many others were numbered in that category – it meant little or nothing. The parliamentary party met to consider the negotiations, during the additional week which the Dáil gave for further exchanges, and gave approval to Haughey without even knowing what he was offering in the way of Government appointments. And Haughey simply ceased to involve his negotiators, choosing to construct his future Government on his own.

He was next faced with the obvious, but even less palatable demand from the Progressive Democrats for two seats in Government. On the principle that Desmond O'Malley's party would be in government as guarantors for the Irish people and not out of any benevolence towards Haughey or a wish to help him or his party, it was essential that there should be a corroboration of this guarantee in the form of a second minister. This was the level of distrust which had to be encompassed. It was given a somewhat ameliorative public interpretation; namely, that the Coalition would have to be seen as a coalition of *parties* and not as a single individual being involved in government. But the reality was more abrasive. O'Malley could not stomach the idea of being on his own with such a gang. There was to be a junior appointment as well, giving the Progressive Democrats a total of three appointments, representing half their parliamentary strength. The negotiations were increasingly conducted by O'Malley and Haughey. O'Malley reported back to the Progressive Democrats at every stage; Haughey not only did not report back, he did not even tell his party or the members of the Government what he was doing. The party tried to hold the deal at one Government appointment, but it was a futile endeavour, ineptly handled. Haughey knew his own strengths where Fianna Fáil members were concerned; and he knew from long and well-rehearsed past experience the weaknesses of the party he had come so comprehensively to possess. They huffed and they puffed, but they let him have his way.

It is a curious phenomenon about the man that, having made such a monumental hash of the whole election, he should then have displayed such brilliant tactics in holding on to power and achieving the single essential of an administration. When the parliamentary party met, in advance of the next sitting of the Dáil, aimed at trying once again to nominate a Taoiseach, Haughey simply told deputies and senators that his negotiations with the Progressive Democrats had not reached any conclusion. Opposition therefore was speculative; there was nothing concrete to block. Some wanted to block any deal at all. Flynn had already expressed his view forcibly in a meeting with Haughey; he simply wanted him to step down. If he did there would be no problem about putting together an administration. Maire Geoghegan-Quinn was incensed at the idea that she might find herself in government with her constituency arch-rival, Robert Molloy. But the meeting was inconclusive. Haughey ordered another for the morning of the Dáil's reassembly and that night met with the party's national executive, again an inconclusive encounter, but one that was important for him, because he could interpret it as tacit approval for the deal he was completing.

He continued to handle the succession of meetings brilliantly. With the national executive, the Government, the parliamentary party and individual supporters he maintained an enigmatic front, insisting on the delicacy of the negotiations and their lack of finality. No one challenged him to clarify key questions. The Dáil was scheduled to sit at three o'clock on 12 July. At ten o'clock that morning Haughey and O'Malley met. Haughey then held a meeting with the Government, mainly to explain that there were still matters to be clarified. He then brought to the parliamentary party meeting the text of the agreement between Fianna Fáil and the Progressive Democrats. This was a lengthy and for the moment totally irrelevant collection of policy agreements and objectives which had nothing to do with party concerns about the strength of Progressive Democrat representation within the Coalition. Nor was it possible to read, digest and debate the contents. But it clearly indicated the closeness of agreement and therefore the means of avoiding another general election. This, at heart, was the single most compelling argument with the vast majority of deputies. In the previous twenty-four hours Haughey had negotiated his way through crucial meetings of the party's organizational committee, the Government, the parliamentary party and the actual sessions with O'Malley. From no single Fianna Fáil grouping had he received any instructions whatever, least of all the one he feared most: not to concede the two Government positions which he had already conceded. He was in the clear. Haughey on his own confirmed with O'Malley, Molloy and Cox their agreement. The Progressive Democrats would have two Government positions and one junior ministry. The four men shook hands. He looked round at them all. 'Nobody but myself could have done it,' he said, with a smile.[1] No one knew the truth of this better than Desmond O'Malley. And out of their prolonged rivalry there now developed a powerful working relationship which set its stamp very quickly on the new administration.

[1] Stephen Collins, op. cit., p. 167.

CHAPTER XXII

THE BEEF SCANDAL

O bloody period!

HAUGHEY'S DEAL WITH the Progressive Democrats sealed his fate as leader of Fianna Fáil. From July 1989, Albert Reynolds, Maire Geoghegan-Quinn, Padraig Flynn, Sean Doherty and others began to work consciously and deliberately to remove him. And they had as their candidate for succession Albert Reynolds himself. It was a re-run, ten years on, of the same strategy that had been used to replace Jack Lynch with Charles Haughey in 1979 and which had done so much damage to Fianna Fáil and the country. Two of the original Gang of Five were involved, but this time they attracted a quite different title of 'the country and western alliance', a reference to Albert Reynolds' endearing propensity to sing country-and-western songs in the bars of his mid-west constituency and the more pronounced west of Ireland independence of deputies like Maire Geoghegan-Quinn and Pádraig Flynn. The title originated in a disparaging remark, from Haughey himself.

While they were embarking on what was to be a long and arduous decapitation of their leader, Desmond O'Malley was restoring credibility and constitutionality to the operation of government. He was also central to its policies, his own party being policy-based anyway, in contrast with Fianna Fáil, which had, under Haughey's leadership, increasingly failed to pursue constructive policies based on any objective analysis of national interests. Though his more dramatic confrontations with his partner in government were rarely, if ever, over items in their joint programme, this still remained the underpinning of the relationship and, in terms of the contribution by the much smaller party, this was seen to be based on a clear set of national targets. The Progressive Democrats had brought to the partnership an emphasis on tax reform. Fianna Fáil sustained a commitment to the reduction of the national debt, but were seen as a party which, in power, relied on the public service for much of its policy. This imbalance between the dominant party and its new partner was further emphasized by the Progressive Democrat insistence on parliamentary and law reforms being part of the programme.

To say that O'Malley swept to power might appear something of an overstatement; he was the leader of a tiny party and his policy remit had been dictated in advance of the formation of the Government. Yet Brian Lenihan, who was deputy leader of the Government (Tánaiste), a formal position stipulated by the Constitution, is on record as stating that 'the real Tánaiste' was O'Malley.[1] This was said in late 1989, not with any rancour; that was to come later.

Patrick Hillery had been President for two seven-year terms. He had succeeded Cearbhaill O Dalaigh, whose resignation had been provoked during the Cosgrave coalition administration in 1976 in highly controversial circumstances. O Dalaigh, in his turn, had succeeded Erskine Childers, who died in office. What was common to all of these men, apart from their sex, was the fact that they were all members, or former members, of the Fianna Fáil Party. Indeed, with the exception of Douglas Hyde's occupation of the office, as the country's first Head of State following the constitutional changes that derived from de Valera's 1937 Constitution, the presidency had *always* been held, with or without electoral competition, by Fianna Fáil.

Dick Spring, the leader of the Labour Party, was determined that this would not happen again and he persuaded Mary Robinson to accept the nomination. Her distinguished background in law, in education and in fighting important minority and human rights issues, often through the European courts, made her an effective candidate. Even so, the prospects for actually getting elected were slim enough. Mary Robinson had been a member of the Labour Party, but had resigned over Northern Ireland policy at the time of the Anglo-Irish Agreement. Before that she had stood for the Dáil, but had shown herself a poor vote-getter. Her political forum was the Senate and her mandate the elitist one of a university seat, representing Trinity College. At the time of her selection by the Labour Party in early April 1990 Haughey was midway through his presidency of the European Community and handling the whole programme of meetings and summits with his usual control over events. He was also doing it with confidence and a certain panache. He underestimated the threat that

---

[1] Cited in Stephen Collins, op. cit., p. 169.

she represented and put off the problem of choosing a Fianna Fáil candidate or of making the appropriate plans for the campaign.

There were preoccupations. 1990, just like other years, brought with it embarrassments and misjudgements. One of these concerned Haughey's erstwhile colleague in the ill-fated 1982 administration, Sean Doherty, who had lost his Dáil seat in the 1989 general election and had come back as a senator. Doherty still carried the dishonourable burden of having been responsible for a number of political mis-demeanours in power, among them the tapping of the telephones of two journalists. His nomination for chairmanship of the Senate, early in 1990, brought with it a whiff of sulphur. Haughey could easily have blocked this and ensured that the other candidate, Des Hanafin, got the appointment. By not doing so there emerged the suspicion that Doherty somehow held over Haughey a residue of power or threat. He was certainly seen widely as unsuitable, yet went forward for the vote in which he tied with Hanafin. Doherty's name was the one drawn from a hat.

Haughey may also have been encouraged in his relaxed attitude towards the presidential contest by the dismal approach of the Fine Gael Party, which handled its own selection process in an inept way. Alan Dukes, the party leader, who had successfully handled the first Haughey period in power, from 1987–89, was in trouble following the setting up of the Haughey–O'Malley coalition. His leadership was increasingly under threat and he had no clear idea of how to handle the presidential race. By nominating Mary Robinson, Dick Spring had ensured that there would be a competition. Fine Gael seemed to have an ideal candidate in Dukes' predecessor, Garret Fitz-Gerald. But FitzGerald had no wish to run. Nor did several other notables within the party. Dick Spring invited them to support Mary Robinson, but almost out of desperation Alan Dukes turned to Austin Currie, already a deputy, though his political background was essen-tially in Northern Ireland politics. Currie had made a wholesome and dynamic impact on political life in the South, but there was undoubtedly resistance to him as a prospective Head of State.

During the whole of the summer of 1990 Mary Robinson followed a gruelling schedule of countrywide election tours. She was schooled for victory in every way: her dress, her speech, her manner, her ideas. The pitfalls of being either left-wing or liberal were carefully skirted. Her appeal to women was strong and she made it central. In no pre-vious presidential election had a candidate laid the foundations so deliberately and with such genuine appeal. By its very seriousness it looked almost amateurish. This dogged woman, with no reputation as a vote-getter, tramped the countryside, proposing a new role for a job which was strictly confined by the Constitution and suggesting a greater say in the affairs of the country by women. It hardly had the appeal from which victories are contrived. Her academic background and her intellectual approach did not inspire public conviction that she would triumph.

Fianna Fáil had two potential candidates, Brian Lenihan and John Wilson. Both were long-serving politicians who had been in several administrations, Brian Lenihan under both Sean Lemass and Jack Lynch. Lenihan had been extremely ill; a life-threatening liver complaint had led to a successful transplant, at the Mayo Clinic in the United States, which had prevented him campaigning in the ill-fated 1989 general election, though it had enhanced his vote-getting appeal, putting him at the top of the poll in his constituency of Dublin West. Being President of Ireland seemed a fitting climax to a long and colourful career in the cockpits of power. He was popular, quick-witted and widely liked and his illness, deriving from the strains of battle and the innumerable encounters and confrontations in which he took such pleasure, added to his appeal. When John Wilson, a man with a different turn of wit, laced with Latin and Greek, also stood for the nomination, it indicated a rich enough choice. The natural strength of Fianna Fáil, set against the unquantifiable challenge of Mary Robinson – who had already pushed Austin Currie into third place – seemed set for victory, despite her conscientious campaigning.

Then Brian Lenihan shot himself in the foot. Badly. He was set up, in the course of a television appearance, and the unlikely architects of his downfall were Fine Gael, not usually a party given to strokes. On this occasion, desperate to raise Austin Currie's profile, Jim Mitchell, who was running the campaign for Fine Gael, orchestrated a television debate during a programme called *Questions and Answers*, in which Garret FitzGerald and Brian Lenihan were participating. The programme consists of a panel of four under the chairmanship of John Bowman, with an audience that includes at least some selected 'guests' of the politicians on the panel. The questions come from the audience. The panellists have some prior knowledge of what they are, or of what they concern, and, though the programme is pre-recorded, it goes out so quickly afterwards that only limited editing is possible. On this occasion Jim Mitchell ensured that the Fine Gael guests were well briefed. Earlier in the campaign the Fine Gael candidate had tried to provoke a debate on Haughey's attempts, through Lenihan, to pre-empt a dissolution of the Dáil. This had happened years earlier, following the collapse of FitzGerald's government in January 1982. Now a question was put to the panel concerning the powers of a president to do this. Brian Lenihan answered it quite openly, saying, correctly, that the option had never been exercised and giving the widely accepted reason, that the Constitution was unclear about the consequences. Garret FitzGerald then raised the almost gratuitous matter of the phone calls to President Hillery. Lenihan denied that they had taken place. Since FitzGerald had been with the President when at least some of the calls came through, he was uniquely placed to challenge the Fianna Fáil presidential candidate, which he did. A further question was asked, this time more direct: had Lenihan made a call to Aras an Uachtaráin on the night in question? Lenihan denied it. Unknown to anyone else involved in the programme, including FitzGerald, the questioner was aware of a taped interview which a research student, James Duffy, had completed with Lenihan as part of his work on a thesis and in that interview Lenihan had spoken quite freely about making such a call and talking with President Hillery. Duffy had published the fruits of his researches already, in a series of articles in *The Irish Times*. He watched the exchanges in total disbelief. The next day he rang the paper. The tape was made available and *The Irish Times*, having claimed that they had incontrovertible proof that Lenihan's denials were incorrect, took the unusual step of summoning a press conference and giving to radio, television and the *other* newspapers details of Duffy's tape, which was then played. What would have been a single-paper scoop became an instant national story of devastating impact.

Lenihan continued his denials, changing the emphasis. What he had said to Duffy had been 'mistaken'. Although he later explained, in a book,[1] that he had been on heavy medication at the time, as a result of complications arising from his liver transplant, this claim was not made at the time. With Haughey's approval, as well as that of the government press secretary, P. J. Mara, Lenihan went out to Montrose and was interviewed for the *Six o'Clock News* on television. 'My mature recollection, at this stage, is that I did not ring President Hillery. I want to put my reputation on the line.' His earnest, crumpled face

[1] Brian Lenihan, op. cit.

and crinkled black hair faced directly into the homes of the Irish people, who had already heard him giving, on tape, a detailed account of the conversation with President Hillery, referring to him as a cautious man whose attitude about his constitutional powers would be strict and conventional. 'Mature recollection' became immediately synonymous with telling lies and the reputation, placed staunchly 'on the line', crumbled. So did his campaign.

His misfortunes, and those of Haughey, did not end with the collapse of his credibility. There was the subsequent danger of the collapse of the Coalition partnership as well. Alan Dukes tabled a no-confidence motion in the Dáil, backing it up with a press statement accusing Lenihan of having told lies and accusing Haughey and three other ministers of having supported those lies. It became immediately clear that the Government was face to face with a major crisis. O'Malley had led the Progressive Democrats into coalition in order to preserve proper standards. They traced their credentials back to the 1970s and George Colley's criticisms of party colleagues with 'low standards in high places'. Moral standards in political life as it had been lived under Lynch's leadership of Fianna Fáil seemed a distant, unattainable ideal, legendary in its strength in Irish political affairs but nevertheless now represented – at least in government – by the tiny Coalition partner. The phrase itself was quoted in justification of the hard line adopted by the Progressive Democrats. They had a guardianship role and their members were united in sticking firm on the issue and not voting confidence in the Government if Lenihan remained a minister.

Haughey was indecisive. Throughout the controversy over the telephone calls it was impossible for him to be dispassionate. His own denials, like those of Lenihan, were simply not credible. And what was at stake, as well as the party's presidential candidate and the future of the Government, was the truths or otherwise relating to a long-buried episode from the GUBU year, 1982, and the long-standing friendship, going back thirty years, between Haughey and Lenihan.

What Haughey wanted was for the Lenihan issue to be left to Fianna Fáil, with the Progressive Democrats continuing their support in the Dáil. O'Malley was quite happy about Fianna Fáil resolving their own problem, but if the party did not do so according to his own party's expectations, then the Progressive Democrats would pull out. The implications were absolutely clear to Haughey: Lenihan would have to resign. And if he did not resign he would have to be dismissed. And this latter, painful course was what indeed happened. But it took an inordinate amount of time and focused massive media attention.

The final act of the saga, including its climax, had a fragmentary beginning, since the key ministers involved, including Haughey, were out of the country on State business and conducted their wranglings through airport press conferences, hastily composed statements and radio interviews. While the Government recognised that Lenihan's resignation was the only solution, Lenihan himself was treated badly, first being confronted by Haughey, then being referred to a group of Fianna Fáil ministers, who told him that his resignation was the only way in which the Government could survive, and then having to face Haughey yet again, this time with a written statement of resignation for him to sign which included the claim that the decision was solely Lenihan's and that he had not been subjected to pressures of any kind.

Lenihan refused. He went ahead with the day's campaigning, travelling to his home territory of Longford with his midlands colleague, Albert Reynolds, who was the only senior member of the party to stand by him, and with his own family, which included his wife, Ann, and his sister, Mary O'Rourke, who was also a member of the Government. They effectively took control of him, preventing access by messengers sent from Dublin, intercepting telephone calls and whipping up a tide of support and sympathy which convincingly persuaded Lenihan to have no truck whatever with the idea of resignation.

It became a saga of epic proportions, a kind of modern Celtic chronicle, monitored hungrily and milked for every syllable and phrase of colour or excitement. It was like nothing so much as one of the giant cattle-raids of Irish legend, armies sweeping across the country to the Shannon, and some being driven beyond, all in pursuit of the great brown bull of Cuailgne. Journalists and politicians were in search of a prize. They were the witnesses of loud and florid confrontations between chieftains. Brian Lenihan, after all, was still himself campaigning for the country's High Kingship and everywhere he went he was followed by a court of supporters, with scribes to record each saying that fell from his lips. And he was justly renowned for colourful language and a ready supply of epithets and witticisms. The sounds of battle and single combat seemed at times to rend the air.

During the course of these journeyings through Longford and Westmeath, two more Government ministers, Pádraig Flynn and Bertie Ahern, travelled down from Dublin and tried to make direct contact with Brian Lenihan, but were prevented by the crowds. 'Are we welcome in Westmeath?' Flynn called out across the crowds, at dusk, in the little town of Moate. 'No, you are not,' shouted back Mary O'Rourke, and she told them to get back across the Shannon. Since they had both travelled from Dublin, where Ahern was based, and were presumably heading back there, with or without their mission accomplished, the advice to cross the river, which was well to the west, has a measure of confusion in it; yet it contains the appropriate territorial sweep, since Shannon waters and Athlone itself were the lands of the Lenihans. Flynn and Ahern followed the cavalcade, however, and were able to speak to Albert Reynolds, and then to Mary O'Rourke, in slightly more civilized circumstances. But still they failed to deliver their ultimatum to Lenihan – that he had to resign – and eventually they returned to Dublin.

Time was running out. The Dáil would begin the debate on Alan Dukes's motion of no confidence the next day, 31 October. If O'Malley had not received a satisfactory answer, his resignation, and the resignations of Bobby Molloy and Mary Harney, would be delivered before the debate started, thus sealing the fate of the Government. The beginning of the debate coincided with the Fianna Fáil parliamentary party meeting and in anticipation of this Mary Harney, junior minister for the Progressive Democrats, was asked by Charles McCreevy to delay any decision to allow for further efforts, essentially to bring Haughey to his senses and ensure that, in the face of Lenihan's refusal to resign, he would exercise his constitutional right and seek the dismissal of the deputy leader of the Government. At one point, Haughey's son, Ciarán, piloted a helicopter down to the Lenihan home, where it circled and hovered, waiting to bring the Tánaiste back to Haughey's home for a final meeting.

Considerable additional pressure was exercised on the party as a whole by an opinion poll in the *Irish Independent* that morning. This showed that Lenihan's presidential prospects had been seriously undermined by his massive self-contradiction and he was now lagging 21 points behind Mary Robinson. Though the damage was mainly to Lenihan himself, the prospect of an election fought in such circumstances, and straddling the final days of the presidential campaign, was unthinkable. It would at best return the party in a minority position and would almost certainly preclude any kind of coalition deal. The somewhat battered party champion returned to Dublin, but refused to attend the party meeting and rejected all visitors from Haughey or attempts to reach him by telephone. Brian Lenihan did send in a statement to the party meeting in which he outlined thirty years of service to Fianna Fáil, referring to the occasions on which he had defended Haughey – and they were many. It ended: 'I do not intend to resign as Tánaiste and Minister for Defence.'

Haughey sought a simple endorsement from the party, that he would be free to take whatever actions were necessary to avoid an election. The party meeting ended with a loosely expressed agreement to this end, that an election would be avoided and that it was up to the Taoiseach. He left that meeting and immediately called in O'Malley to tell him he was dismissing Lenihan. It was shortly afterwards, at 5.45 p.m., that Lenihan rang Haughey. Haughey, for the last time, asked him to resign and, when he again refused, told him he was dismissed. Notification of his removal from the two senior offices he held, signed, no doubt with a full sense of the irony of what he was doing, by Patrick Hillery, was sent out to the house in Rathgar where Lenihan had been waiting.

The vote on the no-confidence motion, with the Progressive Democrats now supporting the Government, was a sombre and emotional occasion. Stephen Collins, who witnessed it, wrote: 'Lenihan made his way into the Dáil before 6.30 p.m., entering the visitors' bar with a group of family and friends. He was greeted there by Seanad Cathaoirleach [Sean Doherty], whom Lenihan had backed when he was under pressure in the Seanad. There were emotional scenes in the bar and in the Chamber when he made his way there to listen to Haughey read out his formal dismissal. There were tears in the eyes of many Fianna Fáil deputies as they marched through the lobbies to vote confidence in their government. After the vote Haughey, his face like a mask, sat stonily in his seat, many of his colleagues avoiding contact with him. Afterwards he asked Lenihan to meet him and the two old friends had an emotional and unacrimonious get-together for a few minutes in the Taoiseach's office.'[1]

Brian Lenihan went back on the campaign trail. He was buoyed up by a wave of public sympathy and all his ancient and endlessly tried resilience came out in the final rallies, interviews and street canvassing. But the invincible warrior, who had in the views of many who had seen him come through his dreadful illness risen, Cuchulain-like, to fight one last great cause, was invincible no more. He failed to raise his vote sufficiently. On the second count Mary Robinson was elected, beating Brian Lenihan by 86,566 votes. She was the first woman to

[1] Stephen Collins, op. cit., p. 193.

win such a campaign. It was the first time Fianna Fáil had ever failed to win a presidential election. It was yet another electoral failure to be laid at Haughey's door.

It was much more than that. Here was a watershed in Irish politics between old and new. 'Nothing will ever be quite the same again after Wednesday's vote,' wrote Conor Cruise O'Brien, and he described the week of her victory as the best he could remember in Irish politics. 'Many people outside Fianna Fáil sympathized with Brian Lenihan as an amiable human being who had been shamefully treated. But they did not lose sight of the fact that the person who had treated him shamefully was the leader of his own party, who was impudently recommending to the people, to fill the highest office in the land, a person whom he had just fired from his own Cabinet. If Mr Lenihan was not fit to be Tánaiste, then he was not fit to be President. The people – outside Fianna Fáil – saw all that quite plainly.'[1] But O'Brien was over-optimistic in his anticipation of Haughey's fall from power, which he predicted would precede the party's annual conference, early the following spring, later bringing this date forward to before Christmas. He also suggested that any alternative leader of Fianna Fáil – including Albert Reynolds, whom he named – would be preferable, in the eyes of the Progressive Democrats. Yet the whole emergence of Reynolds' challenge and his clear desire to be seen as an alternative to Haughey, which was increasingly established in the events surrounding each new crisis, was based on the premise that the new leader would be able to ditch any political partner outright and run for an overall majority.

Yet, if the people saw the lack of logic in the very presentation of Lenihan as a presidential candidate, their vote did not indicate, plainly enough, their rejection of Haughey and his party. The principle of Caligula's horse had been espoused by Haughey. The party's hold on power had been sensationally frustrated. But the feeling remained that the subtle changes achieved by Mary Robinson's campaign and election could be reversed if Fianna Fáil changed its leader. And this underpinned perceptions in the aftermath of her victory. A residual gloom about the future was reinforced by the very poor performance of the second largest party, Fine Gael, which, in the aftermath of the vote, removed Alan Dukes from the leadership and voted in John Bruton.

---

[1] Conor Cruise O'Brien, 'C.J. in terminal trouble', *Irish Independent*, 10 November 1990.

O'Malley's appointment, on the formation of the Government, to the Department of Industry and Commerce, had provided him with a powerful, central responsibility and he had demonstrated his own effectiveness early on by confronting the Goodman meat marketing organization. He had cancelled the export credit insurance cover on Goodman deals with Iraq, in the summer of 1989, and a year later he handled effectively a huge crisis facing the company which threatened the futures of many Irish farmers in a complicated and embarrassing episode for the government that dated from 1987.

Larry Goodman headed the largest beef enterprise in Ireland and beef was the country's largest and most profitable agricultural export. Goodman had been very beneficial to Irish farmers and to Irish agriculture and the food business generally. His aggressive marketing and the good prices he paid had secured jobs throughout the country and had established a much more positive view of the prospects, particularly for Irish beef, which otherwise was all too easily sold into intervention at a preordained price guaranteed by the European Community. He was a major supporter of Fianna Fáil and allegedly a personal friend of Charles Haughey, though Haughey later denied such personal association between them. With Goodman, Haughey launched an elaborate scheme for the development of the Irish beef industry on 18 June 1987. It involved money from Europe and from the Irish Industrial Development Authority, investment from Goodman himself, and State investment, a total of some £260 million.

Although the launching of the scheme was more properly the job of the Minister for Agriculture, Michael O'Kennedy, the anticipated applause was too much for Haughey to resist. He wanted to be seen to have a hands-on involvement and this persuaded him to present the package. This decision relegated O'Kennedy and the junior agriculture minister, Joe Walsh, to subsidiary status and placed the usually retiring Goodman centre-stage. What was on offer was the first unsteady act in a vast, five-act Goodman drama which is still, at the time of writing, providing the public with wonderfully compelling performances and a steady stream of revelations.

What made the first act unsteady was the pitiful outcome of the major announcement. Though much was promised, nothing really came of the grand design announced to the public. And though Goodman companies did go ahead with borrowings based on the plan, the actual investment by the State was not forthcoming. All that seemed to have been achieved was the apparent confirmation of a close relationship between Haughey and Goodman. In the eyes of many this had much less to do with friendship than with deals. The beef industry development scheme became no more than an introductory sub-plot in the drama, which next shifted to Goodman's revealed intention to bid for the Irish Sugar Company through one of his subsidiaries, Food Industries. The Sugar Company was State-owned and was to feature in a later scandal, the Greencore Affair.

The chairman of the parliamentary committee on State-sponsored bodies, which became involved in the Goodman bid, was Liam Lawlor, a director of Food Industries. The potential conflict of interest was raised by a Progressive Democrat deputy, Pat O'Malley, and Liam Lawlor resigned. This was followed by far more serious allegations of irregularities against companies in the group, made in the first instance by the Labour Party deputy Barry Desmond, but then reiterated by the Workers' Party deputy, Tomás MacGiolla. Garda fraud officers had been investigating irregularities and export refunds had been withheld. Desmond also revealed that a fine of £1 million had been imposed by the European Commission on Goodman. Several attempts by journalists to expose activities associated with Goodman company affairs had been frustrated by severe threats of libel action. Now the parliamentary revelations began to emerge, confirmed reluctantly by Government ministers. Michael O'Kennedy, having first defended his department's regulation of affairs in the beef industry, denying legal action against the Goodman organization, then told the Dáil that there had been irregularities which had been reported to the European Commission. And Bobby Molloy then revealed that Goodman was keeping his private jet at the country's main military aerodrome, at Baldonnel, a privilege not available to private individuals. Haughey defended Goodman and Ireland's beef industry, as though they were one and the same thing. Worse followed. Goodman organizations were trading with Iraq and for this required export credit insurance. Cover had been provided by the FitzGerald-led Coalition, but then withdrawn in 1986 by the Fine Gael minister, Michael Noonan, on the grounds that the situation under Saddam Hussein represented too great a risk. In 1987, with the restoration of a Fianna Fáil administration, a massive export credit insurance cover scheme had been reinstated for the company, with apparent special preferences being given to the Goodman companies. Indeed, as the Beef Tribunal was increasingly to show, the cover was set up and maintained for Goodman and his companies, more or less exclusively.

O'Malley became one of the fiercest critics in the Dáil of this preferential treatment given to Goodman. It not only prejudiced other companies in the beef industry, but also unrelated businesses, which needed
comparable protection. He did not envisage that he would be so swiftly
plunged into direct conflict with Goodman, but on his appointment
as Minister for Industry and Commerce he acted swiftly, setting up a
departmental inquiry into the allegations made over the previous two
years. This revealed, among other things, that the insurance cover
had been used for meat sourced in Britain and Northern Ireland and
O'Malley cancelled several policies. It was then reported to him that
Goodman was the beneficial owner of Classic Meats and Goodman
was ordered to dispose of his interests on anti-monopoly grounds.
O'Malley initiated his actions independently, within the law as it
applied to the institutions involved, such as the Industrial Investment
Authority, though with Haughey's and the Government's approval.

Unfortunately, these first moves, and what they uncovered, represented merely the tip of an iceberg. The drama was taking on massive
proportions. The Goodman Group was in fact threatened with collapse. It was massively undermined by a network of debts to a variety
of different banks and banking groups, totalling nearly £500 million.
Iraq, which had just embarked on the ill-fated invasion of Kuwait,
which was to lead to the Gulf War, owed the Goodman organization
£180 million and there was virtually no prospect of this being paid.
Into the bargain, an ill-fated investment in Berisford and Unigate,
on the British Stock Market, had lost Goodman a further substantial sum.

The victims were Irish farmers and saving their investment and
livelihood was the first priority. O'Malley had been presiding in the
Dáil over the rather slow progress of the Companies Bill of 1986. He
extracted from this the relevant section, turned it into a new and
separate piece of legislation and pushed the rescue package through
the Dáil which was recalled in August 1990 expressly for this purpose.
This also represented a rescue for Haughey, who was embarrassed by
the whole affair. He had only himself to blame for the close association
with a man whose actions had been so massively against the national
interest.

The Goodman scandal was the first of several to emerge and was
arguably the most extensive and the most complex. It had many levels
and many dimensions. It involved the FitzGerald administration in the
granting of export insurance cover to begin with, but this had then

been cancelled. After that it seemed to run out of control during the first of the two Haughey administrations, though not specifically as a result of Haughey's own direct involvement. According to Haughey's later evidence, the renewal of insurance cover was decided by Albert Reynolds, independently of the Government and without Haughey's knowledge. The full story might never have emerged due, surprisingly, to O'Malley himself. The row which gave rise to the judicial inquiry was provoked by ITV's *World in Action* programme, which investigated the Goodman Group and its practices and broadcast its findings on 13 May 1991. The revelations, of alleged malpractices within Goodman companies, connivance by state officials and political collusion, seemed to confirm everyone's worst fears about the company. There were related claims that political actions had been taken to support Goodman and give him a preferential position. In the Dáil the following day a new row erupted, with Charles Haughey once again misreading the intensity of public and political dismay and trying to brazen out the questions and allegations. The matter might have been resolved with a relatively anodyne Dáil motion, which reaffirmed confidence in the way the Irish meat industry was being controlled and regulated, essentially through Desmond O'Malley's own department. He approved of the wording himself and seemed prepared to support the motion opposing any judicial investigation. But overnight wiser counsel within the Progressive Democrats prevailed. This was their issue; more than any other it had demonstrated already the restoration of legal and constitutional constraints on the way the country was being run and he was confronted with the need for a more fundamental and far-reaching inquiry. O'Malley put this to Haughey. The two leaders went through the by now familiar ritual, Haughey consulting this time with his Minister for Agriculture. O'Malley, as usual, was backed in the line he took by his parliamentary party. Haughey gave in. A full judicial inquiry was the outcome, announced to the Dáil by the Minister for Agriculture, Michael O'Kennedy, during the course of a speech in which he had extensively defended the Goodman organization. The public sworn inquiry, which became known as the Goodman Tribunal, like some archaic tumbrel of retribution, laden with documents and people, was set on its creaking road of revelation.

The allegations in the Dáil about Goodman were symptomatic, not of Haughey's corruption – though this was implicit in much that was said – but of his bad judgement, ineptitude, loss of authority, the loss indeed of any firm grip over party discipline. He was adrift on a silken sea of uncertainty and vulnerability. He could neither browbeat nor persuade his own party that he was leading effectively. Having weathered violent storms and prodigious battles for control and then for survival, he was now at the whim of innuendo, of detailed and relentless questioning, and of a succession of quite specific charges about the manner in which he was conducting the whole management of the country's affairs. And though the public thrust of this antagonism came from the Opposition, which performed with vigour and courage, the real problem for Haughey lay in the uncertainty within Fianna Fáil. The plotters against him meant business. They had been taught by a master and he was now their target.

A series of scandals in the autumn of 1991 followed on the Goodman row. At the beginning of September, a story in the *Sunday Independent* about Greencore, which had formerly been the Irish Sugar Company, established that substantial profits had been made by company directors and executives at the State's expense. In a storm of controversy the chief executive, Chris Comerford, as well as other senior officers, resigned. These others included Michael Tully, the company secretary, Charles Lyons and Thomas Keleghan, directors, and Charles Garavan, another Greencore executive. All were directors of a company called Gladebrook which was set up for the purpose of purchasing the minority interest in Sugar Distributors. A company called ISM Investments, which had been a subsidiary of Sugar Distributors, had made a loan of £1 million to Gladebrook, approved by Tully and Lyons, in their capacity as a 'majority of the directors' of ISM. As Gladebrook directors they then purchased the interest in Sugar Distributors, reselling, for a substantial financial gain, to the company of which they were also directors, Greencore. Comerford's involvement in this affair was further complicated by the fact that there were conflicting claims about his involvement with another company, Talmino, registered in Jersey, and with a 25 per cent interest in Gladebrook. The whole Greencore scandal would not have become public but for a falling-out between Comerford and one of the other directors, Charles Lyons.

Haughey's own connection was damaging. The company chairman, Bernie Cahill, was a friend of Haughey's; he also happened to be chairman of Feltrim Mining, a company which had been set up by Haughey's son, Conor, and was also chairman of the country's State airline, Aer Lingus. Cahill was not asked to 'step aside' and he resisted the strong public pressures on him to resign. When Haughey turned to his government ministers, however, to get an expression of confidence in Cahill included in a Government statement on the Greencore resignations, this was refused, to his intense annoyance.

The episode raised the spectre of Haughey's financial or personal involvements extending like a spider's web throughout the whole structure of Irish business. This was far-fetched, but it was reinforced almost immediately after the Greencore revelations by another scandal, this time involving a leading Irish businessman, Michael Smurfit, and a highly successful stockbroker, Dermot Desmond.

Desmond seemed to move in a magic circle, where business and politics necessarily had to meet and where deals could be lubricated or cemented through political influence. A good example of this was in the battle for Irish Distillers, between Grand Metropolitan and Pernod. The takeover by Grand Metropolitan seemed absolutely assured, when it swung suddenly to Pernod. In a letter, later published, it emerged that Dermot Desmond had sought a fee of £2 million, which he claimed was for ensuring the changeover, achieved through influence in high places, though it was for other services as well. He received in the end a much-reduced fee. The rapid rise in his fortunes and the flow of government and State work to Desmond's company, National City Brokers, seems to have occurred after the Pernod deal.

Michael Smurfit, one of Ireland's most successful businessmen, was chairman of Telecom, a statutory company set up in 1984 and responsible for telecommunication services throughout the country. His role was seen as a valuable commitment to the country's affairs, over and above his many international business responsibilities. The company had been involved in a complicated property deal involving the premises in Ballsbridge formerly occupied by the Dublin bakery, Johnston, Mooney and O'Brien. And the price for the site was £9.4 million. It emerged that dealings for the property had escalated the price well beyond what Telecom should have paid and that a company in which Smurfit had a beneficial interest was profitably involved in a sequence of sales and transfers.

Desmond was the connection with Haughey. He had been responsible for setting up the property company, United Property Holdings, which had originally bought the site. Smurfit had a 10 per cent interest in this property company. UPH sold it on and companies outside Ireland were involved in the eventual transfer of the Ballsbridge site to Telecom. Representatives for Smurfit had originally denied that he had any financial interest in the site and had used the denial to extract apologies from the *Irish Independent* in February 1990. When it emerged that the chairman of the statutory company was involved in a sale which had seen the property 'rise' in value from approximately £5 to £9 million, mainly on the basis of an assured sale to the State in which Smurfit as chairman had played a part, the Government was faced with yet another crisis.

Haughey reacted sternly to the controversy, but went through none of the required formalities. Instead of meeting with Smurfit and others directly involved, he sought advice from two ministers, Bertie Ahern and Seamus Brennan, from the secretary of his department, Padraig O hUiginn, and from P. J. Mara. Whether he then acted on their counsel or took a different course of action, Haughey's eventual response was poorly judged. He went on radio and suggested that Smurfit should 'step aside' from his chairmanship and that Seamus Parcéir, a former chairman of the Revenue Commission and current chairman of the Custom House Docks Development Board, who was also on the board of the property company, should likewise 'step aside'. Stepping aside had, of course, no legal sense. It was offered on the airwaves in a vague and ameliorative attempt to dismiss the problem rather than solve it. And it was an egregious insult to all concerned to do this without first informing the two prominent figures involved. Parcéir was travelling by car to Belfast to preside over an international conference. Literally stopped in his tracks, he returned immediately to Dublin. He was outraged and resigned immediately; Smurfit resigned two days later; on 3 October Dermot Desmond resigned as chairman of Aer Rianta, the company that owns and runs the country's airports, and also 'stepped aside' as head of his own stockbroking firm. An interim report produced for the Minister for Transport and Tourism, Seamus Brennan, found that there had been direct dealings over the property in which Dermot Desmond and Michael Smurfit were involved, and that proper procedures on valuation and cost comparisons had not been followed.

Haughey also insulted the intelligence of the Fianna Fáil Party. At this stage the party's collective intelligence was increasingly open to question. Nevertheless, there was a strong reaction to his glib comments in the same radio interview about continuing as leader, possibly into his eighties. He made passing reference to the great age of recent Chinese leaders, who remained firmly in control and, while rejecting the idea of staying on until he was ninety, the general drift of these comments reinforced the resentment within the party that he had effectively abandoned all idea of standing down, or even of indicating a willingness to stand down. The spectre grew more hideous with each public utterance, of an obsessive determination to lead on through the growing chaos of electoral débâcles, of increasingly ill-judged and mishandled crises and of his private affairs being enmeshed in the State's business dealings and in other public- or private-sector financial or business arrangements.

Some of these, though trivial by comparison with others, now took on a sour taste as they were regurgitated by circumstance. For more than a year, questions had been asked about the sale of the Carysfort Training College and its land. Originally valued at £3.8 million, the property was subsequently sold to University College, Dublin, for £8 million by Pino Harris, a Dublin truck importer with property inter-ests. He had bought it for £6.25 million. The money for the purchase, with additional funds for the adaptation of the buildings for a post-graduate business school, meant that the State had to provide £9.7 million. There were many irregularities in how the purchase was inves-tigated and agreed, with essential safeguards being ignored and decisions made against formal or official advice. The Department of Finance, for example, opposed the provision of the £9.7 million but was 'handed down' a Government decision on the deal and Haughey himself, though he originally denied any involvement whatever in the purchase, had been directly involved in a number of meetings connec-ted with the sale, seeing the president of the college, Paddy Masterson, and other officials. Opposition politicians, whose views were essentially endorsed by University College, claimed that the college had been 'force-fed' with the funds in order to acquire a property which was far from ideal for its purposes. They also claimed that Pino Harris, the private individual who made £1.75 million from the deal, was 'a politi-cal friend' of Charles Haughey. Haughey denied any 'particular know-ledge of any of the various financial transactions and valuations'. He told the Dáil that his participation was in order to provide extra third-level places for students.

There were particularly angry exchanges over the supposed close political association between Haughey and Harris, Haughey accusing the Labour Party leader, Dick Spring, of lying and of being 'a pro-fessional slanderer'.[1]

More minor, but no less symptomatic of the fiefdom approach of the head of the Government, was the revelation that a wind-powered

---

[1] *Dáil Report*, 11 December 1991.

electricity generator had been installed on Haughey's island home of Innishvichillane, at the State's expense, for experimental purposes.

Further emphasis was placed on the personal aspect of Haughey's rule when the leader of Fine Gael, John Bruton, revealed that a market study conducted by Dermot Desmond's company, National City Brokers, on behalf of Celtic Helicopters, a company owned by the State airline, Aer Lingus, had found its way into the possession of Irish Helicopters, which was owned by Haughey's son, Ciarán, and which was a major rival company.

The scandals were punctuating the life of the country with the dull regular thump of some underground sewage pump, flushing out the evidence of an unplumbed and immeasurable cesspool. And still the defence went on, the determination to survive, the absolute refusal to be shamed out of office. The democratic wranglings went on in the Dáil. The charges were laid, one after another. Yet so long as Haughey could hold his party's allegiance and maintain the coalition deal, he was safe.

Both became focuses for challenge. Throughout the summer – indeed, for many months before that – there had been the clear perception that Albert Reynolds would be the main contender to succeed Haughey, either when he stepped down or when Fianna Fáil eventually decided that it had suffered enough damage at his hands and voted him out of office. Various other figures in the party, conscious of the work being done by Reynolds to build up support, now encouraged or at least 'allowed', speculation on their prospects and ambitions. Mary O'Rourke, Gerard Collins, Michael O'Kennedy and Bertie Ahern were all seen as possible successors and were quizzed at every opportunity. So too was Ireland's Commissioner in Brussels, Ray McSharry, whose claims to succeed Haughey, on grounds of ability and strength, were by far the strongest of any of the names discussed. McSharry ruled himself out emphatically. The others ruled themselves in with varying degrees of deference about whether or not the party would issue a call for their services and of course depending on Haughey's willingness to step down. The improbability of this voluntary resignation rendered the debate sterile and gave to many of the utterances at the time a simpering inconsequentiality which seemed to reach its apogee in the person of Mary O'Rourke.

Mary O'Rourke had good reason to feel resentment towards Haughey over his treatment of her brother, Brian Lenihan, whom she had defended stoutly during the cattle-raid period. She had even better reason to expect some help from *him* in her own aspirations to become the first woman to lead what had always been a very masculine party. Lenihan, however, took quite the opposite view of the situation. Earlier in the year, in anticipation of the annual party conference, he might have transformed the power balance within Fianna Fáil by confronting Haughey for the presidency of the party. This was a symbolic role, with no special purpose other than that of figurehead, but it would still have represented for Lenihan the position of a king-maker figure for the future, with mildly constructive potential. But instead, in a move which was fated from the start to look pointless and ridiculous, he had done the opposite, turning away from this symbolic role and announcing that he too would be a contender for the leadership of the party, if and when it became vacant. Then, in the autumn, he rediscovered his old loyalty towards Haughey and became, bizarrely, his defender.

Lenihan came to Haughey's support when his leadership was directly criticized by four backbenchers who issued a public statement expressing their disquiet over the events of the summer, supporting the various inquiries that had been established, mainly by the leader of the Progressive Democrats, Desmond O'Malley, and insisting that these should be made public. The backbenchers were Sean Power, Liam Fitzgerald, M. J. Nolan and Noel Dempsey. There was immediate speculation about whose stalking-horse they were and what new twist in the hidden conspiracy against Haughey their move represented. The truth was more mundane. The four had met on holiday in the Mediterranean and had agreed that the party was in a parlous state. Their statement anticipated the Dáil resuming in the face of a further tide of attacks and revelations. They also criticized Haughey's handling of the Telecom crisis, deploring his suggestion about 'stepping aside' and directly questioning the failure to extend this to include Bernie Cahill, over the Greencore scandal.

Their statement was issued on 27 September. The Fianna Fáil Party was not due to meet until 9 October. Haughey brought this party meeting forward to 2 October and listened to a catalogue of criticisms of, or more correctly comments on, his leadership. There were several incidents of harsh and bruising treatment meted out to individual deputies. Stephen Collins recounts one of the more colourful of these episodes which concerned Senator Don Lydon, a university teacher and professor of psychology, who was summoned by Haughey after he had made a controversial speech in the Senate on Northern Ireland.

Haughey berated him, in strong language, then dismissed him from his office. Lydon could not find the door in the panelled wall of the room. 'Haughey looked up from his desk a couple of minutes later to find the forlorn senator still in his presence! "What are you still doing here?" he demanded. "I can't find the door, Taoiseach," responded Lydon. "Then why don't you jump out the fucking window," snapped Haughey.'[1]

The short shrift which Haughey gave to his own party members was in marked contrast to the care with which he handled his Coalition partners. He knew he could wheel Fianna Fáil into the lobbies whenever he wanted and outstare them individually or collectively no matter how embarrassing the issue, or how confrontational they at first appeared. But a quite different atmosphere prevailed in relations with the Progressive Democrats and the time prescribed by the coalition agreement between the two parties had now elapsed. Haughey underestimated the implications of this, assuming that the broad success of the working relationship established on Government policy and executive action generally would render such an agreement renewable without too much debate or argument. But this was not the case.

The Progressive Democrats took their role as national guarantors of better government seriously. Although they felt that this had been delivered on many issues, they were also conscious that there was real danger, politically, in their close association with a party and a leader so prone to catastrophe of one kind or another as both Haughey and his closest associates seemed to be. The Progressive Democrats had studiously kept clear of any involvement that was purely 'party', leaving Fianna Fáil to sort out its own embarrassments as best it could. But by its very nature, the larger partner in government, which so often saw itself as the embodiment of the nation itself, seemed to have enmeshed Haughey and Fianna Fáil inextricably with the country, with the business community, with cultural and social life, with land and property, heritage and enterprise. And there were many within the Progressive Democrat party favouring an end to the coalition arrangement just at that time, when the tide of scandals was flowing at flood levels.

It resulted in knife-edge negotiations, with greater pressure on Haughey from his own side than had been the case two years earlier. This time, though he again sought the same free-wheeling mandate

[1] Stephen Collins, op. cit., pp. 212–13.

to conclude a deal, it was frustrated by Albert Reynolds, who had been one of his two negotiators in 1989. Reynolds opposed Haughey. Instead of helping with negotiations, he raised objections on the taxation demands coming from the Progressive Democrats and on the impact the prospective programme would have on public finances. This was seen as part of a challenge, the view being openly expressed that Haughey would be confronted by ministers and asked to step down. Meanwhile Bertie Ahern, who was ambivalent about Reynolds confronting Haughey at such a delicate stage in the coalition arrangements, went ahead and resolved the differences, bringing the deal to a satisfactory conclusion. Haughey's dependence on Ahern was mildly embarrassing to the younger politician. Explaining the deal to political journalists in Government Buildings in Merrion Street, Ahern was interrupted by Haughey, obviously in buoyant mood, who pointed at Ahern and said: 'He's the man. He's the best, the most skilful, the most devious, and the most cunning.' Then he went on his way. 'God, that's all I need,' was Ahern's response.

The very tense and drawn-out negotiations were galling for Fianna Fáil. The party was again being dictated to, by their smaller partners. They were also being shown up. Worse still, they were divided and still apparently incapable of confronting the problem of the future leadership of the party. The nightmare of Chinese leadership had descended to haunt them. Haughey was conscious of this and, since he had got agreement from the Progressive Democrats on a joint programme for government which now covered the balance of the lifetime of the current Dáil, his own personal plans were very much in the minds of all party members. The question was an obvious one: had he set up the deal for himself, or for a successor? The answer was just as obvious and he gave it in what was meant to be a reassuring speech to his parliamentary party on 23 October. He would know, he told them all, when the time had come for his departure; in the meantime there was a heavy programme facing them all.

Once again, the party was being held to ransom by its leader. He knew that there was sufficient jockeying for succession going on to ensure uncertainty and disagreement about any challenge. While all the running had been made by Albert Reynolds, there were others just as deeply committed to keeping Haughey in place until their own chances had improved. And inevitably, even among those who supported Reynolds, or who wanted the present leadership ended, there were doubts and hesitations about timing.

Bertie Ahern had become a pivotal figure in the party. Almost twenty years younger than Albert Reynolds, he had shown considerable ministerial ability, particularly in industrial negotiations. He was a natural negotiator and had been effective in achieving the first phase of the coalition deal with the Progressive Democrats, before Charles Haughey had stepped in and taken over. At that stage he had worked closely with Albert Reynolds. In the autumn of 1991, in the quite different climate created by the succession of scandals, Ahern had worked on his own, since Reynolds was now less committed to the deal and much more openly contemptuous of the continued participation of O'Malley and Molloy in government. He was uncertain about his own ambitions. In the longer term time was on his side. More immediately, he lacked experience, having served in only the one full government post, as Minister for Labour in both the Haughey administrations, 1987–89, and that formed in 1989. It was in his interests to back Reynolds, on the reasonable assumption that he would become the obvious successor. But he made it clear that the time was not right for a challenge.

If ever there was a winter of discontent for the Fianna Fáil Party, it set in now. Nothing went right. Though Reynolds and his closest supporters were ready to challenge Haughey, their backing was insufficient to ensure victory. Several leading figures in the party indicated publicly that Haughey should be permitted to set his own agenda for departure. Privately, those who wanted Reynolds to succeed told him to hold back. Instead of doing this and keeping his counsel until he was ready to move, Reynolds gave an interview in late October in which he both claimed sufficient support to oust Haughey and indicated his preparedness to hold back, in the interests of the party. It was almost as bad as Haughey's own pledges, that he would resign when he felt that his presence at the head of Fianna Fáil was no longer to the party's advantage.

To many backbenchers it seemed that the September statement by the Gang of Four[1] had achieved nothing at all. The long debate, the criticisms, the continued Dáil and newspaper revelations about irregularities involving Haughey had come and gone and the party strife continued. It was now the turn, once again, of Charles McCreevy, whose outspoken criticisms of Haughey predated those of everyone

---

[1] The Gang of Four being Noel Dempsey, Liam Fitzgerald, M. J. Nolan and Sean Power.

else in Fianna Fáil.[1] He made public his view that a vote of confidence should be sought by Haughey. Brian Lenihan then emerged in the highly unexpected role of staunch Haughey supporter. He blocked McCreevy's efforts to have a debate on the leadership, with a view to getting such a confidence motion put down. The result was that one of the Gang of Four, Sean Power, actually did put a motion down and triggered a challenge which in the event played into Haughey's hands. The party chairman, Jim Tunney, summoned a special party meeting for Saturday, 9 November. Reynolds, having given his radio interview about his prospects for defeating Haughey, felt forced now to back the challenge. Two days before the crucial meeting, he announced his support for Power and was dismissed from the Government. Pádraig Flynn than came out in support of the motion and was also dismissed. Three junior ministers then joined them. And there it stopped. A roll-call took place of senior figures in the Government publicly pledging support for Haughey. Key figures on whom Reynolds and his supporters were relying came out against the challenge. Gerard Collins, Minister for Foreign Affairs, made an impassioned appeal on television, warning Reynolds, in almost tearful anxiety, that he would 'burst up' the party.

Albert Reynolds had been manouevred into the position of backing someone else's challenge and was not adequately prepared. The issue of holding the vote in secret became a central one, as did an alternative motion in Haughey's own name. By 55 votes to 22, Haughey won, confounding his critics, demolishing his challengers and once again asserting a late twentieth-century version of the divine right to rule.

---

[1] McCreevy had criticized the party leader in 1981, claiming that 'we seem to be against everything and for nothing'. Threatened with expulsion, he had then resigned the whip for a brief period. (See Chapter 17.)

CHAPTER XXIII

RESIGNATION

for their souls
Another of his fathom they have none
To lead their business.

H AUGHEY CAME OUT of the party meeting, in the early hours
of the morning of Sunday, 10 November 1991, immensely
strengthened. He had once again had his leadership endorsed. His survival over the vote of confidence had been a genuine
rallying of support within the Fianna Fáil Party. Traditionally, the
party had stood opposed to the idea of forcing any leader out. This
had been an argument in previous challenges. It had also been the
historic position and it seemed to manifest itself, in the winter of 1991,
with renewed conviction. Another of the leadership hopefuls, Mary
O'Rourke, gave expression to it: 'We have a very long tradition that,
when the leader is there, in control and in command, you give that
leader time and space to be himself and to express himself freely within
the parliamentary party. I'm content with that. To be otherwise would
be wrong within our ethos.'[1] In reality, the jockeying for support
among other contenders, combined with the fact that Albert Reynolds
had not been happy with the timing, had given Haughey the lifeline
of a substantial majority. But there were loyal supporters who thought
they were in the position to exact a greater reward than Haughey's
gratitude, which on occasion expressed itself in strange ways. Instead
of promoting from among those ministers who had stood out in his
defence, Haughey brought into the Government two backbenchers,
Noel Davern and James McDaid. Davern, an agreeable but undistin-
guished backbencher, first elected to the Dáil in 1969, was given the
exacting and difficult Department of Education. While there was criticism of this in the Dáil on the grounds of his inexperience, and within

[1] Mary O'Rourke speaking in Ballinasloe, 5 January 1992 (reported in *The Irish Times* the
following day).

Fianna Fáil on the grounds of Haughey leap-frogging him over the heads of worthier and more deserving candidates, it did not stir trouble in the way that James McDaid's appointment did.

McDaid was a newcomer to the Dáil, first elected only two years earlier, when he had been spectacularly successful in ousting the sitting Fianna Fáil representative and taking a sizeable slice of Neil Blaney's vote in Donegal. But McDaid had been closely associated with a Provisional IRA escapee from the Maze Prison, James Pius Clarke, appearing with him on the steps of the Four Courts when Clarke, who was a constituent, had successfully appealed against an extradition order before the Supreme Court. Since Haughey was proposing to appoint him to the security-sensitive Department of Defence, there was Dáil uproar and, unusually, exchanges in the House of Commons in Westminster about what was happening in Dublin. The Progressive Democrats indicated that they could not support the appointment and Haughey accepted this. McDaid had to ask the Taoiseach to withdraw his nomination and Haughey then appointed Vincent Brady, his constituency running-mate for many years, as Minister for Defence.

It was an inexplicable mistake. Carelessness had been compounded with the gratuitous insult it represented towards the party as a whole, which had been publicly shamed once more and in humiliating circumstances. Once again Haughey had been directed in what to do by the Progressive Democrats and had treated his own supporters disdainfully. Questioning the survival of the Government under his leadership had again turned into questioning the survival of the Government *because* of his leadership. There was open criticism of him within Fianna Fáil, relentless criticism from outside the party and the setting of clear time-frames for his departure. There was no reactivation of the direct attempts to remove him, but Albert Reynolds, the only contender to have come out into the open and now the party's highest-profile backbencher, planned a series of meetings in Dublin, Cork, Kilkenny and Mayo, through the early months of 1992. Significantly, the schedule ended in April. This was the time limit Reynolds set on Haughey's continued leadership of Fianna Fáil.

Then came a curious development. Sean Doherty, Cathaoirleach of the Senate and former Minister for Justice, responsible for the phone-tapping scandal in the early 1980s, agreed to appear on a late-night television programme called *Nighthawks*, hosted by Shay Healy. The programme, which was set in a studio bar or pub, had a noisy and lively atmosphere and included music and chat as well as interviews. It was not a cradle for political turmoil. It seemed even less so when it moved to Roscommon and included an interview with Doherty among his supporters in a local pub there. But he was asked about the phone-tapping and gave an answer that puzzled Healy. He also reinforced, after the show, the impression that he had gone further in his assertions about the events in 1982 than at any time previously.

'There was a decision taken in Cabinet', Sean Doherty claimed in the interview, 'that the prevention of the leaking of matters from Cabinet must be stopped. I as Minister for Justice had a direct responsibility for doing that – I did that. I do feel that I was let down by the fact that people knew what I was doing.' Later in the interview he claimed that Cabinet colleagues backed him in his moves to detect where the Government leaks were coming from: 'I had an obligation to fulfil – a constitutional obligation to establish who was taking information out of the most important boardroom in the country and making it available without authority to the national media and to others and I felt that that was wrong. So also did my colleagues in Cabinet feel that was wrong and consequently I was required to ensure that that would be stopped and I consulted with the authorities at that time and one of the methods that was decided upon was the tapping of phones and anybody else that says otherwise or tries to abandon himself or herself from that situation is not telling the truth.'

The programme-makers, unsure of the full implications of this, consulted me and I was shown the section containing the interview. I confirmed that this was significant new material and, with the producer's agreement, wrote a story for the *Irish Independent* which appeared on the morning of Wednesday, 15 January, in advance of the showing of *Nighthawks*. Stories appeared in other newspapers, referring to the forthcoming revelations.

I quoted Doherty and went on: 'The latest revelations add further damage to the Taoiseach's credibility, revealing a deliberate misrepresentation of the facts at the time and a subsequent concealment of formal Government knowledge of both the phone-tapping and the actions taken against political journalists and colleagues within his own party.' I quoted Haughey's own denial at the time.[1]

The article, following the detail of what Doherty had asserted, extended the range of responsibility: 'But the embarrassment goes

[1] See Chapter 18. By an oversight, the story did not appear in *The Irish Times*, but was widely covered in other papers.

further, since other members of that Government, according to tonight's Sean Doherty interview, also knew. This includes the present leader of the Progressive Democrats, Desmond O'Malley, as well as former Government Ministers, Albert Reynolds and Pádraig Flynn. At least four Fianna Fáil Ministers in the present Government were members of that Government.'

The article, together with reports in other newspapers, assured *Nighthawks* of a greatly enlarged and countrywide audience. It also provoked a strong denial from Desmond O'Malley that he had known anything at the time of such 'Cabinet decisions'. Others made the same claim. For several days the debate on the implications of Doherty's remarks raged. Then, on Tuesday, 21 January, Doherty called a press conference in the Montrose Hotel, close to the Radio Telefis Eireann station in Donnybrook, and gave full details of what had happened.

Speaking of the events of 1982, he claimed: 'As soon as the transcripts from the taps became available, I took them personally to Mr Haughey in his office and left them in his possession. I understand that the Taoiseach has already denied that this happened, so I wish to reiterate it in specific terms. Mr Ainsworth [Deputy Garda Commissioner at the time] forwarded to me the transcripts relevant to the Cabinet leaks problem, numbering some four or five out of the roughly 12 or 13 total. Each and every one of those relevant transcripts were transported by me to Mr Haughey's office and handed to him directly. He retained all but one of them, making no comment on their content. At no stage did he indicate disapproval of the action which had been taken.' Only Haughey saw them, Doherty went on. 'I did not seek nor did I get any instruction from any member of the Cabinet in this regard, nor did I tell the Cabinet that this action had been taken. Telephone tapping was never discussed in Cabinet.'

Doherty addressed the obvious additional question, of his more recent motivation for speaking out: 'I want to add emphatically that I have never discussed this with Albert Reynolds, nor have I talked to him in the past fortnight.'

A careful reading of Doherty's statement, which is very carefully phrased, reveals that it does not preclude knowledge among colleagues, at the time, of what he was doing. Nor does it rule out the involvement of others in his decision to make the statement in the way he chose, without any question from the press. He used as his reason a sudden conversion to the moral nicety of not lying to the Senate, over which he presided, which was shortly to debate a forthcoming piece of legislation on phone-tapping.

Haughey addressed directly the motive behind Doherty's revelations and the possibility of hidden allies. He had already denied Doherty's earlier, and more general, *Nighthawks* claim. Now, on the day following Doherty's press conference, Haughey gave a comprehensive press conference of his own, claiming that the Senator's comments were part of a campaign that was designed to replace him as leader of Fianna Fáil and Taoiseach, and that the choice of allegations related 'to his own convenience at the present time and not to any exacting standard of truthfulness'. Significantly, he was critical of the fact that Doherty had *only* delivered his statement and had avoided any subsequent interrogation from the press. If he had been interested 'in telling the truth, the whole truth and nothing but the truth', then it was only right that the press should have been given the opportunity to question him about the many inconsistencies between what he had said in the past and what he was now claiming.

Haughey denied absolutely the allegations made by Doherty and referred back to the many statements made at the time, by himself and by his former minister, who had specifically declared that Haughey had had no knowledge. His lengthy statement was a recapitulation of the familiar chronology of phone-tapping in 1982 and the exposure of it the following year, with Haughey quoting himself extensively and offering these quotations – as well as many references to Doherty's quite different evidence in 1983 – as proof of innocence. It was a powerful, gritty performance, conducted by the man on his own. He was seated against the backdrop of a dark curtain, which gave the occasion some of the atmosphere of a Jacobean theatre set – rich, primitive, faintly sinister, as though hidden figures were monitoring the conviction and mapping further speeches of defence. His voice, which in recent months had become increasingly breathless from emphysema, spurted at times like gravel from the wheel of his indignation. Unlike Doherty, and to his added credit in an hour of maximum danger, Haughey took a full thirty minutes of questions during which he played with a small piece of paper, folding it and refolding it endlessly. He had not yet decided on the form of Mr Doherty's execution, whether he would be expelled from Fianna Fáil, or what would be done with him. But there were others who concerned him, people whom he saw lurking with treacherous purpose behind this campaign to get rid of him.

He invited the very large audience of journalists to look with particular care at the role being played by Pádraig Flynn, who, the previous Sunday, in the *Sunday Tribune*, at a time when Sean Doherty had only referred in the *Nighthawks* programme to the bare bones of the matter of who had originated the phone-tapping, had suggested that Doherty would probably be 'clarifying his position'. 'That's a connection I think you should take into account.' He did not directly charge Flynn with involvement, nor did he agree, in so many words, when it was put to him that Albert Reynolds might also be behind the Doherty allegations. But the implication was strongly inferred and in a sense was used as defence.

The people of Ireland looked upon one version of past events, and then looked upon another version, and were ashamed that either might have occurred quite as stated. They were ashamed, too, that they had been governed by these men, that the security of the State had been in their hands, that high office, not just once but repeatedly, had been their responsibility. Most shaming of all was that these men were their choice.

It was the final humiliation. Doherty was believed, not Haughey. The Progressive Democrats indicated that Haughey would have to go and issued an ultimatum to that effect the following day. They made no judgement between the conflicting accounts of the two men concerning events long past; they merely indicated that this, the latest and most serious of a long list of unhappy and politically unacceptable controversies, had undermined the capacity of the Government to work properly and they wanted a swift response from Fianna Fáil 'in order that the credibility and stability of the Government be immediately restored'.[1]

Haughey still fought on. 'Why should I resign for what somebody else did?' was his question. There still seemed some uncertainty within his own party about how this question should be answered, and by whom. They did not bring forward their normal parliamentary party meeting, scheduled for the Wednesday of the following week, nor did any minister or senior member of the party make any public criticism of the leader. Instead, anger was expressed at the reaction of the Progressive Democrats. Their position was exceedingly difficult. The Budget was imminent; they sought its smooth passage and Fianna Fáil were prepared to permit this to go ahead in advance of 'the necessary

---

[1] Statement issued by the Progressive Democrats, on the night of Wednesday, 22 January 1992.

step to restore the authority and effectiveness of the Government'.[1]
But if that necessary step was not taken, there would be a general
election. For Fianna Fáil this would represent a disaster of the greatest
magnitude, to be avoided at all costs. The inevitability of Haughey's
departure was universally accepted by the party. And on the night of
28 January a time-frame for his departure was agreed in advance of
Ahern's Budget speech the next day. Haughey announced his intentions to the Fianna Fáil Party meeting on Thursday, 30 January, and
there followed an array of tributes that stretched through the weekend
and exhausted the range of language possible for such an event.

Though Fianna Fáil deputies still had to choose a successor, the
circumstances were comparatively relaxed. All previous crises over the
leadership had combined two closely related, but distinct requirements:
removing Haughey, then choosing who should replace him. And on
each occasion since 1981, the spark of collective confrontation had
been doused by Haughey's own admirable capacity to survive. With
this resource disposed of and with much of the hidden credit already
belonging to Reynolds, who also offered experience and toughness,
the predicted outcome was comparatively clear. So long as Ahern
remained as a challenger, the prospective contest was serious enough.
But in addition to Ahern's lack of experience – which he freely admitted
– he had no profile comparable to Reynolds' hawkish determination
that Fianna Fáil would recover single-party power in the next election,
reversing the shameful coalition into which Haughey had led the party
in 1989. This was a compelling advantage and not shared by the other
contenders. In addition to Reynolds and Ahern, there were Mary
O'Rourke and Michael Woods, both government ministers with considerable experience. Mary O'Rourke's brother, Brian Lenihan, to
whom she had been so loyal during the presidential crisis, characteristically surprised everyone well before the leadership election took place
by deserting her candidacy and coming out in favour of Bertie Ahern.
Michael Woods had been chief whip under Jack Lynch and had served
with some distinction in several Haughey administrations. The leadership contest, stretched out over weeks because of the time given to
Haughey to implement his resignation, was overshadowed by the

---

[1] Statement issued by the Progressive Democrats, 23 January 1992. The statement followed
a meeting between Haughey and O'Malley at which agreement was reached over the passage
of the Budget resolutions through the Dáil, with the implication that Haughey would step
down afterwards.

Budget. Ahern produced measures, including the broadening of tax bands, which were designed to stabilize the coalition while at the same time following a generally neutral approach, allowing him and the Fianna Fáil party to contemplate with equanimity a general election, should this prove necessary. At the end of January, Ahern was still in the race. But on Saturday, 1 February, with a growing number of deputies declaring their support for Albert Reynolds, he decided that Fianna Fáil unity would be best served if he did the same. On Thursday, 7 February 1992, the leadership election took place. Albert Reynolds secured 61 votes; Michael Woods secured 10; Mary O'Rourke 6.

At the very heart of the traumas that would end his political life, Charles Haughey managed what he described as 'a politics-free day' when his son, Ciarán, married Laura Daly, the reception being held at Abbeville, the groom's father's home in Kinsealy, on the outskirts of the city. Carefully positioning himself before the cameras and film crews of a vastly interested international press, he generously ensured that the limelight fell on his new daughter-in-law, refused all political comment, but treated the visually hungry photographers and film-men to glasses of cold champagne which he poured and handed to them himself. He had always loved their adulation; he had always revelled in its outcome; and he did not let them down in his own hour of distress.

There was speculation about the futures of three of Haughey's closest aides: Martin Mansergh, who had resigned from the Department of Foreign Affairs when Haughey became leader in order to advise him on Northern Ireland; Anthony Cronin, who had been cultural adviser for many years; and P. J. Mara, who was government press secretary. Mara suggested that, like Cincinnatus, he would 'save the empire' and then return to his farm. Neither of the other two made any comment on their futures.

On Tuesday, 11 February, Charles Haughey formally announced his resignation to the Dáil. For the man himself it was an occasion of great emotion, obvious pain and deep disappointment. Although he claimed a deep affection for the Dáil and its traditions, too many of his actions belied this. Although he sought from posterity a demanding accolade, that he would be seen as having served 'all the people to the best of his ability', it was emphatically clear that this perception of him was now shared by very few people, either within Dáil Eireann or outside. He was effusive and wide-ranging in his gratitude. He was relatively modest in the specific achievements he claimed for himself in legislative reform or changes designed to help public representatives. The response of others to his going was a mixed one, coloured by generosity and a sense of the near-tragic terms of his departure, but also mindful of the inevitable reservations felt by the country as a whole and, it had by then to be said, by the vast majority of elected representatives.

The leaders of all the parties in the Dáil paid tribute to him. As for the dreaded media, whose photographers and cameramen he loved, whose commentators and critics he abhorred, their tributes had been exhausted. They were interested now in the new leader of Fianna Fáil.

> I have done the state some service; they know't:
> No more of that.

If, in choosing the character of Othello and drawing upon one of the great moments in Shakespearean drama to summarize his own career, Charles Haughey sought to present himself as a tragic hero, the effort was neither recognized nor accepted. The solemn Dáil occasion was slightly mawkish, the sentiments overblown. He had overstayed and worn out all welcome and support. And with the innate public kindness and consideration that characterizes most official events in Irish political life – indeed, which has characterized Haughey himself in his dealings with so many of his political and other foes – no one knew how to handle this unique occasion on which a leader, in office, had been forced out and dismissed by those closest to him.

If Charles Haughey had some kind of inner flaw or fault, blighting his career as a politician and as leader of Fianna Fáil, then that was recognized, but imperfectly assessed. As one would expect, references that touched on the fact of failure were restrained and oblique. He, of course, accepted no such thing himself.

Unlucky deeds, poor judgement – these do not justify the kind of reaction that Haughey seemed to invite throughout his career, inducing the kind of reservations that dogged him, crossing his path like a wolf in the shadows. There was something more – the abuse of power. He gave a new meaning to the term 'slightly constitutional', which had been applied by leading figures in Fianna Fáil to themselves when they eventually decided to enter the Dáil and abandon militancy. With Haughey it was a belief that he could govern, on occasions, in a manner that seemed to run against the stricter conditions imposed on a Taoiseach by the Constitution. The instances of this are numerous and have been fully detailed in these pages. Individually, they often seem no more than short-cuts, though in certain circumstances they were decidedly more, or worse, than that. Together, they indicate a by-passing of that aspect of democracy that demands strict answerability. And this in a country which had very strong ideas about democracy and its importance. In the end, the conflict between Haughey's way of doing things and the preferred methods of the democratic machinery of government, the law and the Constitution, resulted in a victory for these institutions and defeat for those attempts he made to set them aside.

He certainly gave his name to an era in Irish politics. It embraced the twelve years during which he was leader of the country's largest political party and may be said to have extended beyond that. His was a name to conjure with during the decade of the 1960s, when he represented great promise. His was a name to fear during the 1970s, when he represented a threat to stability within his own party and a threat to the country by virtue of the revelations of the Arms Crisis and the Arms Trial.

When he should have been fulfilling himself and benefiting the country, in four successive administrations during the 1980s, he simply failed to deliver. And what seemed to be, and should have been, the best period of all – between 1987 and 1991 – turned into a long and complicated nightmare, when he succumbed to the tempting but totally misguided idea of calling an election in the summer of 1989.

Such vision as he had was distorted by the fact that his own personal ambition lay at its centre. This made it difficult, if not impossible, to plan any kind of future for the country, for members of his governments, for younger, aspiring politicians, for talented and able public servants or private entrepreneurs. They were all sucked into a web in the centre of which he sat, inscrutable and watchful, expecting that everything should be done for his benefit and should focus on him.

He operated in cycles of great energy and fierce intentions which very swiftly evaporated. He became energized by threat and performed best of all when challenged. The greater the danger – particularly if it threatened his survival – the greater his response. But then the survival became the achieved objective. There was no real sense of what to do until a new challenge emerged. Setting up a government, appointing a team of junior ministers, holding meetings with the 'social partners': these were ends in themselves and were often treated almost flippantly.

He and Margaret Thatcher became heads of the respective governments in the two neighbouring islands in the same year and lasted almost exactly the same period of time. Though she was different, in that she never relinquished power during her twelve years, the two had much in common, including a shared disdain for those under them and a fearful, obsessive concern for control and power. They had initial respect for each other, which soon turned to distrust and an inability to work closely on matters of mutual value or importance.

Haughey's republicanism was political in its motivation and enigmatic. It emerged strongly, in 1970, and was taken to have been there as a covert but intense conviction for years. This perception was not contradicted by Haughey and in the emotional circumstances of the Arms Trial, in the autumn of that year, he heaped praise and endorsement on republicans involved with the IRA. But it was, in reality, a republicanism created to defend a political flank, not out of any burning zeal to confront the British presence in Ireland with all means at his disposal. And in power he was a conventional supporter of peaceful means and agreement as the road forward. When Neil Blaney ceased to be a threat to him, Haughey felt no need to pursue the kind of politics which Blaney had espoused – with much more conviction – during the 1960s.

His views on economics generally, and on specific problems like taxation reform, were informed by an exceptionally sharp mind with a commanding grasp of difficult issues. But he lacked the staying power in planning programmes of political action and he lacked the courage required for difficult and unpopular decisions. He probably appreciated that taxation reform requires a comprehensive system, the lightening of the burden on the individual and no special concessions. But he never addressed the implications of this in reformist, legislative action. Once a politician gives in to sectional interests – such as teachers, nurses, health and postal workers – the prospect of fundamental changes and the broad reduction of tax levels is immediately prejudiced.

All legislative reform follows much the same pattern, and psychologically and emotionally Haughey did not have the patience required for the kind of fundamental changes in society which Ireland's progress during the period in which he held power, both ministerial and as government leader, demanded. There were always vested interests that demanded special satisfaction. And Haughey seems to have been drawn to them as towards some powerful drug. That drug was power itself and the need, as he saw it, in a democracy, to be popular in order to stay in power.

He was and is a secretive man. When Doherty made his statement about the real events in the phone-tapping saga, there was one very telling admission: 'Each and every one of those relevant transcripts were transported by me to Mr Haughey's office and handed to him directly. He retained all but one of them, making no comment on their content. At no stage did he indicate disapproval of the action which had been taken.' A senior former colleague of Haughey's remarked to me how typical it was of him not to comment, not to indicate an attitude, not to criticize or judge, not to *say* anything at all.

Any story of misfortune and bad luck can make painful reading. Yet as teachers often say about Milton's *Paradise Lost*, the most interesting character is Satan himself. Charles Haughey is no Satan. At times brilliantly able, at times woefully misdirected in his energies and actions, he led a turbulent and colourful life in Irish politics with a remarkable number of assets which he deployed with great prodigality. He was generous to the point of profligacy. He was charming and entertaining, witty and mischievous, a patron and supporter of artists, and a man who seemed to embrace, in his rock-hard gaze and his emotive concern, Irish people of every walk of life. Yet Haughey himself walked alone. He was solitary, reclusive, isolated. Few of those people close to him stood up to him, or stood really close to him at all, and this allowed his wilfulness to become damaging. Small of stature, he could strut like Napoleon and seemed often to address those around him with a comparable imperiousness. Every aspect of his character attracts curiosity. No man so dominated his period, in and out of power.

THE NEXT GENERATION

But words are words; I never yet did hear
That the bruised heart was piercèd through the ear

ON BECOMING TAOISEACH, Albert Reynolds swept aside half the previous Government, paying scant regard to experience, seniority, or the relatively obvious need to establish himself firmly with the broad middle ground of the party. He was equally ruthless in the changes at junior minister level. It looked and was savage. It was a breath-taking start to his new administration and the most dramatic sweep of its kind ever witnessed by the people of Ireland. It was, on one level, justified. For more than a year damaging attacks and allegations about Charles Haughey's handling of government had steadily undermined the Government's ability to act effectively in economic and social circumstances which required clear leadership and courage. And the administration as a whole, with some exceptions, had not handled well the latter period of coalition under his leadership. The succession of scandals and crises had clearly demoralized the Fianna Fáil organization and mesmerized those senior ministers who should have performed better. Now that the change had come, some kind of draconian axe was merited. But to make such an approach work requires an iron hand and a first-class political brain. Reynolds had neither. Nor did he have any clear vision of where he wanted to go and what he wanted to do.

He was plunged almost immediately into a crisis that was to remain with him throughout the lifetime of his administration. On the day he received his seal of office and announced the members of his Government, it was also revealed that the Attorney General, Harry Whelehan, had sought and obtained an interim High Court injunction preventing a fourteen-year-old girl from having an abortion in England. The girl had been the victim of an alleged rape and had already gone to England with her parents. But the family returned without the abortion having been carried out.[1] The case came to the Attorney General's attention because the parents sought police advice as to whether the foetus tissue should be tested for DNA or other genetic evidence which might then be used in prosecuting the person suspected of rape. The Attorney General, in going to the High Court, was acting independently of the Government and by virtue of powers conferred on him by law. Normally confined to his constitutional role, as law officer to the Government, the Ministers and Secretaries Act of 1922 gives him also a role as guardian of the public interest. In a Supreme Court judgement of 1988 this special role had been reinforced in the context of the very issue on which he was now acting, when the Supreme Court had described him as 'an especially appropriate person' to vindicate the right to life of the unborn, a right which the Irish people had inserted into the Constitution by referendum in 1983. The Attorney General, further to taking the action, tried to establish a *sub judice* constraint on a debate on these measures, but this was challenged repeatedly in the Dáil.

A High Court Judge, Declan Costello, granted the injunction. The girl was not to be subjected to police surveillance, but was effectively confined to Ireland by the court. The very fears that had been expressed, following the passing of the 1983 referendum – the so-called 'nightmare scenario' – had come to pass. The family decided to appeal the case in the Supreme Court and the State undertook to absolve them from expense in taking this action. But in no sense was the crisis more than temporarily averted. On 26 February the Supreme Court reversed the High Court judgement, released the unnamed girl from the injunction preventing her from travelling to Britain and delivered a judgement that effectively changed the law to make abortion available in certain circumstances. The country was faced with the prospect of another referendum campaign for a fresh constitutional ban on abortion that protected the life of the mother.[2]

At first, it was the wish of most politicians to avoid another referendum; but as the year progressed this became an inevitability. Albert Reynolds began his term as Taoiseach with this major headache. It was to remain with him throughout the year, but Reynolds had other problems, in addition to the abortion issue: unemployment and the

---

[1] It later turned out that the girl had miscarried. A man was subsequently charged with rape.
[2] In the general election of November 1992, Irish voters also dealt with three additional referendum issues, all as a result of what became known as the 'X Case'.

economy; the Northern Ireland talks; the referendum on the Maastricht Treaty; and the European currency crisis in the autumn. He handled these issues competently enough, but needed, in the judgement of most observers, the full two and a half years that were available to him. He was popular enough. His standing in the opinion polls went up rapidly and he was seen to be enjoying the popularity of *not being* Charles Haughey, rather than of being either specially gifted or dynamic as the country's leader. He was sharp, always ready with quick answers, not open to too much debate, but he lacked gravitas. There loomed his forthcoming interrogation before the Beef Tribunal. His actions, back in 1987, were at the heart of the investigation in Dublin Castle, under Judge Liam Hamilton's chairmanship, and the evidence already on the table was not encouraging. As other witnesses, including O'Malley, added to this throughout the year, the questions about his conduct mounted in seriousness and in number.

The dénouement to Reynolds's short administration also involved Charles Haughey and it came about in classic Haughey circumstances. For much of the year following his resignation, Haughey remained in relative obscurity. Then, with the resumption of the Beef Tribunal hearings in Dublin Castle, after the summer break, the appearances of himself, Ray McSharry and Albert Reynolds followed in rapid succession. Haughey delivered a severe indictment of his successor on his first day in the witness box. He declared that the decision taken by Albert Reynolds to reintroduce the export credit insurance cover for Goodman deals with Iraq had been made without the knowledge of himself or the Government. A government spokesman suggested that there was nothing new in this claim and that there would have been nothing unusual about the Minister for Industry and Commerce (the position occupied by Albert Reynolds when he made the decision) taking this action without referring to the Government or to Haughey as head of government. Mr Haughey also denied knowledge of the fact that cover was limited to only two companies.

Haughey brought life and colour to the Tribunal proceedings. He was, in turn, incisive, vague, gracious, intemperate, caustic and benign. He criticized his own critics; he savagely attacked Desmond O'Malley. He defended his position with a mixture of forgetfulness and accurate recall. He could remember some things, but could not, to save his life, remember others. His diary was no help; and the fact that civil servants were often not present for vital, decision-making ministerial and other encounters was a result of the urgency of government business, often conducted at the weekend, at Haughey's mansion north of Dublin.

The collective effect was to load the evidence against Albert Rey-nolds as the man who had been responsible for the decisions over beef which allegedly had been due to the close political and personal association between himself and Larry Goodman. Nevertheless, there was sufficient evidence to throw suspicion upon Charles Haughey to the effect that he had known about and was involved in the decisions. 'The difficulty for the Tribunal', wrote Fintan O'Toole, 'is that Mr Haughey's evidence is entirely ambiguous.'[1]

It seemed to present a trap to Albert Reynolds, who was caught between Haughey, who seemed to be taking revenge for the conspiracy that had removed him, and Desmond O'Malley, whose partnership in government with Reynolds was increasingly a thorn in the side of the Fianna Fáil Party.

When Reynolds appeared before the Beef Tribunal during the last week in October, the emphasis shifted away from the sterile territory of responding to Charles Haughey's denial of knowledge to a quite different battleground – that between the two Coalition partners in government. Albert Reynolds described as 'reckless, irresponsible and dishonest' the evidence that Desmond O'Malley had earlier given the Tribunal, in which he had claimed that Albert Reynolds had put the State at financial risk to the tune of £170 million. The charge was sustained the following day with considerable determination by Albert Reynolds, insisting that he meant what he said under close cross-examination by Adrian Hardiman, counsel for Desmond O'Malley. He would not use the word 'perjury'; he would not withdraw the word 'dishonest'. The morning's newspapers carried the very clear implica-tion that Reynolds was pushing the Coalition to breaking-point. Spokesmen on either side, interpreting for the press the seriousness of what was at stake, made no bones about the impending breakdown in co-operation. The Progressive Democrats regarded as 'outrageous'[2] the charge being made against O'Malley which, 'in the first instance', would be dealt with within the Tribunal by lawyers. On the Govern-ment side Reynolds was described as 'wholly unrepentant'.[3] It was

---

[1] *The Irish Times*, Saturday, 17 October 1992. Fintan O'Toole covered the Beef Tribunal and won a richly deserved A. T. Cross 'Golden Pen' award for his analytical reporting.

[2] Statements made by Progressive Democrat ministers to the press on the night of Tuesday, 27 October 1992, and reported in all Irish daily newspapers.

[3] Statement made by Government spokesperson to the press on the night of Tuesday, 27 October 1992, and reported in all Irish daily newspapers the following morning.

emphasized that he had promised, all along, 'that he would tell it as it was, without any varnish or veneer'.

The atmosphere of crisis was deliberately fostered. Albert Reynolds was accompanied on the second day of his appearance by his three daughters, Andrea, Cathy and Leonie, and a number of members of his administration put in appearances at Dublin Castle in what could only be interpreted as a show of strength. Less committed Reynolds supporters within the Fianna Fáil Party were surprised by his blunt assault on a senior Government colleague and Coalition partner. The Labour Party leader, Dick Spring, said that it would be 'impossible in any normal government to imagine such a charge being levelled without a resignation either being sought or offered. But then,' he added, 'this is no normal government.'[1]

On the third day, with Albert Reynolds sustaining his charge of dishonesty and refusing to accept that 'inaccurate' might be a more appropriate word, the Taoiseach was repeatedly offered the option of withdrawing it by Adrian Hardiman. 'With solemnity', was he saying that the figures were inaccurate or were they dishonest? 'Dishonest'.

More potently, Hardiman put it to Albert Reynolds that by raising in these terms the O'Malley evidence he was distracting attention from the subject-matter of the Tribunal. This referred to the first day's evidence by the Taoiseach, which indicated very serious conflict between himself and departmental officials on the crucial decisions that were made in 1987 concerning the withdrawal of export cover from a non-Goodman company, Halal, on the same day as a letter from Goodman International urged the exclusion from insurance cover of other companies and a substantial increase in the amount of cover for Goodman International.

Reynolds denied receipt of the letter or knowledge of its contents. Yet the head of the export credit section of his department, Joe Timbs, had given sworn evidence in April that it had been Mr Reynolds who produced the letter in the first place and had instructed him to tell the meat company that there would be no additional credit provided. Mr Reynolds, according to Mr Timbs, discussed the Goodman request expressed in the letter that there should be a 'single voice' in Iraq, comments which the two men at the time agreed were 'inappropriate'. More seriously still, Albert Reynolds, on the first day of his evidence, in dealing with matters quite distinct and separate from the charge

[1] *Dáil Report*, 27 October 1992, col. 889.

against O'Malley, contradicted Timbs's sworn evidence as well as departmental documents, when he said he had no recollection of giving the instruction to Timbs to tell Goodman about a substantial increase in insurance cover of £80 million to AIBP and £20 million to Hibernia Meats, both Goodman companies. The commitments were the subject of claims by Goodman against the State on which O'Malley's criticisms of recklessness were based. Reynolds' authority in making them was in doubt and he had been told this by his officials. The new version offered by Reynolds was in conflict with the evidence given by Timbs and with contemporaneous evidence within the Department of Industry and Commerce. To anyone looking at the future implications of this conflict, when the Tribunal eventually came to a conclusion, it augured ill for Reynolds. The earlier evidence, from Charles Haughey, combined with the areas of conflict between himself and his departmental officials, placed him at the centre of responsibility for much of the trouble that had provoked the setting up of the Tribunal in the first place. Although this was unhappily balanced against the quite different threat of a looming general election, it did provoke speculation that the charge of dishonesty against O'Malley was politically motivated.

This was a deliberate attempt to push the Coalition partnership into an irreversible dispute, leading to its break-up and a general election. The chairman of the Tribunal said he found the whole issue unseemly and distasteful. 'It did not form part of the purpose for which the Tribunal was established.' He said he had no intention 'of playing referee in a game of political football'.

For a full week the inevitability of the Dáil's dissolution was the lead in every newspaper and the story on everyone's lips. Then, on Sunday, 1 November, Bobby Molloy, in a statement read, in full, on the 'News at One' programme on RTE, made it clear that without an 'abject' apology from Reynolds, the Progressive Democrats would be pulling out of government.

The enormity of the political conflict towards which the country seemed to be heading by that weekend brought two brief checks in the headlong rush to dissolution. Following Molloy's radio ultimatum, Reynolds suggested that the Progressive Democrats would find his door 'always open' to a meeting, should they want to have one. This was rejected, with some ridicule. Albert Reynolds' judgement was seriously open to question if he thought that two political partners could continue to govern if one thought the other dishonest.

In their turn, the Progressive Democrats seemed to balk at the enormity of what everyone was contemplating. Following the Sunday statement, the resignations of O'Malley and Molloy were expected on the Monday. This move was postponed, ostensibly to support a civil servant from O'Malley's department who was due to give evidence to the Tribunal and to ensure that files related to the Tribunal were not tampered with. It was also to allow a further meeting of the Beef Tribunal at which its chairman, Mr Justice Hamilton, was said to have indicated that he would hear further evidence directly related to the rival versions of events which had been given, in previous months, by O'Malley and Reynolds. Hamilton denied that there would be a 'special investigation', as announced by O'Malley, and stated that O'Malley's use of the term was 'inaccurate and misleading'. Reynolds, through a spokesperson, dismissed as astonishing and disgraceful the suggested need to 'protect' a civil servant.

O'Malley was put in an embarrassing position by this unseemly circle of claims and criticisms, and lost the initiative, which now shifted to the Opposition parties in the Dáil. Fianna Fáil seemed positively eager to accept the Labour Party's motion of no confidence. On the Wednesday night the three Progressive Democrat ministers resigned and the party proclaimed that it would vote against the Government following Thursday's debate on the no-confidence motion.

It then emerged that the troubles between the Coalition partners had been building up over a number of months. O'Malley told a press conference that in September he had written to Reynolds protesting at a departure from Cabinet procedures, which represented 'an emerging pattern of non-consultation'. There had been no reply. The Government's effectiveness, in O'Malley's judgement and that of his colleagues, was sustained only 'by huge sacrifices on our part'. The difficulties, which had intruded into economic decisions, the abortion referendum and the delicate talks on Northern Ireland, were raised to a different level of public dispute by Reynolds' allegations of dishonesty on the part of O'Malley. 'Once it became clear', O'Malley said, 'that the Taoiseach proposed to escalate the barely hidden pattern of behaviour into public attacks on the honesty and integrity of his Cabinet colleagues, it also became clear that my further participation at the Cabinet table was to be publicly rendered meaningless.' He rejected any suggestion that the dispute between the two leaders in government had been personal.

The debate was acrimonious. Reynolds was accused again by John

Bruton of having deliberately destroyed his own Government. Reynolds, in his turn, accused Bruton of being a neo-Unionist and attacked most fiercely the Progressive Democrats, in particular Mary Harney, accusing her of disloyalty over Northern Ireland policy. O'Malley's response to this was a passionate defence of all that she had brought to government and an analysis of some of the more publicly available instances of actions taken in government, by the Fianna Fáil side, that were directly designed to undermine the close working relationship of the Coalition partners. He cited daily newspaper briefings to contradict his own Beef Tribunal evidence, the appearance in a newspaper of a 'government decision' on a report on economic and employment strategy on the morning the decision was to be made, and the abandonment of normal government procedures. 'For some time effective government has been choked by the pursuit of a political agenda directed towards its destruction.'

That destruction was completed at 6.30 p.m. on Thursday, 5 November, when the Presidential Commission, made up of the Chief Justice and the chairmen of the Dáil and Senate, signed the proclamation dissolving the twenty-sixth Dáil. The election was set for 25 November. It was the shortest possible campaign period. The vote would include three abortion referendums – four ballot papers in all.[1] President Mary Robinson, who had earlier completed an official visit to Australia, was on a private visit to New Zealand and had indicated that she would not be returning and did not wish for any communication with the media. It was an occasion on which the President might have exercised the power not to dissolve the Dáil and called in the disputing party leaders to attempt some kind of reconciliation. And no president – with the possible exception of Cearbhaill O Dalaigh – was better equipped to undertake such a delicate task. It may have been debated by the Presidential Commission; but if so the decision to dissolve went ahead.

Charles Haughey and his old adversary, Garret FitzGerald, were

---

[1] There was a substantive amendment proposed for the Constitution, following the Supreme Court decision which allowed for abortion in severely restricted circumstances where the life, as opposed to the health, of the mother was at risk. This was heavily defeated, both by the Pro-Life lobby, which believed it went too far in liberalizing the law, and by the Pro-Choice groups, which felt it did not offer sufficient protection for the mother. There was an amendment giving women the right to information about abortion and one giving them the right to travel – both of which had been the subject of Constitutional restraint or doubt; these were carried by convincing margins.

two former heads of government who would not be contending again for seats. Yet both of them campaigned, FitzGerald on behalf of Fine Gael and a leading activist in women's affairs and a former chairperson both of the Women's Political Association and the Council for the Status of Women, Frances Fitzgerald, running for the seat he was vacating in his Dublin South-East constituency, and Charles Haughey on behalf of his son, Seán. Father and son were on the hustings early, the inevitable photo-call producing a head-start for the family firm. It was not the kind of election that Haughey would have relished, but then his own record in going to the country was an uneven one. Speculation was rife about his thoughts as his successor, Albert Reynolds, ploughed into the field of battle on a programme that had at its heart the elusive target so often missed by Haughey – the overall majority.

Albert Reynolds' standing, and that of his party, had sunk appreciably between his appearance before the Beef Tribunal and the dissolution of the Dáil, but nothing prepared them for the shock of the first opinion polls of the campaign. In the *Irish Independent*, on Monday, 9 November, and in *The Irish Times* the following Thursday, the findings 'visited severe damage', in the words of an opinion poll analyst, on Reynolds and Fianna Fáil. The results showed a huge drop in satisfaction with the Government and widespread scepticism about whether Albert Reynolds' evidence to the Beef Tribunal had been truthful or his allegations about dishonesty credible. The two main options – of an overall majority for Fianna Fáil or a coalition of Fine Gael, Labour and the Progressive Democrats – were evenly balanced.

In the first of the two polls the Fianna Fáil Party itself was seen to be holding its core support; but in the second there was a dramatic change, with that support dropping to 40 per cent. It was worse than any electoral situation ever faced by Haughey. Reynolds had made many blunders. Though not the easiest of politicians to work with, Desmond O'Malley had become a by-word for integrity throughout his long political career and the assault on him was shocking to people of all parties, including Fianna Fáil. There were other lamentable mistakes. In a newspaper interview, and then on television, Reynolds had used the word 'crap', attracting considerable criticism. When it emerged that he did not know its full meaning and also went on to misuse other words, indicating a very basic command of language, this added to the dismay a measure of disdain.

Then, on the first weekend, he went down to his constituency for the selection convention and was chosen, along with Sean Doherty, as part of the team in Longford-Roscommon. It was bad enough to be seen in close collaboration with a man who carried so many political stigmas, including not only the initiation of the phone-tapping, but also the revival of the scandal in order to bring down Haughey. Worse, instead of making only a brief, token appearance at the noisy country-town convention presided over by Pádraig Flynn, now Minister for Industry and Commerce as well as Justice, Reynolds stayed until five o'clock in the morning, at one time climbing out of a window to go for a sleep in his official car.

The press reports of the Sunday night event were lurid enough; there were additional accounts which allegedly had the Minister for Justice advising people that they could drink in the hostelries in the town, directly contrary to licensing laws. It all gave a colourful picture of the country-and-western style of the head of the Government. It did not go down well elsewhere. The very fact that Doherty was standing at all indicated a residual taint, suggested that a debt was being repaid and implied that he might well be on the way back, not just to the Dáil, but to a government position in the event of Reynolds winning his overall majority. This might suit Roscommon. It was definitely not to the liking of the plain people of Ireland.

Reynolds' response to the opinion polls was to suggest that, unlike previous elections, when Fianna Fáil had started well and gone down, he would start down and come up, particularly with the launch of the party programme. It did not happen. And it was clear that Fianna Fáil had little chance of recovery. The outgoing government, which had, until September, worked well and had previously been quite successful under Haughey's control, was a demonstration of the value of coalition. Previous Fianna Fáil administrations, responsible for the scandals and for less effective government, were a signal indication of the foolhardiness of giving the party a solo mandate and Reynolds was the victim of this. He had not given himself time to change the image and direction of the party and he had not established a strongly independent image for himself.

After the sparkling tensions which had provoked the dissolution during the ten days that preceded the election, the campaign itself was a matter of hard winter slogging. There were many manifestos, all of them uncertainly balanced on the cusp of public displeasure, holding out tentative and guarded promises, finding money for the creation of jobs where no money had existed before.

The Labour Party leader ran the best campaign and soon emerged as by far the most popular leader among all contenders. From the outset his party stood to make substantial gains; so much was this the case that it became clear, as the support for Labour grew in the period after nominations had closed, that they had fielded too few candidates. John Bruton, the leader of the second-largest party, Fine Gael, presented a clear prescription for the aftermath – a coalition of Fine Gael, Labour and the Progressive Democrats – and the notion became known as 'the Rainbow Coalition'. Both the title and the idea caught on and a growing mood of panic seized the Fianna Fáil Party. A dreadful mistake appeared to have been made, in timing and in the assessment of the new leader's personal popularity and standing. The style, the grace, the dignity, the fighting spirit, that leathery capacity for survival, which had never deserted Charles Haughey, through many elections and many challenges, were widely missed.

Without him, Fianna Fáil seemed to have so little. It launched several proposals, offering various blandishments to the voters which were then ridiculed by the other parties. A separate manifesto for Dublin, offering several advantages to the capital city which were already contained in the overall election manifesto, attracted further criticism, as did the 'discovery', by the Minister for Education, that he had been considering for some time free third-level education for the whole population and that this too would be available if Fianna Fáil were to be elected.

The party met with bitter recriminations on the doorsteps, about the calling of the election at a time of economic crisis, about high taxation and rising unemployment, but most of all about their party leader. His attack on the honesty of Desmond O'Malley, who had suffered throughout his political career for his integrity and his principles, outraged people from all parties, including Fianna Fáil. The antipathy had other origins as well. There was widespread dismay at the implications of the country-and-western style convention at which Doherty had been nominated and the kind of government which might all too easily contain this restored princeling of past error and misdemeanour. There were clear indications, both from Bobby Molloy at the launch of the Progressive Democrats' manifesto, and from Ken McGuinness, a Northern Ireland Unionist, as well as other Northern Ireland participants, that Albert Reynolds had damaged the progress of the long and difficult debate on Articles 2 and 3 of the Constitution by his intransigent attitude. So much was this the case that Ken

McGuinness, no known lover of Charles Haughey, mentioned in a radio interview the current joke among Unionists in the North: 'Come back, Charlie; all is forgiven.'

Albert Reynolds took all this personally; his wife, Kathleen, even more so. He spoke of personal vilification; she gave a tearful interview about not recognizing her husband in the portrait painted of him by the media. The campaign swept on. Fianna Fáil's standing was stuck fast at a percentage rating that would lose them seats. And lose seats they did, dropping 9, to an eventual total of 68.[1]

The Labour Party more than doubled its representation in the Dáil, from 16 to 33. It was their best result ever and a triumph for individual deputies, some of whom recorded votes which brought in second candidates, and one, Eithne FitzGerald, daughter-in-law of the former Fine Gael Taoiseach, Garret FitzGerald, running in the comparatively affluent middle-class constituency of Dublin South, obtained the highest first-preference vote in the country.[2]

Fine Gael did badly, losing ten seats. The Progressive Democrats improved their representation, from 6 to 10 seats. Seán Haughey took his father's seat and entered the twenty-seventh Dáil. But the result, in his Dublin North-Central constituency, where his father had himself on occasion reached a double quota, carrying in a second deputy almost as a matter of course, was a sign of the times. He was only elected on the *twelfth* count.

Charles Haughey had almost achieved his political apotheosis, his departure regretted after less than a year, his standing confirmed in heroic, if not mythic, terms. As the party he had once led searched for another successor, and seemed to be searching in vain, his own style

[1] The count was greatly extended by a dispute over the final seat in Dublin South Central, which Ben Briscoe won by five votes after recounts which lasted ten days and broke all existing records. Briscoe was first declared the winner with nine votes; then Byrne won by ten votes; then this result was overturned in Briscoe's favour, by five votes. Even this final count result was then challenged and checked, with further discrepancies being discovered, though these were insufficient to justify a further recount.

[2] Her vote totalled two quotas. The Labour Party, the oldest political party in the State, was founded in 1912. It had abstained in the 1918 election and had then formed the main Opposition party to Cumann na nGaedheal (the forerunner of Fine Gael) until, after 1932, it gave support to de Valera. Only in 1948, with the uneasy association between itself and the middle-class Fine Gael Party, did it achieve a participation in power and this began a chequered history for Labour, in which its socialism wavered between extremes. It performed solidly under Corish, in the 1973–77 Coalition, but this was followed by the short leaderships of Frank Cluskey and Michael O'Leary, both unhappy periods for the party. Spring restored credibility and a measure of unity that is likely to be severely tested in the economic circumstances of the 1990s.

and judgement seemed once more to be needed. They had been missed by his adversaries, missed also by his critics and political commentators generally. For him the election was an astonishing outcome. His reputation seemed already cleansed by short memory and an abiding sense of his great personal appeal. It was almost in bad taste to refer at all to the embarrassments and upset that had brought his long career to an unworthy end only ten months earlier. Better by far to see the undoubted qualities, the charm, the appeal, the wry wit, the sharp mind and the overwhelming sense that here was a man of destiny. Perhaps fortunately for the country, that destiny remained only partially fulfilled. Irish democracy, a greater force, a more abiding power, had held him in check and now that he had departed, the people could afford the indulgence of affection coloured by regret, of kindness combined with relief, of judgements which were already being mellowed by time.

Index

Abbeville 4, 13, 52, 69, 83, 281
Aer Lingus 98, 264, 268
Aer Rianta 266
Aer Turas 89
Agnew, Paddy 184
Ahern, Bertie 246, 256–7, 266, 268, 271, 272, 280, 281
Aiken, Frank 21, 57, 71, 100
Ainsworth, Deputy Commissioner Joe 209, 277
Allen, Lorcan 97, 157
Alliance Party (Northern Ireland) 218
Andrews, David 230
Anglo-Irish Agreement (1985) 187, 218, 226–7, 230, 232, 233, 251
Anglo-Irish Council 187
Anglo-Irish Free Trade Area Agreement 48
Aontacht Eireann 105
Aosdána 123, 124, 127
Apprentice Boys' March (1969) 73
Aras an Uachtarain 191, 254
Arms Crisis (1969) 2, 3, 80–92, 129, 145, 283
   trial 93–101
   investigations into funding 102–9, 111–12
   Magill article on 169–70
   Dáil debate (October 1980) 170–1
Arnold, Bruce (author) 203, 209–10, 215, 276
Arnold, Malcolm 61
Arts Bill (1973) 122, 124–6
Arts Council 121–7

'B Specials' 66, 81
Barry, Kevin 34
Battle of the Boyne 72, 76
Beef Scandal 260–4, 289–93
Beef Tribunal 261, 289–93, 295
Beresford, John 52
Berisford International 262
Berry, Peter 29–32, 34–6
   Arms Crisis (1969) 82–5, 89–92, 107, 109, 111, 112, 160

Blaney, Neil 43
   opposes Haughey's appointment as Parliamentary Secretary 29
   spokesman for Taca group 53
   Fianna Fáil leadership contest (1966) 55–60, 78
   appointed Minister of Agriculture 59
   Northern Ireland policy 65–6, 78, 81, 130
   on Northern Ireland sub-committee 75–7
   Arms Crisis and trial (1969) 81–92, 95–100, 102, 104, 105, 106, 110
   dismissal from Government 91–2, 109
   expelled from Fianna Fáil 106, 145
   challenges to Lynch's leadership 105, 108
   as independent Deputy 184, 193, 195, 199, 205, 234, 275
   general election
      (1973) 120
      (1977) 141
      (1981) 184
      (1982) 193
      (1987) 234
Bloody Sunday 114, 118
Bodkin, Thomas 125
Boland, Gerald 14, 30, 97
Boland, Harry 14, 30
Boland, Kevin 29, 43, 75
   association with Taca 52–3
   originator of 'Mohawks' name 53
   Fianna Fáil leadership contest (1966) 55, 57
   Northern Ireland policy 65, 76–7
   redrawing of electoral boundaries 68
   resignation from Government 77, 92
   Arms Crisis and trial (1969) 81, 84, 85, 86, 92, 95–7, 100–1

   resigns seat 101
   resigns from Fianna Fáil 102, 105
   Up Dev! 65, 101
Boland, Bourke and Company 14
Boru, Brian 12
Boundaries Commission 8
Bourke, Michael J. 14
Bowman, John 253
Brady, Seamus
   Terror in Northern Ireland 84
Brady, Vincent 275
Brennan, Joseph 75
Brennan, Paudge 95, 97, 105, 106
Brennan, Seamus 130, 135, 203, 230, 266
Briscoe, Ben 157, 214
British Broadcasting Corporation (BBC) 128, 140
Broadcasting Authority Act (1960) 19
Browne, Dr Noel 18, 141, 170, 171, 177, 184, 189
Browne, Sean 158
Browne, Vincent 13, 60, 146, 148, 149, 158, 181, 182, 215, 219
Bruton, John 189, 190, 259, 268, 293–4, 297
Burke, Raphael 157, 242
Burke, Richard 172, 197–8, 232
Burntollet Massacre 66, 73
by-elections 14–15
   Cavan-Monaghan (1981) 184
   Cork
      (1967) 64
      (1972) 118
      (1979) 152, 154
   Dublin West (1982) 197–8, 232
   East Galway (1982) 201
   Limerick
      (1967) 64
      (1968) 64, 110
   West Mayo (1976) 136–7, 142
Byrne, Alfie 15, 19

Cahill, Bernie 264–5, 269
Callaghan, James 73
Cameron Report 80, 87
Carter, Sir Charles 219
Carysfort Training College 229, 267
Celtic Helicopters 268
Central Bank 67
Chambers, William 52
Charities Bill (1960) 32
Chichester-Clarke, James 73, 114
Childers, Erskine 55, 60, 251
Chubb, Basil 19, 140
Civil Liability Bill (1961) 32–3
Civil Rights Movement (Northern Ireland) 65, 66, 73, 81, 84, 86
Civil Service 21, 22, 35, 40, 51, 60, 118, 125
Civil War (1922) 9, 10, 17, 55, 71
Clann na Poblachta 16–17, 19
Clarke, James Pius 275
Classic Meats 262
Clondalkin Paper Mills 195
Cluskey, Frank 141, 176, 177, 180–4, 232, 234, 236, 241
Colley, George 14, 20, 41, 42, 132, 135, 210, 255
  appointed to Department of Lands 46
  Fianna Fáil leadership contest (1966) 55–60, 78
  appointed to Department of Industry and Commerce 59, 60
  general election (1977) 133
  seen as successor to Lynch 137, 144, 146, 147, 151, 153
  leadership contest (1979) 155–58, 160–3
  as deputy leader 159, 172
  anger at Haughey 160–2
  general election (1982) 191
  dropped from Front Bench 195–6
  receives obscene 'phone calls 203
  as backbencher 216
  death 223
Colley, Harry 14, 20, 41
Collins, Gerard 171, 198, 214, 268, 273
Collins, Michael 8, 9, 10–11, 17
Collins, Stephen 222, 249, 251, 258, 269, 270
Comerford, Chris 264
Commission on Industrial Relations 205
Commission on Taxation 166, 205

Committee of Public Account 35, 104–5, 111–12
Committee on Procedures and Privilege 200
Commonwealth 17, 168
Companies Bill (1986) 262
Condon, Colm 91, 97
Connolly, Ger 157
Connolly, Patrick 201
Coogan, Finlan 27
Coogan, Tim Pat 52, 209
Cooper, Ivan 117
Corish, Brendan 46, 69, 76, 104, 141
Cosgrave, Liam 68, 92, 102–4, 119, 126, 129–31, 135–6, 139, 140, 141
Costello, Declan 68, 288
Costello, John A. 16–19, 23–4, 36, 125
Council for the Status of Women 295
'Country and western alliance' 250, 296, 297
Courts Bill (1961) 32, 34
Cox, Pat 246–9
Coyle, Marion 136
Craig, William 66
Criminal Justice Amendment Bill (1960) 30
Criminal Justice Bill (1963) 40
Criminal Law Jurisdiction Bill (1976) 136, 137–8
Cronin, Anthony 5, 123–4, 127, 206–7, 281
Crowley, Flor 97
Cumann na Gael Party 11
Currie, Austin 252, 253
Customs House Docks Development Board 266

Daly, Laura 281
Davern, Noel 274
de Gaulle, General 64
de Valera, Eamon 30, 100, 148, 216, 251
  general election
    (1948) 16
    (1957) 19–21
  independence (1921) 8
  leadership 13, 17, 20–1, 26, 50–1, 56, 57, 58, 60
  Presidency 77, 90
de Valera, Sile 148–50, 159, 178
Deasy, Rickard 47
Defamation Bill (1961) 32
Dempsey, Noel 269
Department of Agriculture 44–9, 105
Department of Defence 98, 103, 105, 159, 275
Department of Education 274
Department of External Affairs 71, 129

Department of Finance 22, 36, 67, 126, 127, 159, 186, 192, 237, 267
  Arms Crisis see Arms Crisis
Department of Foreign Affairs 72, 168, 186, 228, 281
Department of Health 228
Department of Industry and Commerce 260, 292
Department of Justice 30, 33–44, 46, 98, 127, 159, 196, 209–11
Department of Lands 46
Department of Posts and Telegraphs 19
Department of Tourism and Transport 159
Department of Transport and Power 98
Derry Citizens' Defence Committee 73
Desmond, Barry 224, 228, 261
Desmond, Dermot 265, 266, 268
Devlin, Bernadette 66
Devlin, Paddy 86
Dillon, James 17, 20, 46, 68
Dillon, John 49
Doherty, Kieran 184
Doherty, Sean 172
  Gang of Five conspiracy to unseat Lynch 147, 157
  appointed to Department of Justice 159, 196
  appointed to front bench 186
  telephone tapping scandal 200, 209–12, 214, 215
  plans to remove Haughey as leader 250
  chairmanship of Senate 252, 258
  Nighthawks interview on 'phone-tapping scandal 275–9, 285
  general election (1992) 296
Donegan, Paddy 136, 140
Donlan, Sean 199
Dore, Noel 199
Doyle, Maurice 67
Dublin 52, 53, 297
Duffy, James 254
Dukes, Alan 236, 237, 240–1, 242, 244, 252, 255, 257, 259
Dunlop, Frank 130, 135, 140, 157

Easter Rising 55
Economic Development 24–5
Electoral Amendment Act (1974) 140
Elegant, Robert 61
Emergency Powers Act (1976) 119, 136

European Community 24, 27,
    41, 47, 64, 112, 118, 131,
    207
Beef Scandal 260, 261
Commissioners 172, 197–8,
    268
Presidency 146–7, 148, 150,
    251
European Free Trade Area 24
European Parliament elections
    144, 145, 146, 223, 243
Evening Herald 203
Ewart Biggs, Christopher 135
Extradition Bill (1964) 43

Fagan, Anthony 89, 90, 98
Fahey, Jackie 147, 148, 158
Falklands War (1982) 198–9,
    208
'Farmers' Party' 177
Farrell, Brian 181
Farrell, Joe 178
Farrell, Michael 66
Faulkner, Brian 114, 115, 117,
    118
Faulkner, Padraig 75, 126
FDA 11, 78
Federated Union of Employers
    172
Feeney, John 203
Feltrim Mining 264
Fianna Fáil
    Ard Fheis (annual
        conferences) 1981 1–2,
        53, 104–5, 132, 165–6,
        175–6, 217
    coalitions *see* Governments
    defections to Progressive
        Democrats 229–30
    divisions in party 159, 216,
        223–7
    leadership *see names of leaders*
    policies
        abortion 222
        agriculture 45–6
        Anglo-Irish relations 17,
            48
        divorce 230–2
        economy 21–8, 43, 61, 67,
            69, 133–5, 164–6, 175,
            180, 181, 182, 185, 186,
            191–2, 204–5, 213, 232,
            233, 236–9, 284
        education 63–4, 297
        legislation 34
        Northern Ireland 17, 23,
            48–9, 65–6, 72–9,
            114–19, 136–9, 148–50,
            159, 165–9, 186–9,
            226–31, 233
    Arms Crisis *see* Arms Crisis
    national executive 181–2, 202
    Presidency elections *see*
        Republic of Ireland:
        Presidency

public opinion of 213–14
relationship with Roman
    Catholic Church 224
republicanism within party
    76–7, 81, 105, 115, 119,
    130, 136, 138, 149–50,
    159, 178–9
Taca fund-raising group
    52–3, 156
telephone-tapping
    controversies (1982–83)
    208–12, 215, 275–9
vice-presidents 53, 97
see also by-elections; European
    Parliament elections;
    general elections
Finance Bill
    (1958) 27
    (1969) 72, 121, 122
    (1980) 175
    (1982) 199
Fine Gael 7, 11
    Governments and Coalitions
        see Governments
    leadership 141, 252, 259 *see*
        also names of leaders
    policies 23, 56, 68–9
        economic development
            23–4
        Northern Ireland 119,
            178, 179, 186–7, 207–8,
            213, 216–20, 222, 223,
            230
        Arms Crisis (1969) 95,
            102–4
    Presidency elections *see*
        Republic of Ireland:
        Presidency
    see also by-elections; general
        elections
Fitt, Gerry, 86
Fitzgerald, Eithne 298
Fitzgerald, Frances 295
FitzGerald, Dr Garret 69, 176,
    198, 225
    speech on decimalization 72
    Arms Crisis 103, 104, 106
    becomes leader of Fine Gael
        141
    general election (1981)
        180–4
    as Taoiseach (1981–82)
        186–7, 189, 193
    Northern Ireland policy 130,
        186–7, 207–8, 213,
        216–20, 222, 223, 230
    relationship with Margaret
        Thatcher 187, 191, 218
    fall of Coalition Government
        190–1, 201
    general election (February
        1982) and hung Dáil 2,
        192–3, 195
    general election (November
        1982) 204–8

elected Taoiseach for second
    time (1982–87) 208,
    213
strain of office 222
abortion referendum 222–3
family planning legislation
    224
views of Haughey opposition
    227
disasterous reshuffle of
    Government 228–9
vote of no confidence in
    Government 229–30
divorce referendum 230–1
general election (1987)
    232–4
resigns as leader 236
declines to be nominated for
    President 252
challenges Lenihan on TV
    programme 253–4
does not contend seat at 1992
    general election 294–5
Fitzgerald, Gene 172, 186
Fitzgerald, Liam 269
Flanagan, Oliver J. 224
Flanagan, Seán 30, 57, 60
Fleming, Superintendent John
    89, 111
Flynn, Pádraig 203, 242, 247,
    248, 250, 256–7, 273,
    277, 296
Foley, Des 97, 105
Food Industries 261
Fórsa Cosante Aitiúil (FCA)
    11–12, 13, 78
Forsyth, Frederick 61
Forum for a New Ireland
    218–23, 227
Foster, R. F. 18
Fund for the Relief of Distress
    in Northern Ireland 75,
    80, 87, 99, 104, 105

Gallagher, Denis 158, 216
Gallagher, Eddie 136
Gandon, James 52
Gang of Five conspiracy
    147–55, 158, 169, 186,
    246, 250
Gang of Four 272–3
Garavan, Charles 264
Gargan, Bridie 201
general elections
    (1922) 11
    (1923) 11
    (1927) 11
    (1932) 11
    (1948) 16
    (1951) 14, 18
    (1954) 14
    (1957) 14, 19–21
    (1961) 19, 34
    (1965) 41, 50–1
    (1969) 41, 60, 68–71

(1973) 108, 110, 116, 118,
120, 130
(1977) 133, 138–43, 184
(1981) 2, 175–7, 180–5, 191
(February 1982) 2, 191–4
(November 1982) 204–8
(1987) 232–4
(1989) 2, 211, 242–5
(1992) 292–9
General Secretary of the Irish
Transport and General
Workers Union 195
Geoghegan-Quinn, Maire 159,
247, 248, 250
Gibbons, James 65, 146, 158
Arms Crisis (1969) 82, 84,
90, 91, 98, 99, 104, 105,
106, 107, 129, 170, 171
support for George Colley
57, 146
vote of confidence in 106–9,
115
relationship with Haughey
132, 145, 204
Gladebrook 264
Glenn, Alice 232
Gonne, Maud 16
Goodman Group 262, 263, 291
Goodman, Larry 239
Beef Scandal 260–4, 289–92
Goodman Tribunal 262
Goulding, Cathal 82, 87
Governments 16
Cumann na Gael (1927–32)
11
First Inter-Party Government
(Fine Gael-Labour
Coalition, 1948–51)
16–18, 125
Second Inter-Party
Government (Fine
Gael-Labour Coalition,
1954–57) 18–19
Fianna Fáil (1966–73) see
Lynch, Jack
National Coalition (1973–77)
122, 127–32, 135–6,
139–42
Fianna Fáil (1977–81) see
Lynch, Jack and
Haughey, Charles
Coalition (1981–82) 184–7,
189–91
Fianna Fáil (1987–89) see
Haughey, Charles
Fianna Fáil-Progressive
Democrat Coalition
(1989–92) 2, 244–9,
250–2, 255, 257–9,
268–73, 275, 279–80,
290–4
'Rainbow Coalition' (1922)
297
Government Information
Bureau 129

Grand Metropolitan 265
Grangemore 4, 69
Greencore Affair 261, 264–5,
269
Gregory, Tony 193, 194, 195,
199, 200, 205, 234
Gresham Hotel, Dublin 52
Griffith, Arthur 10
Groome, Joe and Patti 53
Groome's Hotel, Dublin 53

Halal 291
Hamilton, Judge Liam 289, 293
Hanafin, Des 252
Hardiman, Adrian 209, 291
Harney, Mary 203, 204, 223,
227, 244, 257, 294
Harris, Pino 267
Harvard Summer School
Institute 62, 123–4,
126–7
Haughey, Bride (sister) 9
Haughey, Charles (Cathal)
luck 1–2, 175
judgement 2
character 3–4, 25–6, 286,
299
physical appearance 3–4
property deals 4, 52, 69
personal wealth 4–5, 31–2,
52, 69, 156, 206
love affairs 4, 5
friendships 5
family 7–12, 15, 160–1
birth 8
schools 12–13
attends University College,
Dublin 13–14, 28
marriage to Maureen Lemass
13, 28
works at accountant 4, 14, 30
joins Fianna Fáil 14
unsuccessful attempts to enter
Parliament 14–15
takes Dublin North-East seat
(1957) 14, 19
ambition 25–6, 71, 160
attitude to defence forces 11,
13
republican sympathies 3, 14,
77–9, 113, 152, 166, 284
becomes Parliamentary
Secretary to Minister of
Justice 27, 29–35
expensive way of life 31–2
taste in food and drink 31
horse-riding and hunting 31,
32
as Minister of Justice 34–44,
78, 82
political vision 40
interest in the arts 43, 61–2,
121–7, 285
leads 'New Men' in
Government 43

as Minister of Agriculture
44–9
part of 'Mohawks' group
52–4
Fianna Fáil leadership contest
(1966) 55–60, 78
appointed Minister of
Finance 4, 59–64, 71
director of 1969 general
election 68–70
on Northern Ireland
sub-committee 75, 80,
82, 86, 99, 111
controls Northern Ireland
Relief Fund 75, 80, 87,
99, 104
Arms Crisis (1969) 2, 3,
80–92, 129, 145, 283,
284
trial 93–101
investigation into funding
102–9, 110–12
Magill article on 169–70
Dáil debate (October
1980) 170–1
injured in fall from horse 90,
98
dismissal from Government
91–2, 94–6, 111
challenges Lynch as party
leader 99–101
pledges loyalty to Fianna Fáil
106–7, 108–9
political isolation 108–9, 112,
121–32
life on backbenches 110–32
criticism of by Conor Cruise
O'Brien 127, 138, 140
promotes Fianna Fáil around
country 131–2
Gibbons enmity of 132,
145
returns to frontbench as
spokesman on Health
127, 132, 133, 138
general election (1977)
138–43
seen as possible successor to
Lynch 137, 144
Gang of Five conspiracy to
replace Lynch 146–55,
158, 169, 186, 250
Irish Independent article (1979),
on Haughey and
integrity 152–3
leadership contest (1979)
155–8, 160–3
leadership of Fianna Fáil
(1979–81) 78, 107, 109,
115, 152, 163–4
as Taoiseach (1979–81) 1,
158, 160, 177
Colley's anger at 160–1
Opposition criticism of
160–2

Haughey, Charles – *cont.*
relationship with Margaret
Thatcher 175, 177, 178,
182, 183, 186, 198, 208,
239, 284
first summit (May 1980)
167–9, 179
second summit (December
1980) 169, 171, 172–4,
179, 180, 187
general election (1981)
175–7, 180–5
Stardust Ballroom Fire 1–2,
176–8, 183
H-block hunger strikes 2,
173, 178–9, 182, 183,
185
in Opposition 185–93
leadership criticized by
Charles McCreevy
188–9, 193, 202–4
fall of Coalition Government
190–1
general election (February
1982) and hung Dáil
192–4
nominated as Taoiseach
(1982) 193, 195
challenged for leadership by
O'Malley 193–5
Dublin West by-election
(1982) 198
telephone tapping
controversy 199–200,
208–12, 215, 219, 275–9,
285
Bridie Gargan murder
(GUBU affair) 201, 219
motion of no confidence in
leadership 202–4
general election (November
1982) 204–8
believes himself victim of
vilification 206, 219
leads Opposition (1982–87)
213, 216–27
challenge to leadership
(1983) 213–15
announces new front bench
216
press officer's comments on
221–2
challenge to authority by
O'Malley 223–7
tables motion of no
confidence in FitzGerald
Government 229–30
general election (1987)
233–4
nominated Taoiseach for
third time 234–5
launches National Economic
Plan 237–9, 243
passive leadership 239–40
rise in popularity 240, 241, 243

defeat in Government 242
general election (1989)
242–5
coalition with Progressive
Democrats 244–9,
250–2, 255, 257–9,
268–73, 275, 279–90
as caretaker Taoiseach 245–9
European Presidency 251
Dukes motion of no
confidence in coalition
255, 257–9
controversy over Fianna Fáil
presidential candidate
253–9
dismissal of Lenihan 255–9,
268–9
Beef Scandal 260–4, 289–90,
292
Greencore Affair 264–5, 269
Telecom Affair 265–6, 269
intends to continue as leader
266–7, 268
sale of Carysfort Training
College 267
installation of wind generator
on island home 268
contenders for leadership
268–9
leadership challenged by
'Gang of Four'
backbenchers 269–74
controversy over Government
appointments 275–5
Nighthawks interview
resurrects 'phone-tapping
scandal 275–9, 285
forced to resign by
Progressive Democrats
279–81
election for successor 280–1
tributes 282
summary of career 282–5,
298–9
does not contend seat at 1992
general election 294–5
campaigns on behalf of son,
Sean 295
policies
abortion 192, 207, 222–3
Anglo-Irish relations 7, 48
arts and culture 43, 61–2,
113, 121–7
broadcasting 128–9
contraception 144, 145,
224
decimalization 72
divorce 231–2
economy 21–3, 25, 26–8,
43, 61, 67, 69, 133–5,
164–6, 175, 180, 181,
182, 185, 186, 204–5,
213, 232, 233, 236–9,
284
education 64

Europe 49
Falklands crisis 198–9,
208
fisheries 28
Irish neutrality 167–8,
179–80, 199
law reform 37–43
Northern Ireland 3, 7, 15,
37, 48–50, 65–6, 75,
77–9, 94, 112–19, 130,
137–9, 152, 156, 159,
160, 165–9, 178–80,
182–3, 186–7, 198–9,
206–9, 213, 217–21, 223,
226–7, 233, 239, 284
science 62
semi-state organizations
62–3
speeches 27, 33, 112–13,
129
final speech in Dáil 1,
281–2
maiden speech 21, 26
on agriculture 47
on Arts Bill 126
on the State and the Arts
123–4, 126–7
on Budget
(1961) 28
(1969) 61
on divorce 231–2
on economy 21, 26–8, 43,
113
on Fianna Fáil (1983) 217
on fisheries policy 28
on law reform 37, 38–9
on Northern Ireland
49–50, 112–13
on rural-urban split 46–7
on women in society 41
writings
Férinne Fáil 14
Haughey, Ciarán (son) 28, 257,
268, 281
Haughey, Conor (son) 28, 264
Haughey, Eimear 28
Haughey, Eithne (sister) 9, 12
Haughey, Eoghan (brother) 9
Haughey, Maureen (née
Lemass) (wife) 11–12,
28
Haughey, Maureen (sister) 9,
12
Haughey, Padraig 'Jock'
(brother) 9, 87, 104, 157,
215, 217
Haughey, Sarah (née
McWilliams) (mother) 8,
12, 52, 161
Haughey, Seán 'Johnnie'
(father) 8–12, 15
Haughey, Seán (brother) 9
Haughey, Seán (son) 28, 295,
298
Healey, Denis 73

Health (Family Planning) Bill
    (1979) 145
Healy, John 153–4
Healy, Shay 275–6
Heath, Edward 115, 116, 117,
    130
Heenan, Cardinal 49
Hefferon, Colonel Michael 83,
    84, 89, 91
Henchy, Mr Justice 98, 99
Herrema, Tiede 136, 142
Hibernia 49
Hibernia Meats 292
Higgins, James 242
Hillery, Patrick 43, 60
    as Minister for Foreign
        Affairs 72, 105, 118
    Presidency 190–1, 205, 234,
        245, 251, 254–5, 258
Hume, John 86, 117, 186, 218,
    220
Hunt Committee 81, 87
Hussey, Gemma 221, 222, 224,
    228–9, 231
Hyde, Douglas 251

Independence Treaty (1921)
    7–9
Ingham, Bernard 239
Innishvichillane 268
Intoxicating Liquor Bill (1960)
    30, 32
Iraq, beef exports to *see* Beef
    Scandal
Irish Army 8, 9–11
Irish Club, London 49
Irish Distillers 265
Irish Free State 8–11, 17
Irish Helicopters 268
Irish Independent 92, 132, 144,
    152–3, 158, 171, 176,
    179, 188, 205, 206, 214,
    215, 216, 257, 265, 276,
    295
Irish Industrial Development
    Authority 260, 262
Irish Press 51, 52, 56, 150, 209,
    214
Irish Red Cross Society 104
Irish Republican Army (IRA) 7,
    9, 12, 19, 78, 119,
    149–50
    Arms Crisis 80–92, 92, 112
    Official 82, 87
    Provisional 8, 82, 87, 93, 135,
        138, 186, 187, 275
    H-block hunger strikes
        (1981) 2, 173, 178–9,
        182, 184, 185, 191
    see also Northern Ireland: IRA
        campaigns of violence
Irish Sugar Company 261, 264
The Irish Times 9, 50, 53, 154,
    161, 208, 214, 254, 295
ISM Investments 264

James, P. D. 61
Jay, Peter 149
John XXIII, Pope 67
Johnston, Mooney and O'Brien
    265
Joyce, Joe 203, 217
    The Boss 203, 219

Keating, Justin 135, 139
Keleghan, Thomas 264
Kelly, Frank 180
Kelly, Captain James 82, 83, 88,
    89, 91, 97, 98, 99, 104,
    105, 112, 157
Kelly, John 87–8, 90, 97, 98,
    105, 157, 177
Kemmy, Jim 184
Kennedy, Geraldine 188, 203,
    204, 209, 221
Kenny, Edna 137
Kenny, Henry 137
Killilea, Mark 147, 148, 157,
    159, 186
King, Cecil 170

Labour Party 41, 68, 85, 141
    Arms Crisis (1969) 95, 102–4
    Governments and Coalitions
        see Governments
    leadership 177, 204, 207 *see
        also names of leaders*
    policies 55, 69, 76, 119, 178,
        179
    Presidency elections *see*
        Republic of Ireland:
        Presidency
    see also by-elections; general
        elections
Lambert, Gordon 153
Land Commission 10
Law Reform Commission 42
Lawlor, Liam 261
Lee, J. J. 8, 17, 50, 59, 66
Lemass, Eileen 197
Lemass, Kathleen
    (mother-in-law) 28
Lemass, Maureen *see* Haughey,
    Maureen
Lemass, Noel 13
Lemass, Peggy 13
Lemass, Sean (father-in-law)
    Haughey marries daughter
        13, 28
    Fianna Fáil leadership
        (1959–66) 13, 26, 34, 41,
        46, 50–5, 216
    general election (1957) 20
    as Minister for Industry and
        Commerce 13, 21–3
    appoints Haughey
        Parliamentary Secretary
        to Justice Minister
        29–33
    appoints Haughey Minister of
        Justice 34

appoints Haughey Minister of
    Agriculture 44, 45
general election (1965) 50–1
character and background 50,
    55, 237
relinquishes leadership
    55–60, 63
policies
    agriculture 51
    Anglo-Irish Relations 48
    constitutional reform 67–8
    economics 21–6, 43, 51,
        67, 133
    Europe 49
    Northern Ireland 23, 36,
        48, 51, 65, 68, 167
    Irish language 23
Lemass, Sheila 13
Lenihan, Ann 256
Lenihan, Brian 154, 227, 280
    in Department of Justice 42,
        46
    one of 'New Men' in
        Government 43, 53, 55,
        57
    in Ministry for Foreign
        Affairs 179–80, 198
    deputy leader of Government
        251
    Irish Presidency campaign
        253–9
    dismissal by Haughey 268–9
    announces he will contend
        leadership of Fianna Fáil
        269
    on Haughey leadership 215,
        217, 273
Lindsay, Patrick J. 34
Lipper, Mick 141
Lloyd George, David 8
Loftus, Sean 184
Loughnane, William 150, 151,
    204
Luykx, Albert 87, 88, 89, 97,
    98
Lydon, Don 269–70
Lynch, Jack 43
    leadership of Fianna Fáil 50,
        58–60, 63, 102–3,
        107–8, 110–11, 131–2,
        139, 141, 142, 144, 154,
        255
    challenges to 95, 97,
        99–101, 105, 108,
        116–17
    Gang of Five conspiracy
        against 146–55, 158,
        160–3, 169, 186, 250
    resignation 146, 148, 154
    Fianna Fáil leadership contest
        (1966) 55–60, 78
    consultations with wife 58
    political career 58–9, 60
    general election (1969)
        68–71

Lynch, Jack – *cont.*
  Arms Crisis (1969) 3, 81–92,
    170–1
  trial 94–101
  investigation into funding
    102–9, 110–12
  general election (1973) 108,
    110, 116, 118, 120
  general election (1977) 133,
    138–42
  withdraws from Fianna Fáil
    affairs 158
  personality 141
  European Community
    presidency 146–7, 148,
    150
  policies 225
    economics 67, 135
    Northern Ireland 65–6,
    73–9, 99, 105, 112,
    113–17, 130, 136–9,
    148–50, 167, 180,
    227
Lynch, Maureen 58
Lyons, Charles 264

McAleer, Patricia 111
McArthur, Malcolm Edward
  201
MacBride, John 16
MacBride, Seán 16, 17, 18, 19,
  20, 36
McCaffrey, Anne 61
McCarthy, John F. 22–3, 25
Mac Conghial, Muiris 129
McCreevy, Charles 157,
  188–90, 193, 202–4, 257,
  272–3
McDaid, James 274–5
McDowell, Michael 226
McEllistrim, Thomas 147, 150,
  157, 159
MacEntee, Sean 57, 100
MacGiolla, Tomás 261
McGloughlin, Patrick 209
McGuinness, Ken 297–8
McQuaid, Archbishop John
  Charles 39
McQuillan, Jack 28
McSharry, Ray 157, 159, 196,
  204, 213
  in Department of Finance
    201–2, 237, 239
  tape-recording of
    conversation with
    O'Donoghue 209, 214,
    221
  as European Commissioner
    268
  Beef Tribunal 289
Magill 29, 35–6, 83, 92, 101,
  109, 111, 146, 162,
  169–70, 181, 182
Mallon, Seamus 220
Mankievicz, Wolf 61

Mansergh, Martin 5, 10, 12, 15,
  42, 46, 64, 75, 114, 123,
  134, 148, 140, 219, 231,
  281
Mara, P. J. 5, 181, 221–2, 239,
  254, 266
Marxism 69, 87
Masterson, Paddy 267
Mellowes, Liam 8, 11
Mills, Michael 51, 150, 181
Milton, John
  Paradise Lost 285
Ministers and Secretaries Act
  (1922) 288
Mitchell, Jim 197, 199–200,
  210, 253
Molloy, Robert 'Bobby' 59,
  158, 216, 229–30, 246–9,
  257, 261, 272, 292, 297
'Mother-and-Child' scheme 18
Mountbatten, Lord Louis 150
Mountjoy Gaol 34
Moylan, Richard 14
Mulcahy, Richard 10, 17
Murphy, Ned 92
Murray, Charles 24, 67
Murtagh, Peter 203, 208, 217,
  219
  The Boss 203, 219

National City Brokers 265, 268
National College of Art and
  Design 125, 126
National Gallery of Ireland
  123, 125
National Library 123
National Museum 123, 125
National Science Council 62
Nealon, Ted 140
Nighthawks 275–9
Nolan, M. J. 269
Noonan, Michael 209, 211,
  240, 261
Norfolk, Duke of 207, 208
North Atlantic Treaty
  Organisation (NATO)
  17, 168
Northern Ireland
  Bloody Sunday 114, 118
  British Army presence 73, 80,
    82, 87, 114, 116, 118
  calls for withdrawal of British
    presence 136–8, 149,
    199, 217
  civil rights marches 65, 66,
    68, 73, 81
  demands for UN
    peace-keeping force 74,
    75, 113–14, 116
  direct rule 118
  Forum for a New Ireland
    218–23, 227, 232
  H-block hunger strikes
    (1981) 2, 173, 178–9,
    182, 183, 184, 185, 191

internment 114, 115, 116,
  117
IRA campaigns of violence
  (1956) 19
  (1957) 34, 36–7, 40
  (1971) 117
  (1972) 118–19
  (1979) 149–50
  riots 65, 72–3, 76, 78, 114,
    117
  Stormont Government
    (1920) 15
  Sunningdale Agreement
    (1973) 117, 130, 136,
    137, 167
  Thatcher-Fitzgerald summits
    187, 191
  Thatcher-Haughey summits
    167–9, 171, 172–4, 179,
    180, 182, 183, 186, 187,
    198, 239, 284
  unification 3, 49–50, 65,
    67–8, 76, 167, 182
  Unionist Parties 18, 65, 66,
    77, 78, 84, 118, 166, 167,
    217, 230
  see also Anglo-Irish
    Agreement; Arms Crisis

O'Brien, Dr Conor Cruise 75,
  81, 127–30, 149, 201,
  259
  criticism of Haughey 69, 103,
    106, 127, 138, 140, 182
O'Brien, Miriam Hederman
  166
O'Connell, John 144, 152–3,
  159–60, 195
O'Connor, Pat 192
O Dalaigh, Cearbhaill 136, 251,
  294
O'Donoghue, Martin 133, 151
  economic policy 130, 134–5,
    146, 166, 191–2
  moves to replace Lynch 144,
    153
  dropped from front bench
    158, 163, 172
  as spokesmen on finance 186
  leadership challenge (1982)
    195
  appointed to Department of
    Education 196
  resigns from Government
    202
  conversation with McSharry
    taped 209
  Haughey seeks to remove
    party whip from 215
Offences Against the State Act
  19, 119, 131
Official Secrets Act 111, 170
O'Hanlon, Rory 242
O hEochaidh clan 12
O'Higgins, T. F. 34

O hUiginn, Padraig 266
O'Keefe, Mr Justice Andreas 98
O'Kennedy, Michael 136, 137,
    138, 149, 155, 159, 172,
    186, 197, 214, 268
    Beef Scandal 260, 261, 263
O'Leary, Michael 184
O'Malley, Desmond 135, 145,
    295
    elected to Dáil 64, 110
    Arms Crisis and trial 110–12,
        170, 171
    appointed Minister for
        Justice 110–12, 119
    appointed Chief Whip
        110–11
    general election (1977) 133
    seen as possible successor to
        Lynch 137, 144
    leadership contest (1979) 155
    general election (1982) 191
    challenges Haughey's
        leadership (1982) 194–5
    appointed to Trade,
        Commerce and Tourism
        196
    resigns from Government
        202
    on Opposition front bench
        216
    party whip withdrawn from
        221, 223
    challenge to Haughey's
        authority 221, 223–4
    expelled from Fianna Fáil
        224–6
    sets up Progressive Democrat
        Party 225–7, 229–30
    party conference 237–8
    coalition with Fianna Fáil 2,
        244–9, 250–2, 255,
        257–9, 268–73, 275,
        279–80, 290–4
    appointed Minister for
        Industry and Commerce
        260, 262
    Beef Scandal 262–3, 289–91,
        293, 294, 297
    telephone-tapping scandal
        (1982) 277
O'Malley, Donogh 32, 153,
    156
    as Minister for Education
        41–2, 63–4
    one of 'New Men' in
        Government 43, 53
    Fianna Fáil leadership contest
        (1966) 55, 57
    death 64, 110
O'Malley, Pat 261
O Móráin, Micheál 65, 82, 85,
    90, 91, 110
O'Neill, Captain Terence 48,
    49, 51, 65, 66, 73, 76, 94
O'Neill, Tip 227

Orange Order 72
O'Rourke, Mary 238, 256, 257,
    268, 274, 280, 281
O'Sullivan, Father Donal 122
O'Toole, Fintan 290
O Tuathail, Seamus 84

Parcéir, Seamus 266
People's Democracy 66
Pernod 265
Phelan, Angela 31
Power, Patrick 159, 198–9
Power, Seán 269, 273
Prendergast, Peter 200
Presidential Commission 294
Prior, James 198, 207, 208
Prison Welfare Service 39
Progressive Democrat Party
    setting up of 225–7
    Fianna Fáil defections to
        229–30
    Governments and coalitions
        see Governments
    party conferences 237–8
    see also by-elections; general
        elections
    Pro-Life campaign 222

Questions and Answers 253

Radio Eireann 19
Radio Telefís Eireann (RTE)
    128, 153, 181, 208, 277,
    292
Regniorers, Baron William ('Bill
    the Baron') 88
Rent Restriction Bill (1960) 32
Republic of Ireland 17
    Constitution 60, 67–8, 118,
        190–1, 193, 222–3, 251,
        288, 297
    Presidency elections 251–9
    see also Irish Free State
Revenue Commission 61, 122,
    266
Reynolds, Albert 242, 246, 256,
    257, 271
    Gang of Five plot to replace
        Lynch 147, 158
    opposition to Haughey
        leadership 247, 250
    seen as successor to Haughey
        leadership 259, 268,
        271–4, 275
    telephone tapping scandal
        (1982) 277, 279
    Fianna Fáil leadership contest
        (1992) 280–1
    elected leader and Taoiseach
        281, 287, 288–9
    abortion controversy 287–8
    Beef Scandal 263, 289–93,
        295
    motion of no confidence in
        Government 293–4

general election (1992)
    294–9
    opinion poll on 295–6
Reynolds, Andrea, Cathy and
    Leonie 291
Reynolds, Ann 256
Reynolds, Kathleen 298
Robinson, Senator Mary 118,
    294
    Presidency campaign 42,
        251–3, 257, 258–9
Roman Catholic Church
    abortion 192, 222–3
    Church and State 63, 67–8,
        118
    divorce 68, 230–2
    'Mother-and-Child' scheme
        18
    Northern Ireland policy 218
    opposition to law reforms 42
    schools 64
Royal Dublin Society 176
Royal Hibernian Hotel 151
Royal Ulster Constabulary
    (RUC) 73, 81
Russell Hotel, Dublin 53, 153
Ryan, Eoin 202, 221
Ryan, James 21, 24, 27, 202
Ryan, Louden 219
Ryan, Richie 33, 135, 139

Saddam Hussein 261
St Joseph's Christian Brothers
    Secondary School,
    Fairview 12–13
Sands, Bobby 178, 179
Schleuter, Otto 88
Scoil Iosef, Marino 12
Sellars, Peter 61
Shakespeare, William
    Othello 1, 282
    quotations from, passim
Shelbourne Hotel 140, 153
Sheridan, Joe 141
Sherlock, Joe 184
Sherwin, Sean 97, 105
Sinn Fein 8, 11, 191, 193
    Official 82
    Provisional 82, 186, 187, 193
    general elections see general
        elections
Skelly, Liam 197, 232
Smith, Michael 157
Smith, Paddy 45–6, 57
Smurfit, Michael 265–6
Smyth, Esmonde 130
Social, Democratic and Labour
    Party of Northern
    Ireland 86, 117, 217
Society for the Protection of the
    Unborn Child 222
Sorohan, Seamus 14
Spring, Dick 204, 219, 220,
    228, 232, 241, 245, 251,
    252, 267, 291

Squires, John 89
Stardust Ballroom Fire (1981) 1–2, 176–8, 183, 201
Stardust Relatives' Committee 177
Succession Bill (1961) 33, 36, 41, 43
Sugar Distributors 264
Sunday Independent 92, 264
Sunday Tribune 188, 221, 279
Sunningdale Agreement (1973) 117, 130, 136, 137, 167
Sutherland, Peter 222–3
Sweetman, Gerard 20, 22, 23, 27, 68

Taca 52–3, 156
Tallaght strategy 236, 240, 242
Talmino 264
Tansey, Paul 181
Telecom Affair 265–6, 269
Telsis Report 205
Thatcher, Margaret 238
   talks with Jack Lynch (1979) 150
   relationship with Charles Haughey 175, 177, 178, 182, 183, 186, 198, 208, 239, 284
   first summit (May 1980) 167–9, 179

second summit (December 1980) 169, 171, 172–4, 179, 180, 187
   relationship with Garret FitzGerald 187, 191, 217
This Week 116
Thomas, Gordon 61
Thornley, David 50
Timbs, Joe 291–2
The Times 140
Timmons, Eugene 14
Tobin, Thomas 89
Towards a Just Society 68
Traynor, Oscar 14, 29–32, 34–5
Treacy, Sean 234
Treaty of Rome (1957) 24
Tully, Michael 264
Tunney, Jim 215, 273
Tuzo, General Sir Harry 116

Uí Neill, kings of Ulster 12
Ulster Defence Regiment 81
Undeveloped Areas (Amendment) Bill (1959) 27
Unigate 262
United Irishman 84
United Nations Organization 74, 75, 99, 113, 114, 116

United Property Holdings 265
University College, Dublin 13–14, 28, 267

Vanoni Plan 22
Voice of the North 84

Walsh, Judge Brian 43
Walsh, Dick 53, 58, 59, 95, 111, 112, 131–2, 157
Walsh, Joe 260
War of Independence 9
Whelehan, Harry 287
Whitaker, Kenneth 20, 22, 24, 25, 45, 67
Whitelaw, William 118
Williams, Glanville 33
Wilson, Harold 47–8, 49, 73, 76, 115, 136
Wilson, John 126, 200, 214, 253
Women's Political Association 295
Woods, Michael 159, 280, 281
Workers' Party 184, 193, 194, 195, 198, 199, 200, 201, 204, 205
World Bank 25
World in Action 263
Wyse, Pearse 229

Jock
L